MW01601667

Just The

## Textbook Key Facts

Textbook Outlines, Highlights, and Practice Quizzes

---

# Chemistry: The Central Science

## by Theodore E. Brown, 13th Edition

All "Just the Facts101" Material Written or Prepared by Cram101 Textbook Reviews

Title Page

## WHY STOP HERE... THERE'S MORE ONLINE

With technology and experience, we've developed tools that make studying easier and efficient. Like this Facts101 textbook notebook, **JustTheFacts101.com** offers you the highlights from every chapter of your actual textbook. However, unlike this notebook, **JustTheFacts101.com** gives you practice tests for each of the chapters. You also get access to in-depth reference material for writing essays and papers.

### JustTheFacts101.COM FEATURES:

**Outlines & Highlights**
Just like the ones in this notebook, but with links to additional information.

**Integrated Note Taking**
Add your class notes to the Facts101 notes, print them and maximize your study time.

**Problem Solving**
Step-by-step walk throughs for math, stats and other disciplines.

**Practice Exams**
Five different test taking formats for every chapter.

**Easy Access**
Study any of your books, on any computer, anywhere.

**Unlimited Textbooks**
All the features above for virtually all your textbooks, just add them to your account at no additional cost.

Be sure to use the promo code above when registering

on JustTheFacts101.com to get 50% off your membership fees.

# STUDYING MADE EASY

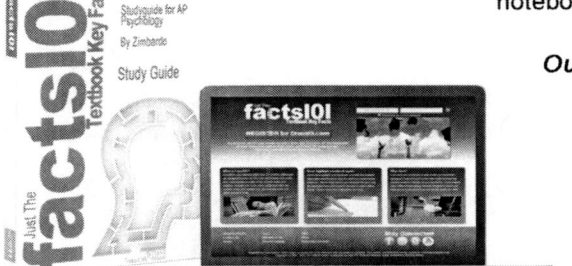

This Facts101 notebook is designed to make studying easier and increase your comprehension of the textbook material. Instead of starting with a blank notebook and trying to write down everything discussed in class lectures, you can use this Facts101 textbook notebook and annotate your notes along with the lecture.

*Our goal is to give you the best tools for success.*

For a supreme understanding of the course, pair your notebook with our online tools. Should you decide you prefer jtfl01.com as your study tool,

*we'd like to offer you a trade...*

Our Trade In program is a simple way for us to keep our promise and provide you the best studying tools, regardless of where you purchased your Facts101 textbook notebook. As long as your notebook is in *Like New Condition\**, you can send it back to us and we will immediately give you a JustTheFacts101.com account free for 120 days!

## Let The *Trade In* Begin!

### THREE SIMPLE STEPS TO TRADE:

**1.** Go to www.jtf101.com/tradein and fill out the packing slip information.

**2.** Submit and print the packing slip and mail it in with your Facts101 textbook notebook.

**3.** Activate your account after you receive your email confirmation.

\* Books must be returned in *Like New Condition*, meaning there is no damage to the book including, but not limited to; ripped or torn pages, markings or writing on pages, or folded / creased pages. Upon receiving the book, Facts101 will inspect it and reserves the right to terminate your free Facts101.com account and return your textbook notebook at the owners expense.

# facts101
## LEARNING SYSTEM

*"Just the Facts101"* is a Content Technologies publication and tool designed to give you all the facts from your textbooks. Visit JustTheFacts101.com for the full practice test for each of your chapters for virtually any of your textbooks.

Facts101 has built custom study tools specific to your textbook. We provide all of the factual testable information and unlike traditional study guides, we will never send you back to your textbook for more information.

*YOU WILL NEVER HAVE TO HIGHLIGHT A BOOK AGAIN!*

## Facts101 StudyGuides
All of the information in this StudyGuide is written specifically for your textbook. We include the key terms, places, people, and concepts... the information you can expect on your next exam!

## Want to take a practice test?
Throughout each chapter of this StudyGuide you will find links to JustTheFacts101.com where you can select specific chapters to take a complete test on, or you can subscribe and get practice tests for up to 12 of your textbooks, along with other exclusive Jtf101.com tools like problem solving labs and reference libraries.

## JustTheFacts101.com
Only Jtf101.com gives you the outlines, highlights, and PRACTICE TESTS specific to your textbook. JustTheFacts101.com is an online application where you'll discover study tools designed to make the most of your limited study time.

By purchasing this book, you get 50% off the normal monthly subscription fee!. Just enter the promotional code **'DK73DW24824'** on the Jtf101.com registration screen.

*www.JustTheFacts101.com*

Copyright © 2014 by Content Technologies, Inc. All rights reserved.

"Just the FACTS101"®, "Cram101"® and "Never Highlight a Book Again!"® are registered trademarks of Content Technologies, Inc.

ISBN(s): 9781497005310. PUBX-5.201451

Chemistry: The Central Science
Theodore E. Brown, 13th

# CONTENTS

# 1. Introduction: Matter and Measurement

CHAPTER OUTLINE: KEY TERMS, PEOPLE, PLACES, CONCEPTS

Enthalpy

Combustion

Chemiluminescence

Period

Binding energy

Acetylsalicylic acid

Aspirin

Atom

Ethanol

Ethylene glycol

Mass spectrum

Molecule

Absorption

Molecular model

Light-emitting diode

Calcium carbonate

Household chemicals

Phosphoric acid

Propene

Sodium hydroxide

Sulfuric acid

# 1. Introduction: Matter and Measurement

CHAPTER OUTLINE: KEY TERMS, PEOPLE, PLACES, CONCEPTS

| | |
|---|---|
| | Chemical industry |
| | State function |
| | Bromine |
| | Calcium |
| | Carbon |
| | Chlorine |
| | Fluorine |
| | Helium |
| | Hydrogen |
| | Iodine |
| | Lithium |
| | Magnesium |
| | Mercury |
| | Nitrogen |
| | Oxygen |
| | Periodic table |
| | Phosphorus |
| | Potassium |
| | Silicon |
| | Sodium |
| | Sulfur |

# 1. Introduction: Matter and Measurement

CHAPTER OUTLINE: KEY TERMS, PEOPLE, PLACES, CONCEPTS

Abundance

Electrochemistry

Lewis structure

Electrolysis

Electrolysis of water

Component

Volume

Intensive property

Physical properties

Nitric acid

Nitrogen dioxide

Evaporation

Distillation

Filtration

Chromatography

Paper chromatography

Candela

Current

Intensity

Luminous intensity

Mole

# 1. Introduction: Matter and Measurement

_____ | Fuel cell _____

_____ | Density _____

_____ | Solid-state _____

_____ | Methane _____

_____ | Nitrous oxide _____

_____ | Propofol _____

_____ | Oxide _____

_____ | Standard deviation _____

_____ | Merck Index _____

CHAPTER HIGHLIGHTS & NOTES: KEY TERMS, PEOPLE, PLACES, CONCEPTS

| | |
|---|---|
| Enthalpy | Enthalpy is a measure of the total energy of a thermodynamic system. It includes the system's internal energy and thermodynamic potential (a state function), as well as its volume and pressure (the energy required to 'make room for it' by displacing its environment, which is an extensive quantity). The unit of measurement for enthalpy in the International System of Units (SI) is the joule, but other historical, conventional units are still in use, such as the British thermal unit and the calorie. |
| Combustion | Combustion or burning is the sequence of exothermic chemical reactions between a fuel and an oxidant accompanied by the production of heat and conversion of chemical species. The release of heat can produce light in the form of either glowing or a flame.<br><br>In a complete combustion reaction, a compound reacts with an oxidizing element, such as oxygen or fluorine, and the products are compounds of each element in the fuel with the oxidizing element. |
| Chemiluminescence | Chemiluminescence is the emission of light (luminescence), as the result of a chemical reaction. There may also be limited emission of heat. Given reactants A and B, with an excited intermediate ?,[A] + [B] ? [?] ? [Products] + light |

For example, if [A] is luminol and [B] is hydrogen peroxide in the presence of a suitable catalyst we have:luminol + $H_2O_2$ ? 3-APA[?] ? 3-APA + light

where:•where 3-APA is 3-aminophthalate•3-APA[?] is the vibronic excited state fluorescing as it decays to a lower energy level.

The decay of this excited state[?] to a lower energy level causes light emission.

| | |
|---|---|
| Period | In the periodic table of the elements, elements are arranged in a series of rows (or periods) so that those with similar properties appear in a column. Elements of the same period have the same number of electron shells; with each group across a period, the elements have one more proton and electron and become less metallic. This arrangement reflects the periodic recurrence of similar properties as the atomic number increases. |
| Binding energy | Binding energy is the mechanical energy required to disassemble a whole into separate parts. A bound system typically has a lower potential energy than the sum of its constituent parts -- this is what keeps the system together. Often this means that energy is released upon the creation of a bound state. |
| Acetylsalicylic acid | Aspirin, also known as acetylsalicylic acid (INN ( ?--?l--i--ik) ASA), is a salicylate drug, often used as an analgesic to relieve minor aches and pains, as an antipyretic to reduce fever, and as an anti-inflammatory medication. The active ingredient of Aspirin was first discovered from the bark of the willow tree in 1763 by Edward Stone of Wadham College, Oxford University. He had discovered salicylic acid, the active metabolite of aspirin. |
| Aspirin | Aspirin, also known as acetylsalicylic acid (INN ( ?--?l--i--ik) ASA), is a salicylate drug, often used as an analgesic to relieve minor aches and pains, as an antipyretic to reduce fever, and as an anti-inflammatory medication. Aspirin was first isolated by Felix Hoffmann, a chemist with the German company Bayer in 1897.<br><br>Salicylic acid, the main metabolite of aspirin, is an integral part of human and animal metabolism. |
| Atom | The atom is a basic unit of matter that consists of a dense central nucleus surrounded by a cloud of negatively charged electrons. The atomic nucleus contains a mix of positively charged protons and electrically neutral neutrons, which means 'uncuttable' or 'the smallest indivisible particle of matter'. Although the Indian and Greek concepts of the atom were based purely on philosophy, modern science has retained the name coined by Democritus. |
| Ethanol | Ethanol, also called ethyl alcohol, pure alcohol, grain alcohol, or drinking alcohol, is a volatile, flammable, colorless liquid with the structural formula $CH_3CH_2OH$, often abbreviated as $C_2H_5OH$ or $C_2H_6O$. |

# 1. Introduction: Matter and Measurement

|  |  |
|---|---|
|  | A psychoactive drug and one of the oldest recreational drugs, ethanol can cause alcohol intoxication when consumed. Best known as the type of alcohol found in alcoholic beverages, it is also used in thermometers, as a solvent, and as a fuel. In common usage, it is often referred to simply as alcohol or spirits. |
| Ethylene glycol | Ethylene glycol is an organic compound primarily used as a raw material in the manufacture of polyester fibers and fabric industry, and polyethylene terephthalate resins (PET) used in bottling. A small percent is also used in industrial applications like antifreeze formulations and other industrial products. It is an odorless, colorless, syrupy, sweet-tasting liquid. |
| Mass spectrum | A mass spectrum is an intensity vs. m/z (mass-to-charge ratio) plot representing a chemical analysis. Hence, the mass spectrum of a sample is a pattern representing the distribution of ions by mass (more correctly: mass-to-charge ratio) in a sample. It is a histogram usually acquired using an instrument called a mass spectrometer. |
| Molecule | A molecule is an electrically neutral group of two or more atoms held together by chemical bonds. Molecules are distinguished from ions by their lack of electrical charge. However, in quantum physics, organic chemistry, and biochemistry, the term molecule is often used less strictly, also being applied to polyatomic ions. |
| Absorption | In chemistry, absorption is a physical or chemical phenomenon or a process in which atoms, molecules, or ions enter some bulk phase - gas, liquid, or solid material. This is a different process from adsorption, since molecules undergoing absorption are taken up by the volume, not by the surface (as in the case for adsorption). A more general term is sorption, which covers absorption, adsorption, and ion exchange. |
| Molecular model | A molecular model, in this article, is a physical model that represents molecules and their processes. The creation of mathematical models of molecular properties and behaviour is molecular modelling, and their graphical depiction is molecular graphics, but these topics are closely linked and each uses techniques from the others. In this article, 'molecular model' will primarily refer to systems containing more than one atom and where nuclear structure is neglected. |
| Light-emitting diode | A light-emitting diode is a semiconductor light source. Light emitting diodes are used as indicator lamps in many devices and are increasingly used for general lighting. Appearing as practical electronic components in 1962, early Light emitting diodes emitted low-intensity red light, but modern versions are available across the visible, ultraviolet, and infrared wavelengths, with very high brightness. |
| Calcium carbonate | Calcium carbonate is a chemical compound with the formula $CaCO_3$. It is a common substance found in rocks in all parts of the world, and is the main component of shells of marine organisms, snails, coal balls, pearls, and eggshells. |

# 1. Introduction: Matter and Measurement

| | |
|---|---|
| Household chemicals | Household chemicals are non-food chemicals that are commonly found and used in and around the average household. They are a type of consumer goods, designed particularly to assist cleaning, pest control and general hygiene purposes.<br><br>Food additives generally do not fall under this category, unless they have a use other than for human consumption. |
| Phosphoric acid | Phosphoric acid is a mineral (inorganic) acid having the chemical formula $H_3PO_4$. Orthophosphoric acid molecules can combine with themselves to form a variety of compounds which are also referred to as phosphoric acids, but in a more general way. The term phosphoric acid can also refer to a chemical or reagent consisting of phosphoric acids, such as pyrophosphoric acid or triphosphoric acid, but usually orthophosphoric acid. |
| Propene | Propene, also known as propylene or methylethylene, is an unsaturated organic compound having the chemical formula $C_3H_6$. It has one double bond, and is the second simplest member of the alkene class of hydrocarbons. |
| Sodium hydroxide | Sodium hydroxide, also known as caustic soda, or lye, is an inorganic compound with the chemical formula NaOH . It is a white solid, and is a highly caustic metallic base and alkali salt. It is available in pellets, flakes, granules, and as prepared solutions at a number of different concentrations. |
| Sulfuric acid | Sulfuric acid is a highly corrosive strong mineral acid with the molecular formula $H_2SO_4$. It is a pungent, colorless to slightly yellow viscous liquid which is soluble in water at all concentrations. Sometimes, it is dyed dark brown during production to alert people to its hazards. |
| Chemical industry | The chemical industry comprises the companies that produce industrial chemicals. Central to the modern world economy, it converts raw materials (oil, natural gas, air, water, metals, and minerals) into more than 70,000 different products. |
| State function | In thermodynamics, a state function, function of state, state quantity, or state variable is a property of a system that depends only on the current state of the system, not on the way in which the system acquired that state . A state function describes the equilibrium state of a system. For example, internal energy, enthalpy, and entropy are state quantities because they describe quantitatively an equilibrium state of a thermodynamic system, irrespective of how the system arrived in that state. |
| Bromine | Bromine is a chemical element with the symbol Br, and atomic number of 35. It is in the halogen group (17). The element was isolated independently by two chemists, Carl Jacob Löwig and Antoine Jerome Balard, in 1825-1826. Elemental bromine is a fuming red-brown liquid at room temperature, corrosive and toxic, with properties between those of chlorine and iodine. |

# 1. Introduction: Matter and Measurement

| | |
|---|---|
| Calcium | Calcium is the chemical element with symbol Ca and atomic number 20. Calcium is a soft gray alkaline earth metal, and is the fifth-most-abundant element by mass in the Earth's crust. Calcium is also the fifth-most-abundant dissolved ion in seawater by both molarity and mass, after sodium, chloride, magnesium, and sulfate. |
| | Calcium is essential for living organisms, in particular in cell physiology, where movement of the calcium ion $Ca^{2+}$ into and out of the cytoplasm functions as a signal for many cellular processes. |
| Carbon | Carbon fiber, alternatively graphite fiber, carbon graphite or CF, is a material consisting of fibers about 5-10 μm in diameter and composed mostly of carbon atoms. The carbon atoms are bonded together in crystals that are more or less aligned parallel to the long axis of the fiber. The crystal alignment gives the fiber high strength-to-volume ratio (making it strong for its size). |
| Chlorine | Chlorine is a chemical element with symbol Cl and atomic number 17. Chlorine is in the halogen group (17) and is the second lightest halogen after fluorine. The element is a yellow-green gas under standard conditions, where it forms diatomic molecules. It has the highest electron affinity and the fourth highest electronegativity of all the reactive elements; for this reason, chlorine is a strong oxidizing agent. |
| Fluorine | Fluorine is the chemical element with symbol F and atomic number 9. At room temperature, the element is a pale yellow gas composed of diatomic molecules, F2. Fluorine is the lightest halogen and the most electronegative element. It requires great care in handling as it is extremely reactive and poisonous. |
| Helium | Helium is a chemical element with symbol He and atomic number 2. It is a colorless, odorless, tasteless, non-toxic, inert, monatomic gas that heads the noble gas group in the periodic table. Its boiling and melting points are the lowest among the elements and it exists only as a gas except in extreme conditions. |
| | Helium is the second lightest element and is the second most abundant element in the observable universe, being present at about 24% of the total elemental mass, which is more than 12 times the mass of all the heavier elements combined. |
| Hydrogen | Hydrogen is a chemical element with chemical symbol H and atomic number 1. With an atomic weight of 1.00794 u, hydrogen is the lightest element and its monatomic form (H) is the most abundant chemical substance, constituting roughly 75% of the Universe's baryonic mass. Non-remnant stars are mainly composed of hydrogen in its plasma state. |
| | At standard temperature and pressure, hydrogen is a colorless, odorless, tasteless, non-toxic, nonmetallic, highly combustible diatomic gas with the molecular formula $H_2$. |
| Iodine | Iodine is a chemical element with symbol I and atomic number 53. The name is from Greek |

??e?d?? ioeides, meaning violet or purple, due to the color of elemental iodine vapor.

Iodine and its compounds are primarily used in nutrition, and industrially in the production of acetic acid and certain polymers. Iodine's relatively high atomic number, low toxicity, and ease of attachment to organic compounds have made it a part of many X-ray contrast materials in modern medicine.

| | |
|---|---|
| Lithium | Lithium is a chemical element with symbol Li and atomic number 3. It is a soft, silver-white metal belonging to the alkali metal group of chemical elements. Under standard conditions it is the lightest metal and the least dense solid element. Like all alkali metals, lithium is highly reactive and flammable. |
| Magnesium | Magnesium is a chemical element with the symbol Mg and atomic number 12. Its common oxidation number is +2. It is an alkaline earth metal and the eighth most abundant element in the Earth's crust and ninth in the known universe as a whole. Magnesium is the fourth most common element in the Earth as a whole (behind iron, oxygen and silicon), making up 13% of the planet's mass and a large fraction of the planet's mantle. The relative abundance of magnesium is related to the fact that it easily builds up in supernova stars from a sequential addition of three helium nuclei to carbon (which in turn is made from three helium nuclei). |
| Mercury | Mercury is a chemical element with the symbol Hg and atomic number 80. It is commonly known as quicksilver and was formerly named hydrargyrum (from Greek 'hydr-' water and 'argyros' silver). A heavy, silvery d-block element, mercury is the only metal that is liquid at standard conditions for temperature and pressure; the only other element that is liquid under these conditions is bromine, though metals such as caesium, gallium, and rubidium melt just above room temperature. With a freezing point of -38.83 °C and boiling point of 356.73 °C, mercury has one of the narrowest ranges of its liquid state of any metal. |
| Nitrogen | Nitrogen, symbol N, is the chemical element of atomic number 7. At room temperature, it is a gas of diatomic molecules and is colorless and odorless. Nitrogen is a common element in the universe, estimated at about seventh in total abundance in our galaxy and the Solar System. On Earth, the element is primarily found as the free element; it forms about 80% of the Earth's atmosphere. |
| Oxygen | Oxygen is a chemical element with symbol O and atomic number 8. It is a member of the chalcogen group on the periodic table and is a highly reactive nonmetallic element and oxidizing agent that readily forms compounds (notably oxides) with most elements. By mass, oxygen is the third-most abundant element in the universe, after hydrogen and helium At STP, two atoms of the element bind to form dioxygen, a diatomic gas that is colorless, odorless, and tasteless; with the formula $O_2$. |

# 1. Introduction: Matter and Measurement

| | |
|---|---|
| Periodic table | The periodic table is a tabular arrangement of the chemical elements, organized on the basis of their atomic numbers, electron configurations, and recurring chemical properties. Elements are presented in order of increasing atomic number (the number of protons in the nucleus). The standard form of the table consists of a grid of elements laid out in 18 columns and 7 rows, with a double row of elements below that. |
| Phosphorus | Phosphorus is a nonmetallic chemical element with symbol P and atomic number 15. A multivalent pnictogen, phosphorus as a mineral is almost always present in its maximally oxidised state, as inorganic phosphate rocks. Elemental phosphorus exists in two major forms--white phosphorus and red phosphorus--but due to its high reactivity, phosphorus is never found as a free element on Earth. |
| | The first form of elemental phosphorus to be produced (white phosphorus, in 1669) emits a faint glow upon exposure to oxygen - hence its name given from Greek mythology, F?sf???? meaning 'light-bearer' (Latin Lucifer), referring to the 'Morning Star', the planet Venus. |
| Potassium | Potassium is a chemical element with symbol K and atomic number 19. Elemental potassium is a soft silvery-white alkali metal that oxidizes rapidly in air and is very reactive with water, generating sufficient heat to ignite the hydrogen emitted in the reaction and burning with a lilac flame. |
| | Because potassium and sodium are chemically very similar, their salts were not at first differentiated. The existence of multiple elements in their salts was suspected from 1702, and this was proven in 1807 when potassium and sodium were individually isolated from different salts by electrolysis. |
| Silicon | Silicon, a tetravalent metalloid, is a chemical element with the symbol Si and atomic number 14. It is less reactive than its chemical analog carbon, the nonmetal directly above it in the periodic table, but more reactive than germanium, the metalloid directly below it in the table. Controversy about silicon's character dates to its discovery; it was first prepared and characterized in pure form in 1823. In 1808, it was given the name silicium (from Latin: silex, hard stone or flint), with an -ium word-ending to suggest a metal, a name which the element retains in several non-English languages. However, its final English name, first suggested in 1817, reflects the more physically similar elements carbon and boron. |
| Sodium | Sodium is a chemical element with the symbol Na and atomic number 11. It is a soft, silver-white, highly reactive metal and is a member of the alkali metals; its only stable isotope is $^{23}Na$. The free metal does not occur in nature, but instead must be prepared from its compounds; it was first isolated by Humphry Davy in 1807 by the electrolysis of sodium hydroxide. Sodium is the sixth most abundant element in the Earth's crust, and exists in numerous minerals such as feldspars, sodalite and rock salt. |
| Sulfur | Sulfur or sulphur is a chemical element with symbol S and atomic number 16. |

It is an abundant, multivalent non-metal. Under normal conditions, sulfur atoms form cyclic octatomic molecules with chemical formula $S_8$. Elemental sulfur is a bright yellow crystalline solid when at room temperature.

| | |
|---|---|
| Abundance | In a chemical reaction, a reactant is considered to be in abundance if the quantity of that substance is high and virtually unchanged by the reaction. Abundance differs from excess in that a reactant in excess is simply any reactant other than the limiting reagent; the amount by which a reactant is in excess is often specified, such as with terms like 'twofold excess', indicating that there is twice the amount of reactant necessary for the limiting reagent to be completely reacted. In this case, should the reaction go to completion, the quantity of the reactant in excess will have halved. |
| Electrochemistry | Electrochemistry is a branch of chemistry that studies chemical reactions which take place in a solution at the interface of an electron conductor and an ionic conductor (the electrolyte). These reactions involve electron transfer between the electrode and the electrolyte or species in solution. |
| | If a chemical reaction is driven by an externally applied voltage, as in electrolysis, or if a voltage is created by a chemical reaction as in a battery, it is an electrochemical reaction. |
| Lewis structure | Lewis structures are diagrams that show the bonding between atoms of a molecule and the lone pairs of electrons that may exist in the molecule. A Lewis structure can be drawn for any covalently bonded molecule, as well as coordination compounds. The Lewis structure was named after Gilbert N |
| Electrolysis | In chemistry and manufacturing, electrolysis is a method of using a direct electric current to drive an otherwise non-spontaneous chemical reaction. Electrolysis is commercially highly important as a stage in the separation of elements from naturally occurring sources such as ores using an electrolytic cell. |
| Electrolysis of water | Electrolysis of water is the decomposition of water into oxygen ($O_2$) and hydrogen gas ($H_2$) due to an electric current being passed through the water. |
| Component | In thermodynamics, a component is a chemically-independent constituent of a system. The number of components represents the minimum number of independent species necessary to define the composition of all phases of the system. |
| | Calculating the number of components in a system is necessary, for example, when applying Gibbs' phase rule in determination of the number of degrees of freedom of a system. |
| Volume | In thermodynamics, the volume of a system is an important extensive parameter for describing its thermodynamic state. The specific volume, an intensive property, is the system's volume per unit of mass. |

# 1. Introduction: Matter and Measurement

| | |
|---|---|
| Intensive property | In thermodynamics and materials science, the physical properties of substances are often described as intensive or extensive, a classification that relates to the dependency of the properties upon the size or extent of the system or object in question. |
| | The distinction is based on the concept that smaller, non-interacting identical subdivisions of the system may be identified so that the property of interest does or does not change when the system is divided, or combined. |
| | An intensive property is a bulk property, meaning that it is a physical property of a system that does not depend on the system size or the amount of material in the system. |
| Physical properties | A physical property is any property that is measurable whose value describes a state of a physical system. The changes in the physical properties of a system can be used to describe its transformations or evolutions between its momentary states. Physical properties are often referred to as observables. |
| Nitric acid | Nitric acid, also known as aqua fortis and spirit of niter, is a highly corrosive strong mineral acid. The pure compound is colorless, but older samples tend to acquire a yellow cast due to decomposition into oxides of nitrogen and water. Most commercially available nitric acid has a concentration of 68%. |
| Nitrogen dioxide | Nitrogen dioxide is the chemical compound with the formula $NO_2$. It is one of several nitrogen oxides. $NO_2$ is an intermediate in the industrial synthesis of nitric acid, millions of tons of which are produced each year. |
| Evaporation | Evaporation is a type of vaporization of a liquid that occurs from the surface of a liquid into a gaseous phase that is not saturated with the evaporating substance. The other type of vaporization is boiling, which, instead, occurs within the entire mass of the liquid and can also take place when the vapor phase is saturated, such as when steam is produced in a boiler. Evaporation that occurs directly from the solid phase below the melting point, as commonly observed with ice at or below freezing or moth crystals (napthalene or paradichlorobenzine), is called sublimation. |
| Distillation | Distillation is a method of separating mixtures based on differences in volatility of components in a boiling liquid mixture. Distillation is a unit operation, or a physical separation process, and not a chemical reaction. |
| | Commercially, distillation has a number of applications. |
| Filtration | Filtration is commonly the mechanical or physical operation which is used for the separation of solids from fluids by interposing a medium through which only the fluid can pass. The fluid that pass through is called a filtrate. |

# 1. Introduction: Matter and Measurement

CHAPTER HIGHLIGHTS & NOTES: KEY TERMS, PEOPLE, PLACES, CONCEPTS

| Chromatography | Chromatography is the collective term for a set of laboratory techniques for the separation of mixtures. The mixture is dissolved in a fluid called the mobile phase, which carries it through a structure holding another material called the stationary phase. The various constituents of the mixture travel at different speeds, causing them to separate. |
| --- | --- |
| Paper chromatography | Paper chromatography is an analytical method technique for separating and identifying mixtures of organic compounds that are or can be coloured, especially pigments. This can also be used in secondary or primary colours in ink experiments. This method has been largely replaced by thin layer chromatography, however it is still a powerful teaching tool. |
| Candela | The candela is the SI base unit of luminous intensity; that is, power emitted by a light source in a particular direction, weighted by the luminosity function (a standardized model of the sensitivity of the human eye to different wavelengths, also known as the luminous efficiency function). A common candle emits light with a luminous intensity of roughly one candela. If emission in some directions is blocked by an opaque barrier, the emission would still be approximately one candela in the directions that are not obscured. |
| Current | A current in a fluid is the magnitude and direction of flow within that fluid. An air current presents the same properties specifically for a gaseous medium.<br><br>Types of fluid currents include•Boundary current•Current a current in a river or stream•Ocean current•Rip current•Subsurface currents•Turbidity current. |
| Intensity | In physics, intensity is the power transferred per unit area. In the SI system, it has units watts per metre squared ($W/m^2$). It is used most frequently with waves (e.g. sound or light), in which case the average power transfer over one period of the wave is used. |
| Luminous intensity | In photometry, luminous intensity is a measure of the wavelength-weighted power emitted by a light source in a particular direction per unit solid angle, based on the luminosity function, a standardized model of the sensitivity of the human eye. The SI unit of luminous intensity is the candela (cd), an SI base unit.<br><br>Photometry deals with the measurement of visible light as perceived by human eyes. |
| Mole | Mole is a unit of measurement used in chemistry to express amounts of a chemical substance, defined as the amount of any substance that contains as many elementary entities (e.g., atoms, molecules, ions, electrons) as there are atoms in 12 grams of pure carbon-12, the isotope of carbon with relative atomic mass 12. This corresponds to the Avogadro constant, which has a value of $6.02214129(27) \times 10^{23}$ elementary entities of the substance. It is one of the base units in the International System of Units, and has the unit symbol mol and corresponds with the dimension symbol N. In honour of the unit, chemists often celebrate October 23 (a reference to the $10^{23}$ part of Avogadro's number) as 'Mole Day'. |

# 1. Introduction: Matter and Measurement

| | |
|---|---|
| Fuel cell | A fuel cell is a device that converts the chemical energy from a fuel into electricity through a chemical reaction with oxygen or another oxidizing agent. Hydrogen is the most common fuel, but hydrocarbons such as natural gas and alcohols like methanol are sometimes used. Fuel cells are different from batteries in that they require a constant source of fuel and oxygen/air to sustain the chemical reaction; however, fuel cells can produce electricity continually for as long as these inputs are supplied. |
| Density | The density, or more precisely, the volumetric mass density, of a substance is its mass per unit volume. The symbol most often used for density is ? (the lower case Greek letter rho). Mathematically, density is defined as mass divided by volume: $\rho = \dfrac{m}{V}$, where ? is the density, m is the mass, and V is the volume. |
| Solid-state | Solid-state electronics are those circuits or devices built entirely from solid materials and in which the electrons, or other charge carriers, are confined entirely within the solid material. The term is often used to contrast with the earlier technologies of vacuum and gas-discharge tube devices and it is also conventional to exclude electro-mechanical devices (relays, switches, hard drives and other devices with moving parts) from the term solid state. While solid-state can include crystalline, polycrystalline and amorphous solids and refer to electrical conductors, insulators and semiconductors, the building material is most often a crystalline semiconductor. |
| Methane | Methane is a chemical compound with the chemical formula $CH_4$ (one atom of carbon and four atoms of hydrogen). It is the simplest alkane and the main component of natural gas. The relative abundance of methane makes it an attractive fuel. |
| Nitrous oxide | Nitrous oxide, commonly known as laughing gas, is a chemical compound with the formula $N_2O$. It is an oxide of nitrogen. At room temperature, it is a colourless, non-flammable gas, with a slightly sweet odour and taste. |
| Propofol | Propofol is a short-acting, intravenously administered hypnotic/amnestic agent. Its uses include the induction and maintenance of general anesthesia, sedation for mechanically ventilated adults, and procedural sedation. Propofol is also commonly used in veterinary medicine. |
| Oxide | An oxide is a chemical compound that contains at least one oxygen atom and one other element in its chemical formula. Metal oxides typically contain an anion of oxygen in the oxidation state of -2. Most of the Earth's crust consists of solid oxides, the result of elements being oxidized by the oxygen in air or in water. Hydrocarbon combustion affords the two principal carbon oxides: carbon monoxide and carbon dioxide. |
| Standard deviation | In statistics and probability theory, the standard deviation shows how much variation or dispersion from the average exists. |

A low standard deviation indicates that the data points tend to be very close to the mean (also called expected value); a high standard deviation indicates that the data points are spread out over a large range of values.

The standard deviation of a random variable, statistical population, data set, or probability distribution is the square root of its variance.

Merck Index | The Merck Index is an encyclopedia of chemicals, drugs and biologicals with over 10,000 monographs on single substances or groups of related compounds. It also includes an appendix with monographs on organic name reactions. It was published by the United States pharmaceutical company Merck & Co. from 1889 until 2013, when the title was acquired by the Royal Society of Chemistry.

CHAPTER QUIZ: KEY TERMS, PEOPLE, PLACES, CONCEPTS

1. _____ or sulphur is a chemical element with symbol S and atomic number 16. It is an abundant, multivalent non-metal. Under normal conditions, _____ atoms form cyclic octatomic molecules with chemical formula $S_8$. Elemental _____ is a bright yellow crystalline solid when at room temperature.

    a. Baryte
    b. Berthierite
    c. Bertrandite
    d. Sulfur

2. In thermodynamics, the _____ of a system is an important extensive parameter for describing its thermodynamic state. The specific _____, an intensive property, is the system's _____ per unit of mass. _____ is a function of state and is interdependent with other thermodynamic properties such as pressure and temperature.

    a. Bioaerosol
    b. Bjerrum length
    c. Volume
    d. Bolaamphiphile

3. . _____ is a measure of the total energy of a thermodynamic system. It includes the system's internal energy and thermodynamic potential (a state function), as well as its volume and pressure (the energy required to 'make room for it' by displacing its environment, which is an extensive quantity). The unit of measurement for _____ in the International System of Units (SI) is the joule, but other historical, conventional units are still in use, such as the British thermal unit and the calorie.

   a. CrystaSulf
   b. Enthalpy
   c. Rectisol
   d. Scrubber

4. In physics, _____ is the power transferred per unit area. In the SI system, it has units watts per metre squared ($W/m^2$). It is used most frequently with waves (e.g. sound or light), in which case the average power transfer over one period of the wave is used.

   a. Bahtinov mask
   b. Bandwidth-limited pulse
   c. Intensity
   d. Beam divergence

5. A _____ in a fluid is the magnitude and direction of flow within that fluid. An air _____ presents the same properties specifically for a gaseous medium.

   Types of fluid _____s include•Boundary _____•_____ a _____ in a river or stream•Ocean _____•Rip _____•Subsurface _____s•Turbidity _____.

   a. Baroclinity
   b. Barotropic fluid
   c. Current
   d. Batchelor scale

**ANSWER KEY**
1. Introduction: Matter and Measurement

**1.** d
**2.** c
**3.** b
**4.** c
**5.** c

---

## You can take the complete Chapter Practice Test

**for 1. Introduction: Matter and Measurement**
on all key terms, persons, places, and concepts.

## Online 99 Cents

## http://www.JustTheFacts101.com

**Use www.JustTheFacts101.com for all your study needs**

**including Facts101's online interactive problem solving labs in**

**chemistry, statistics, mathematics, and more.**

CHAPTER OUTLINE: KEY TERMS, PEOPLE, PLACES, CONCEPTS

| | |
|---|---|
| _____ | Mass spectrum |
| _____ | Physical properties |
| _____ | Atomic theory |
| _____ | Cathode |
| _____ | Charged particle |
| _____ | Fluorescence |
| _____ | Subatomic particle |
| _____ | Thomson |
| _____ | Electron |
| _____ | Curie |
| _____ | Polonium |
| _____ | Radiant energy |
| _____ | Radium |
| _____ | Isotope |
| _____ | Neutron |
| _____ | Proton |
| _____ | Atomic mass |
| _____ | Atomic mass unit |
| _____ | Nuclear reaction |
| _____ | Atomic number |
| _____ | Mass number |

Nuclear force

Abundance

Argon

Chlorine

Helium

Lithium

Neon

Periodic table

Potassium

Sodium

Atom

Spectrum

Nonmetal

Period

Alkali

Chalcogen

Coinage metals

Gold

Halogen

Manganese

Effusion

CHAPTER OUTLINE: KEY TERMS, PEOPLE, PLACES, CONCEPTS

————————————| Astatine

————————————| Boron

————————————| Hydrogen

————————————| Mercury

————————————| Metalloid

————————————| Carbon dioxide

————————————| Carbon monoxide

————————————| Diatomic molecule

————————————| Hydrogen peroxide

————————————| Methane

————————————| Molecule

————————————| Ozone

————————————| Diatomic

————————————| Ball-and-stick model

————————————| Space-filling model

————————————| Product

————————————| Polyatomic ion

————————————| Concentration

————————————| Ionic compound

————————————| Sodium chloride

————————————| Carbon

| | Trace element |
|---|---|
| | Calcium |
| | Carbon group |
| | Inorganic compound |
| | Organic compound |
| | Chromium |
| | Ostwald process |
| | Transition metal |
| | Hypoiodous acid |
| | Oxyanion |
| | Bromide ion |
| | Chloride ion |
| | Cyanide ion |
| | Ice pack |
| | Solubility |
| | Octane rating |
| | Triple point |
| | Binary compound |
| | Alkane |
| | Ethane |
| | Ethanol |

CHAPTER OUTLINE: KEY TERMS, PEOPLE, PLACES, CONCEPTS

_____ | Hydrocarbon

_____ | Methanol

_____ | Octane

_____ | Organic chemistry

_____ | Propane

_____ | 1-Propanol

_____ | Alcohol

_____ | Functional group

_____ | Isomer

_____ | Isopropyl alcohol

_____ | Molecular weight

_____ | Polyethylene

_____ | Benzene

_____ | Diborane

_____ | Glucose

_____ | Silicon tetrachloride

_____ | Tritium

_____ | Cyclohexane

_____ | Cyclohexanol

# 2. Atoms, Molecules, and Ions

| | |
|---|---|
| Mass spectrum | A mass spectrum is an intensity vs. m/z (mass-to-charge ratio) plot representing a chemical analysis. Hence, the mass spectrum of a sample is a pattern representing the distribution of ions by mass (more correctly: mass-to-charge ratio) in a sample. It is a histogram usually acquired using an instrument called a mass spectrometer. |
| Physical properties | A physical property is any property that is measurable whose value describes a state of a physical system. The changes in the physical properties of a system can be used to describe its transformations or evolutions between its momentary states. Physical properties are often referred to as observables. |
| Atomic theory | In chemistry and physics, atomic theory is a scientific theory of the nature of matter, which states that matter is composed of discrete units called atoms, as opposed to the earlier concept which held that matter could be divided into any arbitrarily small quantity. It began as a philosophical concept in ancient Greece (Democritus) and entered the scientific mainstream in the early 19th century when discoveries in the field of chemistry showed that matter did indeed behave as if it were made up of particles. <br><br> The word 'atom' (from the ancient Greek adjective atomos, 'indivisible'. |
| Cathode | A cathode is an electrode through which electric current flows out of a polarized electrical device. The direction of electric current is, by convention, opposite to the direction of electron flow--thus, electrons are considered to flow toward the cathode electrode while current flows away from it. This convention is sometimes remembered using the mnemonic CCD for cathode current departs. |
| Charged particle | In physics, a charged particle is a particle with an electric charge. It may be either a subatomic particle or an ion. A collection of charged particles, or even a gas containing a proportion of charged particles, is called a plasma, which is called the fourth state of matter because its properties are quite different from solids, liquids and gases (plasma is the most common state of matter in the universe). |
| Fluorescence | Fluorescence is the emission of light by a substance that has absorbed light or other electromagnetic radiation. It is a form of luminescence. In most cases, the emitted light has a longer wavelength, and therefore lower energy, than the absorbed radiation. |
| Subatomic particle | In the physical sciences, subatomic particles are the particles smaller than an atom. (although some subatomic particles have mass greater than some atoms). There are two types of subatomic particles: elementary particles, which according to current theories are not made of other particles; and composite particles. |
| Thomson | The thomson is a unit that has appeared infrequently in scientific literature relating to the field of mass spectrometry as a unit of mass-to-charge ratio. The unit was proposed by Cooks and Rockwood naming it in honour of J. J. |

# 2. Atoms, Molecules, and Ions

| | |
|---|---|
| Electron | The electron is a subatomic particle with a negative elementary electric charge. Electrons belong to the first generation of the lepton particle family, and are generally thought to be elementary particles because they have no known components or substructure. The electron has a mass that is approximately 1/1836 that of the proton. |
| Curie | The curie is a non-SI unit of radioactivity the curie is widely used throughout the US government and industry.<br><br>One curie is roughly the activity of 1 gram of the radium isotope $^{226}$Ra, a substance studied by the Curies.<br><br>The SI derived unit of radioactivity is the becquerel (Bq), which equates to one decay per second. |
| Polonium | Polonium is a chemical element with the symbol Po and atomic number 84, discovered in 1898 by Marie Curie and Pierre Curie. A rare and highly radioactive element with no stable isotopes, polonium is chemically similar to bismuth and tellurium, and it occurs in uranium ores. Applications of polonium are few, and include heaters in space probes, antistatic devices, and sources of neutrons and alpha particles. |
| Radiant energy | Radiant energy is the energy of electromagnetic waves. The quantity of radiant energy may be calculated by integrating radiant flux (or power) with respect to time and, like all forms of energy, its SI unit is the joule. The term is used particularly when radiation is emitted by a source into the surrounding environment. |
| Radium | Radium is a chemical element with symbol Ra and atomic number 88. Radium is an almost pure-white alkaline earth metal, but it readily oxidizes on exposure to air, becoming black in color. All isotopes of radium are highly radioactive, with the most stable isotope being radium-226, which has a half-life of 1601 years and decays into radon gas. Because of such instability, radium is luminescent, glowing a faint blue. |
| Isotope | Isotopes are variants of a particular chemical element such that, while all isotopes of a given element have the same number of protons in each atom, they differ in neutron number. The term isotope is formed from the Greek roots isos (?s?? 'equal') and topos (t?p?? 'place'), meaning 'the same place'. Thus, different isotopes of a single element occupy the same position on the periodic table. |
| Neutron | The neutron is a subatomic hadron particle that has the symbol n or n0, no net electric charge and a mass slightly larger than that of a proton. With the exception of hydrogen-1, nuclei of atoms consist of protons and neutrons, which are therefore collectively referred to as nucleons. The number of protons in a nucleus is the atomic number and defines the type of element the atom forms. |

# 2. Atoms, Molecules, and Ions

| | |
|---|---|
| Proton | The proton is a subatomic particle with the symbol p or p+ and a positive electric charge of 1 elementary charge. One or more protons are present in the nucleus of each atom. The number of protons in each atom is its atomic number. |
| Atomic mass | The atomic mass is the mass of an atomic particle, sub-atomic particle, or molecule. It may be expressed in unified atomic mass units; by international agreement, 1 atomic mass unit is defined as 1/12 of the mass of a single carbon-12 atom (at rest). When expressed in such units, the atomic mass is called the relative isotopic mass . |
| Atomic mass unit | The unified atomic mass unit or dalton (symbol: Da) is the standard unit that is used for indicating mass on an atomic or molecular scale (atomic mass). One unified atomic mass unit is approximately the mass of a nucleon and is equivalent to 1 g/mol. It is defined as one twelfth of the mass of an unbound neutral atom of carbon-12 in its nuclear and electronic ground state, and has a value of $1.660538921(73) \times 10^{-27}$ kg. |
| Nuclear reaction | In nuclear physics and nuclear chemistry, a nuclear reaction is semantically considered to be the process in which two nuclei, or else a nucleus of an atom and a subatomic particle from outside the atom, collide to produce one or more nuclides that are different from the nuclide(s) that began the process. Thus, a nuclear reaction must cause a transformation of at least one nuclide to another. If a nucleus interacts with another nucleus or particle and they then separate without changing the nature of any nuclide, the process is simply referred to as a type of nuclear scattering, rather than a nuclear reaction. |
| Atomic number | In chemistry and physics, the atomic number is the number of protons found in the nucleus of an atom and therefore identical to the charge number of the nucleus. It is conventionally represented by the symbol Z. The atomic number uniquely identifies a chemical element. In an atom of neutral charge, the atomic number is also equal to the number of electrons. |
| Mass number | The mass number, also called atomic mass number or nucleon number, is the total number of protons and neutrons (together known as nucleons) in an atomic nucleus. Because protons and neutrons both are baryons, the mass number A is identical with the baryon number B as of the nucleus as of the whole atom or ion. The mass number is different for each different isotope of a chemical element. |
| Nuclear force | The nuclear force is the force between two or more nucleons. Its fundamental laws and constants are unknown unlike the Coulomb and Newton laws. It is responsible for binding protons and neutrons into atomic nuclei. |
| Abundance | In a chemical reaction, a reactant is considered to be in abundance if the quantity of that substance is high and virtually unchanged by the reaction. |

|  | Abundance differs from excess in that a reactant in excess is simply any reactant other than the limiting reagent; the amount by which a reactant is in excess is often specified, such as with terms like 'twofold excess', indicating that there is twice the amount of reactant necessary for the limiting reagent to be completely reacted. In this case, should the reaction go to completion, the quantity of the reactant in excess will have halved. |
|---|---|
| Argon | Argon is a chemical element with symbol Ar and atomic number 18. It is in group 18 of the periodic table and is a noble gas. Argon is the third most common gas in the Earth's atmosphere, at 0.93% (9,300 ppm), making it approximately 23.8 times as abundant as the next most common atmospheric gas, carbon dioxide (390 ppm), and more than 500 times as abundant as the next most common noble gas, neon (18 ppm). Nearly all of this argon is radiogenic argon-40 derived from the decay of potassium-40 in the Earth's crust. |
| Chlorine | Chlorine is a chemical element with symbol Cl and atomic number 17. Chlorine is in the halogen group (17) and is the second lightest halogen after fluorine. The element is a yellow-green gas under standard conditions, where it forms diatomic molecules. It has the highest electron affinity and the fourth highest electronegativity of all the reactive elements; for this reason, chlorine is a strong oxidizing agent. |
| Helium | Helium is a chemical element with symbol He and atomic number 2. It is a colorless, odorless, tasteless, non-toxic, inert, monatomic gas that heads the noble gas group in the periodic table. Its boiling and melting points are the lowest among the elements and it exists only as a gas except in extreme conditions.

Helium is the second lightest element and is the second most abundant element in the observable universe, being present at about 24% of the total elemental mass, which is more than 12 times the mass of all the heavier elements combined. |
| Lithium | Lithium is a chemical element with symbol Li and atomic number 3. It is a soft, silver-white metal belonging to the alkali metal group of chemical elements. Under standard conditions it is the lightest metal and the least dense solid element. Like all alkali metals, lithium is highly reactive and flammable. |
| Neon | Neon is a chemical element with symbol Ne and atomic number 10. It is in group 18 (noble gases) of the periodic table. Neon is a colorless, odorless, inert monatomic gas under standard conditions, with about two-thirds the density of air. It was discovered (along with krypton and xenon) in 1898 as one of the three residual rare inert elements remaining in dry air, after nitrogen, oxygen, argon and carbon dioxide are removed. |
| Periodic table | The periodic table is a tabular arrangement of the chemical elements, organized on the basis of their atomic numbers, electron configurations, and recurring chemical properties. Elements are presented in order of increasing atomic number (the number of protons in the nucleus). |

# 2. Atoms, Molecules, and Ions

| | |
|---|---|
| Potassium | Potassium is a chemical element with symbol K and atomic number 19. Elemental potassium is a soft silvery-white alkali metal that oxidizes rapidly in air and is very reactive with water, generating sufficient heat to ignite the hydrogen emitted in the reaction and burning with a lilac flame. |
| | Because potassium and sodium are chemically very similar, their salts were not at first differentiated. The existence of multiple elements in their salts was suspected from 1702, and this was proven in 1807 when potassium and sodium were individually isolated from different salts by electrolysis. |
| Sodium | Sodium is a chemical element with the symbol Na and atomic number 11. It is a soft, silver-white, highly reactive metal and is a member of the alkali metals; its only stable isotope is $^{23}$Na. The free metal does not occur in nature, but instead must be prepared from its compounds; it was first isolated by Humphry Davy in 1807 by the electrolysis of sodium hydroxide. Sodium is the sixth most abundant element in the Earth's crust, and exists in numerous minerals such as feldspars, sodalite and rock salt. |
| Atom | The atom is a basic unit of matter that consists of a dense central nucleus surrounded by a cloud of negatively charged electrons. The atomic nucleus contains a mix of positively charged protons and electrically neutral neutrons, which means 'uncuttable' or 'the smallest indivisible particle of matter'. Although the Indian and Greek concepts of the atom were based purely on philosophy, modern science has retained the name coined by Democritus. |
| Spectrum | A spectrum is a condition that is not limited to a specific set of values but can vary infinitely within a continuum. The word was first used scientifically within the field of optics to describe the rainbow of colors in visible light when separated using a prism; it has since been applied by analogy to many fields other than optics. Thus, one might talk about the spectrum of political opinion, or the spectrum of activity of a drug, or the autism spectrum. |
| Nonmetal | In chemistry, a nonmetal or non-metal is a chemical element which mostly lacks metallic attributes. Physically, nonmetals tend to be highly volatile (easily vaporised), have low elasticity, and are good insulators of heat and electricity; chemically, they tend to have high ionisation energy and electronegativity values, and gain or share electrons when they react with other elements or compounds. Seventeen elements are generally classified as nonmetals; most are gases (hydrogen, helium, nitrogen, oxygen, fluorine, neon, chlorine, argon, krypton, xenon and radon); one is a liquid (bromine); and a few are solids (carbon, phosphorus, sulfur, selenium, and iodine). |
| Period | In the periodic table of the elements, elements are arranged in a series of rows (or periods) so that those with similar properties appear in a column. Elements of the same period have the same number of electron shells; with each group across a period, the elements have one more proton and electron and become less metallic. This arrangement reflects the periodic recurrence of similar properties as the atomic number increases. |

CHAPTER HIGHLIGHTS & NOTES: KEY TERMS, PEOPLE, PLACES, CONCEPTS

| | |
|---|---|
| Alkali | In chemistry, an alkali is a basic, ionic salt of an alkali metal or alkaline earth metal chemical element. Some authors also define an alkali as a base that dissolves in water. A solution of a soluble base has a pH greater than 7.0. The adjective alkaline is commonly, and alkalescent less often, used in English as a synonym for basic, especially for soluble bases. |
| Chalcogen | The chalcogens are the chemical elements in group 16 of the periodic table. This group is also known as the oxygen family. It consists of the elements oxygen (O), sulfur (S), selenium (Se), tellurium (Te), and the radioactive element polonium (Po). |
| Coinage metals | The coinage metals comprise, at minimum, those metallic chemical elements which have historically been used as components in alloys used to mint coins. The term is not perfectly defined, however, since a number of metals have been used to make 'demonstration coins' which have never been used to make monetized coins for any nation-state, but could be. Some of these elements would make excellent coins in theory (for example, zirconium), but their status as coin metals is not clear. |
| Gold | Gold is a chemical element with the symbol Au and atomic number 79. It is a dense, soft, malleable, and ductile metal with an attractive, bright yellow color and luster that is maintained without tarnishing in air or water. Chemically, gold is a transition metal and a group 11 element. It is one of the least reactive chemical elements, solid under standard conditions. |
| Halogen | The halogens or halogen elements are a group in the periodic table consisting of five chemically related elements, fluorine, chlorine (Cl), bromine (Br), iodine (I), and astatine (At). The artificially created element 117 (ununseptium) may also be a halogen. In the modern IUPAC nomenclature, this group is known as group 17. |
| Manganese | Manganese is a chemical element, designated by the symbol Mn. It has the atomic number 25. It is found as a free element in nature (often in combination with iron), and in many minerals. Manganese is a metal with important industrial metal alloy uses, particularly in stainless steels. |
| Effusion | Effusion is the process in which a gas escapes through a small hole. This occurs if the diameter of the hole is considerably smaller than the mean free path of the molecules. According to Graham's law, the rate at which gases effuse (i.e., how many molecules pass through the hole per second) is dependent on their molecular weight. |
| Astatine | Astatine is a radioactive chemical element with the chemical symbol At and atomic number 85. It occurs on Earth only as the result of the radioactive decay of certain heavier elements. All of its isotopes are short-lived; the most stable is astatine-210, with a half-life of 8.5 hours. Accordingly, much less is known about astatine than most other elements. |
| Boron | Boron is a chemical element with symbol B and atomic number 5. Because boron is produced entirely by cosmic ray spallation and not by stellar nucleosynthesis, it is a low-abundance element in both the solar system and the Earth's crust. |

# 2. Atoms, Molecules, and Ions

|  | |
|---|---|
|  | Boron is concentrated on Earth by the water-solubility of its more common naturally occurring compounds, the borate minerals. These are mined industrially as evaporites, such as borax and kernite. |
| Hydrogen | Hydrogen is a chemical element with chemical symbol H and atomic number 1. With an atomic weight of 1.00794 u, hydrogen is the lightest element and its monatomic form (H) is the most abundant chemical substance, constituting roughly 75% of the Universe's baryonic mass. Non-remnant stars are mainly composed of hydrogen in its plasma state.<br><br>At standard temperature and pressure, hydrogen is a colorless, odorless, tasteless, non-toxic, nonmetallic, highly combustible diatomic gas with the molecular formula $H_2$. |
| Mercury | Mercury is a chemical element with the symbol Hg and atomic number 80. It is commonly known as quicksilver and was formerly named hydrargyrum (from Greek 'hydr-' water and 'argyros' silver). A heavy, silvery d-block element, mercury is the only metal that is liquid at standard conditions for temperature and pressure; the only other element that is liquid under these conditions is bromine, though metals such as caesium, gallium, and rubidium melt just above room temperature. With a freezing point of -38.83 °C and boiling point of 356.73 °C, mercury has one of the narrowest ranges of its liquid state of any metal. |
| Metalloid | A metalloid is a chemical element that has properties that are in between or a mixture of those of metals and nonmetals and is consequently difficult to classify unambiguously as either a metal or a nonmetal. There is no standard definition of a metalloid, nor is there agreement as to which elements are appropriately classified as such. Despite this lack of specificity the term remains in use in chemistry literature. |
| Carbon dioxide | Carbon dioxide is a naturally occurring chemical compound composed of two oxygen atoms each covalently double bonded to a single carbon atom. It is a gas at standard temperature and pressure and exists in Earth's atmosphere in this state, as a trace gas at a concentration of 0.039 per cent by volume.<br><br>As part of the carbon cycle, plants, algae, and cyanobacteria use light energy to photosynthesize carbohydrate from carbon dioxide and water, with oxygen produced as a waste product. |
| Carbon monoxide | Carbon monoxide is a colorless, odorless, and tasteless gas that is slightly less dense than air. It is toxic to humans and animals when encountered in higher concentrations, although it is also produced in normal animal metabolism in low quantities, and is thought to have some normal biological functions. In the atmosphere, it is spatially variable, short lived, having a role in the formation of ground-level ozone. |
| Diatomic molecule | Diatomic molecules are molecules composed only of two atoms, of either the same or different chemical elements. The prefix di- is of Greek origin, meaning two. |

# 2. Atoms, Molecules, and Ions

| | |
|---|---|
| Hydrogen peroxide | Hydrogen peroxide is the simplest peroxide (a compound with an oxygen-oxygen single bond). It is also a strong oxidizer. Hydrogen peroxide is a clear liquid, slightly more viscous than water. |
| Methane | Methane is a chemical compound with the chemical formula $CH_4$ (one atom of carbon and four atoms of hydrogen). It is the simplest alkane and the main component of natural gas. The relative abundance of methane makes it an attractive fuel. |
| Molecule | A molecule is an electrically neutral group of two or more atoms held together by chemical bonds. Molecules are distinguished from ions by their lack of electrical charge. However, in quantum physics, organic chemistry, and biochemistry, the term molecule is often used less strictly, also being applied to polyatomic ions. |
| Ozone | Ozone, or trioxygen, is an inorganic compound with the chemical formula $O_3(\mu\text{-}O)$ (also written [O ($\mu$-O)O] or $O_3$). It is a pale blue gas with a distinctively pungent smell. It is an allotrope of oxygen that is much less stable than the diatomic allotrope $O_2$, breaking down in the lower atmosphere to normal dioxygen. |
| Diatomic | Diatomic molecules are molecules composed of only two atoms, of either the same or different chemical elements. The prefix di- is of Greek origin, meaning 'two'. If a diatomic molecule consists of two atoms of the same element, such as hydrogen ($H_2$) or oxygen ($O_2$), then it is said to be homonuclear. |
| Ball-and-stick model | In chemistry, the ball-and-stick model is a molecular model of a chemical substance which is to display both the three-dimensional position of the atoms and the bonds between them. The atoms are typically represented by spheres, connected by rods which represent the bonds. Double and triple bonds are usually represented by two or three curved rods, respectively. |
| Space-filling model | In chemistry, a space-filling model, also known as a calotte model, is a type of three-dimensional molecular model where the atoms are represented by spheres whose radii are proportional to the radii of the atoms and whose center-to-center distances are proportional to the distances between the atomic nuclei, all in the same scale. Atoms of different chemical elements are usually represented by spheres of different colors.<br><br>Calotte models are distinguished from other 3D representations, such as the ball-and-stick and skeletal models, by the use of 'full size' balls for the atoms. |
| Product | Product are formed during chemical reactions as reagents are consumed. Products have lower energy than the reagents and are produced during the reaction according to the second law of thermodynamics. The released energy comes from changes in chemical bonds between atoms in reagent molecules and may be given off in the form of heat or light. |

# 2. Atoms, Molecules, and Ions

| | |
|---|---|
| Polyatomic ion | A polyatomic ion, also known as a molecular ion, is a charged chemical species composed of two or more atoms covalently bonded or of a metal complex that can be considered to be acting as a single unit. The prefix 'poly-' means 'many,' in Greek, but even ions of two atoms are commonly referred to as polyatomic. In older literature, a polyatomic ion is also referred to as a radical, and less commonly, as a radical group. |
| Concentration | In chemistry, concentration is the abundance of a constituent divided by the total volume of a mixture. Several types of mathematical description can be distinguished: mass concentration, molar concentration, number concentration, and volume concentration. The term concentration can be applied to any kind of chemical mixture, but most frequently it refers to solutes and solvents in solutions. |
| Ionic compound | In chemistry, an ionic compound is a chemical compound in which ions are held together in a lattice structure by ionic bonds. Usually, the positively charged portion consists of metal cations and the negatively charged portion is an anion or polyatomic ion. Ions in ionic compounds are held together by the electrostatic forces between oppositely charged bodies. |
| Sodium chloride | Sodium chloride, also known as salt, common salt, table salt or halite, is an ionic compound with the formula $NaCl$, representing equal proportions of sodium and chlorine. Sodium chloride is the salt most responsible for the salinity of the ocean and of the extracellular fluid of many multicellular organisms. As the major ingredient in edible salt, it is commonly used as a condiment and food preservative. |
| Carbon | Carbon fiber, alternatively graphite fiber, carbon graphite or CF, is a material consisting of fibers about 5-10 μm in diameter and composed mostly of carbon atoms. The carbon atoms are bonded together in crystals that are more or less aligned parallel to the long axis of the fiber. The crystal alignment gives the fiber high strength-to-volume ratio (making it strong for its size). |
| Trace element | In analytical chemistry, a trace element is an element in a sample that has an average concentration of less than 100 parts per million measured in atomic count or less than 100 micrograms per gram.<br><br>In biochemistry, a trace element is a dietary mineral that is needed in very minute quantities for the proper growth, development, and physiology of the organism.<br><br>In geochemistry, a trace element is a chemical element whose concentration is less than 1000 ppm or 0.1% of a rock's composition. |
| Calcium | Calcium is the chemical element with symbol Ca and atomic number 20. Calcium is a soft gray alkaline earth metal, and is the fifth-most-abundant element by mass in the Earth's crust. Calcium is also the fifth-most-abundant dissolved ion in seawater by both molarity and mass, after sodium, chloride, magnesium, and sulfate. |

# 2. Atoms, Molecules, and Ions

| | |
|---|---|
| Carbon group | The carbon group is a periodic table group consisting of carbon, silicon (Si), germanium (Ge), tin (Sn), lead (Pb), and flerovium (Fl).<br><br>In modern IUPAC notation, it is called Group 14. In the field of semiconductor physics, it is still universally called Group IV. The group was once also known as the tetrels (from Greek tetra, four), stemming from the Roman numeral IV in the group names, or (not coincidentally) from the fact that these elements have four valence electrons . The group is sometimes also referred to as tetragens or crystallogens. |
| Inorganic compound | Inorganic compounds are those that lack carbon and hydrogen atoms. Inorganic compounds are traditionally viewed as being synthesized by the agency of geological systems. In contrast, organic compounds are found in biological systems. |
| Organic compound | An organic compound is any member of a large class of gaseous, liquid, or solid chemical compounds whose molecules contain carbon. For historical reasons discussed below, a few types of carbon-containing compounds such as carbides, carbonates, simple oxides of carbon (such as $CO$ and $CO_2$), and cyanides are considered inorganic. The distinction between 'organic' and 'inorganic' carbon compounds, while 'useful in organizing the vast subject of chemistry... is somewhat arbitrary'. |
| Chromium | Chromium is a chemical element which has the symbol Cr and atomic number 24. It is the first element in Group 6. It is a steely-gray, lustrous, hard and brittle metal which takes a high polish, resists tarnishing, and has a high melting point. The name of the element is derived from the Greek word 'chroma' (???μα), meaning colour, because many of its compounds are intensely coloured.<br><br>Chromium oxide was used by the Chinese in the Qin dynasty over 2,000 years ago to coat metal weapons found with the Terracotta Army. |
| Ostwald process | The Ostwald process is a chemical process for making nitric acid . Wilhelm Ostwald developed the process, and he patented it in 1902. The Ostwald process is a mainstay of the modern chemical industry, and it provides the main raw material for the most common type of fertilizer production. Historically and practically, the Ostwald process is closely associated with the Haber process, which provides the requisite raw material, ammonia ($NH_3$). |
| Transition metal | In chemistry, the term transition metal has two possible meanings:•Most scientists describe a 'transition metal' as any element in the d-block of the periodic table (all are metals), which includes groups 3 to 12 on the periodic table. In actual practice, the f-block lanthanide and actinide series are also considered transition metals and are called 'inner transition metals'.<br><br>Jensen reviews the history of the terms 'transition element' (or 'metal') and 'd-block'. |

# 2. Atoms, Molecules, and Ions

| | |
|---|---|
| Hypoiodous acid | Hypoiodous acid is the inorganic compound with the chemical formula HIO. It forms when an aqueous solution of iodine is treated with mercuric or silver salts. It rapidly decomposes by disproportionation:5 HIO ? $HIO_3 + 2I_2 + 2H_2O$<br><br>Hypoiodous acid is a weak acid with a $K_a$ of about $10^{-11}$. The conjugate base is hypoiodite ($IO^-$). |
| Oxyanion | An oxyanion or oxoanion is a chemical compound with the generic formula $A_xO_y^{z-}$. Oxoanions are formed by a large majority of the chemical elements. The formulae of simple oxoanions are determined by the octet rule. |
| Bromide ion | A bromide is a chemical compound containing a bromide ion or ligand. This is a bromine atom with an ionic charge of -1 ($Br^-$); for example, in caesium bromide, caesium cations ($Cs^+$) are electrically attracted to bromide anions ($Br^-$) to form the electrically neutral ionic compound CsBr. The term 'bromide' can also refer to a bromine atom with an oxidation number of -1 in covalent compounds such as sulfur dibromide ($SBr_2$). |
| Chloride ion | The chloride ion is the anion $Cl^-$. It is formed when the element chlorine (a halogen) gains an electron or when a compound such as hydrogen chloride is dissolved in water or other polar solvents. Chlorides salts such as sodium chloride are often very soluble in water. |
| Cyanide ion | A cyanide is any chemical compound that contains monovalent combining group CN. This group, known as the cyano group, consists of a carbon atom triple-bonded to a nitrogen atom.<br><br>In inorganic cyanides, such as sodium cyanide, NaCN, this group is present as the negatively-charged polyatomic cyanide ion; these compounds, which are regarded as salts of hydrocyanic acid, are highly toxic. The cyanide ion is isoelectronic with carbon monoxide and with molecular nitrogen. |
| Ice pack | An ice pack or gel pack is a plastic sac of ice, or of refrigerant gel or liquid. Both the ice pack and the non-toxic gel (which is mostly water) can absorb a considerable amount of heat due to the high enthalpy of fusion of water. These packs are commonly used to keep food cool in coolers for consumption later in the day; or as a cold compress to alleviate the pain of minor injuries; or in insulated shipping containers to keep products cool during transport. |
| Solubility | Solubility is the property of a solid, liquid, or gaseous chemical substance called solute to dissolve in a solid, liquid, or gaseous solvent to form a homogeneous solution of the solute in the solvent. The solubility of a substance fundamentally depends on the physical and chemical properties of the solute and solvent as well as on temperature, pressure and the pH of the solution. |

CHAPTER HIGHLIGHTS & NOTES: KEY TERMS, PEOPLE, PLACES, CONCEPTS

| Octane rating | Octane rating or octane number is a standard measure of the performance of a motor or aviation fuel. The higher the octane number, the more compression the fuel can withstand before detonating. In broad terms, fuels with a higher octane rating are used in high-compression engines that generally have higher performance. |
| --- | --- |
| Triple point | In thermodynamics, the triple point of a substance is the temperature and pressure at which the three phases of that substance coexist in thermodynamic equilibrium. For example, the triple point of mercury occurs at a temperature of -38.8344 °C and a pressure of 0.2 mPa.<br><br>In addition to the triple point between solid, liquid, and gas, there can be triple points involving more than one solid phase, for substances with multiple polymorphs. |
| Binary compound | A binary compound is a chemical compound that contains exactly two different elements. Examples of binary ionic compounds include calcium chloride ($CaCl_2$), sodium fluoride (NaF), and magnesium oxide (MgO), whilst examples of a binary covalent compounds include water ($H_2O$), carbon monoxide (CO), and sulfur hexafluoride ($SF_6$). |
| Alkane | In organic chemistry, an alkane, or paraffin, is a saturated hydrocarbon. Alkanes consist only of hydrogen and carbon atoms, all bonds are single bonds, and the carbon atoms are not joined in cyclic structures but instead form an open chain. They have the general chemical formula $C_nH_{2n+2}$. |
| Ethane | Ethane is a chemical compound with chemical formula $C_2H_6$. At standard temperature and pressure, ethane is a colorless, odorless gas. Ethane is isolated on an industrial scale from natural gas, and as a byproduct of petroleum refining. |
| Ethanol | Ethanol, also called ethyl alcohol, pure alcohol, grain alcohol, or drinking alcohol, is a volatile, flammable, colorless liquid with the structural formula $CH_3CH_2OH$, often abbreviated as $C_2H_5OH$ or $C_2H_6O$. A psychoactive drug and one of the oldest recreational drugs, ethanol can cause alcohol intoxication when consumed. Best known as the type of alcohol found in alcoholic beverages, it is also used in thermometers, as a solvent, and as a fuel. In common usage, it is often referred to simply as alcohol or spirits. |
| Hydrocarbon | In organic chemistry, a hydrocarbon is an organic compound consisting entirely of hydrogen and carbon. Hydrocarbons from which one hydrogen atom has been removed are functional groups, called hydrocarbyls. Aromatic hydrocarbons (arenes), alkanes, alkenes, cycloalkanes and alkyne-based compounds are different types of hydrocarbons. |
| Methanol | Methanol, also known as methyl alcohol, wood alcohol, wood naphtha or wood spirits, is a chemical with the formula $CH_3OH$ . Methanol acquired the name 'wood alcohol' because it was once produced chiefly as a byproduct of the destructive distillation of wood. |

# 2. Atoms, Molecules, and Ions

| | |
|---|---|
| Octane | Octane is a hydrocarbon and an alkane with the chemical formula $C_8H_{18}$, and the condensed structural formula $CH_{36}CH_3$. Octane has many structural isomers that differ by the amount and location of branching in the carbon chain. One of these isomers, 2,2,4-trimethylpentane (isooctane) is used as one of the standard values in the octane rating scale. |
| Organic chemistry | Organic chemistry is a chemistry subdiscipline involving the scientific study of the structure, properties, and reactions of organic compounds and organic materials, i.e., matter in its various forms that contain carbon atoms. Study of structure includes using spectroscopy and other physical and chemical methods to determine the chemical composition and constitution of organic compounds and materials. Study of properties includes both physical properties and chemical properties, and uses similar methods as well as methods to evaluate chemical reactivity, with the aim to understand the behavior of the organic matter in its pure form (when possible), but also in solutions, mixtures, and fabricated forms. |
| Propane | Propane is a three-carbon alkane with the molecular formula C3H8, normally a gas, but compressible to a transportable liquid. A by-product of natural gas processing and petroleum refining, it is commonly used as a fuel for engines, oxy-gas torches, barbecues, portable stoves, and residential central heating. Propane is one of a group of liquefied petroleum gases. |
| 1-Propanol | 1-Propanol is a primary alcohol with the formula $CH_3CH_2CH_2OH$. This colorless liquid is also known as propan-1-ol, 1-propyl alcohol, n-propyl alcohol, n-propanol, or simply propanol. It is an isomer of isopropanol (2-propanol, isopropyl alcohol). It is formed naturally in small amounts during many fermentation processes and used as a solvent in the pharmaceutical industry mainly for resins and cellulose esters. |
| Alcohol | In chemistry, an alcohol is an organic compound in which the hydroxyl functional group is bound to a carbon atom. In particular, this carbon center should be saturated, having single bonds to three other atoms. <br><br> An important class of alcohols are the simple acyclic alcohols, the general formula for which is $C_nH_{2n+1}OH$. Of those, ethanol ($C_2H_5OH$) is the type of alcohol found in alcoholic beverages, and in common speech the word alcohol refers specifically to ethanol. |
| Functional group | In organic chemistry, functional groups are lexicon-specific groups of atoms or bonds within molecules that are responsible for the characteristic chemical reactions of those molecules. The same functional group will undergo the same or similar chemical reaction(s) regardless of the size of the molecule it is a part of. However, its relative reactivity can be modified by nearby functional groups. |
| Isomer | In chemistry, isomers (; from Greek ?s?µe???, isomerès; isos = 'equal', méros = 'part') are molecules with the same molecular formula but different chemical structures. |

That is, isomers contain the same number of atoms of each element, but have different arrangements of their atoms in space. Isomers do not necessarily share similar properties, unless they also have the same functional groups.

| | |
|---|---|
| Isopropyl alcohol | Isopropyl alcohol is a common name for a chemical compound with the molecular formula $C_3H_8O$ or $C_3H_7OH$. It is a colorless, flammable chemical compound with a strong odor. It is the simplest example of a secondary alcohol, where the alcohol carbon atom is attached to two other carbon atoms sometimes shown as $(CH_3)_2CHOH$. It is a structural isomer of propanol. Isopropyl alcohol is denatured for certain uses, in which case the NFPA 704 rating is changed to 2,3,1. |
| Molecular weight | Molecular mass or molecular weight refers to the mass of a molecule. It is calculated as the sum of the mass of each constituent atom multiplied by the number of atoms of that element in the molecular formula. The molecular mass of small to medium size molecules, measured by mass spectrometry, determines stoichiometry. |
| Polyethylene | Polyethylene or polythene (IUPAC name polyethene or poly(methylene)) is the most common plastic. The annual production is approximately 80 million tonnes. Its primary use is in packaging (plastic bag, plastic films, geomembranes, containers including bottles, etc).. |
| Benzene | Benzene is an organic chemical compound with the molecular formula $C_6H_6$. Its molecule is composed of 6 carbon atoms joined in a ring, with 1 hydrogen atom attached to each carbon atom. Because its molecules contain only carbon and hydrogen atoms, benzene is classed as a hydrocarbon. |
| Diborane | Diborane is the chemical compound consisting of boron and hydrogen with the formula $B_2H_6$. It is a colorless gas at room temperature with a repulsively sweet odor. Diborane mixes well with air, easily forming explosive mixtures. |
| Glucose | Glucose, meaning 'sweet'. The suffix '-ose' denotes a sugar. |
| Silicon tetrachloride | Silicon tetrachloride is the inorganic compound with the formula $SiCl_4$. It is a colourless volatile liquid that fumes in air. It is used to produce high purity silicon and silica for commercial applications. |
| Tritium | Tritium is a radioactive isotope of hydrogen. The nucleus of tritium contains one proton and two neutrons, whereas the nucleus of protium (by far the most abundant hydrogen isotope) contains one proton and no neutrons. Naturally occurring tritium is extremely rare on Earth, where trace amounts are formed by the interaction of the atmosphere with cosmic rays. |
| Cyclohexane | Cyclohexane is a cycloalkane with the molecular formula $C_6H_{12}$. Cyclohexane is used as a nonpolar solvent for the chemical industry, and also as a raw material for the industrial production of adipic acid and caprolactam, both of which being intermediates used in the production of nylon. |

# 2. Atoms, Molecules, and Ions

| Cyclohexanol | Cyclohexanol is the organic compound with the formula $(CH_2)_5CHOH$. The molecule is related to cyclohexane ring by replacement of one hydrogen atom by a hydroxyl group. This compound exists as a deliquescent colorless solid, which, when very pure, melts near room temperature. Billions of kilograms are produced annually, mainly as a precursor to nylon. |
|---|---|

1. _____ is a chemical element with the symbol Au and atomic number 79. It is a dense, soft, malleable, and ductile metal with an attractive, bright yellow color and luster that is maintained without tarnishing in air or water. Chemically, _____ is a transition metal and a group 11 element. It is one of the least reactive chemical elements, solid under standard conditions.

   a. Betafite
   b. Bixbyite
   c. Boleite
   d. Gold

2. The _____ is the force between two or more nucleons. Its fundamental laws and constants are unknown unlike the Coulomb and Newton laws. It is responsible for binding protons and neutrons into atomic nuclei.

   a. Baryon number
   b. Beta decay
   c. Nuclear force
   d. Binding energy

3. _____ is the emission of light by a substance that has absorbed light or other electromagnetic radiation. It is a form of luminescence. In most cases, the emitted light has a longer wavelength, and therefore lower energy, than the absorbed radiation.

   a. Fluorescence
   b. Buffering agent
   c. Carbonate alkalinity
   d. Charlot equation

4. . The _____ is a chemical process for making nitric acid . Wilhelm Ostwald developed the process, and he patented it in 1902. The _____ is a mainstay of the modern chemical industry, and it provides the main raw material for the most common type of fertilizer production. Historically and practically, the _____ is closely associated with the Haber process, which provides the requisite raw material, ammonia ($NH_3$).

   a. 3A Molecular sieve

b. Biochemical cascade

c. Bioconversion

d. Ostwald process

5. _____, or trioxygen, is an inorganic compound with the chemical formula $O_3(\mu\text{-}O)$ (also written $[O(\mu\text{-}O)O]$ or $O_3$). It is a pale blue gas with a distinctively pungent smell. It is an allotrope of oxygen that is much less stable than the diatomic allotrope $O_2$, breaking down in the lower atmosphere to normal dioxygen.

a. Disulfur

b. Nanocrystalline silicon

c. Ozone

d. Tin pest

**1.** d
**2.** c
**3.** a
**4.** d
**5.** c

---

## You can take the complete Chapter Practice Test

**for 2. Atoms, Molecules, and Ions**
on all key terms, persons, places, and concepts.

### Online 99 Cents

### http://www.JustTheFacts101.com

**Use www.JustTheFacts101.com for all your study needs**

**including Facts101's online interactive problem solving labs in**

**chemistry, statistics, mathematics, and more.**

# 3. Chemical Reactions and Reaction Stoichiometry

CHAPTER OUTLINE: KEY TERMS, PEOPLE, PLACES, CONCEPTS

Stoichiometry

Absorption

Mass spectrum

Product

Combustion

Mole

Lewis structure

Methane

State function

Combination reaction

Magnesium

Hydrogen

Calcium

Calcium carbonate

Calcium oxide

Sodium azide

Decomposition

Effusion

Molecular weight

Sulfuric acid

Avogadro

Atom

Volume

Barium

Barium azide

Glucose

Insulin

Mesosphere

Particle

Molecule

Mesitylene

Combustion analysis

Ethylene glycol

Isopropyl alcohol

Quantitative analysis

Stock solution

Oxidation

Lithium hydroxide

Oxygen

Adipic acid

Styrene

Aspartame

CHAPTER OUTLINE: KEY TERMS, PEOPLE, PLACES, CONCEPTS

| | |
|---|---|
| | Cadaverine |
| | Caffeine |
| | Epinephrine |
| | Ethyl butyrate |
| | Hydrofluoric acid |
| | Ibuprofen |
| | Menthol |
| | Monosodium glutamate |
| | Nicotine |
| | Sodium silicate |
| | Toluene |
| | Valproic acid |
| | Claus process |
| | Hydrogen sulfide |
| | Acetylsalicylic acid |
| | Aspirin |
| | Hemoglobin |
| | Quantum dot |
| | Serotonin |
| | Vanillin |
| | Concentration |

# 3. Chemical Reactions and Reaction Stoichiometry
## CHAPTER OUTLINE: KEY TERMS, PEOPLE, PLACES, CONCEPTS

| Hydrogen cyanide |

**Stoichiometry**

Stoichiometry is a branch of chemistry that deals with the relative quantities of reactants and products in chemical reactions. In a balanced chemical reaction, the relations among quantities of reactants and products typically form a ratio of positive integers. For example, in a reaction that forms ammonia ($NH_3$), exactly one molecule of nitrogen gas ($N_2$) reacts with three molecules of hydrogen gas ($H_2$) to produce two molecules of $NH_3$: N2 + 3H2 ? 2NH3

This particular kind of stoichiometry - describing the quantitative relationships among substances as they participate in chemical reactions - is known as reaction stoichiometry.

**Absorption**

In chemistry, absorption is a physical or chemical phenomenon or a process in which atoms, molecules, or ions enter some bulk phase - gas, liquid, or solid material. This is a different process from adsorption, since molecules undergoing absorption are taken up by the volume, not by the surface (as in the case for adsorption). A more general term is sorption, which covers absorption, adsorption, and ion exchange.

**Mass spectrum**

A mass spectrum is an intensity vs. m/z (mass-to-charge ratio) plot representing a chemical analysis. Hence, the mass spectrum of a sample is a pattern representing the distribution of ions by mass (more correctly: mass-to-charge ratio) in a sample. It is a histogram usually acquired using an instrument called a mass spectrometer.

**Product**

Product are formed during chemical reactions as reagents are consumed. Products have lower energy than the reagents and are produced during the reaction according to the second law of thermodynamics. The released energy comes from changes in chemical bonds between atoms in reagent molecules and may be given off in the form of heat or light.

**Combustion**

Combustion or burning is the sequence of exothermic chemical reactions between a fuel and an oxidant accompanied by the production of heat and conversion of chemical species. The release of heat can produce light in the form of either glowing or a flame.

In a complete combustion reaction, a compound reacts with an oxidizing element, such as oxygen or fluorine, and the products are compounds of each element in the fuel with the oxidizing element.

| | |
|---|---|
| Mole | Mole is a unit of measurement used in chemistry to express amounts of a chemical substance, defined as the amount of any substance that contains as many elementary entities (e.g., atoms, molecules, ions, electrons) as there are atoms in 12 grams of pure carbon-12, the isotope of carbon with relative atomic mass 12. This corresponds to the Avogadro constant, which has a value of $6.02214129(27) \times 10^{23}$ elementary entities of the substance. It is one of the base units in the International System of Units, and has the unit symbol mol and corresponds with the dimension symbol N. In honour of the unit, chemists often celebrate October 23 (a reference to the $10^{23}$ part of Avogadro's number) as 'Mole Day'.<br><br>The mole is widely used in chemistry instead of units of mass or volume as a convenient way to express amounts of reactants or of products of chemical reactions. |
| Lewis structure | Lewis structures are diagrams that show the bonding between atoms of a molecule and the lone pairs of electrons that may exist in the molecule. A Lewis structure can be drawn for any covalently bonded molecule, as well as coordination compounds. The Lewis structure was named after Gilbert N |
| Methane | Methane is a chemical compound with the chemical formula CH4 (one atom of carbon and four atoms of hydrogen). It is the simplest alkane and the main component of natural gas. The relative abundance of methane makes it an attractive fuel. |
| State function | In thermodynamics, a state function, function of state, state quantity, or state variable is a property of a system that depends only on the current state of the system, not on the way in which the system acquired that state . A state function describes the equilibrium state of a system. For example, internal energy, enthalpy, and entropy are state quantities because they describe quantitatively an equilibrium state of a thermodynamic system, irrespective of how the system arrived in that state. |
| Combination reaction | Those reaction in which two or more elements or compounds combine together to form a single compound are called combination reaction. They may be represented by X + Y ? XY Combination reactions are usually exothermic. For example barium metal and fluorine gas will combine in a highly exothermic reaction to form the salt barium fluoride:<br><br>$Ba + F_2 ? BaF_2$<br><br>Another example is magnesium oxide combining with carbon dioxide to produce magnesium carbonate. |
| Magnesium | Magnesium is a chemical element with the symbol Mg and atomic number 12. Its common oxidation number is +2. It is an alkaline earth metal and the eighth most abundant element in the Earth's crust and ninth in the known universe as a whole. |

# 3. Chemical Reactions and Reaction Stoichiometry

Magnesium is the fourth most common element in the Earth as a whole (behind iron, oxygen and silicon), making up 13% of the planet's mass and a large fraction of the planet's mantle. The relative abundance of magnesium is related to the fact that it easily builds up in supernova stars from a sequential addition of three helium nuclei to carbon (which in turn is made from three helium nuclei).

**Hydrogen**

Hydrogen is a chemical element with chemical symbol H and atomic number 1. With an atomic weight of 1.00794 u, hydrogen is the lightest element and its monatomic form (H) is the most abundant chemical substance, constituting roughly 75% of the Universe's baryonic mass. Non-remnant stars are mainly composed of hydrogen in its plasma state.

At standard temperature and pressure, hydrogen is a colorless, odorless, tasteless, non-toxic, nonmetallic, highly combustible diatomic gas with the molecular formula $H_2$.

**Calcium**

Calcium is the chemical element with symbol Ca and atomic number 20. Calcium is a soft gray alkaline earth metal, and is the fifth-most-abundant element by mass in the Earth's crust. Calcium is also the fifth-most-abundant dissolved ion in seawater by both molarity and mass, after sodium, chloride, magnesium, and sulfate.

Calcium is essential for living organisms, in particular in cell physiology, where movement of the calcium ion $Ca^{2+}$ into and out of the cytoplasm functions as a signal for many cellular processes.

**Calcium carbonate**

Calcium carbonate is a chemical compound with the formula $CaCO_3$. It is a common substance found in rocks in all parts of the world, and is the main component of shells of marine organisms, snails, coal balls, pearls, and eggshells. Calcium carbonate is the active ingredient in agricultural lime, and is created when Ca ions in hard water react with carbonate ions creating limescale.

**Calcium oxide**

Calcium oxide, commonly known as quicklime or burnt lime, is a widely used chemical compound. It is a white, caustic, alkaline crystalline solid at room temperature. The broadly used term 'lime' connotes calcium-containing inorganic materials, which include carbonates, oxides and hydroxides of calcium, silicon, magnesium, aluminium, and iron predominate, such as limestone.

**Sodium azide**

Sodium azide is the inorganic compound with the formula $NaN_3$. This colorless salt is the gas-forming component in many car airbag systems. It is used for the preparation of other azide compounds.

**Decomposition**

Decomposition is the process by which organic substances are broken down into simpler forms of matter. The process is essential for recycling the finite matter that occupies physical space in the biome. Bodies of living organisms begin to decompose shortly after death.

**Effusion**

Effusion is the process in which a gas escapes through a small hole. This occurs if the diameter of the hole is considerably smaller than the mean free path of the molecules.

| | |
|---|---|
| Molecular weight | Molecular mass or molecular weight refers to the mass of a molecule. It is calculated as the sum of the mass of each constituent atom multiplied by the number of atoms of that element in the molecular formula. The molecular mass of small to medium size molecules, measured by mass spectrometry, determines stoichiometry. |
| Sulfuric acid | Sulfuric acid is a highly corrosive strong mineral acid with the molecular formula $H_2SO_4$. It is a pungent, colorless to slightly yellow viscous liquid which is soluble in water at all concentrations. Sometimes, it is dyed dark brown during production to alert people to its hazards. |
| Avogadro | Avogadro is a molecular editor designed for cross-platform use in computational chemistry, molecular modeling, bioinformatics, materials science, and related areas. It is extensible through a plugin architecture. |
| Atom | The atom is a basic unit of matter that consists of a dense central nucleus surrounded by a cloud of negatively charged electrons. The atomic nucleus contains a mix of positively charged protons and electrically neutral neutrons, which means 'uncuttable' or 'the smallest indivisible particle of matter'. Although the Indian and Greek concepts of the atom were based purely on philosophy, modern science has retained the name coined by Democritus. |
| Volume | In thermodynamics, the volume of a system is an important extensive parameter for describing its thermodynamic state. The specific volume, an intensive property, is the system's volume per unit of mass. Volume is a function of state and is interdependent with other thermodynamic properties such as pressure and temperature. |
| Barium | Barium is a chemical element with symbol Ba and atomic number 56. It is the fifth element in Group 2, a soft silvery metallic alkaline earth metal. Because of its high chemical reactivity barium is never found in nature as a free element. Its hydroxide was known in pre-modern history as baryta; this substance does not occur as a mineral, but can be prepared by heating barium carbonate. |
| Barium azide | Barium azide $Ba_2$ is an inorganic azide, is explosive, but less sensitive to mechanical shock than lead azide. |
| Glucose | Glucose, meaning 'sweet'. The suffix '-ose' denotes a sugar. |
| Insulin | Insulin is a peptide hormone, produced by beta cells of the pancreas, and is central to regulating carbohydrate and fat metabolism in the body. Insulin causes cells in the liver, skeletal muscles, and fat tissue to absorb glucose from the blood. In the liver and skeletal muscles, glucose is stored as glycogen, and in fat cells (adipocytes) it is stored as triglycerides. |
| Mesosphere | The mesosphere is the layer of the Earth's atmosphere that is directly above the stratopause and directly below the mesopause. In the mesosphere temperature decreases with increasing height. |

# 3. Chemical Reactions and Reaction Stoichiometry

The upper boundary of the mesosphere is the mesopause, which can be the coldest naturally occurring place on Earth with temperatures below 130 K (-226 °F; -143 °C).

| | |
|---|---|
| Particle | In the physical sciences, a particle is a small localized object to which can be ascribed several physical or chemical properties such as volume or mass. The word is rather general in meaning, and is refined as needed by various scientific fields. Something that is composed of particles may be referred to as particulate, although this term is generally used to refer to a suspension of unconnected particles, rather than a connected particle aggregation. |
| Molecule | A molecule is an electrically neutral group of two or more atoms held together by chemical bonds. Molecules are distinguished from ions by their lack of electrical charge. However, in quantum physics, organic chemistry, and biochemistry, the term molecule is often used less strictly, also being applied to polyatomic ions. |
| Mesitylene | Mesitylene or 1,3,5-trimethylbenzene is a derivative of benzene with three methyl substituents symmetrically placed on the ring. Isomeric trimethylbenzenes include 1,2,4-trimethylbenzene (pseudocumene) and 1,2,3-trimethylbenzene (hemimellitene). All three compounds have the formula $C_6H_3(CH_3)_3$, which is commonly abbreviated $C_6H_3Me_3$. |
| Combustion analysis | Combustion analysis is a method used in both organic chemistry and analytical chemistry to determine the elemental composition of a pure organic compound by combusting the sample under conditions where the resulting combustion products can be quantitatively analyzed. Once the number of moles of each combustion product has been determined the empirical formula or a partial empirical formula of the original compound can be calculated. |
| Ethylene glycol | Ethylene glycol is an organic compound primarily used as a raw material in the manufacture of polyester fibers and fabric industry, and polyethylene terephthalate resins (PET) used in bottling. A small percent is also used in industrial applications like antifreeze formulations and other industrial products. It is an odorless, colorless, syrupy, sweet-tasting liquid. |
| Isopropyl alcohol | Isopropyl alcohol is a common name for a chemical compound with the molecular formula $C_3H_8O$ or $C_3H_7OH$. It is a colorless, flammable chemical compound with a strong odor. It is the simplest example of a secondary alcohol, where the alcohol carbon atom is attached to two other carbon atoms sometimes shown as $(CH_3)_2CHOH$. It is a structural isomer of propanol. Isopropyl alcohol is denatured for certain uses, in which case the NFPA 704 rating is changed to 2,3,1. |
| Quantitative analysis | In chemistry, quantitative analysis is the determination of the absolute or relative abundance of one, several or all particular substance(s) present in a sample. |
| Stock solution | A Stock Solution is a concentrated solution that will be diluted to some lower concentrated for actual use. Stock solutions are used to save preparation time, conserve materials, reduce storage space, and improve the accuracy with which working lower concentration solutions are prepared. |

# 3. Chemical Reactions and Reaction Stoichiometry

| Oxidation | Redox (reduction-oxidation) reactions include all chemical reactions in which atoms have their oxidation state changed; in general, redox reactions involve the transfer of electrons between species. |
| --- | --- |
| | This can be either a simple redox process, such as the oxidation of carbon to yield carbon dioxide or the reduction of carbon by hydrogen to yield methane ($CH_4$), or a complex process such as the oxidation of glucose ($C_6H_{12}O_6$) in the human body through a series of complex electron transfer processes. |
| | The term 'redox' comes from two concepts involved with electron transfer: reduction and oxidation. |
| Lithium hydroxide | Lithium hydroxide is an inorganic compound with the formula LiOH. It is a white hygroscopic crystalline material. It is soluble in water and slightly soluble in ethanol. It is available commercially in anhydrous form and as the monohydrate ($LiOH \cdot H_2O$), both of which are strong bases. |
| Oxygen | Oxygen is a chemical element with symbol O and atomic number 8. It is a member of the chalcogen group on the periodic table and is a highly reactive nonmetallic element and oxidizing agent that readily forms compounds (notably oxides) with most elements. By mass, oxygen is the third-most abundant element in the universe, after hydrogen and helium At STP, two atoms of the element bind to form dioxygen, a diatomic gas that is colorless, odorless, and tasteless; with the formula O2. |
| | Many major classes of organic molecules in living organisms, such as proteins, nucleic acids, carbohydrates, and fats, contain oxygen, as do the major inorganic compounds that are constituents of animal shells, teeth, and bone. |
| Adipic acid | Adipic acid is the organic compound with the formula $(CH_2)_4(COOH)_2$. From an industrial perspective, it is the most important dicarboxylic acid: About 2.5 billion kilograms of this white crystalline powder are produced annually, mainly as a precursor for the production of nylon. Adipic acid otherwise rarely occurs in nature. |
| Styrene | Styrene, also known as vinyl benzene and phenyl ethene, is an organic compound with the chemical formula $C_6H_5CH=CH_2$. This derivative of benzene is a colorless oily liquid that evaporates easily and has a sweet smell, although high concentrations confer a less pleasant odor. Styrene is the precursor to polystyrene and several copolymers. |
| Aspartame | Aspartame is an artificial, non-saccharide sweetener used as a sugar substitute in some foods and beverages. In the European Union, it is codified as E951. Aspartame is a methyl ester of the aspartic acid/phenylalanine dipeptide. It was first sold under the brand name NutraSweet; since 2009 it also has been sold under the brand name AminoSweet. |

# 3. Chemical Reactions and Reaction Stoichiometry

| | |
|---|---|
| Cadaverine | Cadaverine is a foul-smelling diamine compound produced by protein hydrolysis during putrefaction of animal tissue. Cadaverine is a toxic diamine with the formula $NH_2(CH_2)_5NH_2$, which is similar to putrescine. Cadaverine is also known by the names 1,5-pentanediamine and pentamethylenediamine. |
| Caffeine | Caffeine is a bitter, white crystalline xanthine alkaloid and a stimulant drug. Caffeine is found in varying quantities in the seeds, leaves, and fruit of some plants, where it acts as a natural pesticide that paralyzes and kills certain insects feeding on the plants, as well as enhancing the reward memory of pollinators. It is most commonly consumed by humans in infusions extracted from the seed of the coffee plant and the leaves of the tea bush, as well as from various foods and drinks containing products derived from the kola nut. |
| Epinephrine | Epinephrine is a hormone and a neurotransmitter. Epinephrine has many functions in the body, regulating heart rate, blood vessel and air passage diameters, and metabolic shifts; epinephrine release is a crucial component of the fight-or-flight response of the sympathetic nervous system. In chemical terms, epinephrine is one of a group of monoamines called the catecholamines. |
| Ethyl butyrate | Ethyl butyrate, also known as ethyl butanoate, or butyric ether, is an ester with the chemical formula $CH_3CH_2CH_2COOCH_2CH_3$. It is soluble in propylene glycol, paraffin oil, and kerosene. It has a fruity odor, similar to pineapple. |
| Hydrofluoric acid | Hydrofluoric acid is a solution of hydrogen fluoride in water. It is a valued source of fluorine and is a precursor to numerous pharmaceuticals such as fluoxetine (Prozac) and diverse materials such as PTFE (Teflon). |
| | Hydrofluoric acid is a highly corrosive acid, capable of dissolving many materials, especially oxides. |
| Ibuprofen | Ibuprofen is a nonsteroidal anti-inflammatory drug (NSAID) used for pain relief, fever reduction, and for reducing swelling. |
| | Ibuprofen has an antiplatelet effect, though relatively mild and somewhat short-lived compared with aspirin or prescription antiplatelet drugs. In general, ibuprofen also has a vasodilation effect. |
| Menthol | Menthol is an organic compound made synthetically or obtained from cornmint, peppermint or other mint oils. It is a waxy, crystalline substance, clear or white in color, which is solid at room temperature and melts slightly above. The main form of menthol occurring in nature is (-)-menthol, which is assigned the (1R,2S,5R) configuration. |
| Monosodium glutamate | Monosodium glutamate, also known as sodium glutamate, is the sodium salt of glutamic acid, one of the most abundant naturally occurring non-essential amino acids. |
| | MSG was classified by the U.S. |

| | |
|---|---|
| | Food and Drug Administration as generally recognized as safe (GRAS) and by the European Union as a food additive. |
| | MSG has the HS code 29224220 and the E number E621. |
| Nicotine | Nicotine is a potent parasympathomimetic alkaloid found in the nightshade family of plants and a stimulant drug. It is a nicotinic acetylcholine receptor agonist. It is made in the roots and accumulates in the leaves of the plants. |
| Sodium silicate | Sodium silicate is the common name for a compound sodium metasilicate, $Na_2SiO_3$, also known as waterglass or liquid glass. It is available in aqueous solution and in solid form and is used in cements, passive fire protection, refractories, textile and lumber processing, and automobiles. Sodium carbonate and silicon dioxide react when molten to form sodium silicate and carbon dioxide:$Na_2CO_3 + SiO_2$ ? $Na_2SiO_3 + CO_2$ |
| | Anhydrous sodium silicate contains a chain polymeric anion composed of corner shared $\{SiO_4\}$ tetrahedral, and not a discrete $SiO_3^{2-}$ ion. |
| Toluene | Toluene, formerly known as toluol, is a clear, water-insoluble liquid with the typical smell of paint thinners. It is a mono-substituted benzene derivative, i.e., one in which a single hydrogen atom from a group of six atoms from the benzene molecule has been replaced by a univalent group, in this case $CH_3$. As such, its IUPAC systematic name is methylbenzene. |
| Valproic acid | Valproic acid, an acidic chemical compound, has found clinical use as an anticonvulsant and mood-stabilizing drug, primarily in the treatment of epilepsy, bipolar disorder, and, less commonly, major depression. It is also used to treat migraine headaches. VPA is a liquid at room temperature, but it can be reacted with a base such as sodium hydroxide to form the salt sodium valproate, which is a solid. |
| Claus process | The Claus process is the most significant gas desulfurizing process, recovering elemental sulfur from gaseous hydrogen sulfide. First patented in 1883 by the scientist Carl Friedrich Claus, the Claus process has become the industry standard. |
| | The multi-step Claus process recovers sulfur from the gaseous hydrogen sulfide found in raw natural gas and from the by-product gases containing hydrogen sulfide derived from refining crude oil and other industrial processes. |
| Hydrogen sulfide | Hydrogen sulfide is the chemical compound with the formula H2S. It is a colorless gas with the characteristic foul odor of rotten eggs; it is heavier than air, very poisonous, corrosive, flammable and explosive. |

# 3. Chemical Reactions and Reaction Stoichiometry

| | |
|---|---|
| Acetylsalicylic acid | Aspirin, also known as acetylsalicylic acid (INN ( ?--?l--i--ik) ASA), is a salicylate drug, often used as an analgesic to relieve minor aches and pains, as an antipyretic to reduce fever, and as an anti-inflammatory medication. The active ingredient of Aspirin was first discovered from the bark of the willow tree in 1763 by Edward Stone of Wadham College, Oxford University. He had discovered salicylic acid, the active metabolite of aspirin. |
| Aspirin | Aspirin, also known as acetylsalicylic acid (INN ( ?--?l--i--ik) ASA), is a salicylate drug, often used as an analgesic to relieve minor aches and pains, as an antipyretic to reduce fever, and as an anti-inflammatory medication. Aspirin was first isolated by Felix Hoffmann, a chemist with the German company Bayer in 1897.<br><br>Salicylic acid, the main metabolite of aspirin, is an integral part of human and animal metabolism. |
| Hemoglobin | Hemoglobin; also spelled haemoglobin and abbreviated Hb or Hgb, is the iron-containing oxygen-transport metalloprotein in the red blood cells of all vertebrates as well as the tissues of some invertebrates. Hemoglobin in the blood carries oxygen from the respiratory organs (lungs or gills) to the rest of the body (i.e. the tissues) where it releases the oxygen to burn nutrients to provide energy to power the functions of the organism, and collects the resultant carbon dioxide to bring it back to the respiratory organs to be dispensed from the organism.<br><br>In mammals, the protein makes up about 97% of the red blood cells' dry content (by weight), and around 35% of the total content (including water). |
| Quantum dot | A quantum dot is a nanocrystal made of semiconductor materials that are small enough to display quantum mechanical properties, specifically its excitons are confined in all three spatial dimensions. The electronic properties of these materials are intermediate between those of bulk semiconductors and of discrete molecules. Quantum dots were discovered in the early 1980s by Alexei Ekimov in a glass matrix and by Louis E. Brus in colloidal solutions. |
| Serotonin | Serotonin or 5-hydroxytryptamine is a monoamine neurotransmitter. Biochemically derived from tryptophan, serotonin is primarily found in the gastrointestinal (GI) tract, platelets, and in the central nervous system (CNS) of animals, including humans. It is popularly thought to be a contributor to feelings of well-being and happiness. |
| Vanillin | Vanillin is a phenolic aldehyde, which is an organic compound with the molecular formula $C_8H_8O_3$. Its functional groups include aldehyde, ether, and phenol. It is the primary component of the extract of the vanilla bean. |
| Concentration | In chemistry, concentration is the abundance of a constituent divided by the total volume of a mixture. Several types of mathematical description can be distinguished: mass concentration, molar concentration, number concentration, and volume concentration. |

| Hydrogen cyanide | Hydrogen cyanide, sometimes called prussic acid, is an inorganic compound with chemical formula HCN. It is a colorless, extremely poisonous liquid that boils slightly above room temperature, at 26 °C (79 °F). HCN is produced on an industrial scale and is a highly valuable precursor to many chemical compounds ranging from polymers to pharmaceuticals. |
|---|---|

CHAPTER QUIZ: KEY TERMS, PEOPLE, PLACES, CONCEPTS

1. Molecular mass or _____ refers to the mass of a molecule. It is calculated as the sum of the mass of each constituent atom multiplied by the number of atoms of that element in the molecular formula. The molecular mass of small to medium size molecules, measured by mass spectrometry, determines stoichiometry.

   a. Merck Index
   b. Bjerrum length
   c. Boiling-point elevation
   d. Molecular weight

2. _____ is a common name for a chemical compound with the molecular formula $C_3H_8O$ or $C_3H_7OH$. It is a colorless, flammable chemical compound with a strong odor. It is the simplest example of a secondary alcohol, where the alcohol carbon atom is attached to two other carbon atoms sometimes shown as $(CH_3)_2CHOH$. It is a structural isomer of propanol. _____ is denatured for certain uses, in which case the NFPA 704 rating is changed to 2,3,1.

   a. Isopropyl alcohol
   b. Barbicide
   c. Barium borate
   d. BCDMH

3. In chemistry, _____ is the determination of the absolute or relative abundance of one, several or all particular substance(s) present in a sample.

   a. Biomonitoring
   b. Quantitative analysis
   c. Bradford protein assay
   d. Bulk material analyzer

4. . _____ or burning is the sequence of exothermic chemical reactions between a fuel and an oxidant accompanied by the production of heat and conversion of chemical species. The release of heat can produce light in the form of either glowing or a flame.

In a complete _____ reaction, a compound reacts with an oxidizing element, such as oxygen or fluorine, and the products are compounds of each element in the fuel with the oxidizing element.

a. Chalcogel
b. SEAgel
c. Combustion
d. Congelation

5. _____ is a unit of measurement used in chemistry to express amounts of a chemical substance, defined as the amount of any substance that contains as many elementary entities (e.g., atoms, molecules, ions, electrons) as there are atoms in 12 grams of pure carbon-12, the isotope of carbon with relative atomic mass 12. This corresponds to the Avogadro constant, which has a value of $6.02214129(27) \times 10^{23}$ elementary entities of the substance. It is one of the base units in the International System of Units, and has the unit symbol mol and corresponds with the dimension symbol N. In honour of the unit, chemists often celebrate October 23 (a reference to the $10^{23}$ part of Avogadro's number) as '_____ Day'.

The _____ is widely used in chemistry instead of units of mass or volume as a convenient way to express amounts of reactants or of products of chemical reactions.

a. Katal
b. Mole
c. Bisulfide
d. Buffering agent

1. d
2. a
3. b
4. c
5. b

---

## You can take the complete Chapter Practice Test

**for 3. Chemical Reactions and Reaction Stoichiometry**
on all key terms, persons, places, and concepts.

### Online 99 Cents

### http://www.JustTheFacts101.com

**Use www.JustTheFacts101.com for all your study needs**

**including Facts101's online interactive problem solving labs in**

**chemistry, statistics, mathematics, and more.**

# 4. Reactions in Aqueous Solution

CHAPTER OUTLINE: KEY TERMS, PEOPLE, PLACES, CONCEPTS

| | |
|---|---|
| | Aqueous solution |
| | Concentration |
| | Titration |
| | Conductivity |
| | Dissolution |
| | Electrolytic cell |
| | Sodium |
| | Sodium chloride |
| | Solute |
| | Solvent |
| | Volume |
| | Electrolyte |
| | Ionic compound |
| | Sodium sulfate |
| | Solvation |
| | Dissociation |
| | Strong electrolyte |
| | Acetic acid |
| | Hydrochloric acid |
| | Ionization |
| | Strength |

# 4. Reactions in Aqueous Solution

Potassium iodide

Precipitation

Potassium nitrate

Solubility

Charged particle

Spectator ion

Ammonia

Sodium bicarbonate

Hydrogen

Ammonium hydroxide

Citric acid

Diprotic acid

Nitric acid

Weak base

Hydroxide

Chloric acid

Hydrobromic acid

Hydrofluoric acid

Metal hydroxide

Perchloric acid

Sulfuric acid

# 4. Reactions in Aqueous Solution

CHAPTER OUTLINE: KEY TERMS, PEOPLE, PLACES, CONCEPTS

_____ | Alkali

_____ | Alkali metal

_____ | Litmus

_____ | Magnesium hydroxide

_____ | Neutralization

_____ | Sodium hydroxide

_____ | Carbonic acid

_____ | Corrosion

_____ | Hydrogen sulfide

_____ | Absorption

_____ | Oxidation

_____ | Monatomic ion

_____ | Atom

_____ | Calcium

_____ | Lewis structure

_____ | Displacement

_____ | Noble metal

_____ | Redox

_____ | Cobalt

_____ | Mole

_____ | Nernst equation

# 4. Reactions in Aqueous Solution
CHAPTER OUTLINE: KEY TERMS, PEOPLE, PLACES, CONCEPTS

_____ Dilution

_____ Stock solution

_____ Entropy

_____ Stoichiometry

_____ Equivalence point

_____ Phenolphthalein

_____ Standard solution

_____ Acetone

_____ Formic acid

_____ Glycerol

_____ Lanthanum

_____ Tartaric acid

_____ Hard water

_____ Arsenic

_____ Drinking water

# 4. Reactions in Aqueous Solution

CHAPTER HIGHLIGHTS & NOTES: KEY TERMS, PEOPLE, PLACES, CONCEPTS

| | |
|---|---|
| Aqueous solution | An aqueous solution is a solution in which the solvent is water. It is usually shown in chemical equations by appending (aq) to the relevant formula. For example, a solution of ordinary table salt, or sodium chloride (NaCl), in water would be represented as NaCl(aq). |
| Concentration | In chemistry, concentration is the abundance of a constituent divided by the total volume of a mixture. Several types of mathematical description can be distinguished: mass concentration, molar concentration, number concentration, and volume concentration. The term concentration can be applied to any kind of chemical mixture, but most frequently it refers to solutes and solvents in solutions. |
| Titration | Titration, also known as titrimetry, is a common laboratory method of quantitative chemical analysis that is used to determine the unknown concentration of an identified analyte. Since volume measurements play a key role in titration, it is also known as volumetric analysis. A reagent, called the titrant or titrator is prepared as a standard solution. |
| Conductivity | The conductivity of an electrolyte solution is a measure of its ability to conduct electricity. The SI unit of conductivity is siemens per meter (S/m).<br><br>Conductivity measurements are used routinely in many industrial and environmental applications as a fast, inexpensive and reliable way of measuring the ionic content in a solution. |
| Dissolution | Dissolution is the process by which a solute forms a solution in a solvent. The solute, in the case of solids, has its crystalline structure disintegrated as separate ions, atoms, and molecules form. For liquids and gases, the molecules must be adaptable with those of the solvent for a solution to form. |
| Electrolytic cell | An electrolytic cell is an electrochemical cell that undergoes a redox reaction when electrical energy is applied. It is most often used to decompose chemical compounds, in a process called electrolysis--the Greek word lysis means to break up. When electrical energy is added to the system, the chemical energy is increased. |
| Sodium | Sodium is a chemical element with the symbol Na and atomic number 11. It is a soft, silver-white, highly reactive metal and is a member of the alkali metals; its only stable isotope is $^{23}Na$. The free metal does not occur in nature, but instead must be prepared from its compounds; it was first isolated by Humphry Davy in 1807 by the electrolysis of sodium hydroxide. Sodium is the sixth most abundant element in the Earth's crust, and exists in numerous minerals such as feldspars, sodalite and rock salt. |
| Sodium chloride | Sodium chloride, also known as salt, common salt, table salt or halite, is an ionic compound with the formula NaCl, representing equal proportions of sodium and chlorine. Sodium chloride is the salt most responsible for the salinity of the ocean and of the extracellular fluid of many multicellular organisms. |

# 4. Reactions in Aqueous Solution

| | |
|---|---|
| Solute | A solute is a substance that creates a solution when dissolved in a solvent. For example, when sugar (solute) is dissolved in water (solvent).Solute can change its physical state but solvent and solution are of same phase.e.g sugar is solid before getting dissolved in water, and after dissolution it changes its phase to a liquid.<br><br>Etymology: from Latin solutus, past participle of solvere, meaning to loosen. |
| Solvent | A solvent is a substance that dissolves a solute (a chemically different liquid, solid or gas), resulting in a solution. A solvent is usually a liquid but can also be a solid or a gas. The maximum quantity of solute that can dissolve in a specific volume of solvent varies with temperature. |
| Volume | In thermodynamics, the volume of a system is an important extensive parameter for describing its thermodynamic state. The specific volume, an intensive property, is the system's volume per unit of mass. Volume is a function of state and is interdependent with other thermodynamic properties such as pressure and temperature. |
| Electrolyte | An electrolyte is a compound that ionizes when dissolved in suitable ionizing solvents such as water. This includes most soluble salts, acids, and bases. Some gases, such as hydrogen chloride, under conditions of high temperature or low pressure can also function as electrolytes. |
| Ionic compound | In chemistry, an ionic compound is a chemical compound in which ions are held together in a lattice structure by ionic bonds. Usually, the positively charged portion consists of metal cations and the negatively charged portion is an anion or polyatomic ion. Ions in ionic compounds are held together by the electrostatic forces between oppositely charged bodies. |
| Sodium sulfate | Sodium sulfate is the sodium salt of sulfuric acid. When anhydrous, it is a white crystalline solid of formula $Na_2SO_4$ known as the mineral thenardite; the decahydrate $Na_2SO_4 \cdot 10H_2O$ is found naturally as the mineral mirabilite, and in processed form has been known as Glauber's salt or, historically, sal mirabilis since the 17th century. Another solid is the heptahydrate, which transforms to mirabilite when cooled. |
| Solvation | Solvation, also sometimes called dissolution, is the process of attraction and association of molecules of a solvent with molecules or ions of a solute. As ions dissolve in a solvent they spread out and become surrounded by solvent molecules. |
| Dissociation | Dissociation in chemistry and biochemistry is a general process in which ionic compounds separate or split into smaller particles, ions, or radicals, usually in a reversible manner. For instance, when a Brønsted-Lowry acid is put in water, a covalent bond between an electronegative atom and a hydrogen atom is broken by heterolytic fission, which gives a proton and a negative ion. Dissociation is the opposite of association and recombination. |

# 4. Reactions in Aqueous Solution

| | |
|---|---|
| Strong electrolyte | A strong electrolyte is a solute that completely, or almost completely, ionizes or dissociates in a solution. These ions are good conductors of electric current in the solution. |
| | Originally, a 'strong electrolyte' was defined as a chemical that, when in aqueous solution, is a good conductor of electricity. |
| Acetic acid | Acetic acid is an organic compound with the chemical formula $CH_3COOH$ (also written as $CH_3CO_2H$ or $C_2H_4O_2$). It is a colourless liquid that when undiluted is also called glacial acetic acid. Acetic acid is the main component of vinegar (apart from water; vinegar is roughly 8% acetic acid by volume), and has a distinctive sour taste and pungent smell. |
| Hydrochloric acid | Hydrochloric acid is a clear, colorless, highly pungent solution of hydrogen chloride in water. It is a highly corrosive, strong mineral acid with many industrial uses. Hydrochloric acid is found naturally in gastric acid. |
| Ionization | Ionization is the process by which an atom or a molecule acquires a negative or positive charge by gaining or losing electrons. |
| Strength | In explosive materials, strength is the parameter determining the ability of the explosive to move the surrounding material. It is related to the total gas yield of the reaction, and the amount of heat produced. Cf. |
| Potassium iodide | Potassium iodide is an inorganic compound with the chemical formula KI. This white salt is the most commercially significant iodide compound, with approximately 37,000 tons produced in 1985. It is less hygroscopic (absorbs water less readily) than sodium iodide, making it easier to work with. Potassium iodide occurs naturally in Kelp. Kelp's iodide content can range from 89 µg/g to 8165 µg/g. |
| Precipitation | Precipitation is the formation of a solid in a solution or inside another solid during a chemical reaction or by diffusion in a solid. When the reaction occurs in a liquid solution, the solid formed is called the precipitate. The chemical that causes the solid to form is called the precipitant. |
| Potassium nitrate | Potassium nitrate is a chemical compound with the formula $KNO_3$. It is an ionic salt of potassium ions $K^+$ and nitrate ions $NO_3^-$. |
| | It occurs as a mineral niter and is a natural solid source of nitrogen. |
| Solubility | Solubility is the property of a solid, liquid, or gaseous chemical substance called solute to dissolve in a solid, liquid, or gaseous solvent to form a homogeneous solution of the solute in the solvent. The solubility of a substance fundamentally depends on the physical and chemical properties of the solute and solvent as well as on temperature, pressure and the pH of the solution. |

# 4. Reactions in Aqueous Solution

| | |
|---|---|
| Charged particle | In physics, a charged particle is a particle with an electric charge. It may be either a subatomic particle or an ion. A collection of charged particles, or even a gas containing a proportion of charged particles, is called a plasma, which is called the fourth state of matter because its properties are quite different from solids, liquids and gases (plasma is the most common state of matter in the universe). |
| Spectator ion | A spectator ion is an ion that exists as a reactant and a product in a chemical equation. Spectator ions can, for example, be observed in the reaction of aqueous solutions of sodium chloride and copper(II) sulfate but does not affect the equilibrium: $2Na^+_{(aq)} + 2Cl^-_{(aq)} + Cu^{2+}_{(aq)} + SO_4^{2-}_{(aq)} ? 2Na^+_{(aq)} + SO_4^{2-}_{(aq)} + CuCl_{2(s)}$

The $Na^+$ and $SO_4^{2-}$ ions are spectator ions since they remain unchanged on both sides of the equation. They simply 'watch' the other ions react, hence the name. |
| Ammonia | Ammonia or azane is a compound of nitrogen and hydrogen with the formula $NH_3$. It is a colourless gas with a characteristic pungent smell. Ammonia contributes significantly to the nutritional needs of terrestrial organisms by serving as a precursor to food and fertilizers. |
| Sodium bicarbonate | Sodium bicarbonate or sodium hydrogen carbonate is the chemical compound with the formula $NaHCO_3$. Sodium bicarbonate is a white solid that is crystalline but often appears as a fine powder. It has a slightly salty, alkaline taste resembling that of washing soda (sodium carbonate). |
| Hydrogen | Hydrogen is a chemical element with chemical symbol H and atomic number 1. With an atomic weight of 1.00794 u, hydrogen is the lightest element and its monatomic form (H) is the most abundant chemical substance, constituting roughly 75% of the Universe's baryonic mass. Non-remnant stars are mainly composed of hydrogen in its plasma state.

At standard temperature and pressure, hydrogen is a colorless, odorless, tasteless, non-toxic, nonmetallic, highly combustible diatomic gas with the molecular formula $H_2$. |
| Ammonium hydroxide | Ammonia solution, also known as ammonium hydroxide, ammonia water, ammonical liquor, ammonia liquor, aqua ammonia, aqueous ammonia, or simply ammonia, is a solution of ammonia in water. It can be denoted by the symbols $NH_3(aq)$. Although the name ammonium hydroxide suggests an alkali with composition $[NH_4^+][OH^-]$, it is actually impossible to isolate samples of $NH_4OH$, as these ions do not comprise a significant fraction of the total amount of ammonia except in extremely dilute solutions. |
| Citric acid | Citric acid is a weak organic acid with the formula $C_6H_8O_7$. It is a natural preservative/conservative and is also used to add an acidic or sour taste to foods and drinks. |

| Diprotic acid | A diprotic acid is an acid such as $H_2SO_4$ that contains within its molecular structure two hydrogen atoms per molecule capable of dissociating (i.e. ionizable) in water. The complete dissociation of diprotic acids is of the same form as sulfuric acid:$H_2SO_4$ ? $H^+(aq)$ + $HSO_4^-(aq)$ $K_a$ = 1 × $10^3 HSO_4^-$ ? $H^+(aq)$ + $SO_4^{2-}(aq)$ $K_a$ = 1 × $10^{-2}$ <br><br> The dissociation does not happen all at once due to the two stages of dissociation having different $K_a$ values. The first dissociation will, in the case of sulfuric acid, occur completely, but the second one will not. |
|---|---|
| Nitric acid | Nitric acid, also known as aqua fortis and spirit of niter, is a highly corrosive strong mineral acid. The pure compound is colorless, but older samples tend to acquire a yellow cast due to decomposition into oxides of nitrogen and water. Most commercially available nitric acid has a concentration of 68%. |
| Weak base | In chemistry, a weak base is a chemical base that does not ionize fully in an aqueous solution. As Brønsted-Lowry bases are proton acceptors, a weak base may also be defined as a chemical base in which protonation is incomplete. This results in a relatively low pH compared to strong bases. |
| Hydroxide | Hydroxide is a diatomic anion with chemical formula $OH^-$. It consists of an oxygen and a hydrogen atom held together by a covalent bond, and carries a negative electric charge. It is an important but usually minor constituent of water. |
| Chloric acid | Chloric acid, $HClO_3$, is an oxoacid of chlorine, and the formal precursor of chlorate salts. It is a strong acid ($pK_a$ ˜ -1) and oxidizing agent. <br><br> It is prepared by the reaction of sulfuric acid with barium chlorate, the insoluble barium sulfate being removed by precipitation:$Ba(ClO_3)_2$ + $H_2SO_4$ ? $2HClO_3$ + $BaSO_4$ <br><br> Another method is the heating of hypochlorous acid, of which productions include chloric acid and hydrogen chloride:$3HClO$ ? $HClO_3$ + 2 HCl <br><br> It is also produced by the reaction of sulfuric acid with potassium chlorate in the combustion of sugar using potassium chlorate, sulfuric acid, and sugar. |
| Hydrobromic acid | Hydrobromic acid is a strong acid formed by dissolving the diatomic molecule hydrogen bromide in water. 'Constant boiling' hydrobromic acid is an aqueous solution that distills at 124.3 °C and contains 47.6% HBr by weight, which is 8.89 mol/L. Hydrobromic acid has a $pK_a$ of -9, making it a stronger acid than hydrochloric acid, but not as strong as hydroiodic acid. Hydrobromic acid is one of the strongest mineral acids known. |

# 4. Reactions in Aqueous Solution

| | |
|---|---|
| Hydrofluoric acid | Hydrofluoric acid is a solution of hydrogen fluoride in water. It is a valued source of fluorine and is a precursor to numerous pharmaceuticals such as fluoxetine (Prozac) and diverse materials such as PTFE (Teflon).<br><br>Hydrofluoric acid is a highly corrosive acid, capable of dissolving many materials, especially oxides. |
| Metal hydroxide | Metal hydroxide are hydroxides of metals. |
| Perchloric acid | Perchloric acid is an inorganic compound with the formula $HClO_4$. Usually found as an aqueous solution, this colorless compound is a stronger acid than sulfuric and nitric acids. It is a powerful oxidizer, but its aqueous solutions up to approximately 70% are generally safe, only showing strong acid features and no oxidizing properties. |
| Sulfuric acid | Sulfuric acid is a highly corrosive strong mineral acid with the molecular formula $H_2SO_4$. It is a pungent, colorless to slightly yellow viscous liquid which is soluble in water at all concentrations. Sometimes, it is dyed dark brown during production to alert people to its hazards. |
| Alkali | In chemistry, an alkali is a basic, ionic salt of an alkali metal or alkaline earth metal chemical element. Some authors also define an alkali as a base that dissolves in water. A solution of a soluble base has a pH greater than 7.0. The adjective alkaline is commonly, and alkalescent less often, used in English as a synonym for basic, especially for soluble bases. |
| Alkali metal | The alkali metals are a group in the periodic table consisting of the chemical elements lithium, sodium (Na), potassium (K), rubidium (Rb), caesium (Cs), and francium (Fr). This group lies in the s-block of the periodic table as all alkali metals have their outermost electron in an s-orbital. The alkali metals provide the best example of group trends in properties in the periodic table, with elements exhibiting well-characterized homologous behaviour. |
| Litmus | Litmus is a water-soluble mixture of different dyes extracted from lichens, especially Roccella tinctoria. It is often absorbed onto filter paper to produce one of the oldest forms of pH indicator, used to test materials for acidity. Blue litmus paper turns red under acidic conditions and red litmus paper turns blue under basic (i.e. alkaline) conditions, with the color change occurring over the pH range 4.5-8.3 at 25 °C. Neutral litmus paper is purple. |
| Magnesium hydroxide | Magnesium hydroxide is an inorganic compound with the chemical formula of hydrated $Mg_2$. As a suspension in water, it is often called milk of magnesia because of its milk-like appearance. The solid mineral form of magnesium hydroxide is known as brucite. |
| Neutralization | In chemistry, neutralization is a chemical reaction in which an acid and a base react to form a salt. Water is frequently, but not necessarily, produced as well. Neutralizations with Arrhenius acids and bases always produce water where acid-alkali reactions produce water and a metal salt. |

# 4. Reactions in Aqueous Solution

CHAPTER HIGHLIGHTS & NOTES: KEY TERMS, PEOPLE, PLACES, CONCEPTS

| | |
|---|---|
| Sodium hydroxide | Sodium hydroxide, also known as caustic soda, or lye, is an inorganic compound with the chemical formula $NaOH$ . It is a white solid, and is a highly caustic metallic base and alkali salt. It is available in pellets, flakes, granules, and as prepared solutions at a number of different concentrations. |
| Carbonic acid | Not to be confused with carbolic acid, an antiquated name for phenol. Carbonic acid is also an archaic name for carbon dioxide. |
| | Carbonic acid is the chemical compound with the formula $H_2CO_3$ (equivalently $OC_2$). It is also a name sometimes given to solutions of carbon dioxide in water (carbonated water), because such solutions contain small amounts of $H_2CO_3$. Carbonic acid, which is a weak acid, forms two kinds of salts, the carbonates and the bicarbonates. |
| Corrosion | Corrosion is the gradual destruction of materials by chemical reaction with its environment. |
| | In the most common use of the word, this means electrochemical oxidation of metals in reaction with an oxidant such as oxygen. Rusting, the formation of iron oxides, is a well-known example of electrochemical corrosion. |
| Hydrogen sulfide | Hydrogen sulfide is the chemical compound with the formula H2S. It is a colorless gas with the characteristic foul odor of rotten eggs; it is heavier than air, very poisonous, corrosive, flammable and explosive. |
| | Hydrogen sulfide often results from the bacterial breakdown of organic matter in the absence of oxygen, such as in swamps and sewers; this process is commonly known as anaerobic digestion. |
| Absorption | In chemistry, absorption is a physical or chemical phenomenon or a process in which atoms, molecules, or ions enter some bulk phase - gas, liquid, or solid material. This is a different process from adsorption, since molecules undergoing absorption are taken up by the volume, not by the surface (as in the case for adsorption). A more general term is sorption, which covers absorption, adsorption, and ion exchange. |
| Oxidation | Redox (reduction-oxidation) reactions include all chemical reactions in which atoms have their oxidation state changed; in general, redox reactions involve the transfer of electrons between species. |
| | This can be either a simple redox process, such as the oxidation of carbon to yield carbon dioxide or the reduction of carbon by hydrogen to yield methane ($CH_4$), or a complex process such as the oxidation of glucose ($C_6H_{12}O_6$) in the human body through a series of complex electron transfer processes. |
| | The term 'redox' comes from two concepts involved with electron transfer: reduction and oxidation. |

# 4. Reactions in Aqueous Solution

| | |
|---|---|
| Monatomic ion | A monatomic ion is an ion consisting of a single atom. If an ion contains more than 1 atom, even if these atoms are of the same element, it is called a polyatomic ion. For example calcium carbonate consists of the monatomic ion $Ca^{2+}$ and the polyatomic ion $CO_3^{2-}$. |
| Atom | The atom is a basic unit of matter that consists of a dense central nucleus surrounded by a cloud of negatively charged electrons. The atomic nucleus contains a mix of positively charged protons and electrically neutral neutrons, which means 'uncuttable' or 'the smallest indivisible particle of matter'. Although the Indian and Greek concepts of the atom were based purely on philosophy, modern science has retained the name coined by Democritus. |
| Calcium | Calcium is the chemical element with symbol Ca and atomic number 20. Calcium is a soft gray alkaline earth metal, and is the fifth-most-abundant element by mass in the Earth's crust. Calcium is also the fifth-most-abundant dissolved ion in seawater by both molarity and mass, after sodium, chloride, magnesium, and sulfate.<br><br>Calcium is essential for living organisms, in particular in cell physiology, where movement of the calcium ion $Ca^{2+}$ into and out of the cytoplasm functions as a signal for many cellular processes. |
| Lewis structure | Lewis structures are diagrams that show the bonding between atoms of a molecule and the lone pairs of electrons that may exist in the molecule. A Lewis structure can be drawn for any covalently bonded molecule, as well as coordination compounds. The Lewis structure was named after Gilbert N |
| Displacement | In fluid mechanics, displacement occurs when an object is immersed in a fluid, pushing it out of the way and taking its place. The volume of the fluid displaced can then be measured, and from this the volume of the immersed object can be deduced (the volume of the immersed object will be exactly equal to the volume of the displaced fluid).<br><br>An object that sinks displaces an amount of fluid equal to the object's volume. |
| Noble metal | The noble metals are metals that are resistant to corrosion and oxidation in moist air, unlike most base metals. They tend to be precious, often due to their rarity in the Earth's crust. The noble metals are most commonly considered to be ruthenium, rhodium, palladium, silver, osmium, iridium, platinum, and gold. |
| Redox | Redox reactions include all chemical reactions in which atoms have their oxidation state changed; redox reactions generally involve the transfer of electrons between species.<br><br>This can be either a simple redox process, such as the oxidation of carbon to yield carbon dioxide (CO |

2) or the reduction of carbon by hydrogen to yield methane ($CH_4$), or a complex process such as the oxidation of glucose ($C_6H_{12}O_6$) in the human body through a series of complex electron transfer processes.

The term 'redox' comes from two concepts involved with electron transfer: reduction and oxidation.

| | |
|---|---|
| Cobalt | Cobalt is a chemical element with symbol Co and atomic number 27. Like nickel, cobalt in the Earth's crust is found only in chemically combined form, save for small deposits found in alloys of natural meteoric iron. The free element, produced by reductive smelting, is a hard, lustrous, silver-gray metal.<br><br>Cobalt-based blue pigments (cobalt blue) have been used since ancient times for jewelry and paints, and to impart a distinctive blue tint to glass, but the color was later thought by alchemists to be due to the known metal bismuth. |
| Mole | Mole is a unit of measurement used in chemistry to express amounts of a chemical substance, defined as the amount of any substance that contains as many elementary entities (e.g., atoms, molecules, ions, electrons) as there are atoms in 12 grams of pure carbon-12, the isotope of carbon with relative atomic mass 12. This corresponds to the Avogadro constant, which has a value of $6.02214129(27) \times 10^{23}$ elementary entities of the substance. It is one of the base units in the International System of Units, and has the unit symbol mol and corresponds with the dimension symbol N. In honour of the unit, chemists often celebrate October 23 (a reference to the $10^{23}$ part of Avogadro's number) as 'Mole Day'.<br><br>The mole is widely used in chemistry instead of units of mass or volume as a convenient way to express amounts of reactants or of products of chemical reactions. |
| Nernst equation | In electrochemistry, the Nernst equation is an equation that relates the equilibrium reduction potential of a half-cell in an electrochemical cell (or the total voltage for a full cell) to the standard electrode potential, temperature, activity, and reaction quotient of the underlying reactions and species used. It is named after the German physical chemist who first formulated it, Walther Nernst.<br><br>The Nernst equation gives a formula that relates the numerical values of the concentration gradient to the electric gradient that balances it. |
| Dilution | Dilution is a reduction in the concentration of a chemical . It is the process of reducing the concentration of a solute in solution, usually simply by mixing with more solvent. To dilute a solution means to add more solvent without the addition of more solute. |

# 4. Reactions in Aqueous Solution

| | |
|---|---|
| Stock solution | A Stock Solution is a concentrated solution that will be diluted to some lower concentrated for actual use. Stock solutions are used to save preparation time, conserve materials, reduce storage space, and improve the accuracy with which working lower concentration solutions are prepared.<br><br>In chemistry, a stock solution is a large volume of a common reagent, such as hydrochloric acid or sodium hydroxide, at a standardized concentration. |
| Entropy | In thermodynamics, entropy is a measure of the number of specific ways in which a thermodynamic system may be arranged, often taken to be a measure of disorder, or a measure of progressing towards thermodynamic equilibrium. The entropy of an isolated system never decreases, because isolated systems spontaneously evolve towards thermodynamic equilibrium, which is the state of maximum entropy.<br><br>Entropy was originally defined for a thermodynamically reversible process<br><br>as $$\Delta S = \int \frac{dQ_{rev}}{T}$$<br><br>where the entropy is found from the uniform thermodynamic temperature of a closed system dividing an incremental reversible transfer of heat into that system . |
| Stoichiometry | Stoichiometry is a branch of chemistry that deals with the relative quantities of reactants and products in chemical reactions. In a balanced chemical reaction, the relations among quantities of reactants and products typically form a ratio of positive integers. For example, in a reaction that forms ammonia ($NH_3$), exactly one molecule of nitrogen gas ($N_2$) reacts with three molecules of hydrogen gas ($H_2$) to produce two molecules of $NH_3$:N2 + 3H2 ? 2NH3<br><br>This particular kind of stoichiometry - describing the quantitative relationships among substances as they participate in chemical reactions - is known as reaction stoichiometry. |
| Equivalence point | The equivalence point, or stoichiometric point, of a chemical reaction s the point at which an added titrant is stoichiometrically equal to the number of moles of substance present in the sample: the smallest amount of titrant that is sufficient to fully neutralize or react with the analyte. In some cases there are multiple equivalence points, which are multiples of the first equivalence point, such as in the titration of a diprotic acid.<br><br>Acid-Base Equivalence Point - the point at which chemically equivalent quantities of acid and base have been mixed, can be found by means of an indicator<br><br>In a reaction, the equivalence of the reactants as well as products is conserved. |

# 4. Reactions in Aqueous Solution

| | |
|---|---|
| Phenolphthalein | Phenolphthalein is a chemical compound with the formula $C_{20}H_{14}O_4$ and is often written as 'HIn' or 'phph' in shorthand notation. Often used in titrations, it turns colorless in acidic solutions and pink in basic solutions. If the concentration of indicator is particularly strong, it can appear purple. |
| Standard solution | In analytical chemistry, a standard solution is a solution containing a precisely known concentration of an element or a substance i.e., a known weight of solute is dissolved to make a specific volume. It is prepared using a standard substance, such as a primary standard. Standard solutions are used to determine the concentrations of other substances, such as solutions in titrations. |
| Acetone | Acetone is the organic compound with the formula $(CH_3)_2CO$. It is a colorless, mobile, flammable liquid, and is the simplest ketone.<br><br>Acetone is miscible with water and serves as an important solvent in its own right, typically for cleaning purposes in the laboratory. About 6.7 million tonnes were produced worldwide in 2010, mainly for use as a solvent and production of methyl methacrylate and bisphenol A. It is a common building block in organic chemistry. |
| Formic acid | Formic acid is the simplest carboxylic acid. Its chemical formula is $HCOOH$ or $HCO_2H$. It is an important intermediate in chemical synthesis and occurs naturally, most notably in ant venom. In fact, its name comes from the Latin word for ant, formica, referring to its early isolation by the distillation of ant bodies. |
| Glycerol | Glycerol is a simple polyol (sugar alcohol) compound. It is a colorless, odorless, viscous liquid that is widely used in pharmaceutical formulations. Glycerol has three hydroxyl groups that are responsible for its solubility in water and its hygroscopic nature. |
| Lanthanum | Lanthanum is a chemical element with the symbol La and atomic number 57. Lanthanum is a silvery white metallic element and is the first element of the lanthanide series. It is found in some rare-earth minerals, usually in combination with cerium and other rare earth elements. Lanthanum is a malleable, ductile, and soft metal that oxidizes rapidly when exposed to air. |
| Tartaric acid | Tartaric acid is a white crystalline diprotic aldaric acid. It occurs naturally in many plants, particularly grapes, bananas, and tamarinds, is commonly combined with baking soda to function as a leavening agent in recipes, and is one of the main acids found in wine. It is added to other foods to give a sour taste, and is used as an antioxidant. |
| Hard water | Hard water is water that has high mineral content .<br><br>Hard drinking water is generally not harmful to one's health, but can pose serious problems in industrial settings, where water hardness is monitored to avoid costly breakdowns in boilers, cooling towers, and other equipment that handles water. |

# 4. Reactions in Aqueous Solution

| | |
|---|---|
| Arsenic | Arsenic is a chemical element with symbol As and atomic number 33. Arsenic occurs in many minerals, usually in conjunction with sulfur and metals, and also as a pure elemental crystal. It was first documented by Albertus Magnus in 1250. Arsenic is a metalloid. It can exist in various allotropes, although only the gray form has important use in industry. |
| Drinking water | Drinking water or potable water is water safe enough to be consumed by humans or used with low risk of immediate or long term harm. In most developed countries, the water supplied to households, commerce and industry meets drinking water standards, even though only a very small proportion is actually consumed or used in food preparation. Typical uses (for other than potable purposes) include toilet flushing, washing and landscape irrigation. |

CHAPTER QUIZ: KEY TERMS, PEOPLE, PLACES, CONCEPTS

1. _____ is the formation of a solid in a solution or inside another solid during a chemical reaction or by diffusion in a solid. When the reaction occurs in a liquid solution, the solid formed is called the precipitate. The chemical that causes the solid to form is called the precipitant.

   a. Centrifugal extractor
   b. Counterflow centrifugation elutriation
   c. Precipitation
   d. Demister

2. _____ is a unit of measurement used in chemistry to express amounts of a chemical substance, defined as the amount of any substance that contains as many elementary entities (e.g., atoms, molecules, ions, electrons) as there are atoms in 12 grams of pure carbon-12, the isotope of carbon with relative atomic mass 12. This corresponds to the Avogadro constant, which has a value of $6.02214129(27) \times 10^{23}$ elementary entities of the substance. It is one of the base units in the International System of Units, and has the unit symbol mol and corresponds with the dimension symbol N. In honour of the unit, chemists often celebrate October 23 (a reference to the $10^{23}$ part of Avogadro's number) as '_____ Day'.

   The _____ is widely used in chemistry instead of units of mass or volume as a convenient way to express amounts of reactants or of products of chemical reactions.

   a. Katal
   b. Kilogram per cubic metre
   c. Bisulfide
   d. Mole

3. . _____ is a chemical element with symbol As and atomic number 33.

_____ occurs in many minerals, usually in conjunction with sulfur and metals, and also as a pure elemental crystal. It was first documented by Albertus Magnus in 1250. _____ is a metalloid. It can exist in various allotropes, although only the gray form has important use in industry.

a. Bulk material analyzer
b. Biomonitoring
c. Arsenic
d. Bradford protein assay

4. The _____ of an electrolyte solution is a measure of its ability to conduct electricity. The SI unit of _____ is siemens per meter (S/m).

_____ measurements are used routinely in many industrial and environmental applications as a fast, inexpensive and reliable way of measuring the ionic content in a solution.

a. Conductivity
b. Bjerrum length
c. Boiling-point elevation
d. Bolaamphiphile

5. The _____s are metals that are resistant to corrosion and oxidation in moist air, unlike most base metals. They tend to be precious, often due to their rarity in the Earth's crust. The _____s are most commonly considered to be ruthenium, rhodium, palladium, silver, osmium, iridium, platinum, and gold.

a. Noble metal
b. Basic oxygen steelmaking
c. Bimetal
d. Biohydrometallurgy

**1.** c
**2.** d
**3.** c
**4.** a
**5.** a

## You can take the complete Chapter Practice Test

**for 4. Reactions in Aqueous Solution**
on all key terms, persons, places, and concepts.

### Online 99 Cents

### http://www.JustTheFacts101.com

Use www.JustTheFacts101.com for all your study needs

including Facts101's online interactive problem solving labs in

chemistry, statistics, mathematics, and more.

# 5. Thermochemistry

CHAPTER OUTLINE: KEY TERMS, PEOPLE, PLACES, CONCEPTS

| | |
|---|---|
| | Photosynthesis |
| | Solar cell |
| | Thermochemistry |
| | Kinetic energy |
| | Potential energy |
| | Thermodynamic |
| | Chemical energy |
| | Calorie |
| | Thermal energy |
| | Closed system |
| | Isolated system |
| | Lewis structure |
| | First law of thermodynamics |
| | Internal energy |
| | Combustion |
| | Ammonium thiocyanate |
| | Barium hydroxide |
| | State function |
| | Endothermic |
| | Exothermic |
| | Exothermic reaction |

# 5. Thermochemistry

CHAPTER OUTLINE: KEY TERMS, PEOPLE, PLACES, CONCEPTS

_____ | Thermite

_____ | Enthalpy

_____ | Volume

_____ | Effusion

_____ | Thermochemical equation

_____ | Calorimetry

_____ | Heat capacity

_____ | Freezing point

_____ | Calcium

_____ | Calcium carbonate

_____ | Absorption

_____ | Benzoic acid

_____ | Heat of combustion

_____ | Convection

_____ | Evaporation

_____ | Glucose

_____ | Household chemicals

_____ | Water vapor

_____ | Hypothermia

_____ | Methane

_____ | Enthalpy of fusion

# 5. Thermochemistry

CHAPTER OUTLINE: KEY TERMS, PEOPLE, PLACES, CONCEPTS

| | |
|---|---|
| | Enthalpy of vaporization |
| | Vaporization |
| | Acetylene |
| | Benzene |
| | Calcium oxide |
| | Carbon |
| | Carbon monoxide |
| | Hydrogen |
| | Hydrogen bromide |
| | Hydrogen chloride |
| | Hydrogen iodide |
| | Methanol |
| | Propane |
| | Silver chloride |
| | Sodium |
| | Sodium bicarbonate |
| | Sodium bromide |
| | Sodium chloride |
| | Standard enthalpy of formation |
| | Standard state |
| | Bromide |

CHAPTER OUTLINE: KEY TERMS, PEOPLE, PLACES, CONCEPTS

| | Iodide |
|---|---|
| | Ozone |
| | Carbohydrate |
| | Mesosphere |
| | Urea |
| | Bituminous coal |
| | Butane |
| | Ethane |
| | Fossil fuel |
| | Hydrogen fuel |
| | Natural gas |
| | Petroleum |
| | Carbon dioxide |
| | Dioxide |
| | Ethanol |
| | Biofuel |
| | Biodiesel |
| | Nitroglycerin |
| | Sugarcane |
| | Octane |
| | Diethyl ether |

# 5. Thermochemistry

Trimethylamine

| | |
|---|---|
| Photosynthesis | Photosynthesis is a process used by plants and other organisms to convert light energy, normally from the sun, into chemical energy that can be later released to fuel the organisms' activities. This chemical energy is stored in carbohydrate molecules, such as sugars, which are synthesized from carbon dioxide and water - hence the name photosynthesis, from the Greek f??, phos, 'light', and s???es??, synthesis, 'putting together'. In most cases, oxygen is also released as a waste product. |
| Solar cell | A solar cell is an electrical device that converts the energy of light directly into electricity by the photovoltaic effect. It is a form of photoelectric cell (in that its electrical characteristics--e.g. current, voltage, or resistance--vary when light is incident upon it) which, when exposed to light, can generate and support an electric current without being attached to any external voltage source, but do require an external load for power consumption.<br><br>The term 'photovoltaic' comes from the Greek f?? (phos) meaning 'light', and from 'Volt', the unit of electro-motive force, the volt, which in turn comes from the last name of the Italian physicist Alessandro Volta, inventor of the battery (electrochemical cell). |
| Thermochemistry | Thermochemistry is the study of the energy and heat associated with chemical reactions and/or physical transformations. A reaction may release or absorb energy, and a phase change may do the same, such as in melting and boiling. Thermochemistry focuses on these energy changes, particularly on the system's energy exchange with its surroundings. |
| Kinetic energy | In physics, the kinetic energy of an object is the energy which it possesses due to its motion. It is defined as the work needed to accelerate a body of a given mass from rest to its stated velocity. Having gained this energy during its acceleration, the body maintains this kinetic energy unless its speed changes. |
| Potential energy | In physics, potential energy is energy stored in a system of forcefully interacting physical entities. The SI unit for measuring work and energy is the joule (symbol J).<br><br>The term potential energy was introduced by the 19th century Scottish engineer and physicist William Rankine, although it has links to Greek philosopher Aristotle's concept of potentiality. |

| | |
|---|---|
| Thermodynamic | Thermodynamics is a branch of natural science concerned with heat and temperature and their relation to energy and work. It defines macroscopic variables, such as internal energy, entropy, and pressure, that partly describe a body of matter or radiation. It states that the behavior of those variables is subject to general constraints, that are common to all materials, not the peculiar properties of particular materials. |
| Chemical energy | In chemistry, Chemical energy is the potential of a chemical substance to undergo a transformation through a chemical reaction or, to transform other chemical substances. Examples include batteries and light bulbs and cells etc. Breaking or making of chemical bonds involves energy, which may be either absorbed or evolved from a chemical system. |
| Calorie | The name calorie is used for two units of energy. •The small calorie or gram calorie is the approximate amount of energy needed to raise the temperature of one gram of water by one degree Celsius.•The large calorie, kilogram calorie, dietary calorie, nutritionist's calorie or food calorie is the amount of energy needed to raise the temperature of one kilogram of water by one degree Celsius. The large calorie is thus equal to 1000 small calories or one kilocalorie.<br><br>Although these units are part of the metric system, they now have been superseded in the International System of Units by the joule. |
| Thermal energy | Thermal energy is the part of the total potential energy and kinetic energy of an object or sample of matter that results in the system temperature. It is represented by the variable Q, and can be measured in Joules. This quantity may be difficult to determine or even meaningless unless the system has attained its temperature only through warming (heating), and not been subjected to work input or output, or any other energy-changing processes. |
| Closed system | The term closed system refers to a physical system that is closed to certain types of transfers in or out of the system. The specification of what types of transfers are excluded, is different in different contexts. |
| Isolated system | In the natural sciences an isolated system is a physical system without any external exchange - neither matter nor energy can enter or exit, but can only move around inside. Truly isolated systems cannot exist in nature, other than allegedly the universe itself, and they are thus hypothetical concepts only. It obeys, in particular, to the first of the conservation laws: its total energy - mass stays constant. |
| Lewis structure | Lewis structures are diagrams that show the bonding between atoms of a molecule and the lone pairs of electrons that may exist in the molecule. A Lewis structure can be drawn for any covalently bonded molecule, as well as coordination compounds. The Lewis structure was named after Gilbert N |

# 5. Thermochemistry

| | |
|---|---|
| First law of thermodynamics | The first law of thermodynamics is a version of the law of conservation of energy, adapted for thermodynamic systems. The law of conservation of energy states that the total energy of an isolated system is constant; energy can be transformed from one form to another, but cannot be created or destroyed. The first law of thermodynamics recognizes a particular form of energy called internal energy. |
| Internal energy | In thermodynamics, the internal energy is the total energy contained by a thermodynamic system. It is the energy needed to create the system but excludes the energy to displace the system's surroundings, any energy associated with a move as a whole, or due to external force fields. Internal energy has two major components, kinetic energy and potential energy. |
| Combustion | Combustion or burning is the sequence of exothermic chemical reactions between a fuel and an oxidant accompanied by the production of heat and conversion of chemical species. The release of heat can produce light in the form of either glowing or a flame. <br><br> In a complete combustion reaction, a compound reacts with an oxidizing element, such as oxygen or fluorine, and the products are compounds of each element in the fuel with the oxidizing element. |
| Ammonium thiocyanate | Ammonium thiocyanate is an inorganic compound with the formula $NH_4SCN$. It is the salt of the ammonium cation and the thiocyanate anion. |
| Barium hydroxide | Barium hydroxide is the chemical compound with the formula $Ba_2$. Also known as baryta, it is one of the principal compounds of barium. The white granular monohydrate is the usual commercial form. |
| State function | In thermodynamics, a state function, function of state, state quantity, or state variable is a property of a system that depends only on the current state of the system, not on the way in which the system acquired that state . A state function describes the equilibrium state of a system. For example, internal energy, enthalpy, and entropy are state quantities because they describe quantitatively an equilibrium state of a thermodynamic system, irrespective of how the system arrived in that state. |
| Endothermic | In thermodynamics, the term endothermic describes a process or reaction in which the system absorbs energy from its surroundings in the form of heat. It is a modern coinage from Greek roots. The prefix endo- derives from the Greek word 'endon' (??d??) meaning 'within,' and the latter part of the word comes from the Greek word root 'therm' (?e?µ-) meaning 'hot.' The intended sense is that of a reaction that depends on taking in heat if it is to proceed. |
| Exothermic | In thermodynamics, the term exothermic describes a process or reaction that releases energy from the system, usually in the form of heat, but also in a form of light (e.g. a spark, flame, or flash), electricity (e.g. a battery), or sound (e.g. explosion heard when burning hydrogen). |

|  | |
|---|---|
|  | Its etymology stems from the prefix exo (derived from the Greek word ???, exo, 'outside') and the Greek word thermasi (meaning 'to heat'). The term exothermic was first coined by Marcellin Berthelot. |
| Exothermic reaction | An exothermic reaction is a chemical reaction that releases energy in the form of light or heat. It is the opposite of an endothermic reaction.<br><br>Expressed in a chemical equation: reactants ? products + energy |
| Thermite | Thermite is a pyrotechnic composition of metal powder fuel and metal oxide. When ignited by heat, thermite undergoes an exothermic oxidation-reduction reaction. Most varieties are not explosive but can create brief bursts of high temperature in a small area. |
| Enthalpy | Enthalpy is a measure of the total energy of a thermodynamic system. It includes the system's internal energy and thermodynamic potential (a state function), as well as its volume and pressure (the energy required to 'make room for it' by displacing its environment, which is an extensive quantity). The unit of measurement for enthalpy in the International System of Units (SI) is the joule, but other historical, conventional units are still in use, such as the British thermal unit and the calorie. |
| Volume | In thermodynamics, the volume of a system is an important extensive parameter for describing its thermodynamic state. The specific volume, an intensive property, is the system's volume per unit of mass. Volume is a function of state and is interdependent with other thermodynamic properties such as pressure and temperature. |
| Effusion | Effusion is the process in which a gas escapes through a small hole. This occurs if the diameter of the hole is considerably smaller than the mean free path of the molecules. According to Graham's law, the rate at which gases effuse (i.e., how many molecules pass through the hole per second) is dependent on their molecular weight. |
| Thermochemical equation | A Thermochemical Equation is a balanced stoichiometric chemical equation that includes the enthalpy change, ?H. In variable form, a thermochemical equation would look like this:A + B ? C?H = (±) #<br><br>Where {A, B, C} are the usual agents of a chemical equation with coefficients and "(±) #" is a positive or negative numerical value, usually with units of kJ. |
| Calorimetry | Calorimetry is the science or act of measuring changes in parameters of chemical reactions, physical changes and phase transitions, for the purpose of deriving the heat or heat transfer associated with those changes. Calorimetry is performed with a calorimeter. The word calorimetry is derived from the Latin word calor, meaning heat and the Greek word μ?t??? (metron), meaning measure. |

# 5. Thermochemistry

| | |
|---|---|
| Heat capacity | Heat capacity, or thermal capacity, is the measurable physical quantity of heat energy required to change the temperature of an object or body by a given amount. The SI unit of heat capacity is joule per kelvin, $\frac{J}{K}$ and the dimensional form is $M^1L^2T^{-2}T^{-1}$. |
| | Heat capacity is an extensive property of matter, meaning it is proportional to the size of the system. |
| Freezing point | Freezing, or Solidification, is a phase transition in which a liquid turns into a solid when its temperature is lowered below its freezing point. |
| | For most substances, the melting and freezing points are the same temperature; however, certain substances possess differing solid-liquid transition temperatures. For example, agar displays a hysteresis in its melting and freezing temperatures. |
| Calcium | Calcium is the chemical element with symbol Ca and atomic number 20. Calcium is a soft gray alkaline earth metal, and is the fifth-most-abundant element by mass in the Earth's crust. Calcium is also the fifth-most-abundant dissolved ion in seawater by both molarity and mass, after sodium, chloride, magnesium, and sulfate. |
| | Calcium is essential for living organisms, in particular in cell physiology, where movement of the calcium ion $Ca^{2+}$ into and out of the cytoplasm functions as a signal for many cellular processes. |
| Calcium carbonate | Calcium carbonate is a chemical compound with the formula $CaCO_3$. It is a common substance found in rocks in all parts of the world, and is the main component of shells of marine organisms, snails, coal balls, pearls, and eggshells. Calcium carbonate is the active ingredient in agricultural lime, and is created when Ca ions in hard water react with carbonate ions creating limescale. |
| Absorption | In chemistry, absorption is a physical or chemical phenomenon or a process in which atoms, molecules, or ions enter some bulk phase - gas, liquid, or solid material. This is a different process from adsorption, since molecules undergoing absorption are taken up by the volume, not by the surface (as in the case for adsorption). A more general term is sorption, which covers absorption, adsorption, and ion exchange. |
| Benzoic acid | Benzoic acid, $C_7H_6O_2$, is a colorless crystalline solid and a simple aromatic carboxylic acid. The name is derived from gum benzoin, which was for a long time the only source for benzoic acid. Its salts are used as food preservatives and benzoic acid is an important precursor for the synthesis of many other organic substances. |
| Heat of combustion | The heat of combustion is the energy released as heat when a compound undergoes complete combustion with oxygen under standard conditions. The chemical reaction is typically a hydrocarbon reacting with oxygen to form carbon dioxide, water and heat. |

It may be expressed with the quantities:•energy/mole of fuel (kJ/mol)•energy/mass of fuel•energy/volume of fuel

The heat of combustion is conventionally measured with a bomb calorimeter.

| | |
|---|---|
| Convection | Convection is the concerted, collective movement of groups or aggregates of molecules within fluids and rheids, either through advection or through diffusion or as a combination of both of them. Convection of mass cannot take place in solids, since neither bulk current flows nor significant diffusion can take place in solids. Diffusion of heat can take place in solids, but that is called heat conduction. |
| Evaporation | Evaporation is a type of vaporization of a liquid that occurs from the surface of a liquid into a gaseous phase that is not saturated with the evaporating substance. The other type of vaporization is boiling, which, instead, occurs within the entire mass of the liquid and can also take place when the vapor phase is saturated, such as when steam is produced in a boiler. Evaporation that occurs directly from the solid phase below the melting point, as commonly observed with ice at or below freezing or moth crystals (napthalene or paradichlorobenzine), is called sublimation. |
| Glucose | Glucose, meaning 'sweet'. The suffix '-ose' denotes a sugar. |
| Household chemicals | Household chemicals are non-food chemicals that are commonly found and used in and around the average household. They are a type of consumer goods, designed particularly to assist cleaning, pest control and general hygiene purposes.<br><br>Food additives generally do not fall under this category, unless they have a use other than for human consumption. |
| Water vapor | Water vapor or aqueous vapor is the gas phase of water. It is one state of water within the hydrosphere. Water vapor can be produced from the evaporation or boiling of liquid water or from the sublimation of ice. |
| Hypothermia | Hypothermia is a condition in which core temperature drops below the required temperature for normal metabolism and body functions which is defined as 35.0 °C (95.0 °F). Body temperature is usually maintained near a constant level of 36.5-37.5 °C (98-100 °F) through biologic homeostasis or thermoregulation. If exposed to cold and the internal mechanisms are unable to replenish the heat that is being lost, a drop in core temperature occurs. |
| Methane | Methane is a chemical compound with the chemical formula $CH_4$ (one atom of carbon and four atoms of hydrogen). It is the simplest alkane and the main component of natural gas. The relative abundance of methane makes it an attractive fuel. |
| Enthalpy of fusion | The enthalpy of fusion or heat of fusion is the change in enthalpy resulting from heating a given quantity of a substance to change its state from a solid to a liquid. |

# 5. Thermochemistry

| | |
|---|---|
| | The temperature at which this occurs is the melting point. |
| | The 'enthalpy' of fusion is a latent heat, because during melting the introduction of heat cannot be observed as a temperature change, as the temperature remains constant during the process. |
| Enthalpy of vaporization | The enthalpy of vaporization also known as the (latent) heat of vaporization or heat of evaporation, is the enthalpy change required to transform a given quantity of a substance from a liquid into a gas at a given pressure (often atmospheric pressure, as in STP). |
| | It is often measured at the normal boiling point of a substance; although tabulated values are usually corrected to 298 K, the correction is often smaller than the uncertainty in the measured value. |
| | The heat of vaporization is temperature-dependent, though a constant heat of vaporization can be assumed for small temperature ranges and for reduced temperature $T_r<<1.0$. The heat of vaporization diminishes with increasing temperature and it vanishes completely at the critical temperature ($T_r=1$) because above the critical temperature the liquid and vapor phases no longer exist, since the substance is a supercritical fluid. |
| Vaporization | Vaporization of an element or compound is a phase transition from the liquid phase to gas phase. There are two types of vaporization: evaporation and boiling. |
| | Evaporation is a phase transition from the liquid phase to gas phase that occurs at temperatures below the boiling temperature at a given pressure. |
| Acetylene | Acetylene is the chemical compound with the formula $C_2H_2$. It is a hydrocarbon and the simplest alkyne. This colorless gas is widely used as a fuel and a chemical building block. |
| Benzene | Benzene is an organic chemical compound with the molecular formula $C_6H_6$. Its molecule is composed of 6 carbon atoms joined in a ring, with 1 hydrogen atom attached to each carbon atom. Because its molecules contain only carbon and hydrogen atoms, benzene is classed as a hydrocarbon. |
| Calcium oxide | Calcium oxide, commonly known as quicklime or burnt lime, is a widely used chemical compound. It is a white, caustic, alkaline crystalline solid at room temperature. The broadly used term 'lime' connotes calcium-containing inorganic materials, which include carbonates, oxides and hydroxides of calcium, silicon, magnesium, aluminium, and iron predominate, such as limestone. |
| Carbon | Carbon fiber, alternatively graphite fiber, carbon graphite or CF, is a material consisting of fibers about 5-10 µm in diameter and composed mostly of carbon atoms. The carbon atoms are bonded together in crystals that are more or less aligned parallel to the long axis of the fiber. |

# 5. Thermochemistry

| | |
|---|---|
| Carbon monoxide | Carbon monoxide is a colorless, odorless, and tasteless gas that is slightly less dense than air. It is toxic to humans and animals when encountered in higher concentrations, although it is also produced in normal animal metabolism in low quantities, and is thought to have some normal biological functions. In the atmosphere, it is spatially variable, short lived, having a role in the formation of ground-level ozone. |
| Hydrogen | Hydrogen is a chemical element with chemical symbol H and atomic number 1. With an atomic weight of 1.00794 u, hydrogen is the lightest element and its monatomic form (H) is the most abundant chemical substance, constituting roughly 75% of the Universe's baryonic mass. Non-remnant stars are mainly composed of hydrogen in its plasma state. <br><br> At standard temperature and pressure, hydrogen is a colorless, odorless, tasteless, non-toxic, nonmetallic, highly combustible diatomic gas with the molecular formula $H_2$. |
| Hydrogen bromide | Hydrogen bromide is the diatomic molecule HBr. HBr is a gas at standard conditions. Hydrobromic acid forms upon dissolving HBr in water. |
| Hydrogen chloride | The compound hydrogen chloride has the chemical formula HCl. At room temperature, it is a colorless gas, which forms white fumes of hydrochloric acid upon contact with atmospheric humidity. Hydrogen chloride gas and hydrochloric acid are important in technology and industry. |
| Hydrogen iodide | Hydrogen iodide is a diatomic molecule. Aqueous solutions of HI are known as hydroiodic acid or hydriodic acid, a strong acid. Hydrogen iodide and hydroiodic acid are, however, different in that the former is a gas under standard conditions; whereas, the other is an aqueous solution of said gas. |
| Methanol | Methanol, also known as methyl alcohol, wood alcohol, wood naphtha or wood spirits, is a chemical with the formula $CH_3OH$ . Methanol acquired the name 'wood alcohol' because it was once produced chiefly as a byproduct of the destructive distillation of wood. Modern methanol is produced in a catalytic industrial process directly from carbon monoxide, carbon dioxide, and hydrogen. |
| Propane | Propane is a three-carbon alkane with the molecular formula C3H8, normally a gas, but compressible to a transportable liquid. A by-product of natural gas processing and petroleum refining, it is commonly used as a fuel for engines, oxy-gas torches, barbecues, portable stoves, and residential central heating. Propane is one of a group of liquefied petroleum gases. |
| Silver chloride | Silver chloride is a chemical compound with the chemical formula AgCl. This white crystalline solid is well known for its low solubility in water (this behavior being reminiscent of the chlorides of $Tl^+$ and $Pb^{2+}$). Upon illumination or heating, silver chloride converts to silver (and chlorine), which is signaled by greyish or purplish coloration to some samples. |

# 5. Thermochemistry

| | |
|---|---|
| Sodium | Sodium is a chemical element with the symbol Na and atomic number 11. It is a soft, silver-white, highly reactive metal and is a member of the alkali metals; its only stable isotope is $^{23}$Na. The free metal does not occur in nature, but instead must be prepared from its compounds; it was first isolated by Humphry Davy in 1807 by the electrolysis of sodium hydroxide. Sodium is the sixth most abundant element in the Earth's crust, and exists in numerous minerals such as feldspars, sodalite and rock salt. |
| Sodium bicarbonate | Sodium bicarbonate or sodium hydrogen carbonate is the chemical compound with the formula $NaHCO_3$. Sodium bicarbonate is a white solid that is crystalline but often appears as a fine powder. It has a slightly salty, alkaline taste resembling that of washing soda (sodium carbonate). |
| Sodium bromide | Sodium bromide is an inorganic compound with the formula NaBr. It is a high-melting white, crystalline solid that resembles sodium chloride. It is a widely used source of the bromide ion and has many applications. |
| Sodium chloride | Sodium chloride, also known as salt, common salt, table salt or halite, is an ionic compound with the formula NaCl, representing equal proportions of sodium and chlorine. Sodium chloride is the salt most responsible for the salinity of the ocean and of the extracellular fluid of many multicellular organisms. As the major ingredient in edible salt, it is commonly used as a condiment and food preservative. |
| Standard enthalpy of formation | The standard enthalpy of formation or standard heat of formation of a compound is the change of enthalpy from the formation of 1 mole of the compound from its constituent elements, with all substances in their standard states at 101.3 kPa and 298 K. Its symbol is $?H_f^O$ or $?_fH^O$. The superscript theta (zero) on this symbol indicates that the process has been carried out under standard conditions. Standard States are as follows:•For a gas: standard state is a pressure of exactly 1 atmosphere•For a substance present in a solution: a concentration of exactly 1 M at a pressure of 1 atm•For a pure substance in a condensed state (a liquid or a solid): the pure liquid or solid under a pressure of 1 atm•For an element: the form in which the element is most stable under 1 atm of pressure and the specified temperature. |
| Standard state | In chemistry, the standard state of a material is a reference point used to calculate its properties under different conditions. In principle, the choice of standard state is arbitrary, although the International Union of Pure and Applied Chemistry (IUPAC) recommends a conventional set of standard states for general use. IUPAC recommends using a standard pressure $p^o = 10^5$ Pa. |
| Bromide | A bromide is a chemical compound containing a bromide ion or ligand. This is a bromine atom with an ionic charge of -1 (Br); for example, in caesium bromide, caesium cations ($Cs^+$) are electrically attracted to bromide anions (Br) to form the electrically neutral ionic compound CsBr. |

| Iodide | An iodide ion is the ion I⁻. Compounds with iodine in formal oxidation state -1 are called iodides. This page is for the iodide ion and its salts, not organoiodine compounds. |
| --- | --- |
| Ozone | Ozone, or trioxygen, is an inorganic compound with the chemical formula $O_3(\mu-O)$ (also written [O$(\mu-O)O$] or $O_3$). It is a pale blue gas with a distinctively pungent smell. It is an allotrope of oxygen that is much less stable than the diatomic allotrope $O_2$, breaking down in the lower atmosphere to normal dioxygen. |
| Carbohydrate | A carbohydrate is a large biological molecule, or macromolecule, consisting only of carbon, hydrogen (H), and oxygen (O), usually with a hydrogen:oxygen atom ratio of 2:1 (as in water); in other words, with the empirical formula $C_m(H_2O)_n$ (where m could be different from n). Some exceptions exist; for example, deoxyribose, a sugar component of DNA, has the empirical formula $C_5H_{10}O_4$. Carbohydrates are technically hydrates of carbon; structurally it is more accurate to view them as polyhydroxy aldehydes and ketones. |
| Mesosphere | The mesosphere is the layer of the Earth's atmosphere that is directly above the stratopause and directly below the mesopause. In the mesosphere temperature decreases with increasing height. The upper boundary of the mesosphere is the mesopause, which can be the coldest naturally occurring place on Earth with temperatures below 130 K (-226 °F; -143 °C). |
| Urea | Urea or carbamide is an organic compound with the chemical formula $CO_2$. The molecule has two --$NH_2$ groups joined by a carbonyl (C=O) functional group.<br><br>Urea serves an important role in the metabolism of nitrogen-containing compounds by animals and is the main nitrogen-containing substance in the urine of mammals. |
| Bituminous coal | Bituminous coal or black coal is a relatively soft coal containing a tarlike substance called bitumen. It is of higher quality than lignite coal but of poorer quality than anthracite. Formation is usually the result of high pressure being exerted on lignite. |
| Butane | Butane is an organic compound with the formula $C_4H_{10}$ that is an alkane with four carbon atoms. Butane is a gas at room temperature and atmospheric pressure. The term may refer to either of two structural isomers, n-butane or isobutane or to a mixture of these isomers. |
| Ethane | Ethane is a chemical compound with chemical formula $C_2H_6$. At standard temperature and pressure, ethane is a colorless, odorless gas. Ethane is isolated on an industrial scale from natural gas, and as a byproduct of petroleum refining. |
| Fossil fuel | Fossil fuels are fuels formed by natural processes such as anaerobic decomposition of buried dead organisms. The age of the organisms and their resulting fossil fuels is typically millions of years, and sometimes exceeds 650 million years. |

# 5. Thermochemistry

| | |
|---|---|
| Hydrogen fuel | Hydrogen fuel is a zero-emission fuel which uses electrochemical cells, or combustion in internal engines, to power vehicles and electric devices. It is also used in the propulsion of spacecraft and can potentially be mass-produced and commercialized for passenger vehicles and aircraft.<br><br>Hydrogen is the first element on the periodic table, making it the lightest element on earth. |
| Natural gas | Natural gas is a fossil fuel formed when layers of buried plants and animals are exposed to intense heat and pressure over thousands of years. The energy that the plants originally obtained from the sun is stored in the form of carbon in natural gas. Natural gas is a nonrenewable resource because it cannot be replenished on a human time frame. |
| Petroleum | Petroleum (L. petroleum, from Greek: p?t?a + Latin: oleum (oil)) is a naturally occurring, smelly, yellow-to-black liquid consisting of a complex mixture of hydrocarbons of various molecular weights and other liquid organic compounds, that are found in geologic formations beneath the Earth's surface. The name Petroleum covers both naturally occurring unprocessed crude oils and petroleum products that are made up of refined crude oil. A fossil fuel, it is formed when large quantities of dead organisms, usually zooplankton and algae, are buried underneath sedimentary rock and undergo intense heat and pressure. |
| Carbon dioxide | Carbon dioxide is a naturally occurring chemical compound composed of two oxygen atoms each covalently double bonded to a single carbon atom. It is a gas at standard temperature and pressure and exists in Earth's atmosphere in this state, as a trace gas at a concentration of 0.039 per cent by volume.<br><br>As part of the carbon cycle, plants, algae, and cyanobacteria use light energy to photosynthesize carbohydrate from carbon dioxide and water, with oxygen produced as a waste product. |
| Dioxide | An oxide is a chemical compound that contains at least one oxygen atom and one other element in its chemical formula. Metal oxides typically contain an anion of oxygen in the oxidation state of -2. Most of the Earth's crust consists of solid oxides, the result of elements being oxidized by the oxygen in air or in water. Hydrocarbon combustion affords the two principal carbon oxides: carbon monoxide and carbon dioxide. |
| Ethanol | Ethanol, also called ethyl alcohol, pure alcohol, grain alcohol, or drinking alcohol, is a volatile, flammable, colorless liquid with the structural formula $CH_3CH_2OH$, often abbreviated as $C_2H_5OH$ or $C_2H_6O$. A psychoactive drug and one of the oldest recreational drugs, ethanol can cause alcohol intoxication when consumed. Best known as the type of alcohol found in alcoholic beverages, it is also used in thermometers, as a solvent, and as a fuel. In common usage, it is often referred to simply as alcohol or spirits. |
| Biofuel | A biofuel is a fuel that contains energy from geologically recent carbon fixation. These fuels are produced from living organisms. |

CHAPTER HIGHLIGHTS & NOTES: KEY TERMS, PEOPLE, PLACES, CONCEPTS

| | |
|---|---|
| Biodiesel | Biodiesel refers to a vegetable oil- or animal fat-based diesel fuel consisting of long-chain alkyl esters. Biodiesel is typically made by chemically reacting lipids (e.g., vegetable oil, animal fat (tallow)) with an alcohol producing fatty acid esters. |
| | Biodiesel is meant to be used in standard diesel engines and is thus distinct from the vegetable and waste oils used to fuel converted diesel engines. |
| Nitroglycerin | Nitroglycerin, also known as nitroglycerine, trinitroglycerin, trinitroglycerine, or nitro, is more correctly known as glyceryl trinitrate or more formally: 1,2,3-trinitroxypropane. It is a heavy, colorless, oily, explosive liquid most commonly produced by treating glycerol with white fuming nitric acid under conditions appropriate to the formation of the nitric acid ester. Chemically, the substance is an organic nitrate compound rather than a nitro compound, but the traditional name is often retained. |
| Sugarcane | Sugarcane, or Sugar cane, is any of six to 37 species of tall perennial true grasses of the genus Saccharum, tribe Andropogoneae, native to the warm temperate to tropical regions of South Asia. |
| | They have stout jointed fibrous stalks that are rich in sugar, and measure two to six metres (6 to 19 feet) tall. All sugar cane species interbreed and the major commercial cultivars are complex hybrids. |
| Octane | Octane is a hydrocarbon and an alkane with the chemical formula $C_8H_{18}$, and the condensed structural formula $CH_{36}CH_3$. Octane has many structural isomers that differ by the amount and location of branching in the carbon chain. One of these isomers, 2,2,4-trimethylpentane (isooctane) is used as one of the standard values in the octane rating scale. |
| Diethyl ether | Diethyl ether, also known as ethyl ether, sulfuric ether, simply ether, or ethoxyethane, is an organic compound in the ether class with the formula $2O$. It is a colorless, highly volatile flammable liquid. It is commonly used as a solvent and was once used as a general anesthetic. |
| Trimethylamine | Trimethylamine is an organic compound with the formula $N_3$. This colorless, hygroscopic, and flammable tertiary amine has a strong 'fishy' odor in low concentrations and an ammonia-like odor at higher concentrations. It is a gas at room temperature but is usually sold in pressurized gas cylinders or as a 40% solution in water. |

# 5. Thermochemistry

1.  In thermodynamics, the term _____ describes a process or reaction that releases energy from the system, usually in the form of heat, but also in a form of light (e.g. a spark, flame, or flash), electricty (e.g. a battery), or sound (e.g. explosion heard when burning hydrogen). Its etymology stems from the prefix exo (derived from the Greek word ???, exo, 'outside') and the Greek word thermasi (meaning 'to heat'). The term _____ was first coined by Marcellin Berthelot.

    a. Component
    b. Exothermic
    c. Behentrimonium chloride
    d. Cocamidopropyl betaine

2.  _____ is a colorless, odorless, and tasteless gas that is slightly less dense than air. It is toxic to humans and animals when encountered in higher concentrations, although it is also produced in normal animal metabolism in low quantities, and is thought to have some normal biological functions. In the atmosphere, it is spatially variable, short lived, having a role in the formation of ground-level ozone.

    a. Benzoquinonetetracarboxylic dianhydride
    b. Carbon monoxide
    c. Barium acetylacetonate
    d. Cerium acetylacetonate

3.  _____ is a pyrotechnic composition of metal powder fuel and metal oxide. When ignited by heat, _____ undergoes an exothermic oxidation-reduction reaction. Most varieties are not explosive but can create brief bursts of high temperature in a small area.

    a. Panel edge staining
    b. Sibplaz
    c. Thermite
    d. Crown gold

4.  _____ is a measure of the total energy of a thermodynamic system. It includes the system's internal energy and thermodynamic potential (a state function), as well as its volume and pressure (the energy required to 'make room for it' by displacing its environment, which is an extensive quantity). The unit of measurement for _____ in the International System of Units (SI) is the joule, but other historical, conventional units are still in use, such as the British thermal unit and the calorie.

    a. CrystaSulf
    b. Flue-gas desulfurization
    c. Enthalpy
    d. Scrubber

5. . In thermodynamics, a _____, function of state, state quantity, or state variable is a property of a system that depends only on the current state of the system, not on the way in which the system acquired that state . A _____ describes the equilibrium state of a system.

For example, internal energy, enthalpy, and entropy are state quantities because they describe quantitatively an equilibrium state of a thermodynamic system, irrespective of how the system arrived in that state.

a. Backdraft
b. State function
c. Binodal
d. Bjerrum plot

**1.** b
**2.** b
**3.** c
**4.** c
**5.** b

---

## You can take the complete Chapter Practice Test

**for 5. Thermochemistry**
on all key terms, persons, places, and concepts.

### Online 99 Cents

### http://www.JustTheFacts101.com

**Use www.JustTheFacts101.com for all your study needs**

**including Facts101's online interactive problem solving labs in**

**chemistry, statistics, mathematics, and more.**

# 6. Electronic Structure of Atoms

CHAPTER OUTLINE: KEY TERMS, PEOPLE, PLACES, CONCEPTS

| | Electronic structure |
| --- | --- |
| | Light-emitting diode |
| | Potassium |
| | Quantum mechanics |
| | Electromagnetic radiation |
| | Electromagnetic spectrum |
| | Hertz |
| | Radiant energy |
| | Spectrum |
| | Frequency |
| | Blackbody radiation |
| | Bohr model |
| | Photoelectric effect |
| | Photon |
| | Quantization |
| | Einstein |
| | Quantum |
| | Work function |
| | Continuous spectrum |
| | Hydrogen |
| | Neon |

Polychromatic

Hydrogen line

Rydberg constant

Excited state

Ground state

Principal quantum number

Energy level

Atom

Hydrogen atom

Mass spectrum

Diffraction

Electron microscope

Matter wave

Microscope

Momentum

Electron

Electron diffraction

Uncertainty principle

Atomic orbital

Electron density

Wave function

# 6. Electronic Structure of Atoms

CHAPTER OUTLINE: KEY TERMS, PEOPLE, PLACES, CONCEPTS

| | Probability |
|---|---|
| | Angular momentum |
| | Magnetic quantum number |
| | Quantum number |
| | Electron shell |
| | Density |
| | Doping |
| | Pauli exclusion |
| | Pauli exclusion principle |
| | Magnetic resonance imaging |
| | Medical imaging |
| | Nuclear magnetic resonance |
| | Nuclear reactor |
| | Electron configuration |
| | Unpaired electron |
| | Alkali |
| | Condensation reaction |
| | Core electron |
| | Valence electron |
| | Argon |
| | Krypton |

# 6. Electronic Structure of Atoms
CHAPTER OUTLINE: KEY TERMS, PEOPLE, PLACES, CONCEPTS

_____ Lanthanide

_____ Rare earth element

_____ Rubidium

_____ Scandium

_____ Transition metal

_____ Zinc

_____ Actinide

_____ Cerium

_____ Lanthanum

_____ Periodic table

_____ Plutonium

_____ Prasecdymium

_____ Radon

_____ Uranium

_____ Fatty acid

_____ F-block

_____ Bismuth

_____ Halogen

_____ Chromium

_____ Isotope

_____ Molybdenum

# 6. Electronic Structure of Atoms

CHAPTER OUTLINE: KEY TERMS, PEOPLE, PLACES, CONCEPTS

| | |
|---|---|
| | Lyman series |
| | Neutron diffraction |
| | Neutron |
| | Fraunhofer lines |
| | Hafnium |
| | Ozone layer |
| | Zirconium |

CHAPTER HIGHLIGHTS & NOTES: KEY TERMS, PEOPLE, PLACES, CONCEPTS

| | |
|---|---|
| Electronic structure | In quantum chemistry, electronic structure is the state of motion of electrons in an electrostatic field created by stationary nuclei. The term encompass both the wave functions of the electrons and the energies associated with them. Electronic structure is obtained by solving quantum mechanical equations for the aforementioned clamped-nuclei problem. |
| Light-emitting diode | A light-emitting diode is a semiconductor light source. Light emitting diodes are used as indicator lamps in many devices and are increasingly used for general lighting. Appearing as practical electronic components in 1962, early Light emitting diodes emitted low-intensity red light, but modern versions are available across the visible, ultraviolet, and infrared wavelengths, with very high brightness. |
| Potassium | Potassium is a chemical element with symbol K and atomic number 19. Elemental potassium is a soft silvery-white alkali metal that oxidizes rapidly in air and is very reactive with water, generating sufficient heat to ignite the hydrogen emitted in the reaction and burning with a lilac flame. |
| | Because potassium and sodium are chemically very similar, their salts were not at first differentiated. The existence of multiple elements in their salts was suspected from 1702, and this was proven in 1807 when potassium and sodium were individually isolated from different salts by electrolysis. |

# 6. Electronic Structure of Atoms

| | |
|---|---|
| Quantum mechanics | Quantum mechanics is a branch of physics which deals with physical phenomena at microscopic scales, where the action is on the order of the Planck constant. It departs from classical mechanics primarily at the quantum realm of atomic and subatomic length scales. Quantum mechanics provides a mathematical description of much of the dual particle-like and wave-like behavior and interactions of energy and matter. |
| Electromagnetic radiation | Electromagnetic radiation is one of the fundamental phenomena of electromagnetism, behaving as waves propagating through space, and also as photon particles traveling through space, carrying radiant energy. In a vacuum, it propagates at a characteristic speed, the speed of light, normally in straight lines. EMR is emitted and absorbed by charged particles. |
| Electromagnetic spectrum | The electromagnetic spectrum is the range of all possible frequencies of electromagnetic radiation. The 'electromagnetic spectrum' of an object has a different meaning, and is instead the characteristic distribution of electromagnetic radiation emitted or absorbed by that particular object. <br><br> The electromagnetic spectrum extends from below the low frequencies used for modern radio communication to gamma radiation at the short-wavelength (high-frequency) end, thereby covering wavelengths from thousands of kilometers down to a fraction of the size of an atom. |
| Hertz | The hertz is the unit of frequency in the International System of Units (SI). It is defined as one cycle per second. One of its most common uses is the description of the sine wave, particularly those used in radio and audio applications, such as the frequency of musical tones. |
| Radiant energy | Radiant energy is the energy of electromagnetic waves. The quantity of radiant energy may be calculated by integrating radiant flux (or power) with respect to time and, like all forms of energy, its SI unit is the joule. The term is used particularly when radiation is emitted by a source into the surrounding environment. |
| Spectrum | A spectrum is a condition that is not limited to a specific set of values but can vary infinitely within a continuum. The word was first used scientifically within the field of optics to describe the rainbow of colors in visible light when separated using a prism; it has since been applied by analogy to many fields other than optics. Thus, one might talk about the spectrum of political opinion, or the spectrum of activity of a drug, or the autism spectrum. |
| Frequency | Frequency is the number of occurrences of a repeating event per unit time. It is also referred to as temporal frequency, which emphasizes the contrast to spatial frequency and angular frequency. The period is the duration of one cycle in a repeating event, so the period is the reciprocal of the frequency. |
| Blackbody radiation | Black-body radiation is the type of electromagnetic radiation within or surrounding a body in thermodynamic equilibrium with its environment, or emitted by a black body held at constant, uniform temperature. |

The radiation has a specific spectrum and intensity that depends only on the temperature of the body.

The thermal radiation spontaneously emitted by many ordinary objects can be approximated as blackbody radiation.

**Bohr model**

In atomic physics, the Bohr model, introduced by Niels Bohr in 1913, depicts the atom as small, positively charged nucleus surrounded by electrons that travel in circular orbits around the nucleus--similar in structure to the solar system, but with attraction provided by electrostatic forces rather than gravity. After the cubic model .•Quantum ruleThe angular momentum L = $m_e$vr is an integer multiple of h: $m_e v r = n\hbar$ Substituting the expression for the velocity gives an equation for r in terms of n: $\sqrt{Z k_e e^2 m_e} r = n\hbar$ so that the allowed orbit radius at any n is:

$$r_n = \frac{n^2 \hbar^2}{Z k_e e^2 m_e}$$

The smallest possible value of r in the hydrogen atom is called the Bohr radius and is equal to:

$$r_1 = \frac{\hbar^2}{k_e e^2 m_e} \approx 5.29 \times 10^{-11} \, \text{m}$$

The energy of the n-th level for any atom is determined by the radius and quantum number:

$$E = -\frac{Z k_e e^2}{2 r_n} = -\frac{Z^2 (k_e e^2)^2 m_e}{2 \hbar^2 n^2} \approx \frac{-13.6 Z^2}{n^2} \text{eV}$$

An electron in the lowest energy level of hydrogen therefore has about 13.6 eV less energy than a motionless electron infinitely far from the nucleus. The next energy level is -3.4 eV. The third (n = 3) is -1.51 eV, and so on.

**Photoelectric effect**

In the photoelectric effect, electrons are emitted from solids, liquids or gases when they absorb energy from light. Electrons emitted in this manner may be called photoelectrons.

In 1887, Heinrich Hertz discovered that electrodes illuminated with ultraviolet light create electric sparks more easily.

**Photon**

A photon is an elementary particle, the quantum of light and all other forms of electromagnetic radiation, and the force carrier for the electromagnetic force, even when static via virtual photons. The effects of this force are easily observable at both the microscopic and macroscopic level, because the photon has zero rest mass; this allows long distance interactions. Like all elementary particles, photons are currently best explained by quantum mechanics and exhibit wave-particle duality, exhibiting properties of both waves and particles.

**Quantization**

In physics, quantization is the process of transition from a classical understanding of physical phenomena to a newer understanding known as 'quantum mechanics'.

# 6. Electronic Structure of Atoms

| | It is a procedure for constructing a quantum field theory starting from a classical field theory. This is a generalization of the procedure for building quantum mechanics from classical mechanics. |
|---|---|
| Einstein | An einstein is a unit defined as the energy in one mole of photons. Because energy is inversely proportional to wavelength, the unit is frequency dependent. This unit is not part of the International System of Units and is redundant with the joule. |
| Quantum | In physics, a quantum is the minimum amount of any physical entity involved in an interaction. Behind this, one finds the fundamental notion that a physical property may be 'quantized,' referred to as 'the hypothesis of quantization'. This means that the magnitude can take on only certain discrete values. |
| Work function | In solid-state physics, the work function is the minimum thermodynamic work (i.e. energy) needed to remove an electron from a solid to a point in the vacuum immediately outside the solid surface. Here 'immediately' means that the final electron position is far from the surface on the atomic scale, but still too close to the solid to be influenced by ambient electric fields in the vacuum. The work function is not a characteristic of a bulk material, but rather a property of the surface of the material (depending on crystal face and contamination). |
| Continuous spectrum | In physics, a continuous spectrum usually means a set of values for some physical quantity that is best described as an interval of real numbers. It is opposed to discrete spectrum, a set of values that is discrete in the mathematical sense, where there is a positive gap between each value and the next one. |
| | The classical example of a continuous spectrum, from which the name is derived, is the part of the spectrum of the light emitted by excited atoms of hydrogen that is due to free electrons becoming bound to an hydrogen ion, which is smoothly spread over a wide range of wavelengths; in contrast to the discrete lines due to electrons falling from some bound quantum state to a state of lower energy. |
| Hydrogen | Hydrogen is a chemical element with chemical symbol H and atomic number 1. With an atomic weight of 1.00794 u, hydrogen is the lightest element and its monatomic form (H) is the most abundant chemical substance, constituting roughly 75% of the Universe's baryonic mass. Non-remnant stars are mainly composed of hydrogen in its plasma state. |
| | At standard temperature and pressure, hydrogen is a colorless, odorless, tasteless, non-toxic, nonmetallic, highly combustible diatomic gas with the molecular formula $H_2$. |
| Neon | Neon is a chemical element with symbol Ne and atomic number 10. It is in group 18 (noble gases) of the periodic table. Neon is a colorless, odorless, inert monatomic gas under standard conditions, with about two-thirds the density of air. |

# 6. Electronic Structure of Atoms

| | |
|---|---|
| Polychromatic | The term polychromatic means having several colors. |
| | It is used to describe light that exhibits more than one color, which also means that it contains radiation of more than one wavelength. The study of polychromatics is particularly useful in the production of diffraction gratings. |
| Hydrogen line | The hydrogen line, 21 centimeter line or HI line refers to the electromagnetic radiation spectral line that is created by a change in the energy state of neutral hydrogen atoms. This electromagnetic radiation is at the precise frequency of 1420.40575177 MHz, which is equivalent to the vacuum wavelength of 21.10611405413 cm in free space. This wavelength or frequency falls within the microwave radio region of the electromagnetic spectrum, and it is observed frequently in radio astronomy, since those radio waves can penetrate the large clouds of interstellar cosmic dust that are opaque to visible light. |
| Rydberg constant | The Rydberg constant, symbol $R_8$ or $R_H$ is a physical constant relating to atomic spectra, in the science of spectroscopy. The constant first arose as an empirical fitting parameter in the Rydberg formula for the hydrogen spectral series, but Niels Bohr later showed that its value could be calculated from more fundamental constants, explaining the relationship via his 'Bohr model'. As of 2012, $R_8$ is the most accurately measured fundamental physical constant. |
| Excited state | Excitation is an elevation in energy level above an arbitrary baseline energy state. In physics there is a specific technical definition for energy level which is often associated with an atom being excited to an excited state. |
| | In quantum mechanics an excited state of a system (such as an atom, molecule or nucleus) is any quantum state of the system that has a higher energy than the ground state (that is, more energy than the absolute minimum). |
| Ground state | The ground state of a quantum mechanical system is its lowest-energy state; the energy of the ground state is known as the zero-point energy of the system. An excited state is any state with energy greater than the ground state. The ground state of a quantum field theory is usually called the vacuum state or the vacuum. |
| Principal quantum number | The principal quantum number, symbolized as n, is the first of a set of quantum numbers (which includes: the principal quantum number, the azimuthal quantum number, the magnetic quantum number, and the spin quantum number) of an atomic orbital. The principal quantum number can only have positive integer values. As n increases, the orbital becomes larger and the electron spends more time farther from the nucleus. |
| Energy level | A quantum mechanical system or particle that is bound--that is, confined spatially--can only take on certain discrete values of energy. This contrasts with classical particles, which can have any energy. |

# 6. Electronic Structure of Atoms

| | |
|---|---|
| Atom | The atom is a basic unit of matter that consists of a dense central nucleus surrounded by a cloud of negatively charged electrons. The atomic nucleus contains a mix of positively charged protons and electrically neutral neutrons, which means 'uncuttable' or 'the smallest indivisible particle of matter'. Although the Indian and Greek concepts of the atom were based purely on philosophy, modern science has retained the name coined by Democritus. |
| Hydrogen atom | A hydrogen atom is an atom of the chemical element hydrogen. The electrically neutral atom contains a single positively charged proton and a single negatively charged electron bound to the nucleus by the Coulomb force. Atomic hydrogen constitutes about 75% of the elemental mass of the universe. |
| Mass spectrum | A mass spectrum is an intensity vs. m/z (mass-to-charge ratio) plot representing a chemical analysis. Hence, the mass spectrum of a sample is a pattern representing the distribution of ions by mass (more correctly: mass-to-charge ratio) in a sample. It is a histogram usually acquired using an instrument called a mass spectrometer. |
| Diffraction | Diffraction refers to various phenomena which occur when a wave encounters an obstacle. In classical physics, the diffraction phenomenon is described as the apparent bending of waves around small obstacles and the spreading out of waves past small openings. Similar effects occur when a light wave travels through a medium with a varying refractive index, or a sound wave travels through one with varying acoustic impedance. |
| Electron microscope | An electron microscope is a type of microscope that uses an electron beam to illuminate a specimen and produce a magnified image. <br><br> An EM has greater resolving power than a light microscope and can reveal the structure of smaller objects because electrons have wavelengths about 100,000 times shorter than visible light photons. They can achieve better than 50 pm resolution and magnifications of up to about 10,000,000x whereas ordinary, non-confocal light microscopes are limited by diffraction to about 200 nm resolution and useful magnifications below 2000x. |
| Matter wave | In quantum mechanics, the concept of matter waves or de Broglie waves reflects the wave-particle duality of matter. The theory was proposed by Louis de Broglie in 1924 in his PhD thesis. The de Broglie relations show that the wavelength is inversely proportional to the momentum of a particle and is also called de Broglie wavelength. |
| Microscope | A microscope is an instrument used to see objects that are too small for the naked eye. The science of investigating small objects using such an instrument is called microscopy. Microscopic means invisible to the eye unless aided by a microscope. |
| Momentum | In classical mechanics, linear momentum or translational momentum is the product of the mass and velocity of an object. |

|  |  |
|---|---|
|  | For example, a heavy truck moving fast has a large momentum--it takes a large and prolonged force to get the truck up to this speed, and it takes a large and prolonged force to bring it to a stop afterwards. If the truck were lighter, or moving more slowly, then it would have less momentum. |
| Electron | The electron is a subatomic particle with a negative elementary electric charge. Electrons belong to the first generation of the lepton particle family, and are generally thought to be elementary particles because they have no known components or substructure. The electron has a mass that is approximately 1/1836 that of the proton. |
| Electron diffraction | Electron diffraction refers to the wave nature of electrons. However, from a technical or practical point of view, it may be regarded as a technique used to study matter by firing electrons at a sample and observing the resulting interference pattern. This phenomenon is commonly known as the wave-particle duality, which states that the behavior of a particle of matter (in this case the incident electron) can be described by a wave. |
| Uncertainty principle | In quantum mechanics, the uncertainty principle is any of a variety of mathematical inequalities asserting a fundamental limit to the precision with which certain pairs of physical properties of a particle known as complementary variables, such as position x and momentum p, can be known simultaneously. For instance, the more precisely the position of some particle is determined, the less precisely its momentum can be known, and vice versa. The original heuristic argument that such a limit should exist was given by Werner Heisenberg in 1927, after whom it is sometimes named the Heisenberg principle. |
| Atomic orbital | An atomic orbital is a mathematical function that describes the wave-like behavior of either one electron or a pair of electrons in an atom. This function can be used to calculate the probability of finding any electron of an atom in any specific region around the atom's nucleus. The term may also refer to the physical region or space where the electron can be calculated to be present, as defined by the particular mathematical form of the orbital. |
| Electron density | Electron density is the measure of the probability of an electron being present at a specific location. |
|  | In molecules, regions of electron density are usually found around the atom, and its bonds. In de-localized or conjugated systems, such as phenol, benzene and compounds such as hemoglobin and chlorophyll, the electron density covers an entire region, i.e., in benzene they are found above and below the planar ring. |
| Wave function | A wave function or wavefunction in quantum mechanics describes the quantum state of a particle and how it behaves. Typically, its values are complex numbers and, for a single particle, it is a function of space and time. The Schrödinger equation describes how the wave function evolves over time. |
| Probability | Probability is a measure of the likeliness that an event will occur. |

# 6. Electronic Structure of Atoms

| | |
|---|---|
| | Probability is used to quantify an attitude of mind towards some proposition of whose truth we are not certain. The proposition of interest is usually of the form 'Will a specific event occur?' The attitude of mind is of the form 'How certain are we that the event will occur?' The certainty we adopt can be described in terms of a numerical measure and this number, between 0 and 1 (where 0 indicates impossibility and 1 indicates certainty), we call probability. |
| Angular momentum | In physics, angular momentum, moment of momentum, or rotational momentum is a measure of the amount of rotation an object has, taking into account its mass, shape and speed. It is a vector quantity that represents the product of a body's rotational inertia and rotational velocity about a particular axis. The angular momentum of a system of particles (e.g. a rigid body) is the sum of angular momenta of the individual particles. |
| Magnetic quantum number | In atomic physics, the magnetic quantum number is the third of a set of quantum numbers (the principal quantum number, the azimuthal quantum number, the magnetic quantum number, and the spin quantum number) which describe the unique quantum state of an electron and is designated by the letter m. The magnetic quantum number denotes the energy levels available within a subshell. |
| Quantum number | Quantum numbers describe values of conserved quantities in the dynamics of a quantum system. Perhaps the most peculiar aspect of quantum mechanics is the quantization of observable quantities, since quantum numbers are discrete sets of integers or half-integers. This is distinguished from classical mechanics where the values can range continuously. |
| Electron shell | In chemistry and atomic physics, an electron shell, also called a principle energy level may be thought of as an orbit followed by electrons around an atom's nucleus. The closest shell to the nucleus is called the '1 shell' (also called 'K shell'), followed by the '2 shell' (or 'L shell'), then the '3 shell' (or 'M shell'), and so on farther and farther from the nucleus. The shells correspond with the principal quantum numbers (1, 2, 3, 4.).. |
| Density | The density, or more precisely, the volumetric mass density, of a substance is its mass per unit volume. The symbol most often used for density is ? (the lower case Greek letter rho). Mathematically, density is defined as mass divided by volume: $$\rho = \frac{m}{V},$$ where ? is the density, m is the mass, and V is the volume. |
| Doping | In semiconductor production, doping intentionally introduces impurities into an extremely pure semiconductor for the purpose of modulating its electrical properties. The impurities are dependent upon the type of semiconductor. Lightly and moderately doped semiconductors are referred to as extrinsic. |

| | |
|---|---|
| Pauli exclusion | The Pauli exclusion principle is the quantum mechanical principle that no two identical fermions may occupy the same quantum state simultaneously. In the case of electrons, it can be stated as follows, It is impossible for two electrons of a poly-electron atom to have the same values of the four quantum numbers (n, l, $m_l$ and $m_s$). For two electrons residing in the same orbital, n, l, and $m_l$ are the same, so $m_s$ must be different and the electrons have opposite spins. |
| Pauli exclusion principle | The Pauli exclusion principle is the quantum mechanical principle that no two identical fermions may occupy the same quantum state simultaneously. A more rigorous statement is that the total wave function for two identical fermions is anti-symmetric with respect to exchange of the particles. The principle was formulated by Austrian physicist Wolfgang Pauli in 1925. |
| Magnetic resonance imaging | Magnetic resonance imaging, nuclear magnetic resonance imaging or magnetic resonance tomography (MRT) is a medical imaging technique used in radiology to visualize the internal structures of the body to investigate both anatomy and function in health and disease. The technique is widely used in hospitals for medical diagnosis, staging of disease and for follow-up. There has been a 10% annual growth in MR usage over the last decade and, although the technique avoids ionizing radiation, there are concerns about cost effectiveness and overdiagnosis. |
| Medical imaging | Medical imaging is the technique and process used to create images of the human body for clinical purposes (medical procedures seeking to reveal, diagnose, or examine disease) or medical science (including the study of normal anatomy and physiology). Although imaging of removed organs and tissues can be performed for medical reasons, such procedures are not usually referred to as medical imaging, but rather are a part of pathology. As a discipline and in its widest sense, it is part of biological imaging and incorporates Radiology, Magnetic Resonance Imaging, Nuclear medicine, medical Ultrasonography or Ultrasound, Endoscopy, Elastography, Tactile Imaging, Thermography and medical photography. |
| Nuclear magnetic resonance | Nuclear magnetic resonance is a physical phenomenon in which nuclei in a magnetic field absorb and re-emit electromagnetic radiation. This energy is at a specific resonance frequency which depends on the strength of the magnetic field and the magnetic properties of the isotope of the atoms; in practical applications, the frequency is similar to VHF and UHF television broadcasts (60-1000 MHz). Nuclear magnetic resonance allows the observation of specific quantum mechanical magnetic properties of the atomic nucleus. |
| Nuclear reactor | A nuclear reactor is a device to initiate and control a sustained nuclear chain reaction. Nuclear reactors are used at nuclear power plants for electricity generation and in propulsion of ships. Heat from nuclear fission is passed to a working fluid (water or gas), which runs through turbines. |
| Electron configuration | In atomic physics and quantum chemistry, the electron configuration is the distribution of electrons of an atom or molecule in atomic or molecular orbitals. For example, the electron configuration of the neon atom is $1s^2\,2s^2\,2p^6$. |

# 6. Electronic Structure of Atoms

| | |
|---|---|
| Unpaired electron | In chemistry, an unpaired electron is an electron that occupies an orbital of an atom singly, rather than as part of an electron pair. As the formation of electron pairs is often energetically favourable, either in the form of a chemical bond or as a lone pair, unpaired electrons are relatively uncommon in chemistry, because an entity that carries an unpaired electron is usually rather reactive. In organic chemistry they typically only occur briefly during a reaction on an entity called a radical; however, they play an important role in explaining reaction pathways. |
| Alkali | In chemistry, an alkali is a basic, ionic salt of an alkali metal or alkaline earth metal chemical element. Some authors also define an alkali as a base that dissolves in water. A solution of a soluble base has a pH greater than 7.0. The adjective alkaline is commonly, and alkalescent less often, used in English as a synonym for basic, especially for soluble bases. |
| Condensation reaction | A condensation reaction, also commonly referred to as dehydration synthesis, is a chemical reaction in which two molecules or moieties combine to form a larger molecule, together with the loss of a small molecule. Possible small molecules lost are water, hydrogen chloride, methanol, or acetic acid. The word 'condensation' suggests a process in which two or more things are brought 'together' (Latin 'con') to form something 'dense', like in condensation from gaseous to liquid state of matter; this does not imply, however, that condensation reaction products have greater density than reactants. |
| Core electron | Core electrons are the electrons in an atom that are not valence electrons and therefore do not participate in bonding. An example: the carbon atom has a total of 6 electrons, 4 of them being valence electrons. So the remaining 2 electrons must be core electrons. |
| Valence electron | In chemistry, a valence electron is an electron that is associated with an atom, and that can participate in the formation of a chemical bond; in a single covalent bond, both atoms in the bond contribute one valence electron in order to form a shared pair. The presence of valence electrons can determine the element's chemical properties and whether it may bond with other elements: For a main group element, a valence electron can only be in the outermost electron shell. In a transition metal, a valence electron can also be in an inner shell. |
| Argon | Argon is a chemical element with symbol Ar and atomic number 18. It is in group 18 of the periodic table and is a noble gas. Argon is the third most common gas in the Earth's atmosphere, at 0.93% (9,300 ppm), making it approximately 23.8 times as abundant as the next most common atmospheric gas, carbon dioxide (390 ppm), and more than 500 times as abundant as the next most common noble gas, neon (18 ppm). Nearly all of this argon is radiogenic argon-40 derived from the decay of potassium-40 in the Earth's crust. |
| Krypton | Krypton is a chemical element with symbol Kr and atomic number 36. It is a member of group 18 (noble gases) elements. A colorless, odorless, tasteless noble gas, krypton occurs in trace amounts in the atmosphere, is isolated by fractionally distilling liquified air, and is often used with other rare gases in fluorescent lamps. |

| | |
|---|---|
| Lanthanide | The lanthanide or lanthanoid series of chemical elements comprises the fifteen metallic chemical elements with atomic numbers 57 through 71, from lanthanum through lutetium. These fifteen lanthanide elements, along with the chemically similar elements scandium and yttrium, are often collectively known as the rare earth elements.<br><br>The informal chemical symbol Ln is used in general discussions of lanthanide chemistry to refer to any lanthanide. |
| Rare earth element | As defined by IUPAC, rare earth elements or rare earth metals are a set of seventeen chemical elements in the periodic table, specifically the fifteen lanthanides plus scandium and yttrium. Scandium and yttrium are considered rare earth elements since they tend to occur in the same ore deposits as the lanthanides and exhibit similar chemical properties.<br><br>Despite their name, rare earth elements (with the exception of the radioactive promethium) are relatively plentiful in the Earth's crust, with cerium being the 25th most abundant element at 68 parts per million (similar to copper). |
| Rubidium | Rubidium is a chemical element with the symbol Rb and atomic number 37. Rubidium is a soft, silvery-white metallic element of the alkali metal group, with an atomic mass of 85.4678. Elemental rubidium is highly reactive, with properties similar to those of other alkali metals, such as very rapid oxidation in air. Natural rubidium is a mix of two isotopes: $^{85}$Rb, the only stable one, constitutes 72% of it, and 28% is accounted for slightly radioactive $^{87}$Rb with a half-life of 49 billion years--more than three times longer than the estimated age of the universe.<br><br>German chemists Robert Bunsen and Gustav Kirchhoff discovered rubidium in 1861 by the newly developed method of flame spectroscopy. |
| Scandium | Scandium is a chemical element with symbol Sc and atomic number 21. A silvery-white metallic transition metal, it has historically been sometimes classified as a rare earth element, together with yttrium and the lanthanoids. It was discovered in 1879 by spectral analysis of the minerals euxenite and gadolinite from Scandinavia.<br><br>Scandium is present in most of the deposits of rare earth and uranium compounds, but it is extracted from these ores in only a few mines worldwide. |
| Transition metal | In chemistry, the term transition metal has two possible meanings:•Most scientists describe a 'transition metal' as any element in the d-block of the periodic table (all are metals), which includes groups 3 to 12 on the periodic table. In actual practice, the f-block lanthanide and actinide series are also considered transition metals and are called 'inner transition metals'.<br><br>Jensen reviews the history of the terms 'transition element' (or 'metal') and 'd-block'. |

# 6. Electronic Structure of Atoms

| | |
|---|---|
| Zinc | Zinc, in commerce also spelter, is a metallic chemical element; it has the symbol Zn and atomic number 30. It is the first element of group 12 of the periodic table. Zinc is, in some respects, chemically similar to magnesium, because its ion is of similar size and its only common oxidation state is +2. Zinc is the 24th most abundant element in the Earth's crust and has five stable isotopes. The most common zinc ore is sphalerite (zinc blende), a zinc sulfide mineral. |
| Actinide | The actinide or actinoid series encompasses the 15 metallic chemical elements with atomic numbers from 89 to 103, actinium through lawrencium.<br><br>The actinide series derives its name from the group 3 element actinium. The informal chemical symbol An is used in general discussions of actinide chemistry to refer to any actinide. |
| Cerium | Cerium is a chemical element with symbol Ce and atomic number 58. It is a soft, silvery, ductile metal which easily oxidizes in air. Cerium was named after the dwarf planet Ceres (itself named for the Roman goddess of agriculture). Cerium is the most abundant of the rare earth elements, making up about 0.0046% of the Earth's crust by weight. |
| Lanthanum | Lanthanum is a chemical element with the symbol La and atomic number 57. Lanthanum is a silvery white metallic element and is the first element of the lanthanide series. It is found in some rare-earth minerals, usually in combination with cerium and other rare earth elements. Lanthanum is a malleable, ductile, and soft metal that oxidizes rapidly when exposed to air. |
| Periodic table | The periodic table is a tabular arrangement of the chemical elements, organized on the basis of their atomic numbers, electron configurations, and recurring chemical properties. Elements are presented in order of increasing atomic number (the number of protons in the nucleus). The standard form of the table consists of a grid of elements laid out in 18 columns and 7 rows, with a double row of elements below that. |
| Plutonium | Plutonium is a transuranic radioactive chemical element with the symbol Pu and atomic number 94. It is an actinide metal of silvery-gray appearance that tarnishes when exposed to air, and forms a dull coating when oxidized. The element normally exhibits six allotropes and four oxidation states. It reacts with carbon, halogens, nitrogen, silicon and hydrogen. |
| Praseodymium | Praseodymium is a chemical element that has the symbol Pr and atomic number 59. Praseodymium is a soft, silvery, malleable and ductile metal in the lanthanide group. It is too reactive to be found in native form, and when artificially prepared, it slowly develops a green oxide coating.<br><br>The element was named for the color of its primary oxide. |
| Radon | Radon is a chemical element with symbol Rn and atomic number 86. |

It is a radioactive, colorless, odorless, tasteless noble gas, occurring naturally as an indirect decay product of uranium or thorium. Its most stable isotope, $^{222}$Rn, has a half-life of 3.8 days. Radon is one of the densest substances that remains a gas under normal conditions.

| | |
|---|---|
| Uranium | Uranium is a silvery-white metallic chemical element in the actinide series of the periodic table, with symbol U and atomic number 92. A uranium atom has 92 protons and 92 electrons, of which 6 are valence electrons. Uranium is weakly radioactive because all its isotopes are unstable. The most common isotopes of uranium are uranium-238 (which has 146 neutrons) and uranium-235 (which has 143 neutrons). |
| Fatty acid | In chemistry, and especially in biochemistry, a fatty acid is a carboxylic acid with a long aliphatic tail, which is either saturated or unsaturated. Most naturally occurring fatty acids have a chain of an even number of carbon atoms, from 4 to 28. Fatty acids are usually derived from triglycerides or phospholipids. When they are not attached to other molecules, they are known as 'free' fatty acids. |
| F-block | The f-block of the periodic table of the elements consists of those elements whose atoms or ions have valence electrons in f-orbitals. Actual electronic configurations may be slightly different from what is predicted by the Aufbau principle. The elements are also known as inner transition elements, although that term is normally taken to include lutetium and lawrencium as well, which are part of the d-block. |
| Bismuth | Bismuth is a chemical element with symbol Bi and atomic number 83. Bismuth, a pentavalent poor metal, chemically resembles arsenic and antimony. Elemental bismuth may occur naturally, although its sulfide and oxide form important commercial ores. The free element is 86% as dense as lead. |
| Halogen | The halogens or halogen elements are a group in the periodic table consisting of five chemically related elements, fluorine, chlorine (Cl), bromine (Br), iodine (I), and astatine (At). The artificially created element 117 (ununseptium) may also be a halogen. In the modern IUPAC nomenclature, this group is known as group 17. |
| Chromium | Chromium is a chemical element which has the symbol Cr and atomic number 24. It is the first element in Group 6. It is a steely-gray, lustrous, hard and brittle metal which takes a high polish, resists tarnishing, and has a high melting point. The name of the element is derived from the Greek word 'chroma' (???μα), meaning colour, because many of its compounds are intensely coloured. Chromium oxide was used by the Chinese in the Qin dynasty over 2,000 years ago to coat metal weapons found with the Terracotta Army. |
| Isotope | Isotopes are variants of a particular chemical element such that, while all isotopes of a given element have the same number of protons in each atom, they differ in neutron number. |

# 6. Electronic Structure of Atoms

| | |
|---|---|
| | The term isotope is formed from the Greek roots isos (?s?? 'equal') and topos (t?p?? 'place'), meaning 'the same place'. Thus, different isotopes of a single element occupy the same position on the periodic table. |
| Molybdenum | Molybdenum is a Group 6 chemical element with the symbol Mo and atomic number 42. The name is from Neo-Latin Molybdaenum, from Ancient Greek ????ßd?? molybdos, meaning lead, since its ores were confused with lead ores. Molybdenum minerals have been known into prehistory, but the element was discovered (in the sense of differentiating it as a new entity from the mineral salts of other metals) in 1778 by Carl Wilhelm Scheele. The metal was first isolated in 1781 by Peter Jacob Hjelm. |
| Lyman series | In physics and chemistry, the Lyman series is the series of transitions and resulting ultraviolet emission lines of the hydrogen atom as an electron goes from $n = 2$ to $n = 1$ the lowest energy level of the electron. The transitions are named sequentially by Greek letters: from $n = 2$ to $n = 1$ is called Lyman-alpha, 3 to 1 is Lyman-beta, 4 to 1 is Lyman-gamma, etc. The series is named after its discoverer, Theodore Lyman. |
| Neutron diffraction | Neutron diffraction or elastic neutron scattering is the application of neutron scattering to the determination of the atomic and/or magnetic structure of a material. A sample to be examined is placed in a beam of thermal or cold neutrons to obtain a diffraction pattern that provides information of the structure of the material. The technique is similar to X-ray diffraction but due to their different scattering properties, neutrons and X-rays provide complementary information. |
| Neutron | The neutron is a subatomic hadron particle that has the symbol n or n0, no net electric charge and a mass slightly larger than that of a proton. With the exception of hydrogen-1, nuclei of atoms consist of protons and neutrons, which are therefore collectively referred to as nucleons. The number of protons in a nucleus is the atomic number and defines the type of element the atom forms. |
| Fraunhofer lines | In physics and optics, the Fraunhofer lines are a set of spectral lines named after the German physicist Joseph von Fraunhofer . The lines were originally observed as dark features (absorption lines) in the optical spectrum of the Sun. |
| Hafnium | Hafnium is a chemical element with the symbol Hf and atomic number 72. A lustrous, silvery gray, tetravalent transition metal, hafnium chemically resembles zirconium and is found in zirconium minerals. Its existence was predicted by Dmitri Mendeleev in 1869. Hafnium was the penultimate stable isotope element to be discovered (rhenium was identified two years later). Hafnium is named after Hafnia, the Latin name for Copenhagen, where it was discovered. |
| Ozone layer | The ozone layer is a layer in Earth's atmosphere that absorbs most of the Sun's UV radiation. |

It contains relatively high concentrations of ozone ($O_3$), although it is still very small with regard to ordinary oxygen, and is less than ten parts per million, the average ozone concentration in Earth's atmosphere being only about 0.6 parts per million. The ozone layer is mainly found in the lower portion of the stratosphere from approximately 20 to 30 kilometres (12 to 19 mi) above Earth, though the thickness varies seasonally and geographically.

| | |
|---|---|
| Zirconium | Zirconium is a chemical element with the symbol Zr, atomic number 40 and atomic mass of 91.224. The name of zirconium is taken from the mineral zircon, the most important source of zirconium, and from the Persian word 'zargun - ?????', meaning 'gold colored'. It is a lustrous, grey-white, strong transition metal that resembles titanium. Zirconium is mainly used as a refractory and opacifier, although it is used in small amounts as an alloying agent for its strong resistance to corrosion. |

1. _____ is a Group 6 chemical element with the symbol Mo and atomic number 42. The name is from Neo-Latin Molybdaenum, from Ancient Greek ????ßd?? molybdos, meaning lead, since its ores were confused with lead ores. _____ minerals have been known into prehistory, but the element was discovered (in the sense of differentiating it as a new entity from the mineral salts of other metals) in 1778 by Carl Wilhelm Scheele. The metal was first isolated in 1781 by Peter Jacob Hjelm.

   a. Barium
   b. Berkelium
   c. Beryllium
   d. Molybdenum

2. The _____ is a basic unit of matter that consists of a dense central nucleus surrounded by a cloud of negatively charged electrons. The atomic nucleus contains a mix of positively charged protons and electrically neutral neutrons, which means 'uncuttable' or 'the smallest indivisible particle of matter'. Although the Indian and Greek concepts of the _____ were based purely on philosophy, modern science has retained the name coined by Democritus.

   a. 3-Deazaneplanocin A
   b. Atom
   c. Calibration curve
   d. Bulk material analyzer

3. . The _____ is the unit of frequency in the International System of Units (SI). It is defined as one cycle per second. One of its most common uses is the description of the sine wave, particularly those used in radio and audio applications, such as the frequency of musical tones.

a. Merck Index
b. Cosmic ray
c. Hertz
d. Dose profile

4. _____ is the energy of electromagnetic waves. The quantity of _____ may be calculated by integrating radiant flux (or power) with respect to time and, like all forms of energy, its SI unit is the joule. The term is used particularly when radiation is emitted by a source into the surrounding environment.

a. Bidirectional scattering distribution function
b. Bolometer
c. Crookes radiometer
d. Radiant energy

5. In quantum chemistry, _____ is the state of motion of electrons in an electrostatic field created by stationary nuclei. The term encompass both the wave functions of the electrons and the energies associated with them. _____ is obtained by solving quantum mechanical equations for the aforementioned clamped-nuclei problem.

a. Electronic structure
b. Cunningham correction factor
c. Deodorant
d. Nebulizer

**ANSWER KEY**
6. Electronic Structure of Atoms

1. d
2. b
3. c
4. d
5. a

*You can take the complete Chapter Practice Test*

**for 6. Electronic Structure of Atoms**
on all key terms, persons, places, and concepts.

*Online 99 Cents*

*http://www.JustTheFacts101.com*

Use www.JustTheFacts101.com for all your study needs

including Facts101's online interactive problem solving labs in

chemistry, statistics, mathematics, and more.

# 7. Periodic Properties of the Elements

CHAPTER OUTLINE: KEY TERMS, PEOPLE, PLACES, CONCEPTS

_____ | Electron configuration

_____ | Molecular geometry

_____ | Periodic table

_____ | Technetium

_____ | Atom

_____ | Atomic number

_____ | Effective nuclear charge

_____ | Gallium

_____ | Germanium

_____ | Binding energy

_____ | Valence electron

_____ | Concentration

_____ | Bond length

_____ | Iodine

_____ | Atomic radius

_____ | Radius

_____ | Natural gas

_____ | Periodic trends

_____ | Effusion

_____ | Boron

_____ | Anode

_____ | Cathode

_____ | Graphite

_____ | Lithium cobalt oxide

_____ | Ionization energy

_____ | Silicon

_____ | Ionization

_____ | Lewis structure

_____ | Electron

_____ | Electron affinity

_____ | Precipitation

_____ | Halogen

_____ | Hydrogen

_____ | Chromium

_____ | Metalloid

_____ | Tungsten

_____ | Nonmetal

_____ | Sulfur

_____ | Dopant

_____ | Semiconductor

_____ | Sulfur dioxide

_____ | Absorption

# 7. Periodic Properties of the Elements

CHAPTER OUTLINE: KEY TERMS, PEOPLE, PLACES, CONCEPTS

Carbon dioxide

Alkali

Hydride

Sulfide

Alkali metal

Flame test

Potassium superoxide

Rubidium

Superoxide

Barium

Strontium

Uric acid

Alkaline earth metal

Lithium

Calcium

Calcium carbonate

Chlorine

Magnesium

Oxide

Oxyanion

Hydrochloric acid

Ozone

Polonium

Tellurium

Allotropes of oxygen

Astatine

Hydrogen peroxide

Oxygen

Fluorine

Half-reaction

Hypochlorous acid

Krypton

Radon

Xenon

Bismuth

Bismuth subsalicylate

Strontium oxide

Chalcogen

Electron transfer

Compound semiconductor

Enzyme

Spectroscopy

| | |
|---|---|
| Electron configuration | In atomic physics and quantum chemistry, the electron configuration is the distribution of electrons of an atom or molecule in atomic or molecular orbitals. For example, the electron configuration of the neon atom is $1s^2\ 2s^2\ 2p^6$.<br><br>Electronic configurations describe electrons as each moving independently in an orbital, in an average field created by all other orbitals. |
| Molecular geometry | Molecular geometry is the three-dimensional arrangement of the atoms that constitute a molecule. It determines several properties of a substance including its reactivity, polarity, phase of matter, color, magnetism, and biological activity. The angles between bonds that an atom forms depend only weakly on the rest of molecule, i.e. they can be understood as approximately local and hence transferable properties. |
| Periodic table | The periodic table is a tabular arrangement of the chemical elements, organized on the basis of their atomic numbers, electron configurations, and recurring chemical properties. Elements are presented in order of increasing atomic number (the number of protons in the nucleus). The standard form of the table consists of a grid of elements laid out in 18 columns and 7 rows, with a double row of elements below that. |
| Technetium | Technetium is the chemical element with atomic number 43 and the symbol Tc. It is the lowest atomic number element without any stable isotopes; every form of it is radioactive. Nearly all technetium is produced synthetically, and only minute amounts are found in nature. |
| Atom | The atom is a basic unit of matter that consists of a dense central nucleus surrounded by a cloud of negatively charged electrons. The atomic nucleus contains a mix of positively charged protons and electrically neutral neutrons, which means 'uncuttable' or 'the smallest indivisible particle of matter'. Although the Indian and Greek concepts of the atom were based purely on philosophy, modern science has retained the name coined by Democritus. |
| Atomic number | In chemistry and physics, the atomic number is the number of protons found in the nucleus of an atom and therefore identical to the charge number of the nucleus. It is conventionally represented by the symbol Z. The atomic number uniquely identifies a chemical element. In an atom of neutral charge, the atomic number is also equal to the number of electrons. |
| Effective nuclear charge | The effective nuclear charge is the net positive charge experienced by an electron in a multi-electron atom. The term 'effective' is used because the shielding effect of negatively charged electrons prevents higher orbital electrons from experiencing the full nuclear charge by the repelling effect of inner-layer electrons. The effective nuclear charge experienced by the outer shell electron is also called the core charge. |
| Gallium | Gallium is a chemical element with symbol Ga and atomic number 31. |

Elemental gallium does not occur in free form in nature, but as the gallium(III) compounds that are in trace amounts in zinc ores and in bauxite. Gallium is a soft silvery metal, and elemental gallium is a brittle solid at low temperatures. If it is held in the human hand long enough, gallium will melt, since it melts at the temperature of about 29.76 °C (85.57 °F) (slightly above room temperature).

| | |
|---|---|
| Germanium | Germanium is a chemical element with symbol Ge and atomic number 32. It is a lustrous, hard, grayish-white metalloid in the carbon group, chemically similar to its group neighbors tin and silicon. Purified germanium is a semiconductor, with an appearance most similar to elemental silicon. Like silicon, germanium naturally reacts and forms complexes with oxygen in nature. |
| Binding energy | Binding energy is the mechanical energy required to disassemble a whole into separate parts. A bound system typically has a lower potential energy than the sum of its constituent parts -- this is what keeps the system together. Often this means that energy is released upon the creation of a bound state. |
| Valence electron | In chemistry, a valence electron is an electron that is associated with an atom, and that can participate in the formation of a chemical bond; in a single covalent bond, both atoms in the bond contribute one valence electron in order to form a shared pair. The presence of valence electrons can determine the element's chemical properties and whether it may bond with other elements: For a main group element, a valence electron can only be in the outermost electron shell. In a transition metal, a valence electron can also be in an inner shell. |
| Concentration | In chemistry, concentration is the abundance of a constituent divided by the total volume of a mixture. Several types of mathematical description can be distinguished: mass concentration, molar concentration, number concentration, and volume concentration. The term concentration can be applied to any kind of chemical mixture, but most frequently it refers to solutes and solvents in solutions. |
| Bond length | In molecular geometry, bond length or bond distance is the average distance between nuclei of two bonded atoms in a molecule. It is a transferable property of a bond between atoms of fixed types, relatively independent of the rest of the molecule. |
| Iodine | Iodine is a chemical element with symbol I and atomic number 53. The name is from Greek ??e?d?? ioeides, meaning violet or purple, due to the color of elemental iodine vapor. |
| | Iodine and its compounds are primarily used in nutrition, and industrially in the production of acetic acid and certain polymers. Iodine's relatively high atomic number, low toxicity, and ease of attachment to organic compounds have made it a part of many X-ray contrast materials in modern medicine. |
| Atomic radius | The atomic radius of a chemical element is a measure of the size of its atoms, usually the mean or typical distance from the nucleus to the boundary of the surrounding cloud of electrons. |

Since the boundary is not a well-defined physical entity, there are various non-equivalent definitions of atomic radius. Three widely used definitions of atomic radius are Van der Waals radius, ionic radius, and covalent radius.

**Radius**

In classical geometry, the radius of a circle or sphere is the length of a line segment from its center to its perimeter. The name comes from Latin radius, meaning 'ray' but also the spoke of a chariot wheel. The plural of radius can be either radii (from the Latin plural) or the conventional English plural radiuses.

**Natural gas**

Natural gas is a fossil fuel formed when layers of buried plants and animals are exposed to intense heat and pressure over thousands of years. The energy that the plants originally obtained from the sun is stored in the form of carbon in natural gas. Natural gas is a nonrenewable resource because it cannot be replenished on a human time frame.

**Periodic trends**

In chemistry, periodic trends are the tendencies of certain elemental characteristics to increase or decrease as one progresses along a row or column of the periodic table of elements.

All periodic trends of the chemicals are based on Coulomb's law $F_C = \dfrac{kq_1q_2}{d^2}$ . As distance from the protons in the nucleus to the valence electrons increases values associated with attributes such as electron affinity, ionization energy, and electronegativity decrease.

**Effusion**

Effusion is the process in which a gas escapes through a small hole. This occurs if the diameter of the hole is considerably smaller than the mean free path of the molecules. According to Graham's law, the rate at which gases effuse (i.e., how many molecules pass through the hole per second) is dependent on their molecular weight.

**Boron**

Boron is a chemical element with symbol B and atomic number 5. Because boron is produced entirely by cosmic ray spallation and not by stellar nucleosynthesis, it is a low-abundance element in both the solar system and the Earth's crust. Boron is concentrated on Earth by the water-solubility of its more common naturally occurring compounds, the borate minerals. These are mined industrially as evaporites, such as borax and kernite.

**Anode**

An anode is an electrode through which electric current flows into a polarized electrical device. The direction of electric current is, by convention, opposite to the direction of electron flow. In other words, the electrons flow from the anode into, for example, an electrical circuit.

**Cathode**

A cathode is an electrode through which electric current flows out of a polarized electrical device. The direction of electric current is, by convention, opposite to the direction of electron flow--thus, electrons are considered to flow toward the cathode electrode while current flows away from it. This convention is sometimes remembered using the mnemonic CCD for cathode current departs.

# 7. Periodic Properties of the Elements

| | |
|---|---|
| Graphite | The mineral graphite is an allotrope of carbon. It was named by Abraham Gottlob Werner in 1789 from the Ancient Greek ???f? (grapho), 'to draw/write', for its use in pencils, where it is commonly called lead (not to be confused with the metallic element lead). Unlike diamond (another carbon allotrope), graphite is an electrical conductor, a semimetal. |
| Lithium cobalt oxide | Lithium cobalt oxide is a chemical compound commonly used in the positive electrodes of lithium-ion batteries. The structure of $LiCoO_2$ is known theoretically and has been confirmed with techniques like x-ray diffraction, electron microscopy, neutron powder diffraction, and EXAFS: it consists of layers of lithium that lie between slabs of octahedra formed by cobalt and oxygen atoms. The space group is $R\bar{3}m$ in Hermann-Mauguin notation, signifying a rhombus-like unit cell with threefold improper rotational symmetry and a mirror plane. |
| Ionization energy | The ionization energy of an atom or molecule describes the amount of energy required to remove an electron from the atom or molecule in the gaseous state. $X + energy\ ?\ X^+ + e^-$<br><br>The term ionization potential has been used in the past but is not recommended.<br><br>The units for ionization energy vary from discipline to discipline. |
| Silicon | Silicon, a tetravalent metalloid, is a chemical element with the symbol Si and atomic number 14. It is less reactive than its chemical analog carbon, the nonmetal directly above it in the periodic table, but more reactive than germanium, the metalloid directly below it in the table. Controversy about silicon's character dates to its discovery; it was first prepared and characterized in pure form in 1823. In 1808, it was given the name silicium (from Latin: silex, hard stone or flint), with an -ium word-ending to suggest a metal, a name which the element retains in several non-English languages. However, its final English name, first suggested in 1817, reflects the more physically similar elements carbon and boron. |
| Ionization | Ionization is the process by which an atom or a molecule acquires a negative or positive charge by gaining or losing electrons. |
| Lewis structure | Lewis structures are diagrams that show the bonding between atoms of a molecule and the lone pairs of electrons that may exist in the molecule. A Lewis structure can be drawn for any covalently bonded molecule, as well as coordination compounds. The Lewis structure was named after Gilbert N |
| Electron | The electron is a subatomic particle with a negative elementary electric charge. Electrons belong to the first generation of the lepton particle family, and are generally thought to be elementary particles because they have no known components or substructure. The electron has a mass that is approximately 1/1836 that of the proton. |

| | |
|---|---|
| Electron affinity | In chemistry and atomic physics, the electron affinity of an atom or molecule is defined as the energy change when an electron is added to a neutral atom or molecule to form a negative ion. X + e⁻ ? X⁻ + energy |
| | In solid state physics, the electron affinity for a surface is defined somewhat differently . |
| Precipitation | Precipitation is the formation of a solid in a solution or inside another solid during a chemical reaction or by diffusion in a solid. When the reaction occurs in a liquid solution, the solid formed is called the precipitate. The chemical that causes the solid to form is called the precipitant. |
| Halogen | The halogens or halogen elements are a group in the periodic table consisting of five chemically related elements, fluorine, chlorine (Cl), bromine (Br), iodine (I), and astatine (At). The artificially created element 117 (ununseptium) may also be a halogen. In the modern IUPAC nomenclature, this group is known as group 17. |
| Hydrogen | Hydrogen is a chemical element with chemical symbol H and atomic number 1. With an atomic weight of 1.00794 u, hydrogen is the lightest element and its monatomic form (H) is the most abundant chemical substance, constituting roughly 75% of the Universe's baryonic mass. Non-remnant stars are mainly composed of hydrogen in its plasma state. |
| | At standard temperature and pressure, hydrogen is a colorless, odorless, tasteless, non-toxic, nonmetallic, highly combustible diatomic gas with the molecular formula $H_2$. |
| Chromium | Chromium is a chemical element which has the symbol Cr and atomic number 24. It is the first element in Group 6. It is a steely-gray, lustrous, hard and brittle metal which takes a high polish, resists tarnishing, and has a high melting point. The name of the element is derived from the Greek word 'chroma' (???μα), meaning colour, because many of its compounds are intensely coloured. |
| | Chromium oxide was used by the Chinese in the Qin dynasty over 2,000 years ago to coat metal weapons found with the Terracotta Army. |
| Metalloid | A metalloid is a chemical element that has properties that are in between or a mixture of those of metals and nonmetals and is consequently difficult to classify unambiguously as either a metal or a nonmetal. There is no standard definition of a metalloid, nor is there agreement as to which elements are appropriately classified as such. Despite this lack of specificity the term remains in use in chemistry literature. |
| Tungsten | Tungsten, also known as wolfram, is a chemical element with the chemical symbol W and atomic number 74. The word tungsten comes from the Swedish language tung sten directly translatable to heavy stone, though the name is volfram in Swedish to distinguish it from Scheelite, which in Swedish is alternatively named tungsten. |

# 7. Periodic Properties of the Elements

|  |  |
|---|---|
|  | A hard, rare metal under standard conditions when uncombined, tungsten is found naturally on Earth only in chemical compounds. It was identified as a new element in 1781, and first isolated as a metal in 1783. Its important ores include wolframite and scheelite. |
| Nonmetal | In chemistry, a nonmetal or non-metal is a chemical element which mostly lacks metallic attributes. Physically, nonmetals tend to be highly volatile (easily vaporised), have low elasticity, and are good insulators of heat and electricity; chemically, they tend to have high ionisation energy and electronegativity values, and gain or share electrons when they react with other elements or compounds. Seventeen elements are generally classified as nonmetals; most are gases (hydrogen, helium, nitrogen, oxygen, fluorine, neon, chlorine, argon, krypton, xenon and radon); one is a liquid (bromine); and a few are solids (carbon, phosphorus, sulfur, selenium, and iodine). |
| Sulfur | Sulfur or sulphur is a chemical element with symbol S and atomic number 16. It is an abundant, multivalent non-metal. Under normal conditions, sulfur atoms form cyclic octatomic molecules with chemical formula $S_8$. Elemental sulfur is a bright yellow crystalline solid when at room temperature. |
| Dopant | A dopant, also called a doping agent, is a trace impurity element that is inserted into a substance in order to alter the electrical properties or the optical properties of the substance. In the case of crystalline substances, the atoms of the dopant very commonly take the place of elements that were in the crystal lattice of the material. These materials are very commonly either crystals of a semiconductor (silicon, germanium, etc)., for use in solid-state electronics; or else transparent crystals that are used to make lasers of various types. |
| Semiconductor | A semiconductor is a material which has electrical conductivity to a degree between that of a metal and that of an insulator (such as glass). Semiconductors are the foundation of modern electronics, including transistors, solar cells, light-emitting diodes (LEDs), quantum dots and digital and analog integrated circuits.<br><br>A semiconductor may have a number of unique properties, one of which is the ability to change conductivity by the addition of impurities ('doping') or by interaction with another phenomenon, such as an electric field or light; this ability makes a semiconductor very useful for constructing a device that can amplify, switch, or convert an energy input. |
| Sulfur dioxide | Sulfur dioxide is the chemical compound with the formula SO2. At standard atmosphere it is a toxic gas with a pungent, irritating and rotten smell. The triple point is 197.69 K and 1.67Kpa. |
| Absorption | In chemistry, absorption is a physical or chemical phenomenon or a process in which atoms, molecules, or ions enter some bulk phase - gas, liquid, or solid material. This is a different process from adsorption, since molecules undergoing absorption are taken up by the volume, not by the surface (as in the case for adsorption). |

CHAPTER HIGHLIGHTS & NOTES: KEY TERMS, PEOPLE, PLACES, CONCEPTS

| | |
|---|---|
| Carbon dioxide | Carbon dioxide is a naturally occurring chemical compound composed of two oxygen atoms each covalently double bonded to a single carbon atom. It is a gas at standard temperature and pressure and exists in Earth's atmosphere in this state, as a trace gas at a concentration of 0.039 per cent by volume. |
| | As part of the carbon cycle, plants, algae, and cyanobacteria use light energy to photosynthesize carbohydrate from carbon dioxide and water, with oxygen produced as a waste product. |
| Alkali | In chemistry, an alkali is a basic, ionic salt of an alkali metal or alkaline earth metal chemical element. Some authors also define an alkali as a base that dissolves in water. A solution of a soluble base has a pH greater than 7.0. The adjective alkaline is commonly, and alkalescent less often, used in English as a synonym for basic, especially for soluble bases. |
| Hydride | In chemistry, a hydride is the anion of hydrogen, $H^-$, or, more commonly, an alloy, or compound in which one or more hydrogen centres have nucleophilic, reducing, or basic properties. In compounds that are regarded as hydrides, hydrogen is bonded to a more electropositive element or group. Compounds containing hydrogen bonded to metals or metalloid may be referred to as hydrides, even though these hydrogen centres can have a protic character. |
| Sulfide | Sulfide is an inorganic anion with the chemical formula $S^{2-}$. It contributes no color to sulfide salts. Sulfide is the main component of niningerite (niningerite is roughly 47% sulfide by mass), and contributes no odor to sulfide salts. |
| Alkali metal | The alkali metals are a group in the periodic table consisting of the chemical elements lithium, sodium (Na), potassium (K), rubidium (Rb), caesium (Cs), and francium (Fr). This group lies in the s-block of the periodic table as all alkali metals have their outermost electron in an s-orbital. The alkali metals provide the best example of group trends in properties in the periodic table, with elements exhibiting well-characterized homologous behaviour. |
| Flame test | A flame test is an analytic procedure used in chemistry to detect the presence of certain elements, primarily metal ions, based on each element's characteristic emission spectrum. The color of flames in general also depends on temperature; see flame color. |
| | The test involves introducing a sample of the element or compound to a hot, non-luminous flame, and observing the color of the flame that results. |
| Potassium superoxide | Potassium superoxide is the inorganic compound with the formula $KO_2$. It is a yellow solid that decomposes in moist air. It is a rare example of a stable salt of the superoxide ion. |
| Rubidium | Rubidium is a chemical element with the symbol Rb and atomic number 37. Rubidium is a soft, silvery-white metallic element of the alkali metal group, with an atomic mass of 85.4678. |

|  | Elemental rubidium is highly reactive, with properties similar to those of other alkali metals, such as very rapid oxidation in air. Natural rubidium is a mix of two isotopes: $^{85}$Rb, the only stable one, constitutes 72% of it, and 28% is accounted for slightly radioactive $^{87}$Rb with a half-life of 49 billion years--more than three times longer than the estimated age of the universe.<br><br>German chemists Robert Bunsen and Gustav Kirchhoff discovered rubidium in 1861 by the newly developed method of flame spectroscopy. |
|---|---|
| Superoxide | A superoxide, also known by the obsolete name hyperoxide, is a compound that contains the superoxide anion with the chemical formula $O_2^-$. The systematic name of the anion is dioxide(1-). Superoxide anion is particularly important as the product of the one-electron reduction of dioxygen $O_2$, which occurs widely in nature. |
| Barium | Barium is a chemical element with symbol Ba and atomic number 56. It is the fifth element in Group 2, a soft silvery metallic alkaline earth metal. Because of its high chemical reactivity barium is never found in nature as a free element. Its hydroxide was known in pre-modern history as baryta; this substance does not occur as a mineral, but can be prepared by heating barium carbonate. |
| Strontium | Strontium is a chemical element with symbol Sr and atomic number 38. An alkaline earth metal, strontium is a soft silver-white or yellowish metallic element that is highly reactive chemically. The metal turns yellow when it is exposed to air. Strontium has physical and chemical properties similar to those of its two neighbors calcium and barium. |
| Uric acid | Uric acid is a heterocyclic compound of carbon, nitrogen, oxygen, and hydrogen with the formula $C_5H_4N_4O_3$. It forms ions and salts known as urates and acid urates such as ammonium acid urate. Uric acid is a product of the metabolic breakdown of purine nucleotides. |
| Alkaline earth metal | The alkaline earth metals are a group of chemical elements in the periodic table with very similar properties. They are all shiny, silvery-white, somewhat reactive metals at standard temperature and pressure and readily lose their two outermost electrons to form cations with charge 2+ and an oxidation state, or oxidation number of +2. In the modern IUPAC nomenclature, the alkaline earth metals comprise the group 2 elements.<br><br>The alkaline earth metals are beryllium (Be), magnesium (Mg), calcium (Ca), strontium (Sr), barium (Ba), and radium (Ra). |
| Lithium | Lithium is a chemical element with symbol Li and atomic number 3. It is a soft, silver-white metal belonging to the alkali metal group of chemical elements. Under standard conditions it is the lightest metal and the least dense solid element. Like all alkali metals, lithium is highly reactive and flammable. |

| | |
|---|---|
| Calcium | Calcium is the chemical element with symbol Ca and atomic number 20. Calcium is a soft gray alkaline earth metal, and is the fifth-most-abundant element by mass in the Earth's crust. Calcium is also the fifth-most-abundant dissolved ion in seawater by both molarity and mass, after sodium, chloride, magnesium, and sulfate.<br><br>Calcium is essential for living organisms, in particular in cell physiology, where movement of the calcium ion $Ca^{2+}$ into and out of the cytoplasm functions as a signal for many cellular processes. |
| Calcium carbonate | Calcium carbonate is a chemical compound with the formula $CaCO_3$. It is a common substance found in rocks in all parts of the world, and is the main component of shells of marine organisms, snails, coal balls, pearls, and eggshells. Calcium carbonate is the active ingredient in agricultural lime, and is created when Ca ions in hard water react with carbonate ions creating limescale. |
| Chlorine | Chlorine is a chemical element with symbol Cl and atomic number 17. Chlorine is in the halogen group (17) and is the second lightest halogen after fluorine. The element is a yellow-green gas under standard conditions, where it forms diatomic molecules. It has the highest electron affinity and the fourth highest electronegativity of all the reactive elements; for this reason, chlorine is a strong oxidizing agent. |
| Magnesium | Magnesium is a chemical element with the symbol Mg and atomic number 12. Its common oxidation number is +2. It is an alkaline earth metal and the eighth most abundant element in the Earth's crust and ninth in the known universe as a whole. Magnesium is the fourth most common element in the Earth as a whole (behind iron, oxygen and silicon), making up 13% of the planet's mass and a large fraction of the planet's mantle. The relative abundance of magnesium is related to the fact that it easily builds up in supernova stars from a sequential addition of three helium nuclei to carbon (which in turn is made from three helium nuclei). |
| Oxide | An oxide is a chemical compound that contains at least one oxygen atom and one other element in its chemical formula. Metal oxides typically contain an anion of oxygen in the oxidation state of -2. Most of the Earth's crust consists of solid oxides, the result of elements being oxidized by the oxygen in air or in water. Hydrocarbon combustion affords the two principal carbon oxides: carbon monoxide and carbon dioxide. |
| Oxyanion | An oxyanion or oxoanion is a chemical compound with the generic formula $A_xO_y^{z-}$. Oxoanions are formed by a large majority of the chemical elements. The formulae of simple oxoanions are determined by the octet rule. |
| Hydrochloric acid | Hydrochloric acid is a clear, colorless, highly pungent solution of hydrogen chloride in water. It is a highly corrosive, strong mineral acid with many industrial uses. Hydrochloric acid is found naturally in gastric acid. |
| Ozone | Ozone, or trioxygen, is an inorganic compound with the chemical formula O |

# 7. Periodic Properties of the Elements

| | |
|---|---|
| | $3(\mu\text{-}O)$ (also written $[O(\mu\text{-}O)O]$ or $O3$). It is a pale blue gas with a distinctively pungent smell. It is an allotrope of oxygen that is much less stable than the diatomic allotrope $O2$, breaking down in the lower atmosphere to normal dioxygen. |
| Polonium | Polonium is a chemical element with the symbol Po and atomic number 84, discovered in 1898 by Marie Curie and Pierre Curie. A rare and highly radioactive element with no stable isotopes, polonium is chemically similar to bismuth and tellurium, and it occurs in uranium ores. Applications of polonium are few, and include heaters in space probes, antistatic devices, and sources of neutrons and alpha particles. |
| Tellurium | Tellurium is a chemical element with symbol Te and atomic number 52. A brittle, mildly toxic, rare, silver-white metalloid which looks similar to tin, tellurium is chemically related to selenium and sulfur. It is occasionally found in native form, as elemental crystals. Tellurium is far more common in the universe as a whole than it is on Earth. |
| Allotropes of oxygen | There are several known allotropes of oxygen. The most familiar is molecular oxygen ($O_2$), present at significant levels in Earth's atmosphere and also known as dioxygen or triplet oxygen. Another is the highly reactive ozone ($O_3$). |
| Astatine | Astatine is a radioactive chemical element with the chemical symbol At and atomic number 85. It occurs on Earth only as the result of the radioactive decay of certain heavier elements. All of its isotopes are short-lived; the most stable is astatine-210, with a half-life of 8.5 hours. Accordingly, much less is known about astatine than most other elements. |
| Hydrogen peroxide | Hydrogen peroxide is the simplest peroxide (a compound with an oxygen-oxygen single bond). It is also a strong oxidizer. Hydrogen peroxide is a clear liquid, slightly more viscous than water. |
| Oxygen | Oxygen is a chemical element with symbol O and atomic number 8. It is a member of the chalcogen group on the periodic table and is a highly reactive nonmetallic element and oxidizing agent that readily forms compounds (notably oxides) with most elements. By mass, oxygen is the third-most abundant element in the universe, after hydrogen and helium At STP, two atoms of the element bind to form dioxygen, a diatomic gas that is colorless, odorless, and tasteless; with the formula $O2$.<br><br>Many major classes of organic molecules in living organisms, such as proteins, nucleic acids, carbohydrates, and fats, contain oxygen, as do the major inorganic compounds that are constituents of animal shells, teeth, and bone. |
| Fluorine | Fluorine is the chemical element with symbol F and atomic number 9. At room temperature, the element is a pale yellow gas composed of diatomic molecules, $F2$. Fluorine is the lightest halogen and the most electronegative element. |

| Half-reaction | A half reaction is either the oxidation or reduction reaction component of a redox reaction. A half reaction is obtained by considering the change in oxidation states of individual substances involved in the redox reaction. |
| --- | --- |
| | Often, the concept of half-reactions is used to describe what occurs in an electrochemical cell, such as a Galvanic cell battery. |
| Hypochlorous acid | Hypochlorous acid is a weak acid with the chemical formula HClO. It forms when chlorine dissolves in water. It cannot be isolated in pure form due to rapid equilibration with its precursor. HOCl is an oxidizer, and as its sodium salt sodium hypochlorite, (NaClO), or its calcium salt calcium hypochlorite, ($Ca(ClO)_2$) is used as a bleach, a deodorant, and a disinfectant. |
| Krypton | Krypton is a chemical element with symbol Kr and atomic number 36. It is a member of group 18 (noble gases) elements. A colorless, odorless, tasteless noble gas, krypton occurs in trace amounts in the atmosphere, is isolated by fractionally distilling liquified air, and is often used with other rare gases in fluorescent lamps. Krypton is inert for most practical purposes. |
| Radon | Radon is a chemical element with symbol Rn and atomic number 86. It is a radioactive, colorless, odorless, tasteless noble gas, occurring naturally as an indirect decay product of uranium or thorium. Its most stable isotope, $^{222}Rn$, has a half-life of 3.8 days. Radon is one of the densest substances that remains a gas under normal conditions. |
| Xenon | Xenon is a chemical element with the symbol Xe and atomic number 54. It is a colorless, heavy, odorless noble gas, that occurs in the Earth's atmosphere in trace amounts. Although generally unreactive, xenon can undergo a few chemical reactions such as the formation of xenon hexafluoroplatinate, the first noble gas compound to be synthesized. |
| | Naturally occurring xenon consists of eight stable isotopes. |
| Bismuth | Bismuth is a chemical element with symbol Bi and atomic number 83. Bismuth, a pentavalent poor metal, chemically resembles arsenic and antimony. Elemental bismuth may occur naturally, although its sulfide and oxide form important commercial ores. The free element is 86% as dense as lead. |
| Bismuth subsalicylate | Bismuth subsalicylate, with the empirical chemical formula of $C_7H_5BiO_4$, is a colloidal substance obtained by hydrolysis of bismuth salicylate ($Bi\{C_6H_4CO_2\}_3$). The actual structure is unknown and the formulation is only approximate. Recent evidence indicates that it is composed of a bismuth oxide core structure with salicylate ions attached to the surface. |
| Strontium oxide | Strontium oxide or strontia, SrO, is formed when strontium reacts with oxygen. Burning strontium in air results in a mixture of strontium oxide and strontium nitride. |

# 7. Periodic Properties of the Elements

| | |
|---|---|
| Chalcogen | The chalcogens are the chemical elements in group 16 of the periodic table. This group is also known as the oxygen family. It consists of the elements oxygen (O), sulfur (S), selenium (Se), tellurium (Te), and the radioactive element polonium (Po). |
| Electron transfer | Electron transfer occurs when an electron moves from an atom or a chemical species (e.g. a molecule) to another atom or chemical species. ET is a mechanistic description of the thermodynamic concept of redox, wherein the oxidation states of both reaction partners change.<br><br>Numerous biological processes involve ET reactions. |
| Compound semiconductor | A compound semiconductor is a semiconductor compound composed of elements from two or more different groups of the periodic table. These semiconductors typically form in groups 13-15 (old groups III-V), for example of elements from group 13 (old group III, boron, aluminium, gallium, indium) and from group 15 (old group V, nitrogen, phosphorus, arsenic, antimony, bismuth). The range of possible formulae is quite broad because these elements can form binary (two elements, e.g. gallium(III) arsenide (GaAs)), ternary (three elements, e.g. indium gallium arsenide (InGaAs)) and quaternary (four elements, e.g. aluminium gallium indium phosphide (AlInGaP)) alloys. |
| Enzyme | Enzymes are large biological molecules responsible for the thousands of metabolic processes that sustain life. They are highly selective catalysts, greatly accelerating both the rate and specificity of metabolic reactions, from the digestion of food to the synthesis of DNA. Most enzymes are proteins, although some catalytic RNA molecules have been identified. Enzymes adopt a specific three-dimensional structure, and may employ organic (e.g. biotin) and inorganic (e.g. magnesium ion) cofactors to assist in catalysis. |
| Spectroscopy | Spectroscopy is the study of the interaction between matter and radiated energy. Historically, spectroscopy originated through the study of visible light dispersed according to its wavelength, e.g., by a prism. Later the concept was expanded greatly to comprise any interaction with radiative energy as a function of its wavelength or frequency. |

1.  In chemistry, an _____ is a basic, ionic salt of an _____ metal or alkaline earth metal chemical element. Some authors also define an _____ as a base that dissolves in water. A solution of a soluble base has a pH greater than 7.0. The adjective alkaline is commonly, and alkalescent less often, used in English as a synonym for basic, especially for soluble bases.

    a. 18-Electron rule
    b. Crucible
    c. Cross-validation
    d. Alkali

2.  _____ is a chemical element with symbol Kr and atomic number 36. It is a member of group 18 (noble gases) elements. A colorless, odorless, tasteless noble gas, _____ occurs in trace amounts in the atmosphere, is isolated by fractionally distilling liquified air, and is often used with other rare gases in fluorescent lamps. _____ is inert for most practical purposes.

    a. Barium
    b. Krypton
    c. Beryllium
    d. Bismuth

3.  The _____ is a subatomic particle with a negative elementary electric charge. _____s belong to the first generation of the lepton particle family, and are generally thought to be elementary particles because they have no known components or substructure. The _____ has a mass that is approximately 1/1836 that of the proton.

    a. Compton wavelength
    b. Electron
    c. Bohr model
    d. Bohr magneton

4.  In atomic physics and quantum chemistry, the _____ is the distribution of electrons of an atom or molecule in atomic or molecular orbitals. For example, the _____ of the neon atom is $1s^2\ 2s^2\ 2p^6$.

    Electronic configurations describe electrons as each moving independently in an orbital, in an average field created by all other orbitals.

    a. Bohr magneton
    b. Electron configuration
    c. Boson
    d. Bremsstrahlung

5. .  A half reaction is either the oxidation or reduction reaction component of a redox reaction. A half reaction is obtained by considering the change in oxidation states of individual substances involved in the redox reaction.

Often, the concept of _____s is used to describe what occurs in an electrochemical cell, such as a Galvanic cell battery.

a. Biophotovoltaic
b. Bipolar electrochemistry
c. Half-reaction
d. Cell notation

**1.** d
**2.** b
**3.** b
**4.** b
**5.** c

---

## You can take the complete Chapter Practice Test

**for 7. Periodic Properties of the Elements**
on all key terms, persons, places, and concepts.

### Online 99 Cents

### *http://www.JustTheFacts101.com*

Use www.JustTheFacts101.com for all your study needs

including Facts101's online interactive problem solving labs in

chemistry, statistics, mathematics, and more.

# 8. Basic Concepts of Chemical Bonding

CHAPTER OUTLINE: KEY TERMS, PEOPLE, PLACES, CONCEPTS

Chemical bond

Covalent

Entropy

Lewis structure

Octet rule

Valence electron

Electron

Bromine

Electron transfer

Ionization energy

Ionization

Ionic compound

Lattice energy

Sodium

Sodium chloride

Crystal structure

Titration

Product

Alkali

Chloride

Electron configuration

# 8. Basic Concepts of Chemical Bonding

_____ | P-block

_____ | Concentration

_____ | Electron density

_____ | Density

_____ | Molecule

_____ | Double bond

_____ | Nitrogen

_____ | Triple bond

_____ | Electron affinity

_____ | Electronegativity

_____ | Charged particle

_____ | Phosphorus

_____ | Debye

_____ | Diatomic

_____ | Diatomic molecule

_____ | Dipole

_____ | Polar molecules

_____ | Bond length

_____ | Hydrogen

_____ | Hydrogen chloride

_____ | Halide

CHAPTER OUTLINE: KEY TERMS, PEOPLE, PLACES, CONCEPTS

| | Manganese oxide |
|---|---|
| | Polyatomic ion |
| | Chlorine |
| | Cyanide ion |
| | Formal charge |
| | Oxidation |
| | Ozone |
| | Benzene |
| | Resonance |
| | Hypervalent molecule |
| | Phosphorus pentafluoride |
| | Enthalpy |
| | Strength |
| | Nitroglycerin |
| | Phosgene |
| | Naphthalene |
| | Chlorine monoxide |
| | Haber process |
| | Triazine |
| | Ethane |
| | Methane |

# 8. Basic Concepts of Chemical Bonding

| | Acetylene |
|---|---|
| | Barium azide |
| | Chloral hydrate |

CHAPTER HIGHLIGHTS & NOTES: KEY TERMS, PEOPLE, PLACES, CONCEPTS

| | |
|---|---|
| Chemical bond | A chemical bond is an attraction between atoms that allows the formation of chemical substances that contain two or more atoms. The bond is caused by the electrostatic force of attraction between opposite charges, either between electrons and nuclei, or as the result of a dipole attraction. The strength of chemical bonds varies considerably; there are 'strong bonds' such as covalent or ionic bonds and 'weak bonds' such as dipole-dipole interactions, the London dispersion force and hydrogen bonding. |
| Covalent | A covalent bond is a chemical bond that involves the sharing of electron pairs between atoms. The stable balance of attractive and repulsive forces between atoms when they share electrons is known as covalent bonding. For many molecules, the sharing of electrons allows each atom to attain the equivalent of a full outer shell, corresponding to a stable electronic configuration. |
| Entropy | In thermodynamics, entropy is a measure of the number of specific ways in which a thermodynamic system may be arranged, often taken to be a measure of disorder, or a measure of progressing towards thermodynamic equilibrium. The entropy of an isolated system never decreases, because isolated systems spontaneously evolve towards thermodynamic equilibrium, which is the state of maximum entropy.<br><br>Entropy was originally defined for a thermodynamically reversible process<br><br>as $$\Delta S = \int \frac{dQ_{rev}}{T}$$<br><br>where the entropy is found from the uniform thermodynamic temperature of a closed system dividing an incremental reversible transfer of heat into that system . |
| Lewis structure | Lewis structures are diagrams that show the bonding between atoms of a molecule and the lone pairs of electrons that may exist in the molecule. A Lewis structure can be drawn for any covalently bonded molecule, as well as coordination compounds. |

# 8. Basic Concepts of Chemical Bonding

CHAPTER HIGHLIGHTS & NOTES: KEY TERMS, PEOPLE, PLACES, CONCEPTS

| Octet rule | The octet rule is a chemical rule of thumb that states that atoms of low atomic number tend to combine in such a way that they each have eight electrons in their valence shells, giving them the same electronic configuration as a noble gas. The rule is applicable to the main-group elements, especially carbon, nitrogen, oxygen, and the halogens, but also to metals such as sodium or magnesium. |
| :--- | :--- |
| | The valence electrons can be counted using a Lewis electron dot diagram as shown at the right for carbon dioxide. |
| Valence electron | In chemistry, a valence electron is an electron that is associated with an atom, and that can participate in the formation of a chemical bond; in a single covalent bond, both atoms in the bond contribute one valence electron in order to form a shared pair. The presence of valence electrons can determine the element's chemical properties and whether it may bond with other elements: For a main group element, a valence electron can only be in the outermost electron shell. In a transition metal, a valence electron can also be in an inner shell. |
| Electron | The electron is a subatomic particle with a negative elementary electric charge. Electrons belong to the first generation of the lepton particle family, and are generally thought to be elementary particles because they have no known components or substructure. The electron has a mass that is approximately 1/1836 that of the proton. |
| Bromine | Bromine is a chemical element with the symbol Br, and atomic number of 35. It is in the halogen group (17). The element was isolated independently by two chemists, Carl Jacob Löwig and Antoine Jerome Balard, in 1825-1826. Elemental bromine is a fuming red-brown liquid at room temperature, corrosive and toxic, with properties between those of chlorine and iodine. Free bromine does not occur in nature, but occurs as colorless soluble crystalline mineral halide salts, analogous to table salt. |
| Electron transfer | Electron transfer occurs when an electron moves from an atom or a chemical species (e.g. a molecule) to another atom or chemical species. ET is a mechanistic description of the thermodynamic concept of redox, wherein the oxidation states of both reaction partners change. |
| | Numerous biological processes involve ET reactions. |
| Ionization energy | The ionization energy of an atom or molecule describes the amount of energy required to remove an electron from the atom or molecule in the gaseous state. $X + energy \rightarrow X^+ + e^-$ |
| | The term ionization potential has been used in the past but is not recommended. |
| | The units for ionization energy vary from discipline to discipline. |

# 8. Basic Concepts of Chemical Bonding

| | |
|---|---|
| Ionization | Ionization is the process by which an atom or a molecule acquires a negative or positive charge by gaining or losing electrons. |
| Ionic compound | In chemistry, an ionic compound is a chemical compound in which ions are held together in a lattice structure by ionic bonds. Usually, the positively charged portion consists of metal cations and the negatively charged portion is an anion or polyatomic ion. Ions in ionic compounds are held together by the electrostatic forces between oppositely charged bodies. |
| Lattice energy | The lattice energy of an ionic solid is a measure of the strength of bonds in that ionic compound. It is usually defined as the enthalpy of formation of the ionic compound from gaseous ions and as such is invariably exothermic. Lattice energy may also be defined as the energy required to completely separate one mole of a solid ionic compound into gaseous ionic constituents. |
| Sodium | Sodium is a chemical element with the symbol Na and atomic number 11. It is a soft, silver-white, highly reactive metal and is a member of the alkali metals; its only stable isotope is $^{23}$Na. The free metal does not occur in nature, but instead must be prepared from its compounds; it was first isolated by Humphry Davy in 1807 by the electrolysis of sodium hydroxide. Sodium is the sixth most abundant element in the Earth's crust, and exists in numerous minerals such as feldspars, sodalite and rock salt. |
| Sodium chloride | Sodium chloride, also known as salt, common salt, table salt or halite, is an ionic compound with the formula NaCl, representing equal proportions of sodium and chlorine. Sodium chloride is the salt most responsible for the salinity of the ocean and of the extracellular fluid of many multicellular organisms. As the major ingredient in edible salt, it is commonly used as a condiment and food preservative. |
| Crystal structure | In mineralogy and crystallography, crystal structure is a unique arrangement of atoms or molecules in a crystalline liquid or solid. A crystal structure is composed of a pattern, a set of atoms arranged in a particular way, and a lattice exhibiting long-range order and symmetry. Patterns are located upon the points of a lattice, which is an array of points repeating periodically in three dimensions. |
| Titration | Titration, also known as titrimetry, is a common laboratory method of quantitative chemical analysis that is used to determine the unknown concentration of an identified analyte. Since volume measurements play a key role in titration, it is also known as volumetric analysis. A reagent, called the titrant or titrator is prepared as a standard solution. |
| Product | Product are formed during chemical reactions as reagents are consumed. Products have lower energy than the reagents and are produced during the reaction according to the second law of thermodynamics. The released energy comes from changes in chemical bonds between atoms in reagent molecules and may be given off in the form of heat or light. |

CHAPTER HIGHLIGHTS & NOTES: KEY TERMS, PEOPLE, PLACES, CONCEPTS

| | |
|---|---|
| Alkali | In chemistry, an alkali is a basic, ionic salt of an alkali metal or alkaline earth metal chemical element. Some authors also define an alkali as a base that dissolves in water. A solution of a soluble base has a pH greater than 7.0. The adjective alkaline is commonly, and alkalescent less often, used in English as a synonym for basic, especially for soluble bases. |
| Chloride | The chloride ion is formed when the element chlorine gains an electron to form an anion (negatively charged ion) $Cl^-$. The salts of hydrochloric acid contain chloride ions and can also be called chlorides. The chloride ion, and its salts such as sodium chloride, are very soluble in water. |
| Electron configuration | In atomic physics and quantum chemistry, the electron configuration is the distribution of electrons of an atom or molecule in atomic or molecular orbitals. For example, the electron configuration of the neon atom is $1s^2\ 2s^2\ 2p^6$. |
| | Electronic configurations describe electrons as each moving independently in an orbital, in an average field created by all other orbitals. |
| P-block | The p-block of the periodic table of the elements consists of the last six groups except helium . In the elemental form of the p-block elements, the highest energy electron occupies a p-orbital. The p-block contains all of the nonmetals (except for hydrogen and helium, which are in the s-block) and semimetals, as well as the poor metals. |
| Concentration | In chemistry, concentration is the abundance of a constituent divided by the total volume of a mixture. Several types of mathematical description can be distinguished: mass concentration, molar concentration, number concentration, and volume concentration. The term concentration can be applied to any kind of chemical mixture, but most frequently it refers to solutes and solvents in solutions. |
| Electron density | Electron density is the measure of the probability of an electron being present at a specific location. |
| | In molecules, regions of electron density are usually found around the atom, and its bonds. In de-localized or conjugated systems, such as phenol, benzene and compounds such as hemoglobin and chlorophyll, the electron density covers an entire region, i.e., in benzene they are found above and below the planar ring. |
| Density | The density, or more precisely, the volumetric mass density, of a substance is its mass per unit volume. The symbol most often used for density is ? (the lower case Greek letter rho). Mathematically, density is defined as mass divided by volume: $$\rho = \frac{m}{V},$$ where ? is the density, m is the mass, and V is the volume. |
| Molecule | A molecule is an electrically neutral group of two or more atoms held together by chemical bonds. |

# 8. Basic Concepts of Chemical Bonding

|  | Molecules are distinguished from ions by their lack of electrical charge. However, in quantum physics, organic chemistry, and biochemistry, the term molecule is often used less strictly, also being applied to polyatomic ions. |
|---|---|
| Double bond | A double bond in chemistry is a chemical bond between two chemical elements involving four bonding electrons instead of the usual two. The most common double bond, that is between two carbon atoms, can be found in alkenes. Many types of double bonds exist between two different elements. |
| Nitrogen | Nitrogen, symbol N, is the chemical element of atomic number 7. At room temperature, it is a gas of diatomic molecules and is colorless and odorless. Nitrogen is a common element in the universe, estimated at about seventh in total abundance in our galaxy and the Solar System. On Earth, the element is primarily found as the free element; it forms about 80% of the Earth's atmosphere. |
| Triple bond | A triple bond in chemistry is a chemical bond between two atoms involving six bonding electrons instead of the usual two in a covalent single bond. The most common triple bond, that between two carbon atoms, can be found in alkynes. Other functional groups containing a triple bond are cyanides and isocyanides. |
| Electron affinity | In chemistry and atomic physics, the electron affinity of an atom or molecule is defined as the energy change when an electron is added to a neutral atom or molecule to form a negative ion. X + e⁻ ? X⁻ + energy<br><br>In solid state physics, the electron affinity for a surface is defined somewhat differently . |
| Electronegativity | Electronegativity, symbol ?, is a chemical property that describes the tendency of an atom or a functional group to attract electrons towards itself. An atom's electronegativity is affected by both its atomic number and the distance that its valence electrons reside from the charged nucleus. The higher the associated electronegativity number, the more an element or compound attracts electrons towards it. |
| Charged particle | In physics, a charged particle is a particle with an electric charge. It may be either a subatomic particle or an ion. A collection of charged particles, or even a gas containing a proportion of charged particles, is called a plasma, which is called the fourth state of matter because its properties are quite different from solids, liquids and gases (plasma is the most common state of matter in the universe). |
| Phosphorus | Phosphorus is a nonmetallic chemical element with symbol P and atomic number 15. A multivalent pnictogen, phosphorus as a mineral is almost always present in its maximally oxidised state, as inorganic phosphate rocks. |

|  | Elemental phosphorus exists in two major forms--white phosphorus and red phosphorus--but due to its high reactivity, phosphorus is never found as a free element on Earth.

The first form of elemental phosphorus to be produced (white phosphorus, in 1669) emits a faint glow upon exposure to oxygen - hence its name given from Greek mythology, F?sf???? meaning 'light-bearer' (Latin Lucifer), referring to the 'Morning Star', the planet Venus. |
|---|---|
| Debye | The debye is a CGS unit (a non-SI metric unit) of electric dipole moment named in honour of the physicist Peter J. W. Debye. It is defined as $1 \times 10^{-18}$ statcoulomb-centimetre. Historically the debye was defined as the dipole moment resulting from two charges of opposite sign but an equal magnitude of $10^{-10}$ statcoulomb (generally called e.s.u. |
| Diatomic | Diatomic molecules are molecules composed of only two atoms, of either the same or different chemical elements. The prefix di- is of Greek origin, meaning 'two'. If a diatomic molecule consists of two atoms of the same element, such as hydrogen ($H_2$) or oxygen ($O_2$), then it is said to be homonuclear. |
| Diatomic molecule | Diatomic molecules are molecules composed only of two atoms, of either the same or different chemical elements. The prefix di- is of Greek origin, meaning two. |
| Dipole | In physics, there are several kinds of dipole:

Dipoles can be characterized by their dipole moment, a vector quantity. For the simple electric dipole given above, the electric dipole moment points from the negative charge towards the positive charge, and has a magnitude equal to the strength of each charge times the separation between the charges. (To be precise: for the definition of the dipole moment, one should always consider the 'dipole limit', where e.g. the distance of the generating charges should converge to 0, while simultaneously the charge strength should diverge to infinity in such a way that the product remains a positive constant). |
| Polar molecules | In chemistry, polarity refers to a separation of electric charge leading to a molecule or its chemical groups having an electric dipole or multipole moment. Polar molecules interact through dipole-dipole intermolecular forces and hydrogen bonds. Molecular polarity is dependent on the difference in electronegativity between atoms in a compound and the asymmetry of the compound's structure. |
| Bond length | In molecular geometry, bond length or bond distance is the average distance between nuclei of two bonded atoms in a molecule. It is a transferable property of a bond between atoms of fixed types, relatively independent of the rest of the molecule. |
| Hydrogen | Hydrogen is a chemical element with chemical symbol H and atomic number 1. With an atomic weight of 1.00794 u, hydrogen is the lightest element and its monatomic form (H) is the most abundant chemical substance, constituting roughly 75% of the Universe's baryonic mass. |

# 8. Basic Concepts of Chemical Bonding

| | |
|---|---|
| | Non-remnant stars are mainly composed of hydrogen in its plasma state |
| | At standard temperature and pressure, hydrogen is a colorless, odorless, tasteless, non-toxic, nonmetallic, highly combustible diatomic gas with the molecular formula $H_2$. |
| Hydrogen chloride | The compound hydrogen chloride has the chemical formula HCl. At room temperature, it is a colorless gas, which forms white fumes of hydrochloric acid upon contact with atmospheric humidity. Hydrogen chloride gas and hydrochloric acid are important in technology and industry. |
| Halide | A halide is a binary compound, of which one part is a halogen atom and the other part is an element or radical that is less electronegative than the halogen, to make a fluoride, chloride, bromide, iodide, or astatide compound. Many salts are halides. All Group 1 metals form halides which are white solids at room temperature. |
| Manganese oxide | Manganese oxide is any of a variety of manganese oxides and hydroxides. This includes •Manganese(II) oxide, MnO•Manganese(II,III) oxide, $Mn_3O_4$•Manganese(III) oxide, $Mn_2O_3$•Manganese dioxide, (manganese(IV) oxide), $MnO_2$•Manganese(VII) oxide, $Mn_2O_7$

It may refer more specifically to the following manganese minerals:•Birnessite•Hausmannite•Manganite•Manganosite•Psilomelane•Pyrolusite

Manganese may also form mixed oxides with other metals such as Fe, Nb, Ta, ... :•Bixbyite, a manganese iron oxide mineral•Jacobsite, a manganese iron oxide mineral•Columbite, also called niobite, niobite-tantalite and columbate•Tantalite, a mineral group close to columbite•Coltan, a mixture of columbite and tantalite•Galaxite, a spinel mineral•Todorokite a rare complex hydrous manganese oxide mineral. |
| Polyatomic ion | A polyatomic ion, also known as a molecular ion, is a charged chemical species composed of two or more atoms covalently bonded or of a metal complex that can be considered to be acting as a single unit. The prefix 'poly-' means 'many,' in Greek, but even ions of two atoms are commonly referred to as polyatomic. In older literature, a polyatomic ion is also referred to as a radical, and less commonly, as a radical group. |
| Chlorine | Chlorine is a chemical element with symbol Cl and atomic number 17. Chlorine is in the halogen group (17) and is the second lightest halogen after fluorine. The element is a yellow-green gas under standard conditions, where it forms diatomic molecules. It has the highest electron affinity and the fourth highest electronegativity of all the reactive elements; for this reason, chlorine is a strong oxidizing agent. |
| Cyanide ion | A cyanide is any chemical compound that contains monovalent combining group CN. This group, known as the cyano group, consists of a carbon atom triple-bonded to a nitrogen atom. |

In inorganic cyanides, such as sodium cyanide, NaCN, this group is present as the negatively-charged polyatomic cyanide ion; these compounds, which are regarded as salts of hydrocyanic acid, are highly toxic. The cyanide ion is isoelectronic with carbon monoxide and with molecular nitrogen.

**Formal charge**

In chemistry, a formal charge is the charge assigned to an atom in a molecule, assuming that electrons in a chemical bond are shared equally between atoms, regardless of relative electronegativity.

The formal charge of any atom in a molecule can be calculated by the following equation:

$$FC = V - (N + \frac{B}{2})$$

Where V is the number of valence electrons of the atom in isolation (atom in ground state); N is the number of non-bonding valence electrons on this atom in the molecule; and B is the total number of electrons shared in covalent bonds with other atoms in the molecule. There are two electrons shared per single covalent bond.

**Oxidation**

Redox (reduction-oxidation) reactions include all chemical reactions in which atoms have their oxidation state changed; in general, redox reactions involve the transfer of electrons between species.

This can be either a simple redox process, such as the oxidation of carbon to yield carbon dioxide or the reduction of carbon by hydrogen to yield methane ($CH_4$), or a complex process such as the oxidation of glucose ($C_6H_{12}O_6$) in the human body through a series of complex electron transfer processes.

The term 'redox' comes from two concepts involved with electron transfer: reduction and oxidation.

**Ozone**

Ozone, or trioxygen, is an inorganic compound with the chemical formula O3(μ-O) (also written [O(μ-O)O] or O3). It is a pale blue gas with a distinctively pungent smell. It is an allotrope of oxygen that is much less stable than the diatomic allotrope O2, breaking down in the lower atmosphere to normal dioxygen.

**Benzene**

Benzene is an organic chemical compound with the molecular formula $C_6H_6$. Its molecule is composed of 6 carbon atoms joined in a ring, with 1 hydrogen atom attached to each carbon atom. Because its molecules contain only carbon and hydrogen atoms, benzene is classed as a hydrocarbon.

# 8. Basic Concepts of Chemical Bonding

| | |
|---|---|
| Resonance | In physics, resonance is the tendency of a system to oscillate with greater amplitude at some frequencies than at others. Frequencies at which the response amplitude is a relative maximum are known as the system's resonant frequencies, or resonance frequencies. At these frequencies, even small periodic driving forces can produce large amplitude oscillations, because the system stores vibrational energy. |
| Hypervalent molecule | A hypervalent molecule is a molecule that contains one or more main group elements formally bearing more than eight electrons in their valence shells. Phosphorus pentachloride ($PCl_5$), sulfur hexafluoride ($SF_6$), chlorine trifluoride ($ClF_3$), and the triiodide ($I_3^-$) ion are examples of hypervalent molecules. |
| Phosphorus pentafluoride | Phosphorus pentafluoride, $PF_5$, is a phosphorus halide. It is a colourless gas at room temperature and pressure. |
| Enthalpy | Enthalpy is a measure of the total energy of a thermodynamic system. It includes the system's internal energy and thermodynamic potential (a state function), as well as its volume and pressure (the energy required to 'make room for it' by displacing its environment, which is an extensive quantity). The unit of measurement for enthalpy in the International System of Units (SI) is the joule, but other historical, conventional units are still in use, such as the British thermal unit and the calorie |
| Strength | In explosive materials, strength is the parameter determining the ability of the explosive to move the surrounding material. It is related to the total gas yield of the reaction, and the amount of heat produced. Cf. |
| Nitroglycerin | Nitroglycerin, also known as nitroglycerine, trinitroglycerin, trinitroglycerine, or nitro, is more correctly known as glyceryl trinitrate or more formally: 1,2,3-trinitroxypropane. It is a heavy, colorless, oily, explosive liquid most commonly produced by treating glycerol with white fuming nitric acid under conditions appropriate to the formation of the nitric acid ester. Chemically, the substance is an organic nitrate compound rather than a nitro compound, but the traditional name is often retained. |
| Phosgene | Phosgene is the chemical compound with the formula $COCl_2$. This colorless gas gained infamy as a chemical weapon during World War I. It is also a valued industrial reagent and building block in synthesis of pharmaceuticals and other organic compounds. In low concentrations, its odor resembles freshly cut hay or grass. |
| Naphthalene | Naphthalene is an organic compound with formula C10H8. It is the simplest polycyclic aromatic hydrocarbon, and is a white crystalline solid with a characteristic odor that is detectable at concentrations as low as 0.08 ppm by mass. As an aromatic hydrocarbon, naphthalene's structure consists of a fused pair of benzene rings. |

| Chlorine monoxide | Chlorine monoxide is a chemical radical with the formula ClO. It plays an important role in the process of ozone depletion. In the stratosphere, chlorine atoms react with ozone molecules to form chlorine monoxide and oxygen. $Cl \cdot + O_3 \rightarrow ClO \cdot + O_2$

This reaction causes the depletion of the ozone layer. |
| --- | --- |
| Haber process | The Haber process, also called the Haber-Bosch process, is the industrial implementation of the reaction of nitrogen gas and hydrogen gas. It is the main industrial route to ammonia: $N_2 + 3 H_2 \rightarrow 2 NH_3$ ($\Delta H = -92.4$ kJ·mol$^{-1}$)

Nitrogen is a critical limiting mineral nutrient in plant growth. Carbon and oxygen are also critical, but are easily obtained by plants from soil and air. |
| Triazine | A triazine is one of three organic chemicals, isomeric with each other, whose molecular formula is $C_3H_3N_3$ and whose empirical formula is CHN. |
| Ethane | Ethane is a chemical compound with chemical formula $C_2H_6$. At standard temperature and pressure, ethane is a colorless, odorless gas. Ethane is isolated on an industrial scale from natural gas, and as a byproduct of petroleum refining. |
| Methane | Methane is a chemical compound with the chemical formula CH4 (one atom of carbon and four atoms of hydrogen). It is the simplest alkane and the main component of natural gas. The relative abundance of methane makes it an attractive fuel. |
| Acetylene | Acetylene is the chemical compound with the formula $C_2H_2$. It is a hydrocarbon and the simplest alkyne. This colorless gas is widely used as a fuel and a chemical building block. |
| Barium azide | Barium azide Ba$_2$ is an inorganic azide, is explosive, but less sensitive to mechanical shock than lead azide. |
| Chloral hydrate | Chloral hydrate is an organic compound with the formula $C_2H_3Cl_3O_2$. It is a colourless solid. It was once used as sedative and hypnotic drug. |

# 8. Basic Concepts of Chemical Bonding

1. In chemistry, a _____ is the charge assigned to an atom in a molecule, assuming that electrons in a chemical bond are shared equally between atoms, regardless of relative electronegativity.

   The _____ of any atom in a molecule can be calculated by the following

   $$FC = V - (N + \frac{B}{2})$$
   equation:

   Where V is the number of valence electrons of the atom in isolation (atom in ground state); N is the number of non-bonding valence electrons on this atom in the molecule; and B is the total number of electrons shared in covalent bonds with other atoms in the molecule. There are two electrons shared per single covalent bond.

   a. Triple bond
   b. Formal charge
   c. 2,6-Dihydroxypyridine
   d. Bismuth

2. In atomic physics and quantum chemistry, the _____ is the distribution of electrons of an atom or molecule in atomic or molecular orbitals. For example, the _____ of the neon atom is $1s^2$ $2s^2$ $2p^6$.

   Electronic configurations describe electrons as each moving independently in an orbital, in an average field created by all other orbitals.

   a. Bohr magneton
   b. Bohr model
   c. Boson
   d. Electron configuration

3. The _____ of the periodic table of the elements consists of the last six groups except helium . In the elemental form of the _____ elements, the highest energy electron occupies a p-orbital. The _____ contains all of the nonmetals (except for hydrogen and helium, which are in the s-block) and semimetals, as well as the poor metals.

   a. Boron group
   b. Carbon group
   c. P-block
   d. D-block

4. . The _____ of an ionic solid is a measure of the strength of bonds in that ionic compound. It is usually defined as the enthalpy of formation of the ionic compound from gaseous ions and as such is invariably exothermic. _____ may also be defined as the energy required to completely separate one mole of a solid ionic compound into gaseous ionic constituents.

   a. Biaxial nematic
   b. Lattice energy
   c. Borrmann effect

5. _____ molecules are molecules composed of only two atoms, of either the same or different chemical elements. The prefix di- is of Greek origin, meaning 'two'. If a _____ molecule consists of two atoms of the same element, such as hydrogen ($H_2$) or oxygen ($O_2$), then it is said to be homonuclear.

a. Merck Index
b. Berkelium
c. Beryllium
d. Diatomic

**1.** b
**2.** d
**3.** c
**4.** b
**5.** d

---

## You can take the complete Chapter Practice Test

**for 8. Basic Concepts of Chemical Bonding**
on all key terms, persons, places, and concepts.

## Online 99 Cents

## http://www.JustTheFacts101.com

Use www.JustTheFacts101.com for all your study needs

including Facts101's online interactive problem solving labs in

chemistry, statistics, mathematics, and more.

# 9. Molecular Geometry and Bonding Theories

CHAPTER OUTLINE: KEY TERMS, PEOPLE, PLACES, CONCEPTS

Molecular geometry

Statin

Space-filling model

Tetrahedral molecular geometry

Linear molecular geometry

Octahedral molecular geometry

Phosgene

Atomic radius

Electron

Molecule

Square planar

Square planar molecular geometry

Acetic acid

Poly

Vinyl alcohol

Polar molecules

Absorption

Covalent

Lewis structure

Orbital overlap

Hybrid orbitals

Hydrochloric acid

Doping

Ball-and-stick model

Double bond

Strength

Triple bond

Diazine

Formaldehyde

Delocalized

Retinal

Molecular orbital

Molecular orbital theory

Antibonding

Hydrogen

Bond order

Helium

Diatomic

Diatomic molecule

Homonuclear

Electron configuration

Atomic orbital

# 9. Molecular Geometry and Bonding Theories

CHAPTER OUTLINE: KEY TERMS, PEOPLE, PLACES, CONCEPTS

_____ Phase diagram

_____ Wave function

_____ Diamagnetism

_____ Paramagnetism

_____ Heteronuclear

_____ Heteronuclear molecule

_____ Low-density polyethylene

_____ Nitric oxide

_____ Electron excitation

_____ Oxide

_____ Titanium dioxide

_____ Difluoromethane

_____ Acetylsalicylic acid

_____ Aspirin

_____ Ethyl acetate

_____ Propene

_____ Cisplatin

_____ Xenon hexafluoride

_____ Azobenzene

_____ Butadiene

_____ Ozone

# 9. Molecular Geometry and Bonding Theories
CHAPTER OUTLINE: KEY TERMS, PEOPLE, PLACES, CONCEPTS

| | |
|---|---|
| | 1-Butene |
| | 2-Butene |
| | Carbon monoxide |
| | Sulfur tetrafluoride |
| | Anthracene |
| | Methyl isocyanate |
| | Naphthalene |
| | Tetracene |

CHAPTER HIGHLIGHTS & NOTES: KEY TERMS, PEOPLE, PLACES, CONCEPTS

| | |
|---|---|
| Molecular geometry | Molecular geometry is the three-dimensional arrangement of the atoms that constitute a molecule. It determines several properties of a substance including its reactivity, polarity, phase of matter, color, magnetism, and biological activity. The angles between bonds that an atom forms depend only weakly on the rest of molecule, i.e. they can be understood as approximately local and hence transferable properties. |
| Statin | Statins are a class of drugs used to lower cholesterol levels by inhibiting the enzyme HMG-CoA reductase, which plays a central role in the production of cholesterol in the liver. Increased cholesterol levels have been associated with cardiovascular disease, and statins have been found to prevent cardiovascular disease in those who are at high risk. Research has found that statins are most effective for treating cardiovascular disease (CVD) as a secondary prevention strategy (treatment in the early stages of a disease), with questionable benefit in those with elevated cholesterol levels but without previous CVD. Statins have some side effects including a mildly increased risk of diabetes and abnormalities in liver enzyme tests. |
| Space-filling model | In chemistry, a space-filling model, also known as a calotte model, is a type of three-dimensional molecular model where the atoms are represented by spheres whose radii are proportional to the radii of the atoms and whose center-to-center distances are proportional to the distances between the atomic nuclei, all in the same scale. |

Atoms of different chemical elements are usually represented by spheres of different colors.

Calotte models are distinguished from other 3D representations, such as the ball-and-stick and skeletal models, by the use of 'full size' balls for the atoms.

| | |
|---|---|
| Tetrahedral molecular geometry | In a tetrahedral molecular geometry a central atom is located at the center with four substituents that are located at the corners of a tetrahedron. The bond angles are $\cos^{-1}(-1/3)$ ~ 109.5° when all four substituents are the same, as in $CH_4$. This molecular geometry is common throughout the first half of the periodic table. |
| Linear molecular geometry | In chemistry, the Linear molecular geometry describes the arrangement of three or more atoms placed at an expected bond angle of 180°. Linear organic molecules, e.g. acetylene, are often described by invoking sp orbital hybridization for the carbon centers. Many linear molecules exist, prominent examples include $CO_2$, HCN, and xenon difluoride. |
| Octahedral molecular geometry | In chemistry, octahedral molecular geometry describes the shape of compounds wherein six atoms or groups of atoms or ligands are symmetrically arranged around a central atom, defining the vertices of an octahedron. The octahedron has eight faces, hence the prefix octa. The octahedron is one of the Platonic solids, although octahedral molecules typically have an atom in their centre and no bonds between the ligand atoms. |
| Phosgene | Phosgene is the chemical compound with the formula $COCl_2$. This colorless gas gained infamy as a chemical weapon during World War I. It is also a valued industrial reagent and building block in synthesis of pharmaceuticals and other organic compounds. In low concentrations, its odor resembles freshly cut hay or grass. |
| Atomic radius | The atomic radius of a chemical element is a measure of the size of its atoms, usually the mean or typical distance from the nucleus to the boundary of the surrounding cloud of electrons. Since the boundary is not a well-defined physical entity, there are various non-equivalent definitions of atomic radius. Three widely used definitions of atomic radius are Van der Waals radius, ionic radius, and covalent radius. |
| Electron | The electron is a subatomic particle with a negative elementary electric charge. Electrons belong to the first generation of the lepton particle family, and are generally thought to be elementary particles because they have no known components or substructure. The electron has a mass that is approximately 1/1836 that of the proton. |
| Molecule | A molecule is an electrically neutral group of two or more atoms held together by chemical bonds. Molecules are distinguished from ions by their lack of electrical charge. However, in quantum physics, organic chemistry, and biochemistry, the term molecule is often used less strictly, also being applied to polyatomic ions. |

# 9. Molecular Geometry and Bonding Theories

| | |
|---|---|
| Square planar | The square planar molecular geometry in chemistry describes the stereochemistry that is adopted by certain chemical compounds. As the name suggests, molecules of this geometry have their atoms positioned at the corners of a square on the same plane about a central atom. |
| Square planar molecular geometry | The square planar molecular geometry in chemistry describes the stereochemistry that is adopted by certain chemical compounds. As the name suggests, molecules of this geometry have their atoms positioned at the corners of a square on the same plane about a central atom. |
| Acetic acid | Acetic acid is an organic compound with the chemical formula $CH_3COOH$ (also written as $CH_3CO_2H$ or $C_2H_4O_2$). It is a colourless liquid that when undiluted is also called glacial acetic acid. Acetic acid is the main component of vinegar (apart from water; vinegar is roughly 8% acetic acid by volume), and has a distinctive sour taste and pungent smell. |
| Poly | Poly(p-phenylene ether) (PPE) is a high-temperature thermoplastic. It is rarely used in its pure form due to difficulties in processing. It is mainly used as blend with polystyrene, high impact styrene-butadiene copolymer or polyamide. |
| Vinyl alcohol | Vinyl alcohol, also called ethenol, is an alcohol. It is not to be confused with the drinking alcohol, ethanol. With the formula $CH_2CHOH$, vinyl alcohol is an isomer of acetaldehyde and ethylene oxide. |
| Polar molecules | In chemistry, polarity refers to a separation of electric charge leading to a molecule or its chemical groups having an electric dipole or multipole moment. Polar molecules interact through dipole-dipole intermolecular forces and hydrogen bonds. Molecular polarity is dependent on the difference in electronegativity between atoms in a compound and the asymmetry of the compound's structure. |
| Absorption | In chemistry, absorption is a physical or chemical phenomenon or a process in which atoms, molecules, or ions enter some bulk phase - gas, liquid, or solid material. This is a different process from adsorption, since molecules undergoing absorption are taken up by the volume, not by the surface (as in the case for adsorption). A more general term is sorption, which covers absorption, adsorption, and ion exchange. |
| Covalent | A covalent bond is a chemical bond that involves the sharing of electron pairs between atoms. The stable balance of attractive and repulsive forces between atoms when they share electrons is known as covalent bonding. For many molecules, the sharing of electrons allows each atom to attain the equivalent of a full outer shell, corresponding to a stable electronic configuration. |
| Lewis structure | Lewis structures are diagrams that show the bonding between atoms of a molecule and the lone pairs of electrons that may exist in the molecule. A Lewis structure can be drawn for any covalently bonded molecule, as well as coordination compounds. The Lewis structure was named after Gilbert N |

# 9. Molecular Geometry and Bonding Theories

| Orbital overlap | Orbital overlap is a concept used in theories of the chemical bond. It refers to the concentration of orbitals on adjacent atoms in the same region(s) of space, which can lead to bond formation. The importance of orbital overlap was emphasized by Linus Pauling to explain the molecular bond angles observed through experimentation and is the basis for the concept of orbital hybridisation. |
| --- | --- |
| Hybrid orbitals | In chemistry, hybridisation is the concept of mixing atomic orbitals into new hybrid orbitals suitable for the pairing of electrons to form chemical bonds in valence bond theory. Hybrid orbitals are very useful in the explanation of molecular geometry and atomic bonding properties. Although sometimes taught together with the valence shell electron-pair repulsion (VSEPR) theory, valence bond and hybridisation are in fact not related to the VSEPR model. |
| Hydrochloric acid | Hydrochloric acid is a clear, colorless, highly pungent solution of hydrogen chloride in water. It is a highly corrosive, strong mineral acid with many industrial uses. Hydrochloric acid is found naturally in gastric acid. |
| Doping | In semiconductor production, doping intentionally introduces impurities into an extremely pure semiconductor for the purpose of modulating its electrical properties. The impurities are dependent upon the type of semiconductor. Lightly and moderately doped semiconductors are referred to as extrinsic. |
| Ball-and-stick model | In chemistry, the ball-and-stick model is a molecular model of a chemical substance which is to display both the three-dimensional position of the atoms and the bonds between them. The atoms are typically represented by spheres, connected by rods which represent the bonds. Double and triple bonds are usually represented by two or three curved rods, respectively. |
| Double bond | A double bond in chemistry is a chemical bond between two chemical elements involving four bonding electrons instead of the usual two. The most common double bond, that is between two carbon atoms, can be found in alkenes. Many types of double bonds exist between two different elements. |
| Strength | In explosive materials, strength is the parameter determining the ability of the explosive to move the surrounding material. It is related to the total gas yield of the reaction, and the amount of heat produced. Cf. |
| Triple bond | A triple bond in chemistry is a chemical bond between two atoms involving six bonding electrons instead of the usual two in a covalent single bond. The most common triple bond, that between two carbon atoms, can be found in alkynes. Other functional groups containing a triple bond are cyanides and isocyanides. |
| Diazine | Diazine refers to a group of organic compounds having the molecular formula $C_4H_4N_2$. Each contains a benzene ring in which two of the C-H fragments have been replaced by isolobal nitrogen. |

# 9. Molecular Geometry and Bonding Theories

| | |
|---|---|
| Formaldehyde | Formaldehyde is an organic compound with the formula $CH_2O$ or HCHO. It is the simplest aldehyde, hence its systematic name methanal. The common name of the substance comes from its similarity and relation to formic acid.<br><br>A gas at room temperature, formaldehyde is colorless and has a characteristic pungent, irritating odor. |
| Delocalized | In chemistry, delocalized electrons are electrons in a molecule, ion or solid metal that are not associated with a single atom or one covalent bond. Delocalized electrons are contained within an orbital that extends over several adjacent atoms. Classically, delocalized electrons can be found in conjugated systems and mesoionic compounds. |
| Retinal | Retinal, also called retinaldehyde or vitamin A aldehyde, is one of the many forms of vitamin A . Retinal is a polyene chromophore, and bound to proteins called opsins, is the chemical basis of animal vision. Bound to proteins called type 1 rhodopsins, retinal allows certain microorganisms to convert light into metabolic energy. |
| Molecular orbital | In chemistry, a molecular orbital is a mathematical function describing the wave-like behavior of an electron in a molecule. This function can be used to calculate chemical and physical properties such as the probability of finding an electron in any specific region. The term orbital was introduced by Robert S. Mulliken in 1932 as an abbreviation for one-electron orbital wave function. |
| Molecular orbital theory | In chemistry, molecular orbital theory is a method for determining molecular structure in which electrons are not assigned to individual bonds between atoms, but are treated as moving under the influence of the nuclei in the whole molecule. In this theory, each molecule has a set of molecular orbitals, in which it is assumed that the molecular orbital wave function $\psi_j$ can be written as a simple weighted sum of the n constituent atomic orbitals $\chi_i$, according to the following equation: $$\psi_j = \sum_{i=1}^{n} c_{ij}\chi_i.$$<br>The $c_{ij}$ coefficients may be determined numerically by substitution of this equation into the Schrödinger equation and application of the variational principle. This method is called the linear combination of atomic orbitals (LCAO) approximation and is used in computational chemistry. |
| Antibonding | Antibonding is a type of chemical bonding. An antibonding orbital is a form of molecular orbital (MO) that is located outside the region of two distinct nuclei. The overlap of the constituent atomic orbitals is said to be out of phase, and as such the electrons present in each antibonding orbital are repulsive and act to destabilize the molecule as a whole. |
| Hydrogen | Hydrogen is a chemical element with chemical symbol H and atomic number 1. With an atomic weight of 1.007 |

94 u, hydrogen is the lightest element and its monatomic form (H) is the most abundant chemical substance, constituting roughly 75% of the Universe's baryonic mass. Non-remnant stars are mainly composed of hydrogen in its plasma state.

At standard temperature and pressure, hydrogen is a colorless, odorless, tasteless, non-toxic, nonmetallic, highly combustible diatomic gas with the molecular formula $H_2$.

| | |
|---|---|
| Bond order | Bond order is the number of chemical bonds between a pair of atoms. For example, in diatomic nitrogen N≡N the bond order is 3, in acetylene H-C≡C-H the bond order between the two carbon atoms is also 3, and the C-H bond order is 1. Bond order gives an indication to the stability of a bond. |
| | In molecules that have resonance or nonclassical bonding, bond order does not need to be an integer. |
| Helium | Helium is a chemical element with symbol He and atomic number 2. It is a colorless, odorless, tasteless, non-toxic, inert, monatomic gas that heads the noble gas group in the periodic table. Its boiling and melting points are the lowest among the elements and it exists only as a gas except in extreme conditions. |
| | Helium is the second lightest element and is the second most abundant element in the observable universe, being present at about 24% of the total elemental mass, which is more than 12 times the mass of all the heavier elements combined. |
| Diatomic | Diatomic molecules are molecules composed of only two atoms, of either the same or different chemical elements. The prefix di- is of Greek origin, meaning 'two'. If a diatomic molecule consists of two atoms of the same element, such as hydrogen ($H_2$) or oxygen ($O_2$), then it is said to be homonuclear. |
| Diatomic molecule | Diatomic molecules are molecules composed only of two atoms, of either the same or different chemical elements. The prefix di- is of Greek origin, meaning two. |
| Homonuclear | Homonuclear molecules, or homonuclear species, are molecules composed of only one type of element. Homonuclear molecules may consist of various numbers of atoms, depending on the element's properties. Some elements form molecules of more than one size. |
| Electron configuration | In atomic physics and quantum chemistry, the electron configuration is the distribution of electrons of an atom or molecule in atomic or molecular orbitals. For example, the electron configuration of the neon atom is $1s^2 2s^2 2p^6$. |

# 9. Molecular Geometry and Bonding Theories

| | |
|---|---|
| Atomic orbital | An atomic orbital is a mathematical function that describes the wave-like behavior of either one electron or a pair of electrons in an atom. This function can be used to calculate the probability of finding any electron of an atom in any specific region around the atom's nucleus. The term may also refer to the physical region or space where the electron can be calculated to be present, as defined by the particular mathematical form of the orbital. |
| Phase diagram | A phase diagram in physical chemistry, engineering, mineralogy, and materials science is a type of chart used to show conditions at which thermodynamically distinct phases can occur at equilibrium. In mathematics and physics, 'phase diagram' is used with a different meaning: a synonym for a phase space. |
| Wave function | A wave function or wavefunction in quantum mechanics describes the quantum state of a particle and how it behaves. Typically, its values are complex numbers and, for a single particle, it is a function of space and time. The Schrödinger equation describes how the wave function evolves over time. |
| Diamagnetism | Diamagnetism is the property of an object or material that causes it to create a magnetic field in opposition to an externally applied magnetic field. It is a quantum mechanical effect that occurs in all materials; where it is the only contribution to the magnetism the material is called a diamagnet. Unlike a ferromagnet, a diamagnet is not a permanent magnet. |
| Paramagnetism | Paramagnetism is a form of magnetism whereby certain materials are attracted by an externally applied magnetic field. In contrast with this behavior, diamagnetic materials are repelled by magnetic fields. Paramagnetic materials include most chemical elements and some compounds; they have a relative magnetic permeability greater than or equal to 1 (i.e., a positive magnetic susceptibility) and hence are attracted to magnetic fields. |
| Heteronuclear | Heteronuclear molecules, or heteronuclear species, are molecules composed of more than one type of element, for example, HCl. In heteronuclear molecules e.g. HCl where bonded atoms are of different elements, the molecules become polar due to electronegatity difference. |
| Heteronuclear molecule | Heteronuclear molecules, or heteronuclear species, are molecules composed of more than one type of element, for example, HCl. |
| Low-density polyethylene | Low-density polyethylene is a thermoplastic made from the monomer ethylene. It was the first grade of polyethylene, produced in 1933 by Imperial Chemical Industries (ICI) using a high pressure process via free radical polymerization. Its manufacture employs the same method today. |
| Nitric oxide | Nitric oxide, or nitrogen oxide, also known as nitrogen monoxide, is a molecule with chemical formula NO. It is a free radical and is an important intermediate in the chemical industry. Nitric oxide is a by-product of combustion of substances in the air, as in automobile engines, fossil fuel power plants, and is produced naturally during the electrical discharges of lightning in thunderstorms. |

| | |
|---|---|
| Electron excitation | Electron excitation is the transfer of a bound electron to a more energetic, but still bound state. This can be done by photoexcitation (PE), where the electron absorbs a photon and gains all its energy or by electrical excitation (EE), where the electron receives energy from another, energetic electron. Within a semiconductor crystal lattice, thermal excitation is a process where lattice vibrations provide enough energy to transfer electrons to a higher energy band. |
| Oxide | An oxide is a chemical compound that contains at least one oxygen atom and one other element in its chemical formula. Metal oxides typically contain an anion of oxygen in the oxidation state of -2. Most of the Earth's crust consists of solid oxides, the result of elements being oxidized by the oxygen in air or in water. Hydrocarbon combustion affords the two principal carbon oxides: carbon monoxide and carbon dioxide. |
| Titanium dioxide | Titanium dioxide, also known as titanium oxide or titania, is the naturally occurring oxide of titanium, chemical formula $TiO2$. When used as a pigment, it is called titanium white, Pigment White 6 (PW6), or CI 77891. Generally it is sourced from ilmenite, rutile and anatase. It has a wide range of applications, from paint to sunscreen to food colouring. |
| Difluoromethane | Difluoromethane, also called HFC-32 or R-32, is an organic compound of the dihalogenoalkane variety. It is based on methane, except that two of the four hydrogen atoms have been replaced by fluorine atoms. Hence the formula is $CH_2F_2$ instead of $CH_4$ for normal methane. |
| Acetylsalicylic acid | Aspirin, also known as acetylsalicylic acid (INN ( ?--?l--i--ik) ASA), is a salicylate drug, often used as an analgesic to relieve minor aches and pains, as an antipyretic to reduce fever, and as an anti-inflammatory medication. The active ingredient of Aspirin was first discovered from the bark of the willow tree in 1763 by Edward Stone of Wadham College, Oxford University. He had discovered salicylic acid, the active metabolite of aspirin. |
| Aspirin | Aspirin, also known as acetylsalicylic acid (INN ( ?--?l--i--ik) ASA), is a salicylate drug, often used as an analgesic to relieve minor aches and pains, as an antipyretic to reduce fever, and as an anti-inflammatory medication. Aspirin was first isolated by Felix Hoffmann, a chemist with the German company Bayer in 1897.<br><br>Salicylic acid, the main metabolite of aspirin, is an integral part of human and animal metabolism. |
| Ethyl acetate | Ethyl acetate is the organic compound with the formula $CH_3$-COO-$CH_2$-$CH_3$. This colorless liquid has a characteristic sweet smell (similar to pear drops) and is used in glues, nail polish removers, decaffeinating tea and coffee, and cigarettes . Ethyl acetate is the ester of ethanol and acetic acid; it is manufactured on a large scale for use as a solvent. |
| Propene | Propene, also known as propylene or methylethylene, is an unsaturated organic compound having the chemical formula $C_3H_6$. It has one double bond, and is the second simplest member of the alkene class of hydrocarbons. |

# 9. Molecular Geometry and Bonding Theories

| | |
|---|---|
| Cisplatin | Cisplatin, cisplatinum, or cis-diamminedichloridoplatinum (CDDP) is a chemotherapy drug. It was the first member of a class of platinum-containing anti-cancer drugs, which now also includes carboplatin and oxaliplatin. These platinum complexes react in vivo, binding to and causing crosslinking of DNA, which ultimately triggers apoptosis (programmed cell death). |
| Xenon hexafluoride | Xenon hexafluoride is a noble gas compound with the formula $XeF_6$ and the highest of the three known binary fluorides of xenon, the other two being $XeF_2$ and $XeF_4$. All known are exergonic and stable at normal temperatures. $XeF_6$ is the strongest fluorinating agent of the series. |
| Azobenzene | Azobenzene is a chemical compound composed of two phenyl rings linked by a N=N double bond. It is the simplest example of an azo compound. The term 'azobenzene' or simply 'azo' is often used to refer to a wide class of molecules that share the core azobenzene structure, with different chemical functional groups extending from the phenyl rings. |
| Butadiene | 1,3-Butadiene is a simple conjugated diene with the formula $C_4H_6$. It is an important industrial chemical used as a monomer in the production of synthetic rubber. When the word butadiene is used, most of the time it refers to 1,3-butadiene. |
| Ozone | Ozone, or trioxygen, is an inorganic compound with the chemical formula O3(μ-O) (also written [O(μ-O)O] or O3). It is a pale blue gas with a distinctively pungent smell. It is an allotrope of oxygen that is much less stable than the diatomic allotrope O2, breaking down in the lower atmosphere to normal dioxygen. |
| 1-Butene | 1-Butene is an organic chemical compound, linear alpha-olefin, and one of the isomers of butene. The formula is C4H8. |
| 2-Butene | 2-Butene is an acyclic alkene with four carbon atoms. It is the simplest alkene exhibiting cis/trans-isomerism (also known as (E/Z)-isomerism); that is, it exists as two geometrical isomers cis-2-butene ((Z)-2-butene) and trans-2-butene ((E)-2-butene).<br><br>It is a petrochemical, produced by the catalytic cracking of crude oil or the dimerization of ethylene. |
| Carbon monoxide | Carbon monoxide is a colorless, odorless, and tasteless gas that is slightly less dense than air. It is toxic to humans and animals when encountered in higher concentrations, although it is also produced in normal animal metabolism in low quantities, and is thought to have some normal biological functions. In the atmosphere, it is spatially variable, short lived, having a role in the formation of ground-level ozone. |
| Sulfur tetrafluoride | Sulfur tetrafluoride is the chemical compound with the formula $SF_4$. This species exists as a gas at standard conditions. It is a corrosive species that releases dangerous HF upon exposure to water or moisture. |

| Anthracene | Anthracene is a solid polycyclic aromatic hydrocarbon of formula $C_{14}H_{10}$, consisting of three fused benzene rings. It is a component of coal tar. Anthracene is used in the production of the red dye alizarin and other dyes. |
| --- | --- |
| Methyl isocyanate | Methyl isocyanate is an organic compound with the molecular formula $CH_3NCO$. Synonyms are isocyanatomethane, methyl carbylamine, and MIC. Methyl isocyanate is an intermediate chemical in the production of carbamate pesticides (such as carbaryl, carbofuran, methomyl, and aldicarb). It has also been used in the production of rubbers and adhesives. As a highly toxic and irritating material, it is extremely hazardous to human health. |
| Naphthalene | Naphthalene is an organic compound with formula C10H8. It is the simplest polycyclic aromatic hydrocarbon, and is a white crystalline solid with a characteristic odor that is detectable at concentrations as low as 0.08 ppm by mass. As an aromatic hydrocarbon, naphthalene's structure consists of a fused pair of benzene rings. |
| Tetracene | Tetracene, also called naphthacene, is a polycyclic aromatic hydrocarbon. It has the appearance of a pale orange powder. Tetracene is the four-ringed member of the series of acenes, the previous one being anthracene (tricene) and the next one being pentacene. |

CHAPTER QUIZ: KEY TERMS, PEOPLE, PLACES, CONCEPTS

1. _____ is the property of an object or material that causes it to create a magnetic field in opposition to an externally applied magnetic field. It is a quantum mechanical effect that occurs in all materials; where it is the only contribution to the magnetism the material is called a diamagnet. Unlike a ferromagnet, a diamagnet is not a permanent magnet.

   a. Constitutive equation
   b. Diamagnetism
   c. Chalcogel
   d. SEAgel

2. . _____ molecules, or _____ species, are molecules composed of more than one type of element, for example, HCl. In _____ molecules e.g. HCl where bonded atoms are of different elements, the molecules become polar due to electronegatity difference.

   a. homonuclear
   b. Heteronuclear
   c. 2,6-Dihydroxypyridine

3. _____s are diagrams that show the bonding between atoms of a molecule and the lone pairs of electrons that may exist in the molecule. A _____ can be drawn for any covalently bonded molecule, as well as coordination compounds. The _____ was named after Gilbert N

   a. Bond energy
   b. covalent
   c. Lewis structure
   d. Formal charge

4. _____, also called naphthacene, is a polycyclic aromatic hydrocarbon. It has the appearance of a pale orange powder. _____ is the four-ringed member of the series of acenes, the previous one being anthracene (tricene) and the next one being pentacene.

   a. Tetracene
   b. Catenane
   c. Diindenoperylene
   d. Hexacene

5. _____ is an organic compound with the chemical formula $CH_3COOH$ (also written as $CH_3CO_2H$ or $C_2H_4O_2$). It is a colourless liquid that when undiluted is also called glacial _____. _____ is the main component of vinegar (apart from water; vinegar is roughly 8% _____ by volume), and has a distinctive sour taste and pungent smell.

   a. Bisulfide
   b. Acetic acid
   c. Carbonate alkalinity
   d. Charlot equation

**ANSWER KEY**
9. Molecular Geometry and Bonding Theories

1. b
2. b
3. c
4. a
5. b

*You can take the complete Chapter Practice Test*

**for 9. Molecular Geometry and Bonding Theories**
on all key terms, persons, places, and concepts.

*Online 99 Cents*

*http://www.JustTheFacts101.com*

Use www.JustTheFacts101.com for all your study needs

including Facts101's online interactive problem solving labs in

chemistry, statistics, mathematics, and more.

# 10. Gases

CHAPTER OUTLINE: KEY TERMS, PEOPLE, PLACES, CONCEPTS

Atmosphere

Nitrogen

Nuclear force

Ammonia

Argon

Carbon dioxide

Carbon monoxide

Hydrogen cyanide

Hydrogen sulfide

Methane

Nitrogen dioxide

Nitrous oxide

Oxygen

Propane

Sulfur dioxide

Diatomic

Effusion

Millimeter of mercury

Manometer

Ball-and-stick model

Gas law

# 10. Gases

CHAPTER OUTLINE: KEY TERMS, PEOPLE, PLACES, CONCEPTS

- State function
- Mole
- Absolute zero
- Avogadro
- Thomson
- Volume
- Ideal gas
- Calcium carbonate
- Standard state
- Combined gas law
- Density
- Carbon tetrachloride
- Carbon
- Dioxide
- Partial pressure
- Sodium azide
- Mole fraction
- Glucose
- Molecular diffusion
- Mean free path
- Uranium

## 10. Gases



CHAPTER OUTLINE: KEY TERMS, PEOPLE, PLACES, CONCEPTS

- Isotope
- Intermolecular force
- Van der Waals equation
- Van der Waals constants
- Cyanogen
- Mercury
- Calcium hydride
- Hydrogen
- Magnesium
- Greenhouse effect
- Absorption
- Ammonium chloride
- Chlorine dioxide
- Cyclopropane
- Iodine pentafluoride
- Natural gas

# 10. Gases

| | |
|---|---|
| Atmosphere | The standard atmosphere is an international reference pressure defined as 101325 Pa and used as a unit of pressure. |
| Nitrogen | Nitrogen, symbol N, is the chemical element of atomic number 7. At room temperature, it is a gas of diatomic molecules and is colorless and odorless. Nitrogen is a common element in the universe, estimated at about seventh in total abundance in our galaxy and the Solar System. On Earth, the element is primarily found as the free element; it forms about 80% of the Earth's atmosphere. |
| Nuclear force | The nuclear force is the force between two or more nucleons. Its fundamental laws and constants are unknown unlike the Coulomb and Newton laws. It is responsible for binding protons and neutrons into atomic nuclei. |
| Ammonia | Ammonia or azane is a compound of nitrogen and hydrogen with the formula $NH_3$. It is a colourless gas with a characteristic pungent smell. Ammonia contributes significantly to the nutritional needs of terrestrial organisms by serving as a precursor to food and fertilizers. |
| Argon | Argon is a chemical element with symbol Ar and atomic number 18. It is in group 18 of the periodic table and is a noble gas. Argon is the third most common gas in the Earth's atmosphere, at 0.93% (9,300 ppm), making it approximately 23.8 times as abundant as the next most common atmospheric gas, carbon dioxide (390 ppm), and more than 500 times as abundant as the next most common noble gas, neon (18 ppm). Nearly all of this argon is radiogenic argon-40 derived from the decay of potassium-40 in the Earth's crust. |
| Carbon dioxide | Carbon dioxide is a naturally occurring chemical compound composed of two oxygen atoms each covalently double bonded to a single carbon atom. It is a gas at standard temperature and pressure and exists in Earth's atmosphere in this state, as a trace gas at a concentration of 0.039 per cent by volume. <br><br> As part of the carbon cycle, plants, algae, and cyanobacteria use light energy to photosynthesize carbohydrate from carbon dioxide and water, with oxygen produced as a waste product. |
| Carbon monoxide | Carbon monoxide is a colorless, odorless, and tasteless gas that is slightly less dense than air. It is toxic to humans and animals when encountered in higher concentrations, although it is also produced in normal animal metabolism in low quantities, and is thought to have some normal biological functions. In the atmosphere, it is spatially variable, short lived, having a role in the formation of ground-level ozone. |
| Hydrogen cyanide | Hydrogen cyanide, sometimes called prussic acid, is an inorganic compound with chemical formula HCN. It is a colorless, extremely poisonous liquid that boils slightly above room temperature, at 26 °C (79 °F). HCN is produced on an industrial scale and is a highly valuable precursor to many chemical compounds ranging from polymers to pharmaceuticals. |

| | |
|---|---|
| Hydrogen sulfide | Hydrogen sulfide is the chemical compound with the formula $H_2S$. It is a colorless gas with the characteristic foul odor of rotten eggs; it is heavier than air, very poisonous, corrosive, flammable and explosive. |
| | Hydrogen sulfide often results from the bacterial breakdown of organic matter in the absence of oxygen, such as in swamps and sewers; this process is commonly known as anaerobic digestion. |
| Methane | Methane is a chemical compound with the chemical formula $CH_4$ (one atom of carbon and four atoms of hydrogen). It is the simplest alkane and the main component of natural gas. The relative abundance of methane makes it an attractive fuel. |
| Nitrogen dioxide | Nitrogen dioxide is the chemical compound with the formula $NO_2$. It is one of several nitrogen oxides. $NO_2$ is an intermediate in the industrial synthesis of nitric acid, millions of tons of which are produced each year. |
| Nitrous oxide | Nitrous oxide, commonly known as laughing gas, is a chemical compound with the formula $N_2O$. It is an oxide of nitrogen. At room temperature, it is a colourless, non-flammable gas, with a slightly sweet odour and taste. |
| Oxygen | Oxygen is a chemical element with symbol O and atomic number 8. It is a member of the chalcogen group on the periodic table and is a highly reactive nonmetallic element and oxidizing agent that readily forms compounds (notably oxides) with most elements. By mass, oxygen is the third-most abundant element in the universe, after hydrogen and helium At STP, two atoms of the element bind to form dioxygen, a diatomic gas that is colorless, odorless, and tasteless; with the formula $O_2$. |
| | Many major classes of organic molecules in living organisms, such as proteins, nucleic acids, carbohydrates, and fats, contain oxygen, as do the major inorganic compounds that are constituents of animal shells, teeth, and bone. |
| Propane | Propane is a three-carbon alkane with the molecular formula $C_3H_8$, normally a gas, but compressible to a transportable liquid. A by-product of natural gas processing and petroleum refining, it is commonly used as a fuel for engines, oxy-gas torches, barbecues, portable stoves, and residential central heating. Propane is one of a group of liquefied petroleum gases. |
| Sulfur dioxide | Sulfur dioxide is the chemical compound with the formula $SO_2$. At standard atmosphere it is a toxic gas with a pungent, irritating and rotten smell. The triple point is 197.69 K and 1.67Kpa. |
| Diatomic | Diatomic molecules are molecules composed of only two atoms, of either the same or different chemical elements. The prefix di- is of Greek origin, meaning 'two'. |

# 10. Gases

| | |
|---|---|
| Effusion | Effusion is the process in which a gas escapes through a small hole. This occurs if the diameter of the hole is considerably smaller than the mean free path of the molecules. According to Graham's law, the rate at which gases effuse (i.e., how many molecules pass through the hole per second) is dependent on their molecular weight. |
| Millimeter of mercury | A millimeter of mercury is a manometric unit of pressure, formerly defined as the extra pressure generated by a column of mercury one millimetre high. It is now defined precisely as $13.5951 \times 9.80665 = 133.322387415$ pascals. It is denoted by the symbol 'mmHg'. |
| Manometer | Many techniques have been developed for the measurement of pressure and vacuum. Instruments used to measure pressure are called pressure gauges or vacuum gauges.<br><br>A manometer is an instrument that uses a column of liquid to measure pressure, although the term is often used nowadays to mean any pressure measuring instrument. |
| Ball-and-stick model | In chemistry, the ball-and-stick model is a molecular model of a chemical substance which is to display both the three-dimensional position of the atoms and the bonds between them. The atoms are typically represented by spheres, connected by rods which represent the bonds. Double and triple bonds are usually represented by two or three curved rods, respectively. |
| Gas law | The early gas laws were developed at the end of the 18th century, when scientists began to realize that relationships between the pressure, volume and temperature of a sample of gas could be obtained which would hold for all gases. Gases behave in a similar way over a wide variety of conditions because to a good approximation they all have molecules which are widely spaced, and nowadays the equation of state for an ideal gas is derived from kinetic theory. The earlier gas laws are now considered as special cases of the ideal gas equation, with one or more of the variables held constant. |
| State function | In thermodynamics, a state function, function of state, state quantity, or state variable is a property of a system that depends only on the current state of the system, not on the way in which the system acquired that state . A state function describes the equilibrium state of a system. For example, internal energy, enthalpy, and entropy are state quantities because they describe quantitatively an equilibrium state of a thermodynamic system, irrespective of how the system arrived in that state. |
| Mole | Mole is a unit of measurement used in chemistry to express amounts of a chemical substance, defined as the amount of any substance that contains as many elementary entities (e.g., atoms, molecules, ions, electrons) as there are atoms in 12 grams of pure carbon-12, the isotope of carbon with relative atomic mass 12. This corresponds to the Avogadro constant, which has a value of $6.02214129(27) \times 10^{23}$ elementary entities of the substance. It is one of the base units in the International System of Units, and has the unit symbol mol and corresponds with the dimension symbol N. |

In honour of the unit, chemists often celebrate October 23 (a reference to the $10^{23}$ part of Avogadro's number) as 'Mole Day'.

The mole is widely used in chemistry instead of units of mass or volume as a convenient way to express amounts of reactants or of products of chemical reactions.

| | |
|---|---|
| Absolute zero | Absolute zero is the lowest temperature possible. More formally, it is the temperature at which entropy reaches its minimum value. The laws of thermodynamics state that absolute zero cannot be reached using only thermodynamic means. |
| Avogadro | Avogadro is a molecular editor designed for cross-platform use in computational chemistry, molecular modeling, bioinformatics, materials science, and related areas. It is extensible through a plugin architecture. |
| Thomson | The thomson is a unit that has appeared infrequently in scientific literature relating to the field of mass spectrometry as a unit of mass-to-charge ratio. The unit was proposed by Cooks and Rockwood naming it in honour of J. J. Thomson who measured the mass-to-charge ratio of electrons and ions. |
| Volume | In thermodynamics, the volume of a system is an important extensive parameter for describing its thermodynamic state. The specific volume, an intensive property, is the system's volume per unit of mass. Volume is a function of state and is interdependent with other thermodynamic properties such as pressure and temperature. |
| Ideal gas | An ideal gas is a theoretical gas composed of a set of randomly moving, non-interacting point particles. The ideal gas concept is useful because it obeys the ideal gas law, a simplified equation of state, and is amenable to analysis under statistical mechanics.<br><br>At normal conditions such as standard temperature and pressure, most real gases behave qualitatively like an ideal gas. |
| Calcium carbonate | Calcium carbonate is a chemical compound with the formula $CaCO_3$. It is a common substance found in rocks in all parts of the world, and is the main component of shells of marine organisms, snails, coal balls, pearls, and eggshells. Calcium carbonate is the active ingredient in agricultural lime, and is created when Ca ions in hard water react with carbonate ions creating limescale. |
| Standard state | In chemistry, the standard state of a material is a reference point used to calculate its properties under different conditions. In principle, the choice of standard state is arbitrary, although the International Union of Pure and Applied Chemistry (IUPAC) recommends a conventional set of standard states for general use. IUPAC recommends using a standard pressure $p^{o} = 10^5$ Pa. |

# 10. Gases

| | |
|---|---|
| Combined gas law | The combined gas law is a gas law which combines Charles's law, Boyle's law, and Gay-Lussac's law. There is no official founder for this law; it is merely an amalgamation of the three previously discovered laws. These laws each relate one thermodynamic variable to another mathematically while holding everything else constant. |
| Density | The density, or more precisely, the volumetric mass density, of a substance is its mass per unit volume. The symbol most often used for density is ? (the lower case Greek letter rho). Mathematically, density is defined as mass divided by volume: $$\rho = \frac{m}{V},$$ where ? is the density, m is the mass, and V is the volume. |
| Carbon tetrachloride | Carbon tetrachloride, also known by many other names, is the organic compound with the formula $CCl_4$. It was formerly widely used in fire extinguishers, as a precursor to refrigerants, and as a cleaning agent. It is a colourless liquid with a 'sweet' smell that can be detected at low levels. |
| Carbon | Carbon fiber, alternatively graphite fiber, carbon graphite or CF, is a material consisting of fibers about 5-10 μm in diameter and composed mostly of carbon atoms. The carbon atoms are bonded together in crystals that are more or less aligned parallel to the long axis of the fiber. The crystal alignment gives the fiber high strength-to-volume ratio (making it strong for its size). |
| Dioxide | An oxide is a chemical compound that contains at least one oxygen atom and one other element in its chemical formula. Metal oxides typically contain an anion of oxygen in the oxidation state of -2. Most of the Earth's crust consists of solid oxides, the result of elements being oxidized by the oxygen in air or in water. Hydrocarbon combustion affords the two principal carbon oxides: carbon monoxide and carbon dioxide. |
| Partial pressure | In a mixture of gases, each gas has a partial pressure which is the hypothetical pressure of that gas if it alone occupied the volume of the mixture at the same temperature. The total pressure of an ideal gas mixture is the sum of the partial pressures of each individual gas in the mixture. It relies on the following isotherm relation: $V_x \times p_{tot} = V_{tot} \times p_x$ •$V_x$ is the partial volume of any individual gas component (X)•$V_{tot}$ is the total volume in gas mixture•$p_x$ is the partial pressure of gas X•$p_{tot}$ is the total pressure of gas mixture•$n_x$ is the amount of substance of a gas (X)•$n_{tot}$ is the total amount of substance in gas mixture The partial pressure of a gas is a measure of thermodynamic activity of the gas's molecules. |
| Sodium azide | Sodium azide is the inorganic compound with the formula $NaN_3$. This colorless salt is the gas-forming component in many car airbag systems. |

| Mole fraction | In chemistry, the mole fraction $x_i$ is defined as the amount of a constituent $n_i$ divided by the total amount of all constituents in a mixture $n_{tot}$ : $$x_i = \frac{n_i}{n_{tot}}$$ The sum of all the mole fractions is equal to 1: $$\sum_{i=1}^{N} n_i = n_{tot}; \quad \sum_{i=1}^{N} x_i = 1$$ The mole fraction is also called the amount fraction. It is identical to the number fraction, which is defined as the number of molecules of a constituent $N_i$ divided by the total number of all molecules $N_{tot}$ . It is one way of expressing the composition of a mixture with a dimensionless quantity (mass fraction is another). |
|---|---|
| Glucose | Glucose, meaning 'sweet'. The suffix '-ose' denotes a sugar. |
| Molecular diffusion | 'Molecular diffusion', often simply called diffusion, is the thermal motion of all particles at temperatures above absolute zero. The rate of this movement is a function of temperature, viscosity of the fluid and the size (mass) of the particles. Diffusion explains the net flux of molecules from a region of higher concentration to one of lower concentration, but diffusion also occurs when there is no concentration gradient. |
| Mean free path | In physics, the mean free path is the average distance travelled by a moving particle between successive impacts (collisions), which modify its direction or energy or other particle properties. |
| Uranium | Uranium is a silvery-white metallic chemical element in the actinide series of the periodic table, with symbol U and atomic number 92. A uranium atom has 92 protons and 92 electrons, of which 6 are valence electrons. Uranium is weakly radioactive because all its isotopes are unstable. The most common isotopes of uranium are uranium-238 (which has 146 neutrons) and uranium-235 (which has 143 neutrons). |
| Isotope | Isotopes are variants of a particular chemical element such that, while all isotopes of a given element have the same number of protons in each atom, they differ in neutron number. The term isotope is formed from the Greek roots isos (?s?? 'equal') and topos (t?p?? 'place'), meaning 'the same place'. Thus, different isotopes of a single element occupy the same position on the periodic table. |
| Intermolecular force | Intermolecular forces are forces of attraction or repulsion which act between neighboring particles . They are weak compared to the intramolecular forces, the forces which keep a molecule together. |

# 10. Gases

| | |
|---|---|
| Van der Waals equation | The van der Waals equation is an equation of state for a fluid composed of particles that have a non-zero volume and a pairwise attractive inter-particle force . It was derived in 1873 by Johannes Diderik van der Waals, who received the Nobel prize in 1910 for 'his work on the equation of state for gases and liquids'. The equation is based on a modification of the ideal gas law and approximates the behavior of real fluids, taking into account the nonzero size of molecules and the attraction between them. |
| Van der Waals constants | The following table lists the van der Waals constants for a number of common gases and volatile liquids. <br><br> Units:1 $J \cdot m^3/mol^2$ = 1 $m^6 \cdot Pa/mol^2$ = 10 $L^2 \cdot bar/mol^2$1 $L^2 atm/mol^2$ = 101 325 $J \cdot m^3/kmol^2$ = 101 325 $Pa \cdot m^6/kmol^2$1 $dm^3/mol$ = 1 L/mol = 1 $m^3/kmol$ (where kmol is kilomoles = 1000 moles) <br><br> Source: Weast. R. C. (Ed)., Handbook of Chemistry and Physics (53rd Edn)., Cleveland:Chemical Rubber Co., 1972. |
| Cyanogen | Cyanogen is the chemical compound with the formula $(CN)_2$. It is a colorless, toxic gas with a pungent odor. The molecule is a pseudohalogen. |
| Mercury | Mercury is a chemical element with the symbol Hg and atomic number 80. It is commonly known as quicksilver and was formerly named hydrargyrum (from Greek 'hydr-' water and 'argyros' silver). A heavy, silvery d-block element, mercury is the only metal that is liquid at standard conditions for temperature and pressure; the only other element that is liquid under these conditions is bromine, though metals such as caesium, gallium, and rubidium melt just above room temperature. With a freezing point of -38.83 °C and boiling point of 356.73 °C, mercury has one of the narrowest ranges of its liquid state of any metal. |
| Calcium hydride | Calcium hydride is the chemical compound with the formula $CaH_2$. This grey powder (white if pure, which is rare) reacts vigorously with water liberating hydrogen gas. $CaH_2$ is thus used as a drying agent, i.e. a desiccant. |
| Hydrogen | Hydrogen is a chemical element with chemical symbol H and atomic number 1. With an atomic weight of 1.00794 u, hydrogen is the lightest element and its monatomic form (H) is the most abundant chemical substance, constituting roughly 75% of the Universe's baryonic mass. Non-remnant stars are mainly composed of hydrogen in its plasma state. <br><br> At standard temperature and pressure, hydrogen is a colorless, odorless, tasteless, non-toxic, nonmetallic, highly combustible diatomic gas with the molecular formula $H_2$. |
| Magnesium | Magnesium is a chemical element with the symbol Mg and atomic number 12. Its common oxidation number is +2. |

It is an alkaline earth metal and the eighth most abundant element in the Earth's crust and ninth in the known universe as a whole. Magnesium is the fourth most common element in the Earth as a whole (behind iron, oxygen and silicon), making up 13% of the planet's mass and a large fraction of the planet's mantle. The relative abundance of magnesium is related to the fact that it easily builds up in supernova stars from a sequential addition of three helium nuclei to carbon (which in turn is made from three helium nuclei).

| | |
|---|---|
| Greenhouse effect | The greenhouse effect is a process by which thermal radiation from a planetary surface is absorbed by atmospheric greenhouse gases, and is re-radiated in all directions. Since part of this re-radiation is back towards the surface and the lower atmosphere, it results in an elevation of the average surface temperature above what it would be in the absence of the gases.<br><br>Solar radiation at the frequencies of visible light largely passes through the atmosphere to warm the planetary surface, which then emits this energy at the lower frequencies of infrared thermal radiation. |
| Absorption | In chemistry, absorption is a physical or chemical phenomenon or a process in which atoms, molecules, or ions enter some bulk phase - gas, liquid, or solid material. This is a different process from adsorption, since molecules undergoing absorption are taken up by the volume, not by the surface (as in the case for adsorption). A more general term is sorption, which covers absorption, adsorption, and ion exchange. |
| Ammonium chloride | Ammonium chloride, an inorganic compound with the formula $NH_4Cl$, is a white crystalline salt, highly soluble in water. Solutions of ammonium chloride are mildly acidic. Sal ammoniac is a name of the natural, mineralogical form of ammonium chloride. |
| Chlorine dioxide | Chlorine dioxide is a chemical compound with the formula $ClO_2$. This yellowish-green gas crystallizes as bright orange crystals at -59 °C. As one of several oxides of chlorine, it is a potent and useful oxidizing agent used in water treatment and in bleaching. |
| Cyclopropane | Cyclopropane is a cycloalkane molecule with the molecular formula $C_3H_6$, consisting of three carbon atoms linked to each other to form a ring, with each carbon atom bearing two hydrogen atoms resulting in $D_{3h}$ molecular symmetry. Cyclopropane and propene have the same molecular formula but have different structures, making them structural isomers.<br><br>Cyclopropane is an anaesthetic when inhaled. |
| Iodine pentafluoride | Iodine pentafluoride is an interhalogen compound with chemical formula $IF_5$. It is a fluoride of iodine. It is a colourless or yellow liquid with a density of 3.250 g $cm^{-3}$. |

# 10. Gases

| Natural gas | Natural gas is a fossil fuel formed when layers of buried plants and animals are exposed to intense heat and pressure over thousands of years. The energy that the plants originally obtained from the sun is stored in the form of carbon in natural gas. Natural gas is a nonrenewable resource because it cannot be replenished on a human time frame. |
|---|---|

1. _____ is a colorless, odorless, and tasteless gas that is slightly less dense than air. It is toxic to humans and animals when encountered in higher concentrations, although it is also produced in normal animal metabolism in low quantities, and is thought to have some normal biological functions. In the atmosphere, it is spatially variable, short lived, having a role in the formation of ground-level ozone.

   a. Carbon monoxide
   b. Carbon hexoxide
   c. Barium acetylacetonate
   d. Cerium acetylacetonate

2. The standard _____ is an international reference pressure defined as 101325 Pa and used as a unit of pressure.

   a. Atmosphere
   b. Chemical engineering
   c. Synthetic membrane
   d. Barium acetylacetonate

3. Many techniques have been developed for the measurement of pressure and vacuum. Instruments used to measure pressure are called pressure gauges or vacuum gauges.

   A _____ is an instrument that uses a column of liquid to measure pressure, although the term is often used nowadays to mean any pressure measuring instrument.

   a. Merck Index
   b. Manometer
   c. Diagnosis Mercury: Money, Politics and Poison
   d. Mercury battery

4. . An _____ is a theoretical gas composed of a set of randomly moving, non-interacting point particles. The _____ concept is useful because it obeys the _____ law, a simplified equation of state, and is amenable to analysis under statistical mechanics.

At normal conditions such as standard temperature and pressure, most real gases behave qualitatively like an

_____ .

a. Bisulfide
b. Buffer solution
c. Buffering agent
d. Ideal gas

5.  _____ is a chemical compound with the formula $CaCO_3$. It is a common substance found in rocks in all parts of the world, and is the main component of shells of marine organisms, snails, coal balls, pearls, and eggshells.
_____ is the active ingredient in agricultural lime, and is created when Ca ions in hard water react with carbonate ions creating limescale.

a. Badab-e Surt
b. Calcium carbonate
c. Beachrock
d. Bear Gulch Limestone

**1.** a
**2.** a
**3.** b
**4.** d
**5.** b

---

## You can take the complete Chapter Practice Test

**for 10. Gases**
on all key terms, persons, places, and concepts.

### Online 99 Cents

### http://www.JustTheFacts101.com

Use www.JustTheFacts101.com for all your study needs

including Facts101's online interactive problem solving labs in

chemistry, statistics, mathematics, and more.

# 11. Liquids and Intermolecular Forces

CHAPTER OUTLINE: KEY TERMS, PEOPLE, PLACES, CONCEPTS

Intermolecular force

Phase diagram

Effusion

Covalent

Iodine

Mass spectrum

Sodium

Sodium chloride

Room temperature

Boiling-point elevation

Hydrogen

Hydrogen chloride

Lithium

Benzene

Boiling point

Phenol

Toluene

London dispersion

London dispersion force

Polar molecules

Polarizability

CHAPTER OUTLINE: KEY TERMS, PEOPLE, PLACES, CONCEPTS

| | Halogen |
| --- | --- |
| | Acetonitrile |
| | Molecular geometry |
| | Neopentane |
| | Dimethyl ether |
| | Lewis structure |
| | Molecular weight |
| | Propane |
| | Combustion |
| | Enthalpy |
| | Hydrogen bond |
| | 1-Propanol |
| | Acetic acid |
| | Ethylammonium nitrate |
| | Ionic liquid |
| | Octane |
| | Viscosity |
| | Capillary action |
| | Meniscus |
| | Surface tension |
| | Condensation |

_____ | Deposition

_____ | Enthalpy of fusion

_____ | Sublimation

_____ | Vaporization

_____ | Supercooling

_____ | Water heating

_____ | Ammonia

_____ | Argon

_____ | Carbon dioxide

_____ | Hydrogen sulfide

_____ | Oxygen

_____ | Phosphine

_____ | Supercritical fluid

_____ | Supercritical fluid extraction

_____ | Vapor pressure

_____ | Absorption

_____ | Dynamic equilibrium

_____ | Volatility

_____ | Concentration

_____ | Diethyl ether

_____ | Ethylene glycol

## 11. Liquids and Intermolecular Forces



CHAPTER OUTLINE: KEY TERMS, PEOPLE, PLACES, CONCEPTS

- Critical point
- Freezing point
- Melting point
- Triple point
- Cholesteryl benzoate
- Liquid crystal
- Electronic paper
- Acetone
- Isopropyl alcohol
- Chlorofluorocarbon
- Gallium
- Adenine
- Cytosine
- DNA double helix
- Dichloromethane
- Guanine
- Thymine
- Hexafluorobenzene
- Methyl iodide
- Butane

# 11. Liquids and Intermolecular Forces

| | |
|---|---|
| Intermolecular force | Intermolecular forces are forces of attraction or repulsion which act between neighboring particles . They are weak compared to the intramolecular forces, the forces which keep a molecule together. For example, the covalent bond present within HCl molecules is much stronger than the forces present between the neighboring molecules, which exist when the molecules are sufficiently close to each other. |
| Phase diagram | A phase diagram in physical chemistry, engineering, mineralogy, and materials science is a type of chart used to show conditions at which thermodynamically distinct phases can occur at equilibrium. In mathematics and physics, 'phase diagram' is used with a different meaning: a synonym for a phase space. |
| Effusion | Effusion is the process in which a gas escapes through a small hole. This occurs if the diameter of the hole is considerably smaller than the mean free path of the molecules. According to Graham's law, the rate at which gases effuse (i.e., how many molecules pass through the hole per second) is dependent on their molecular weight. |
| Covalent | A covalent bond is a chemical bond that involves the sharing of electron pairs between atoms. The stable balance of attractive and repulsive forces between atoms when they share electrons is known as covalent bonding. For many molecules, the sharing of electrons allows each atom to attain the equivalent of a full outer shell, corresponding to a stable electronic configuration. |
| Iodine | Iodine is a chemical element with symbol I and atomic number 53. The name is from Greek ??e? d?? ioeides, meaning violet or purple, due to the color of elemental iodine vapor. <br><br> Iodine and its compounds are primarily used in nutrition, and industrially in the production of acetic acid and certain polymers. Iodine's relatively high atomic number, low toxicity, and ease of attachment to organic compounds have made it a part of many X-ray contrast materials in modern medicine. |
| Mass spectrum | A mass spectrum is an intensity vs. m/z (mass-to-charge ratio) plot representing a chemical analysis. Hence, the mass spectrum of a sample is a pattern representing the distribution of ions by mass (more correctly: mass-to-charge ratio) in a sample. It is a histogram usually acquired using an instrument called a mass spectrometer. |
| Sodium | Sodium is a chemical element with the symbol Na and atomic number 11. It is a soft, silver-white, highly reactive metal and is a member of the alkali metals; its only stable isotope is $^{23}$Na. The free metal does not occur in nature, but instead must be prepared from its compounds; it was first isolated by Humphry Davy in 1807 by the electrolysis of sodium hydroxide. Sodium is the sixth most abundant element in the Earth's crust, and exists in numerous minerals such as feldspars, sodalite and rock salt. |

| | |
|---|---|
| Sodium chloride | Sodium chloride, also known as salt, common salt, table salt or halite, is an ionic compound with the formula NaCl, representing equal proportions of sodium and chlorine. Sodium chloride is the salt most responsible for the salinity of the ocean and of the extracellular fluid of many multicellular organisms. As the major ingredient in edible salt, it is commonly used as a condiment and food preservative. |
| Room temperature | Room temperature is a common term to denote a certain temperature to which humans are accustomed. It is, under normal conditions, 21 °C (70°F). |
| Boiling-point elevation | Boiling-point elevation describes the phenomenon that the boiling point of a liquid will be higher when another compound is added, meaning that a solution has a higher boiling point than a pure solvent. This happens whenever a non-volatile solute, such as a salt, is added to a pure solvent, such as water. The boiling point can be measured accurately using an ebullioscope. |
| Hydrogen | Hydrogen is a chemical element with chemical symbol H and atomic number 1. With an atomic weight of 1.00794 u, hydrogen is the lightest element and its monatomic form (H) is the most abundant chemical substance, constituting roughly 75% of the Universe's baryonic mass. Non-remnant stars are mainly composed of hydrogen in its plasma state. At standard temperature and pressure, hydrogen is a colorless, odorless, tasteless, non-toxic, nonmetallic, highly combustible diatomic gas with the molecular formula $H_2$. |
| Hydrogen chloride | The compound hydrogen chloride has the chemical formula HCl. At room temperature, it is a colorless gas, which forms white fumes of hydrochloric acid upon contact with atmospheric humidity. Hydrogen chloride gas and hydrochloric acid are important in technology and industry. |
| Lithium | Lithium is a chemical element with symbol Li and atomic number 3. It is a soft, silver-white metal belonging to the alkali metal group of chemical elements. Under standard conditions it is the lightest metal and the least dense solid element. Like all alkali metals, lithium is highly reactive and flammable. |
| Benzene | Benzene is an organic chemical compound with the molecular formula $C_6H_6$. Its molecule is composed of 6 carbon atoms joined in a ring, with 1 hydrogen atom attached to each carbon atom. Because its molecules contain only carbon and hydrogen atoms, benzene is classed as a hydrocarbon. |
| Boiling point | The boiling point of a substance is the temperature at which the vapor pressure of the liquid equals the pressure surrounding the liquid and the liquid changes into a vapor. A liquid in a vacuum has a lower boiling point than when that liquid is at atmospheric pressure. A liquid at high-pressure has a higher boiling point than when that liquid is at atmospheric pressure. |

# 11. Liquids and Intermolecular Forces

| | |
|---|---|
| Phenol | Phenol -- also known as carbolic acid -- is an aromatic organic compound with the molecular formula $C_6H_5OH$. It is a white crystalline solid that is volatile. The molecule consists of a phenyl group ($-C_6H_5$) bonded to a hydroxyl group ($-OH$). It is mildly acidic, but requires careful handling due to its propensity to cause burns. |
| Toluene | Toluene, formerly known as toluol, is a clear, water-insoluble liquid with the typical smell of paint thinners. It is a mono-substituted benzene derivative, i.e., one in which a single hydrogen atom from a group of six atoms from the benzene molecule has been replaced by a univalent group, in this case $CH_3$. As such, its IUPAC systematic name is methylbenzene. |
| London dispersion | London dispersion forces are a type of force acting between atoms and molecules. They are part of the van der Waals forces. The LDF is named after the German-American physicist Fritz London. |
| London dispersion force | London dispersion forces are a type of force acting between atoms and molecules. They are part of the van der Waals forces. The London dispersion force is named after the German-American physicist Fritz London. |
| Polar molecules | In chemistry, polarity refers to a separation of electric charge leading to a molecule or its chemical groups having an electric dipole or multipole moment. Polar molecules interact through dipole-dipole intermolecular forces and hydrogen bonds. Molecular polarity is dependent on the difference in electronegativity between atoms in a compound and the asymmetry of the compound's structure. |
| Polarizability | Polarizability is the ability for a molecule to be polarized. It is a property of matter. Polarizabilities determine the dynamical response of a bound system to external fields, and provide insight into a molecule's internal structure. |
| Halogen | The halogens or halogen elements are a group in the periodic table consisting of five chemically related elements, fluorine, chlorine (Cl), bromine (Br), iodine (I), and astatine (At). The artificially created element 117 (ununseptium) may also be a halogen. In the modern IUPAC nomenclature, this group is known as group 17. |
| Acetonitrile | Acetonitrile is the chemical compound with the formula CH3CN. This colourless liquid is the simplest organic nitrile (hydrogen cyanide is a simpler nitrile, but the cyanide anion is not classed as organic). It is produced mainly as a byproduct of acrylonitrile manufacture. |
| Molecular geometry | Molecular geometry is the three-dimensional arrangement of the atoms that constitute a molecule. It determines several properties of a substance including its reactivity, polarity, phase of matter, color, magnetism, and biological activity. The angles between bonds that an atom forms depend only weakly on the rest of molecule, i.e. they can be understood as approximately local and hence transferable properties. |

| Neopentane | Neopentane, also called 2,2-dimethylpropane, is a double-branched-chain alkane with five carbon atoms. Neopentane is an extremely flammable gas at room temperature and pressure which can condense into a highly volatile liquid on a cold day, in an ice bath, or when compressed to a higher pressure.<br><br>Neopentane is the simplest alkane with a quaternary carbon. |
| --- | --- |
| Dimethyl ether | Dimethyl ether, also known as methoxymethane, is the organic compound with the formula $CH_3OCH_3$. The simplest ether, it is a colourless gas that is a useful precursor to other organic compounds and an aerosol propellant. |
| Lewis structure | Lewis structures are diagrams that show the bonding between atoms of a molecule and the lone pairs of electrons that may exist in the molecule. A Lewis structure can be drawn for any covalently bonded molecule, as well as coordination compounds. The Lewis structure was named after Gilbert N |
| Molecular weight | Molecular mass or molecular weight refers to the mass of a molecule. It is calculated as the sum of the mass of each constituent atom multiplied by the number of atoms of that element in the molecular formula. The molecular mass of small to medium size molecules, measured by mass spectrometry, determines stoichiometry. |
| Propane | Propane is a three-carbon alkane with the molecular formula $C_3H_8$, normally a gas, but compressible to a transportable liquid. A by-product of natural gas processing and petroleum refining, it is commonly used as a fuel for engines, oxy-gas torches, barbecues, portable stoves, and residential central heating. Propane is one of a group of liquefied petroleum gases. |
| Combustion | Combustion or burning is the sequence of exothermic chemical reactions between a fuel and an oxidant accompanied by the production of heat and conversion of chemical species. The release of heat can produce light in the form of either glowing or a flame.<br><br>In a complete combustion reaction, a compound reacts with an oxidizing element, such as oxygen or fluorine, and the products are compounds of each element in the fuel with the oxidizing element. |
| Enthalpy | Enthalpy is a measure of the total energy of a thermodynamic system. It includes the system's internal energy and thermodynamic potential (a state function), as well as its volume and pressure (the energy required to 'make room for it' by displacing its environment, which is an extensive quantity). The unit of measurement for enthalpy in the International System of Units (SI) is the joule, but other historical, conventional units are still in use, such as the British thermal unit and the calorie. |

# 11. Liquids and Intermolecular Forces

| | |
|---|---|
| Hydrogen bond | A hydrogen bond is the electromagnetic attractive interaction between polar molecules in which hydrogen is bound to a highly electronegative atom, such as nitrogen (N), oxygen (O) or fluorine (F). The name hydrogen bond is something of a misnomer, as it is not a true bond but a particularly strong dipole-dipole attraction, and should not be confused with a covalent bond.<br><br>These hydrogen-bond attractions can occur between molecules (intermolecular) or within different parts of a single molecule (intramolecular). |
| 1-Propanol | 1-Propanol is a primary alcohol with the formula $CH_3CH_2CH_2OH$. This colorless liquid is also known as propan-1-ol, 1-propyl alcohol, n-propyl alcohol, n-propanol, or simply propanol. It is an isomer of isopropanol (2-propanol, isopropyl alcohol). It is formed naturally in small amounts during many fermentation processes and used as a solvent in the pharmaceutical industry mainly for resins and cellulose esters. |
| Acetic acid | Acetic acid is an organic compound with the chemical formula $CH_3COOH$ (also written as $CH_3CO_2H$ or $C_2H_4O_2$). It is a colourless liquid that when undiluted is also called glacial acetic acid. Acetic acid is the main component of vinegar (apart from water; vinegar is roughly 8% acetic acid by volume), and has a distinctive sour taste and pungent smell. |
| Ethylammonium nitrate | Ethylammonium nitrate or ethylamine nitrate is a salt with formula C2H8N2O3 or $(C2H5)NH+3·NO-3$. It is an odorless and colorless to slightly yellowish liquid with a melting point of 12 °C. This compound was described by Paul Walden in 1914, and is believed to be the earliest reported example of a room-temperature ionic liquid. |
| Ionic liquid | An ionic liquid is a salt in the liquid state. In some contexts, the term has been restricted to salts whose melting point is below some arbitrary temperature, such as 100 °C (212 °F). While ordinary liquids such as water and gasoline are predominantly made of electrically neutral molecules, ionic liquids are largely made of ions and short-lived ion pairs. |
| Octane | Octane is a hydrocarbon and an alkane with the chemical formula $C_8H_{18}$, and the condensed structural formula CH36CH3. Octane has many structural isomers that differ by the amount and location of branching in the carbon chain. One of these isomers, 2,2,4-trimethylpentane (isooctane) is used as one of the standard values in the octane rating scale. |
| Viscosity | The viscosity of a fluid is a measure of its resistance to gradual deformation by shear stress or tensile stress. For liquids, it corresponds to the informal notion of 'thickness'. For example, honey has a higher viscosity than water. |
| Capillary action | Capillary action is the ability of a liquid to flow in narrow spaces without the assistance of, and in opposition to, external forces like gravity. The effect can be seen in the drawing up of liquids between the hairs of a paint-brush, in a thin tube, in porous materials such as paper, in some non-porous materials such as liquified carbon fiber, or in a cell. |

# 11. Liquids and Intermolecular Forces

| | |
|---|---|
| Meniscus | The meniscus is the curve in the upper surface of a liquid close to the surface of the container or another object, caused by surface tension. It can be either convex or concave, depending on the liquid and the surface.<br><br>A convex meniscus occurs when the particles in the liquid have a stronger attraction to each other (cohesion) than to the material of the container (adhesion). |
| Surface tension | Surface tension is a contractive tendency of the surface of a liquid that allows it to resist an external force. It is revealed, for example, in the floating of some objects on the surface of water, even though they are denser than water, and in the ability of some insects (e.g. water striders) to run on the water surface. This property is caused by cohesion of similar molecules, and is responsible for many of the behaviors of liquids. |
| Condensation | Condensation is the change of the physical state of matter from gas phase into liquid phase, and is the reverse of vaporization. It can also be defined as the change in the state of water vapor to water/any liquid when in contact with any surface. When the transition happens from the gaseous phase into the solid phase directly, the change is called deposition. |
| Deposition | Deposition, also known as desublimation, is a thermodynamic process, a phase transition in which gas transforms into solid. The reverse of deposition is sublimation.<br><br>One example of deposition is the process by which, in sub-freezing air, water vapor changes directly to ice without first becoming a liquid. |
| Enthalpy of fusion | The enthalpy of fusion or heat of fusion is the change in enthalpy resulting from heating a given quantity of a substance to change its state from a solid to a liquid. The temperature at which this occurs is the melting point.<br><br>The 'enthalpy' of fusion is a latent heat, because during melting the introduction of heat cannot be observed as a temperature change, as the temperature remains constant during the process. |
| Sublimation | Sublimation is the transition of a substance directly from the solid to the gas phase without passing through an intermediate liquid phase. Sublimation is an endothermic phase transition that occurs at temperatures and pressures below a substance's triple point in its phase diagram. The reverse process of sublimation is desublimation, or deposition. |
| Vaporization | Vaporization of an element or compound is a phase transition from the liquid phase to gas phase. There are two types of vaporization: evaporation and boiling.<br><br>Evaporation is a phase transition from the liquid phase to gas phase that occurs at temperatures below the boiling temperature at a given pressure. |

# 11. Liquids and Intermolecular Forces

| | |
|---|---|
| Supercooling | Supercooling, also known as undercooling, is the process of lowering the temperature of a liquid or a gas below its freezing point without it becoming a solid. |
| | A liquid below its standard freezing point will crystallize in the presence of a seed crystal or nucleus around which a crystal structure can form creating a solid. However, lacking any such nuclei, the liquid phase can be maintained all the way down to the temperature at which crystal homogeneous nucleation occurs. |
| Water heating | Water heating is a thermodynamic process that uses an energy source to heat water above its initial temperature. Typical domestic uses of hot water include cooking, cleaning, bathing, and space heating. In industry, hot water and water heated to steam have many uses. |
| Ammonia | Ammonia or azane is a compound of nitrogen and hydrogen with the formula $NH_3$. It is a colourless gas with a characteristic pungent smell. Ammonia contributes significantly to the nutritional needs of terrestrial organisms by serving as a precursor to food and fertilizers. |
| Argon | Argon is a chemical element with symbol Ar and atomic number 18. It is in group 18 of the periodic table and is a noble gas. Argon is the third most common gas in the Earth's atmosphere, at 0.93% (9,300 ppm), making it approximately 23.8 times as abundant as the next most common atmospheric gas, carbon dioxide (390 ppm), and more than 500 times as abundant as the next most common noble gas, neon (18 ppm). Nearly all of this argon is radiogenic argon-40 derived from the decay of potassium-40 in the Earth's crust. |
| Carbon dioxide | Carbon dioxide is a naturally occurring chemical compound composed of two oxygen atoms each covalently double bonded to a single carbon atom. It is a gas at standard temperature and pressure and exists in Earth's atmosphere in this state, as a trace gas at a concentration of 0.039 per cent by volume. |
| | As part of the carbon cycle, plants, algae, and cyanobacteria use light energy to photosynthesize carbohydrate from carbon dioxide and water, with oxygen produced as a waste product. |
| Hydrogen sulfide | Hydrogen sulfide is the chemical compound with the formula H2S. It is a colorless gas with the characteristic foul odor of rotten eggs; it is heavier than air, very poisonous, corrosive, flammable and explosive. |
| | Hydrogen sulfide often results from the bacterial breakdown of organic matter in the absence of oxygen, such as in swamps and sewers; this process is commonly known as anaerobic digestion. |
| Oxygen | Oxygen is a chemical element with symbol O and atomic number 8. It is a member of the chalcogen group on the periodic table and is a highly reactive nonmetallic element and oxidizing agent that readily forms compounds (notably oxides) with most elements. |

By mass, oxygen is the third-most abundant element in the universe, after hydrogen and helium At STP, two atoms of the element bind to form dioxygen, a diatomic gas that is colorless, odorless, and tasteless; with the formula O2.

Many major classes of organic molecules in living organisms, such as proteins, nucleic acids, carbohydrates, and fats, contain oxygen, as do the major inorganic compounds that are constituents of animal shells, teeth, and bone.

| | |
|---|---|
| Phosphine | Phosphine is the compound with the chemical formula $PH_3$. It is a colorless, flammable, toxic gas. Pure phosphine is odorless, but technical grade samples have a highly unpleasant odor like garlic or rotting fish, due to the presence of substituted phosphine and diphosphane ($P_2H_4$). |
| Supercritical fluid | A supercritical fluid is any substance at a temperature and pressure above its critical point, where distinct liquid and gas phases do not exist. It can effuse through solids like a gas, and dissolve materials like a liquid. In addition, close to the critical point, small changes in pressure or temperature result in large changes in density, allowing many properties of a supercritical fluid to be 'fine-tuned'. |
| Supercritical fluid extraction | Supercritical Fluid Extraction is the process of separating one component (the extractant) from another (the matrix) using supercritical fluids as the extracting solvent. Extraction is usually from a solid matrix, but can also be from liquids. Supercritical fluid extraction can be used as a sample preparation step for analytical purposes, or on a larger scale to either strip unwanted material from a product (e.g. decaffeination) or collect a desired product (e.g. essential oils). |
| Vapor pressure | Vapor pressure or equilibrium vapor pressure is the pressure exerted by a vapor in thermodynamic equilibrium with its condensed phases at a given temperature in a closed system. The equilibrium vapor pressure is an indication of a liquid's evaporation rate. It relates to the tendency of particles to escape from the liquid (or a solid). |
| Absorption | In chemistry, absorption is a physical or chemical phenomenon or a process in which atoms, molecules, or ions enter some bulk phase - gas, liquid, or solid material. This is a different process from adsorption, since molecules undergoing absorption are taken up by the volume, not by the surface (as in the case for adsorption). A more general term is sorption, which covers absorption, adsorption, and ion exchange. |
| Dynamic equilibrium | A dynamic equilibrium exists once a reversible reaction ceases to change its ratio of reactants/products, but substances move between the chemicals at an equal rate, meaning there is no net change. It is a particular example of a system in a steady state. In thermodynamics a closed system is in thermodynamic equilibrium when reactions occur at such rates that the composition of the mixture does not change with time. |
| Volatility | In chemistry and physics, volatility is the tendency of a substance to vaporize. |

# 11. Liquids and Intermolecular Forces

Volatility is directly related to a substance's vapor pressure. At a given temperature, a substance with higher vapor pressure vaporizes more readily than a substance with a lower vapor pressure.

| | |
|---|---|
| Concentration | In chemistry, concentration is the abundance of a constituent divided by the total volume of a mixture. Several types of mathematical description can be distinguished: mass concentration, molar concentration, number concentration, and volume concentration. The term concentration can be applied to any kind of chemical mixture, but most frequently it refers to solutes and solvents in solutions. |
| Diethyl ether | Diethyl ether, also known as ethyl ether, sulfuric ether, simply ether, or ethoxyethane, is an organic compound in the ether class with the formula 2O. It is a colorless, highly volatile flammable liquid. It is commonly used as a solvent and was once used as a general anesthetic. |
| Ethylene glycol | Ethylene glycol is an organic compound primarily used as a raw material in the manufacture of polyester fibers and fabric industry, and polyethylene terephthalate resins (PET) used in bottling. A small percent is also used in industrial applications like antifreeze formulations and other industrial products. It is an odorless, colorless, syrupy, sweet-tasting liquid. |
| Critical point | In physical chemistry, thermodynamics, chemistry and condensed matter physics, a critical point, also known as a critical state, occurs under conditions at which no phase boundaries exist. There are multiple types of critical points, including vapor-liquid critical points and liquid-liquid critical points. |
| Freezing point | Freezing, or Solidification, is a phase transition in which a liquid turns into a solid when its temperature is lowered below its freezing point.<br><br>For most substances, the melting and freezing points are the same temperature; however, certain substances possess differing solid-liquid transition temperatures. For example, agar displays a hysteresis in its melting and freezing temperatures. |
| Melting point | The melting point of a solid is the temperature at which it changes state from solid to liquid at atmospheric pressure. At the melting point the solid and liquid phase exist in equilibrium. The melting point of a substance depends (usually slightly) on pressure and is usually specified at standard pressure. |
| Triple point | In thermodynamics, the triple point of a substance is the temperature and pressure at which the three phases of that substance coexist in thermodynamic equilibrium. For example, the triple point of mercury occurs at a temperature of -38.8344 °C and a pressure of 0.2 mPa.<br><br>In addition to the triple point between solid, liquid, and gas, there can be triple points involving more than one solid phase, for substances with multiple polymorphs. |

CHAPTER HIGHLIGHTS & NOTES: KEY TERMS, PEOPLE, PLACES, CONCEPTS

| | |
|---|---|
| Cholesteryl benzoate | Cholesteryl benzoate, also called 5-cholesten-3-yl benzoate, is an organic chemical, an ester of cholesterol and benzoic acid. It is a liquid crystal material forming cholesteric liquid crystals with helical structure.<br><br>It can be used with cholesteryl nonanoate and cholesteryl oleyl carbonate in some thermochromic liquid crystals. |
| Liquid crystal | Liquid crystals are matter in a state that has properties between those of conventional liquid and those of solid crystal. For instance, a liquid crystal may flow like a liquid, but its molecules may be oriented in a crystal-like way. There are many different types of liquid-crystal phases, which can be distinguished by their different optical properties (such as birefringence). |
| Electronic paper | Electronic paper, e-paper and electronic ink are display technologies which are designed to mimic the appearance of ordinary ink on paper. Unlike conventional backlit flat panel displays which emit light, electronic paper displays reflect light like ordinary paper, theoretically making it more comfortable to read, and giving the surface a wider viewing angle compared to conventional displays. The contrast ratio in available displays as of 2008 might be described as similar to that of newspaper, though newly developed displays are slightly better. |
| Acetone | Acetone is the organic compound with the formula $(CH_3)_2CO$. It is a colorless, mobile, flammable liquid, and is the simplest ketone.<br><br>Acetone is miscible with water and serves as an important solvent in its own right, typically for cleaning purposes in the laboratory. About 6.7 million tonnes were produced worldwide in 2010, mainly for use as a solvent and production of methyl methacrylate and bisphenol A. It is a common building block in organic chemistry. |
| Isopropyl alcohol | Isopropyl alcohol is a common name for a chemical compound with the molecular formula $C_3H_8O$ or $C_3H_7OH$. It is a colorless, flammable chemical compound with a strong odor. It is the simplest example of a secondary alcohol, where the alcohol carbon atom is attached to two other carbon atoms sometimes shown as $(CH_3)_2CHOH$. It is a structural isomer of propanol. Isopropyl alcohol is denatured for certain uses, in which case the NFPA 704 rating is changed to 2,3,1. |
| Chlorofluorocarbon | A chlorofluorocarbon is an organic compound that contains only carbon, chlorine, and fluorine, produced as a volatile derivative of methane and ethane. They are also commonly known by the DuPont brand name Freon. The most common representative is dichlorodifluoromethane (R-12 or Freon-12). |
| Gallium | Gallium is a chemical element with symbol Ga and atomic number 31. Elemental gallium does not occur in free form in nature, but as the gallium(III) compounds that are in trace amounts in zinc ores and in bauxite. Gallium is a soft silvery metal, and elemental gallium is a brittle solid at low temperatures. |

# 11. Liquids and Intermolecular Forces

| | |
|---|---|
| | If it is held in the human hand long enough, gallium will melt, since it melts at the temperature of about 29.76 °C (85.57 °F) (slightly above room temperature). |
| Adenine | Adenine is a nucleobase (a purine derivative) with a variety of roles in biochemistry including cellular respiration, in the form of both the energy-rich adenosine triphosphate (ATP) and the cofactors nicotinamide adenine dinucleotide (NAD) and flavin adenine dinucleotide (FAD), and protein synthesis, as a chemical component of DNA and RNA. The shape of adenine is complementary to either thymine in DNA or uracil in RNA. |
| Cytosine | Cytosine is one of the four main bases found in DNA and RNA, along with adenine, guanine, and thymine (uracil in RNA). It is a pyrimidine derivative, with a heterocyclic aromatic ring and two substituents attached (an amine group at position 4 and a keto group at position 2). The nucleoside of cytosine is cytidine. |
| DNA double helix | In molecular biology, the term double helix refers to the structure formed by double-stranded molecules of nucleic acids such as DNA and RNA. The double helical structure of a nucleic acid complex arises as a consequence of its secondary structure, and is a fundamental component in determining its tertiary structure. The term entered popular culture with the publication in 1968 of The Double Helix: A Personal Account of the Discovery of the Structure of DNA, by James Watson.<br><br>The DNA double helix polymer of nucleic acids, held together by nucleotides which base pair together. |
| Dichloromethane | Dichloromethane --or methylene chloride--is an organic compound with the formula $CH_2Cl_2$. This colorless, volatile liquid with a moderately sweet aroma is widely used as a solvent. Although it is not miscible with water, it is miscible with many organic solvents. |
| Guanine | Guanine is one of the four main nucleobases found in the nucleic acids DNA and RNA, the others being adenine, cytosine, and thymine (uracil in RNA). In DNA, guanine is paired with cytosine. With the formula $C_5H_5N_5O$, guanine is a derivative of purine, consisting of a fused pyrimidine-imidazole ring system with conjugated double bonds. |
| Thymine | Thymine is one of the four nucleobases in the nucleic acid of DNA that are represented by the letters G-C-A-T. The others are adenine, guanine, and cytosine. Thymine is also known as 5-methyluracil, a pyrimidine nucleobase. |
| Hexafluorobenzene | Hexafluorobenzene, HFB, C6F6, or perfluorobenzene is an organic, aromatic compound. In this derivative of benzene all hydrogen atoms have been replaced by fluorine atoms. The technical uses of the compound are limited, although it is recommended as a solvent in a number of Photochemical reactions. |

| Methyl iodide | Methyl iodide, also called iodomethane, and commonly abbreviated 'MeI', is the chemical compound with the formula $CH_3I$. It is a dense, colorless, volatile liquid. In terms of chemical structure, it is related to methane by replacement of one hydrogen atom by an atom of iodine. It is naturally emitted by rice plantations in small amounts. |
| --- | --- |
| Butane | Butane is an organic compound with the formula $C_4H_{10}$ that is an alkane with four carbon atoms. Butane is a gas at room temperature and atmospheric pressure. The term may refer to either of two structural isomers, n-butane or isobutane or to a mixture of these isomers. |

1. A _____ is an intensity vs. m/z (mass-to-charge ratio) plot representing a chemical analysis. Hence, the _____ of a sample is a pattern representing the distribution of ions by mass (more correctly: mass-to-charge ratio) in a sample. It is a histogram usually acquired using an instrument called a mass spectrometer.

   a. Berkeley Geochronology Center
   b. Mass spectrum
   c. Calutron
   d. Canadian Penning Trap Mass Spectrometer

2. _____s are diagrams that show the bonding between atoms of a molecule and the lone pairs of electrons that may exist in the molecule. A _____ can be drawn for any covalently bonded molecule, as well as coordination compounds. The _____ was named after Gilbert N

   a. Bond energy
   b. covalent
   c. Lewis structure
   d. Formal charge

3. _____s are matter in a state that has properties between those of conventional liquid and those of solid crystal. For instance, a _____ may flow like a liquid, but its molecules may be oriented in a crystal-like way. There are many different types of liquid-crystal phases, which can be distinguished by their different optical properties (such as birefringence).

   a. Blue phase mode LCD
   b. British Liquid Crystal Society
   c. Cholesteric liquid crystal
   d. Liquid crystal

# 11. Liquids and Intermolecular Forces

4. _____ or azane is a compound of nitrogen and hydrogen with the formula $NH_3$. It is a colourless gas with a characteristic pungent smell. _____ contributes significantly to the nutritional needs of terrestrial organisms by serving as a precursor to food and fertilizers.

   a. Barium acetylacetonate
   b. Cerium acetylacetonate
   c. Dysprosium acetylacetonate
   d. Ammonia

5. A _____ is any substance at a temperature and pressure above its critical point, where distinct liquid and gas phases do not exist. It can effuse through solids like a gas, and dissolve materials like a liquid. In addition, close to the critical point, small changes in pressure or temperature result in large changes in density, allowing many properties of a _____ to be 'fine-tuned'.

   a. Band mapping
   b. Supercritical fluid
   c. Bloch wave
   d. Bosenova

1. b
2. c
3. d
4. d
5. b

---

## You can take the complete Chapter Practice Test

**for 11. Liquids and Intermolecular Forces**
on all key terms, persons, places, and concepts.

### Online 99 Cents

### *http://www.JustTheFacts101.com*

**Use www.JustTheFacts101.com for all your study needs**

**including Facts101's online interactive problem solving labs in**

**chemistry, statistics, mathematics, and more.**

# 12. Solids and Modern Materials

CHAPTER OUTLINE: KEY TERMS, PEOPLE, PLACES, CONCEPTS

Light-emitting diode

Mass spectrum

Polymer

Semiconductor

Amorphous solid

Lewis structure

Molecular solid

Valence electron

Benzene

Delocalized

Nanotechnology

Phenol

Spectrum

Toluene

Obsidian

Quartz

Sodium

Volcanic glass

Parallelepiped

Graphene

Crystal structure

Diffraction

Diffraction grating

X-ray crystallography

Chromium

Conductivity

Ductility

Gold leaf

Thermal conductivity

Efficiency

Brass

Stainless steel

Sterling silver

Pewter

Plumber

Alloy steel

Cementite

Ferrochrome

Pearlite

Solid solution

Vanadium

Entropy

# 12. Solids and Modern Materials



CHAPTER OUTLINE: KEY TERMS, PEOPLE, PLACES, CONCEPTS

- Intermetallic
- Magnesium
- Phosphorus
- Silicon
- Sulfur
- Electron pair
- Gold
- Physical properties
- Band gap
- Molecular orbital
- Calcium
- Electronic band structure
- Alkali
- Alkali metal
- Ionic compound
- Melting point
- Alkali metal halide
- Coordination number
- Halide
- Ionic crystal
- Metal halides

# 12. Solids and Modern Materials
CHAPTER OUTLINE: KEY TERMS, PEOPLE, PLACES, CONCEPTS

_____ | Sodium chloride

_____ | Magnesium fluoride

_____ | Scandium fluoride

_____ | Sodium fluoride

_____ | Environment

_____ | Density

_____ | Stoichiometry

_____ | Iridium

_____ | Boron nitride

_____ | Germanium

_____ | Silicon carbide

_____ | Compound semiconductor

_____ | Conduction band

_____ | Gallium arsenide

_____ | Indium

_____ | Valence band

_____ | Dopant

_____ | Doping

_____ | Cellulose

_____ | Monomer

_____ | Polymerization

CHAPTER OUTLINE: KEY TERMS, PEOPLE, PLACES, CONCEPTS

| | |
|---|---|
| | Elastomer |
| | Polyethylene |
| | Thermoplastic |
| | Carboxylic acid |
| | Nylon |
| | Polyester |
| | Condensation |
| | Addition polymer |
| | Condensation polymer |
| | Copolymer |
| | Diamine |
| | Polycarbonate |
| | Polypropylene |
| | Polystyrene |
| | Polyurethane |
| | Adipic acid |
| | Low-density polyethylene |
| | High-density polyethylene |
| | Crystallinity |
| | Macromolecule |
| | Isoprene |

| | Double bond |
| --- | --- |
| | Lipid |
| | Vulcanization |
| | Quantum dot |
| | Photoluminescence |
| | Polyphosphate |
| | Quantum well |
| | Quantum wire |
| | Quantum |
| | Carbon |
| | Carbon nanotube |
| | Fullerene |
| | Polyacetylene |
| | Semimetal |
| | Rutile |
| | Clausthalite |
| | Cadmium telluride |
| | Natural gas |
| | Nomex |
| | Polyacrylonitrile |
| | Spinel |

| | |
|---|---|
| Light-emitting diode | A light-emitting diode is a semiconductor light source. Light emitting diodes are used as indicator lamps in many devices and are increasingly used for general lighting. Appearing as practical electronic components in 1962, early Light emitting diodes emitted low-intensity red light, but modern versions are available across the visible, ultraviolet, and infrared wavelengths, with very high brightness. |
| Mass spectrum | A mass spectrum is an intensity vs. m/z (mass-to-charge ratio) plot representing a chemical analysis. Hence, the mass spectrum of a sample is a pattern representing the distribution of ions by mass (more correctly: mass-to-charge ratio) in a sample. It is a histogram usually acquired using an instrument called a mass spectrometer. |
| Polymer | A polymer is a large molecule composed of many repeated subunits, known as monomers. Because of their broad range of properties, both synthetic and natural polymers play an essential and ubiquitous role in everyday life. Polymers range from familiar synthetic plastics such as polystyrene (or styrofoam) to natural biopolymers such as DNA and proteins that are fundamental to biological structure and function. |
| Semiconductor | A semiconductor is a material which has electrical conductivity to a degree between that of a metal and that of an insulator (such as glass). Semiconductors are the foundation of modern electronics, including transistors, solar cells, light-emitting diodes (LEDs), quantum dots and digital and analog integrated circuits.<br><br>A semiconductor may have a number of unique properties, one of which is the ability to change conductivity by the addition of impurities ('doping') or by interaction with another phenomenon, such as an electric field or light; this ability makes a semiconductor very useful for constructing a device that can amplify, switch, or convert an energy input. |
| Amorphous solid | In condensed matter physics, an amorphous or non-crystalline solid is a solid that lacks the long-range order characteristic of a crystal.<br><br>In some older books, the term has been used synonymously with glass. Nowadays, 'amorphous solid' is considered to be the overarching concept, and glass the more special case: A glass is an amorphous solid that exhibits a glass transition. |
| Lewis structure | Lewis structures are diagrams that show the bonding between atoms of a molecule and the lone pairs of electrons that may exist in the molecule. A Lewis structure can be drawn for any covalently bonded molecule, as well as coordination compounds. The Lewis structure was named after Gilbert N |
| Molecular solid | Molecular solid is a solid composed of molecules held together by the van der Waals forces. Because these dipole forces are weaker than covalent or ionic bonds, molecular solids are soft and have relatively low melting temperature. |

# 12. Solids and Modern Materials

| | |
|---|---|
| Valence electron | In chemistry, a valence electron is an electron that is associated with an atom, and that can participate in the formation of a chemical bond; in a single covalent bond, both atoms in the bond contribute one valence electron in order to form a shared pair. The presence of valence electrons can determine the element's chemical properties and whether it may bond with other elements: For a main group element, a valence electron can only be in the outermost electron shell. In a transition metal, a valence electron can also be in an inner shell. |
| Benzene | Benzene is an organic chemical compound with the molecular formula $C_3H_6$. Its molecule is composed of 6 carbon atoms joined in a ring, with 1 hydrogen atom attached to each carbon atom. Because its molecules contain only carbon and hydrogen atoms, benzene is classed as a hydrocarbon. |
| Delocalized | In chemistry, delocalized electrons are electrons in a molecule, ion or solid metal that are not associated with a single atom or one covalent bond. Delocalized electrons are contained within an orbital that extends over several adjacent atoms. Classically, delocalized electrons can be found in conjugated systems and mesoionic compounds. |
| Nanotechnology | Nanotechnology is the manipulation of matter on an atomic and molecular scale. The earliest, widespread description of nanotechnology referred to the particular technological goal of precisely manipulating atoms and molecules for fabrication of macroscale products, also now referred to as molecular nanotechnology. A more generalized description of nanotechnology was subsequently established by the National Nanotechnology Initiative, which defines nanotechnology as the manipulation of matter with at least one dimension sized from 1 to 100 nanometers. |
| Phenol | Phenol -- also known as carbolic acid -- is an aromatic organic compound with the molecular formula $C_6H_5OH$. It is a white crystalline solid that is volatile. The molecule consists of a phenyl group ($-C_6H_5$) bonded to a hydroxyl group ($-OH$). It is mildly acidic, but requires careful handling due to its propensity to cause burns. |
| Spectrum | A spectrum is a condition that is not limited to a specific set of values but can vary infinitely within a continuum. The word was first used scientifically within the field of optics to describe the rainbow of colors in visible light when separated using a prism; it has since been applied by analogy to many fields other than optics. Thus, one might talk about the spectrum of political opinion, or the spectrum of activity of a drug, or the autism spectrum. |
| Toluene | Toluene, formerly known as toluol, is a clear, water-insoluble liquid with the typical smell of paint thinners. It is a mono-substituted benzene derivative, i.e., one in which a single hydrogen atom from a group of six atoms from the benzene molecule has been replaced by a univalent group, in this case $CH_3$. As such, its IUPAC systematic name is methylbenzene. |
| Obsidian | Obsidian is a naturally occurring volcanic glass formed as an extrusive igneous rock. |

It is produced when felsic lava extruded from a volcano cools rapidly with minimum crystal growth. Obsidian is commonly found within the margins of rhyolitic lava flows known as obsidian flows, where the chemical composition (high silica content) induces a high viscosity and polymerization degree of the lava.

| Quartz | Quartz is the second most abundant mineral in the Earth's continental crust, after feldspar. It is made up of a continuous framework of $SiO_4$ silicon-oxygen tetrahedra, with each oxygen being shared between two tetrahedra, giving an overall formula $SiO_2$.

There are many different varieties of quartz, several of which are semi-precious gemstones. |

| Sodium | Sodium is a chemical element with the symbol Na and atomic number 11. It is a soft, silver-white, highly reactive metal and is a member of the alkali metals; its only stable isotope is $^{23}Na$. The free metal does not occur in nature, but instead must be prepared from its compounds; it was first isolated by Humphry Davy in 1807 by the electrolysis of sodium hydroxide. Sodium is the sixth most abundant element in the Earth's crust, and exists in numerous minerals such as feldspars, sodalite and rock salt. |

| Volcanic glass | Volcanic glass is the amorphous product of rapidly cooling magma. Like all types of glass, it is a state of matter intermediate between the close-packed, highly ordered array of a crystal and the highly disordered array of gas. Volcanic glass can refer to the interstitial, or matrix material in an aphanitic (fine grained) volcanic rock or can refer to any of several types of vitreous igneous rocks. |

| Parallelepiped | In geometry, a parallelepiped is a three-dimensional figure formed by six parallelograms. (The term rhomboid is also sometimes used with this meaning). By analogy, it relates to a parallelogram just as a cube relates to a square or as a cuboid to a rectangle. |

| Graphene | Graphene is one of the crystalline forms of carbon, alongside diamond, graphite, carbon nanotubes and fullerenes. In this material, carbon atoms are arranged in a regular hexagonal pattern. Graphene can be described as a one-atom thick layer of the layered mineral graphite. |

| Crystal structure | In mineralogy and crystallography, crystal structure is a unique arrangement of atoms or molecules in a crystalline liquid or solid. A crystal structure is composed of a pattern, a set of atoms arranged in a particular way, and a lattice exhibiting long-range order and symmetry. Patterns are located upon the points of a lattice, which is an array of points repeating periodically in three dimensions. |

| Diffraction | Diffraction refers to various phenomena which occur when a wave encounters an obstacle. In classical physics, the diffraction phenomenon is described as the apparent bending of waves around small obstacles and the spreading out of waves past small openings. |

# 12. Solids and Modern Materials

| | |
|---|---|
| Diffraction grating | In optics, a diffraction grating is an optical component with a periodic structure, which splits and diffracts light into several beams travelling in different directions. The directions of these beams depend on the spacing of the grating and the wavelength of the light so that the grating acts as the dispersive element. Because of this, gratings are commonly used in monochromators and spectrometers. |
| X-ray crystallography | X-ray crystallography is a method used for determining the atomic and molecular structure of a crystal, in which the crystalline atoms cause a beam of X-rays to diffract into many specific directions. By measuring the angles and intensities of these diffracted beams, a crystallographer can produce a three-dimensional picture of the density of electrons within the crystal. From this electron density, the mean positions of the atoms in the crystal can be determined, as well as their chemical bonds, their disorder and various other information. |
| Chromium | Chromium is a chemical element which has the symbol Cr and atomic number 24. It is the first element in Group 6. It is a steely-gray, lustrous, hard and brittle metal which takes a high polish, resists tarnishing, and has a high melting point. The name of the element is derived from the Greek word 'chroma' (???μα), meaning colour, because many of its compounds are intensely coloured.<br><br>Chromium oxide was used by the Chinese in the Qin dynasty over 2,000 years ago to coat metal weapons found with the Terracotta Army. |
| Conductivity | The conductivity of an electrolyte solution is a measure of its ability to conduct electricity. The SI unit of conductivity is siemens per meter (S/m).<br><br>Conductivity measurements are used routinely in many industrial and environmental applications as a fast, inexpensive and reliable way of measuring the ionic content in a solution. |
| Ductility | In materials science, ductility is a solid material's ability to deform under tensile stress; this is often characterized by the material's ability to be stretched into a wire. Malleability, a similar property, is a material's ability to deform under compressive stress; this is often characterized by the material's ability to form a thin sheet by hammering or rolling. Both of these mechanical properties are aspects of plasticity, the extent to which a solid material can be plastically deformed without fracture. |
| Gold leaf | Gold leaf is gold that has been hammered into extremely thin sheets by goldbeating and is often used for gilding. Gold leaf is available in a wide variety of karats and shades. 22-karat yellow gold is the most commonly used.<br><br>Gold leaf is sometimes confused with metal leaf but they are different products. |
| Thermal conductivity | In physics, thermal conductivity is the property of a material to conduct heat. It is evaluated primarily in terms of Fourier's Law for heat conduction. |

| Efficiency | Efficiency in general, describes the extent to which time, effort or cost is well used for the intended task or purpose. It is often used with the specific purpose of relaying the capability of a specific application of effort to produce a specific outcome effectively with a minimum amount or quantity of waste, expense, or unnecessary effort. 'Efficiency' has widely varying meanings in different disciplines. |
|---|---|
| Brass | Brass is an alloy made of copper and zinc; the proportions of zinc and copper can be varied to create a range of brasses with varying properties.<br><br>By comparison, bronze is principally an alloy of copper and tin. Bronze does not necessarily contain tin, and a variety of alloys of copper, including alloys with arsenic, phosphorus, aluminium, manganese, and silicon, are commonly termed 'bronze'. |
| Stainless steel | In metallurgy, stainless steel, also known as inox steel or inox from French 'inoxydable', is a steel alloy with a minimum of 10.5% chromium content by mass.<br><br>Stainless steel does not readily corrode, rust or stain with water as ordinary steel does, but despite the name it is not fully stain-proof, most notably under low oxygen, high salinity, or poor circulation environments. There are different grades and surface finishes of stainless steel to suit the environment the alloy must endure. |
| Sterling silver | Sterling silver is an alloy of silver containing 92.5% by mass of silver and 7.5% by mass of other metals, usually copper. The sterling silver standard has a minimum millesimal fineness of 925.<br><br>Fine silver, for example 99.9% pure silver, is generally too soft for producing functional objects; therefore, the silver is usually alloyed with copper to give it strength while preserving the ductility and beauty of the precious metal. |
| Pewter | Pewter is a malleable metal alloy, traditionally 85-99% tin, with the remainder consisting of copper, antimony, bismuth and sometimes, less commonly today, lead. Silver is also sometimes used. Copper and antimony act as hardeners while lead is common in the lower grades of pewter, which have a bluish tint. |
| Plumber | A plumber is a tradesperson who specializes in installing and maintaining systems used for potable water, sewage, and drainage in plumbing systems. The term dates from ancient times, and is related to the Latin word for lead, 'plumbum.' |
| Alloy steel | Alloy steel is steel that is alloyed with a variety of elements in total amounts between 1.0% and 50% by weight to improve its mechanical properties. Alloy steels are broken down into two groups: low-alloy steels and high-alloy steels. The difference between the two is somewhat arbitrary: Smith and Hashemi define the difference at 4.0%, while Degarmo, et al., define it at 8.0%. |

# 12. Solids and Modern Materials

| | |
|---|---|
| Cementite | Cementite, also known as iron carbide, is a chemical compound of iron and carbon, with the formula $Fe_3C$. By weight, it is 6.67% carbon and 93.3% iron. It has an orthorhombic crystal structure. |
| Ferrochrome | Ferrochrome is an alloy of chromium and iron containing between 50% and 70% chromium. The ferrochrome is produced by electric arc melting of chromite, an iron magnesium chromium oxide and the most important chromium ore. Most of the world's ferrochrome is produced in South Africa, Kazakhstan and India, which have large domestic chromite resources. |
| Pearlite | Pearlite is a two-phased, lamellar structure composed of alternating layers of alpha-ferrite (88 wt%) and cementite (12 wt%) that occurs in some steels and cast irons. In fact, the lamellar appearance is misleading since the individual lamellae within a colony are connected in three dimensions; a single colony is therefore an interpenetrating bicrystal of ferrite and cementite. In an iron-carbon alloy, during slow cooling pearlite forms by a eutectoid reaction as austenite cools below 727 °C (1,341 °F) (the eutectoid temperature). |
| Solid solution | A solid solution is a solid-state solution of one or more solutes in a solvent. Such a mixture is considered a solution rather than a compound when the crystal structure of the solvent remains unchanged by addition of the solutes, and when the mixture remains in a single homogeneous phase. This often happens when the two elements (generally metals) involved are close together on the periodic table; conversely, a chemical compound is generally a result of the non-proximity of the two metals involved on the periodic table. |
| Vanadium | Vanadium is a chemical element with the symbol V and atomic number 23. It is a hard, silvery gray, ductile and malleable transition metal. The element is found only in chemically combined form in nature, but once isolated artificially, the formation of an oxide layer stabilizes the free metal somewhat against further oxidation. |
| | Andrés Manuel del Río discovered compounds of vanadium in 1801 by analyzing a new lead-bearing mineral he called 'brown lead,' and presumed its qualities were due to the presence of a new element, which he named erythronium (Greek for 'red') since, upon heating, most of its salts turned from their initial color to red. |
| Entropy | In thermodynamics, entropy is a measure of the number of specific ways in which a thermodynamic system may be arranged, often taken to be a measure of disorder, or a measure of progressing towards thermodynamic equilibrium. The entropy of an isolated system never decreases, because isolated systems spontaneously evolve towards thermodynamic equilibrium, which is the state of maximum entropy. |
| | Entropy was originally defined for a thermodynamically reversible process as |

$$\Delta S = \int \frac{dQ_{rev}}{T}$$

where the entropy is found from the uniform thermodynamic temperature of a closed system dividing an incremental reversible transfer of heat into that system .

**Intermetallic**

Intermetallic compound is a term that is used in a number of different ways. Most commonly it refers to solid-state phases involving metals. There is a 'research definition' adhered to generally in scientific publications, and a wider 'common use' term.

**Magnesium**

Magnesium is a chemical element with the symbol Mg and atomic number 12. Its common oxidation number is +2. It is an alkaline earth metal and the eighth most abundant element in the Earth's crust and ninth in the known universe as a whole. Magnesium is the fourth most common element in the Earth as a whole (behind iron, oxygen and silicon), making up 13% of the planet's mass and a large fraction of the planet's mantle. The relative abundance of magnesium is related to the fact that it easily builds up in supernova stars from a sequential addition of three helium nuclei to carbon (which in turn is made from three helium nuclei).

**Phosphorus**

Phosphorus is a nonmetallic chemical element with symbol P and atomic number 15. A multivalent pnictogen, phosphorus as a mineral is almost always present in its maximally oxidised state, as inorganic phosphate rocks. Elemental phosphorus exists in two major forms--white phosphorus and red phosphorus--but due to its high reactivity, phosphorus is never found as a free element on Earth.

The first form of elemental phosphorus to be produced (white phosphorus, in 1669) emits a faint glow upon exposure to oxygen - hence its name given from Greek mythology, F?sf???? meaning 'light-bearer' (Latin Lucifer), referring to the 'Morning Star', the planet Venus.

**Silicon**

Silicon, a tetravalent metalloid, is a chemical element with the symbol Si and atomic number 14. It is less reactive than its chemical analog carbon, the nonmetal directly above it in the periodic table, but more reactive than germanium, the metalloid directly below it in the table. Controversy about silicon's character dates to its discovery; it was first prepared and characterized in pure form in 1823. In 1808, it was given the name silicium (from Latin: silex, hard stone or flint), with an -ium word-ending to suggest a metal, a name which the element retains in several non-English languages. However, its final English name, first suggested in 1817, reflects the more physically similar elements carbon and boron.

**Sulfur**

Sulfur or sulphur is a chemical element with symbol S and atomic number 16. It is an abundant, multivalent non-metal. Under normal conditions, sulfur atoms form cyclic octatomic molecules with chemical formula $S_8$. Elemental sulfur is a bright yellow crystalline solid when at room temperature.

# 12. Solids and Modern Materials

| | |
|---|---|
| Electron pair | In chemistry, an electron pair consists of two electrons that occupy the same orbital but have opposite spins. The electron pair concept was introduced in a 1916 paper of Gilbert N. Lewis.<br><br>Because electrons are fermions, the Pauli exclusion principle forbids these particles from having exactly the same quantum numbers. |
| Gold | Gold is a chemical element with the symbol Au and atomic number 79. It is a dense, soft, malleable, and ductile metal with an attractive, bright yellow color and luster that is maintained without tarnishing in air or water. Chemically, gold is a transition metal and a group 11 element. It is one of the least reactive chemical elements, solid under standard conditions. |
| Physical properties | A physical property is any property that is measurable whose value describes a state of a physical system. The changes in the physical properties of a system can be used to describe its transformations or evolutions between its momentary states. Physical properties are often referred to as observables. |
| Band gap | In solid-state physics, a band gap, also called an energy gap or bandgap, is an energy range in a solid where no electron states can exist. In graphs of the electronic band structure of solids, the band gap generally refers to the energy difference (in electron volts) between the top of the valence band and the bottom of the conduction band in insulators and semiconductors. This is equivalent to the energy required to free an outer shell electron from its orbit about the nucleus to become a mobile charge carrier, able to move freely within the solid material, so the band gap is a major factor determining the electrical conductivity of a solid. |
| Molecular orbital | In chemistry, a molecular orbital is a mathematical function describing the wave-like behavior of an electron in a molecule. This function can be used to calculate chemical and physical properties such as the probability of finding an electron in any specific region. The term orbital was introduced by Robert S. Mulliken in 1932 as an abbreviation for one-electron orbital wave function. |
| Calcium | Calcium is the chemical element with symbol Ca and atomic number 20. Calcium is a soft gray alkaline earth metal, and is the fifth-most-abundant element by mass in the Earth's crust. Calcium is also the fifth-most-abundant dissolved ion in seawater by both molarity and mass, after sodium, chloride, magnesium, and sulfate.<br><br>Calcium is essential for living organisms, in particular in cell physiology, where movement of the calcium ion $Ca^{2+}$ into and out of the cytoplasm functions as a signal for many cellular processes. |
| Electronic band structure | In solid-state physics, the electronic band structure of a solid describes those ranges of energy that an electron within the solid may have (called energy bands, allowed bands, or simply bands), and ranges of energy that it may not have (called band gaps or forbidden bands). Band theory derives these bands and band gaps by examining the allowed quantum mechanical wave functions for an electron in a large, periodic lattice of atoms or molecules. |

| | |
|---|---|
| Alkali | In chemistry, an alkali is a basic, ionic salt of an alkali metal or alkaline earth metal chemical element. Some authors also define an alkali as a base that dissolves in water. A solution of a soluble base has a pH greater than 7.0. The adjective alkaline is commonly, and alkalescent less often, used in English as a synonym for basic, especially for soluble bases. |
| Alkali metal | The alkali metals are a group in the periodic table consisting of the chemical elements lithium, sodium (Na), potassium (K), rubidium (Rb), caesium (Cs), and francium (Fr). This group lies in the s-block of the periodic table as all alkali metals have their outermost electron in an s-orbital. The alkali metals provide the best example of group trends in properties in the periodic table, with elements exhibiting well-characterized homologous behaviour. |
| Ionic compound | In chemistry, an ionic compound is a chemical compound in which ions are held together in a lattice structure by ionic bonds. Usually, the positively charged portion consists of metal cations and the negatively charged portion is an anion or polyatomic ion. Ions in ionic compounds are held together by the electrostatic forces between oppositely charged bodies. |
| Melting point | The melting point of a solid is the temperature at which it changes state from solid to liquid at atmospheric pressure. At the melting point the solid and liquid phase exist in equilibrium. The melting point of a substance depends (usually slightly) on pressure and is usually specified at standard pressure. |
| Alkali metal halide | Alkali metal halides are the family of inorganic compounds with the chemical formula MX, where M is an alkali metal and X is a halogen. These compounds are the often commercially significant sources of these metals and halides. The best known of these compounds is sodium chloride, table salt. |
| Coordination number | In chemistry and crystallography, the coordination number of a central atom in a molecule or crystal is the number of its nearest neighbours. This number is determined somewhat differently for molecules than for crystals.<br><br>In chemistry, the emphasis is on bonding structure in molecules or ions and the coordination number of an atom is determined by simply counting the other atoms to which it is bonded (by either single or multiple bonds). |
| Halide | A halide is a binary compound, of which one part is a halogen atom and the other part is an element or radical that is less electronegative than the halogen, to make a fluoride, chloride, bromide, iodide, or astatide compound. Many salts are halides. All Group 1 metals form halides which are white solids at room temperature. |
| Ionic crystal | An ionic crystal is a crystal consisting of ions bound together by their electrostatic attraction. |

# 12. Solids and Modern Materials

Examples of such crystals are the alkali halides, including potassium fluoride, potassium chloride, potassium bromide, potassium iodide, sodium fluoride, and other combinations of sodium, caesium, rubidium, or lithium ions with fluoride, bromide, chloride or iodide ions. NaCl has a 6:6 co-ordination.

| | |
|---|---|
| Metal halides | Metal halides are compounds between metals and halogens. Some, such as sodium chloride are ionic, while others are covalently bonded. Covalently bonded metal halides may be discrete molecules, such as uranium hexafluoride, or they may form polymeric structures, such as palladium chloride. |
| Sodium chloride | Sodium chloride, also known as salt, common salt, table salt or halite, is an ionic compound with the formula NaCl, representing equal proportions of sodium and chlorine. Sodium chloride is the salt most responsible for the salinity of the ocean and of the extracellular fluid of many multicellular organisms. As the major ingredient in edible salt, it is commonly used as a condiment and food preservative. |
| Magnesium fluoride | Magnesium fluoride is an inorganic compound with the formula $MgF_2$. The compound is a white crystalline salt and is transparent over a wide range of wavelengths, with commercial uses in optics that are also used in space telescopes. It occurs naturally as the rare mineral sellaite. |
| Scandium fluoride | Scandium fluoride, $ScF_3$, is an ionic compound. It is slightly soluble in water but dissolves in the presence of excess fluoride to form $ScF_6^{3-}$. $ScF_3$ can be produced by reacting scandium and fluorine. |
| Sodium fluoride | Sodium fluoride is an inorganic chemical compound with the formula NaF. A colorless solid, it is a source of the fluoride ion in diverse applications. Sodium fluoride is less expensive and less hygroscopic than the related salt potassium fluoride. |
| Environment | In science and engineering, a system is the part of the universe that is being studied, while the environment is the remainder of the universe that lies outside the boundaries of the system. It is also known as the surroundings, and in thermodynamics, as the reservoir. Depending on the type of system, it may interact with the environment by exchanging mass, energy (including heat and work), linear momentum, angular momentum, electric charge, or other conserved properties. |
| Density | The density, or more precisely, the volumetric mass density, of a substance is its mass per unit volume. The symbol most often used for density is ? (the lower case Greek letter rho). Mathematically, density is defined as mass divided by volume: $$\rho = \frac{m}{V},$$ where ? is the density, m is the mass, and V is the volume. |

| | |
|---|---|
| Stoichiometry | Stoichiometry is a branch of chemistry that deals with the relative quantities of reactants and products in chemical reactions. In a balanced chemical reaction, the relations among quantities of reactants and products typically form a ratio of positive integers. For example, in a reaction that forms ammonia ($NH_3$), exactly one molecule of nitrogen gas ($N_2$) reacts with three molecules of hydrogen gas ($H_2$) to produce two molecules of $NH_3$: $N2 + 3H2 ? 2NH3$<br><br>This particular kind of stoichiometry - describing the quantitative relationships among substances as they participate in chemical reactions - is known as reaction stoichiometry. |
| Iridium | Iridium is the chemical element with symbol Ir and atomic number 77. A very hard, brittle, silvery-white transition metal of the platinum family, iridium is the second-densest element (after osmium) and is the most corrosion-resistant metal, even at temperatures as high as 2000 °C. Although only certain molten salts and halogens are corrosive to solid iridium, finely divided iridium dust is much more reactive and can be flammable.<br><br>Iridium was discovered in 1803 among insoluble impurities in natural platinum. Smithson Tennant, the primary discoverer, named the iridium for the Greek goddess Iris, personification of the rainbow, because of the striking and diverse colors of its salts. |
| Boron nitride | Boron nitride is a chemical compound with chemical formula BN, consisting of equal numbers of boron and nitrogen atoms. BN is isoelectronic to a similarly structured carbon lattice and thus exists in various crystalline forms. The hexagonal form corresponding to graphite is the most stable and softest among BN polymorphs, and is therefore used as a lubricant and an additive to cosmetic products. |
| Germanium | Germanium is a chemical element with symbol Ge and atomic number 32. It is a lustrous, hard, grayish-white metalloid in the carbon group, chemically similar to its group neighbors tin and silicon. Purified germanium is a semiconductor, with an appearance most similar to elemental silicon. Like silicon, germanium naturally reacts and forms complexes with oxygen in nature. |
| Silicon carbide | Silicon carbide, also known as carborundum, is a compound of silicon and carbon with chemical formula SiC. It occurs in nature as the extremely rare mineral moissanite. Silicon carbide powder has been mass-produced since 1893 for use as an abrasive. Grains of silicon carbide can be bonded together by sintering to form very hard ceramics that are widely used in applications requiring high endurance, such as car brakes, car clutches and ceramic plates in bulletproof vests. |
| Compound semiconductor | A compound semiconductor is a semiconductor compound composed of elements from two or more different groups of the periodic table. These semiconductors typically form in groups 13-15 (old groups III-V), for example of elements from group 13 (old group III, boron, aluminium, gallium, indium) and from group 15 (old group V, nitrogen, phosphorus, arsenic, antimony, bismuth). The range of possible formulae is quite broad because these elements can form binary (two elements, e.g. gallium(III) arsenide (GaAs)), ternary (three elements, e.g. |

indium gallium arsenide (InGaAs)) and quaternary (four elements, e.g. aluminium gallium indium phosphide (AlInGaP)) alloys.

| | |
|---|---|
| Conduction band | The conduction band is the range of electron energies enough to free an electron from binding with its atom to move freely within the atomic lattice of the material as a 'delocalized electron'. Various materials may be classified by their band gap: this is defined as the difference between the valence and conduction bands. •In non-conductors, commonly known as insulators, the conduction band is higher than that of the valence band, so it takes infeasibly high energies to delocalize their valence electrons. |
| Gallium arsenide | Gallium arsenide is a compound of the elements gallium and arsenic. It is a III/V semiconductor, and is used in the manufacture of devices such as microwave frequency integrated circuits, monolithic microwave integrated circuits, infrared light-emitting diodes, laser diodes, solar cells and optical windows. |
| | GaAs is often used as a substrate material for the epitaxial growth of other III-V semiconductors including: InGaAs and GaInNAs. |
| Indium | Indium is a chemical element with symbol In and atomic number 49. This rare, very soft, malleable and easily fusible poor metal is chemically similar to gallium and thallium, and shows intermediate properties between these two. Indium was discovered in 1863 and named for the indigo blue line in its spectrum that was the first indication of its existence in zinc ores, as a new and unknown element. The metal was first isolated in the following year. |
| Valence band | In solids, the valence band is the highest range of electron energies in which electrons are normally present at absolute zero temperature. |
| | The valence electrons are bound to individual atoms, as opposed to conduction electrons, which can move freely within the atomic lattice of the material. On a graph of the electronic band structure of a material, the valence band is located below the conduction band, separated from it in insulators and semiconductors by a band gap. |
| Dopant | A dopant, also called a doping agent, is a trace impurity element that is inserted into a substance in order to alter the electrical properties or the optical properties of the substance. In the case of crystalline substances, the atoms of the dopant very commonly take the place of elements that were in the crystal lattice of the material. These materials are very commonly either crystals of a semiconductor (silicon, germanium, etc)., for use in solid-state electronics; or else transparent crystals that are used to make lasers of various types. |
| Doping | In semiconductor production, doping intentionally introduces impurities into an extremely pure semiconductor for the purpose of modulating its electrical properties. The impurities are dependent upon the type of semiconductor. |

| Cellulose | Cellulose is an organic compound with the formula n, a polysaccharide consisting of a linear chain of several hundred to over ten thousand ß(1?4) linked -glucose units. Cellulose is an important structural component of the primary cell wall of green plants, many forms of algae and the oomycetes. Some species of bacteria secrete it to form biofilms. |
|---|---|
| Monomer | A monomer, pronounced mon'?-m?r, or MON-uh-mer, is a molecule that may bind chemically to other molecules to form a polymer. The term 'monomeric protein' may also be used to describe one of the proteins making up a multiprotein complex. The most common natural monomer is glucose, which is linked by glycosidic bonds into polymers such as cellulose and starch, and is over 77% of the mass of all plant matter. |
| Polymerization | In polymer chemistry, polymerization is a process of reacting monomer molecules together in a chemical reaction to form polymer chains or three-dimensional networks. There are many forms of polymerization and different systems exist to categorize them. |
| Elastomer | An elastomer is a polymer with viscoelasticity, generally having low Young's modulus and high failure strain compared with other materials. The term, which is derived from elastic polymer, is often used interchangeably with the term rubber, although the latter is preferred when referring to vulcanisates. Each of the monomers which link to form the polymer is usually made of carbon, hydrogen, oxygen and/or silicon. |
| Polyethylene | Polyethylene or polythene (IUPAC name polyethene or poly(methylene)) is the most common plastic. The annual production is approximately 80 million tonnes. Its primary use is in packaging (plastic bag, plastic films, geomembranes, containers including bottles, etc).. |
| Thermoplastic | A thermoplastic, or thermosoftening plastic, is a polymer that becomes pliable or moldable above a specific temperature, and returns to a solid state upon cooling. Most thermoplastics have a high molecular weight. The polymer chains associate through intermolecular forces, which permits thermoplastics to be remolded because the intermolecular interactions increase upon cooling and restore the bulk properties. |
| Carboxylic acid | A carboxylic acid is an organic acid characterized by the presence of at least one carboxyl group. The general formula of a carboxylic acid is R-COOH, where R is some monovalent functional group. A carboxyl group (or carboxy) is a functional group consisting of a carbonyl (RR'C=O) and a hydroxyl (R-O-H), which has the formula -C(=O)OH, usually written as -COOH or $-CO_2H$. <br><br> Carboxylic acids are Brønsted-Lowry acids because they are proton ($H^+$) donors. |
| Nylon | Nylon is a generic designation for a family of synthetic polymers known generically as aliphatic polyamides, first produced on February 28, 1935, by Wallace Carothers at DuPont's research facility at the DuPont Experimental Station. Nylon is one of the most commonly used polymers. |

# 12. Solids and Modern Materials

| | |
|---|---|
| Polyester | Polyester is a category of polymers which contain the ester functional group in their main chain. Although there are many polyesters, the term 'polyester' as a specific material most commonly refers to polyethylene terephthalate (PET). Polyesters include naturally occurring chemicals, such as in the cutin of plant cuticles, as well as synthetics through step-growth polymerization such as polycarbonate and polybutyrate. |
| Condensation | Condensation is the change of the physical state of matter from gas phase into liquid phase, and is the reverse of vaporization. It can also be defined as the change in the state of water vapor to water/any liquid when in contact with any surface. When the transition happens from the gaseous phase into the solid phase directly, the change is called deposition. |
| Addition polymer | An addition polymer is a polymer which is formed by an addition reaction, where many monomers bond together via rearrangement of bonds without the loss of any atom or molecule. This is in contrast to a condensation polymer which is formed by a condensation reaction where a molecule, usually water, is lost during the formation. |
| Condensation polymer | Condensation polymers are any kind of polymers formed through a condensation reaction--where molecules join together--losing small molecules as by-products such as water or methanol, as opposed to addition polymers which involve the reaction of unsaturated monomers. Types of condensation polymers include polyamides, polyacetals and polyesters.

Condensation polymerization, a form of step-growth polymerization, is a process by which two molecules join together, resulting loss of small molecules which is often water. |
| Copolymer | A heteropolymer or copolymer is a polymer derived from two monomeric species, as opposed to a homopolymer where only one monomer is used. Copolymerization refers to methods used to chemically synthesize a copolymer.

Commercially relevant copolymers include ABS plastic, SBR, Nitrile rubber, styrene-acrylonitrile, styrene-isoprene-styrene (SIS) and ethylene-vinyl acetate. |
| Diamine | A diamine is a type of polyamine with exactly two amino groups. Diamines are mainly used as monomers to prepare polyamides, polyimides and polyureas. In terms of quantities produced, 1,6-diaminohexane, a precursor to Nylon 6-6, is most important, followed by ethylenediamine. |
| Polycarbonate | Polycarbonates, known by the trademarked names Lexan, Makrolon, Makroclear and others, are a particular group of thermoplastic polymers. They are easily worked, molded, and thermoformed. Because of these properties, polycarbonates find many applications. |

| | |
|---|---|
| Polypropylene | Polypropylene, also known as polypropene, is a thermoplastic polymer used in a wide variety of applications including packaging and labeling, textiles (e.g., ropes, thermal underwear and carpets), stationery, plastic parts and reusable containers of various types, laboratory equipment, loudspeakers, automotive components, and polymer banknotes. An addition polymer made from the monomer propylene, it is rugged and unusually resistant to many chemical solvents, bases and acids. <br><br> In 2008, the global market for polypropylene had a volume of 45.1 million metric tons, which led to a turnover of about $65 billion (~ €47.4 billion). |
| Polystyrene | Polystyrene is a synthetic aromatic polymer made from the monomer styrene, a liquid petrochemical. Polystyrene can be rigid or foamed. General purpose polystyrene is clear, hard and brittle. |
| Polyurethane | Polyurethane is a polymer composed of a chain of organic units joined by carbamate (urethane) links. While most polyurethanes are thermosetting polymers that do not melt when heated, thermoplastic polyurethanes are also available. <br><br> Polyurethane polymers are formed by reacting an isocyanate with a polyol. |
| Adipic acid | Adipic acid is the organic compound with the formula $(CH_2)_4(COOH)_2$. From an industrial perspective, it is the most important dicarboxylic acid: About 2.5 billion kilograms of this white crystalline powder are produced annually, mainly as a precursor for the production of nylon. Adipic acid otherwise rarely occurs in nature. |
| Low-density polyethylene | Low-density polyethylene is a thermoplastic made from the monomer ethylene. It was the first grade of polyethylene, produced in 1933 by Imperial Chemical Industries (ICI) using a high pressure process via free radical polymerization. Its manufacture employs the same method today. |
| High-density polyethylene | High-density polyethylene or polyethylene high-density (PEHD) is a polyethylene thermoplastic made from petroleum. Known for its large strength to density ratio, HDPE is commonly used in the production of plastic bottles, corrosion-resistant piping, geomembranes, and plastic lumber. HDPE is commonly recycled, and has the number '2' as its recycling symbol. |
| Crystallinity | Crystallinity refers to the degree of structural order in a solid. In a crystal, the atoms or molecules are arranged in a regular, periodic manner. The degree of crystallinity has a big influence on hardness, density, transparency and diffusion. |
| Macromolecule | A macromolecule is a very large molecule commonly created by polymerization of smaller subunits. In biochemistry, the term is applied to the four conventional biopolymers (nucleic acids, proteins, and carbohydrates), as well as non-polymeric molecules with large molecular mass such as lipids and macrocycles. |

# 12. Solids and Modern Materials

| | |
|---|---|
| Isoprene | Isoprene, or 2-methyl-1,3-butadiene, is a common organic compound with the formula $CH_2=CCH=CH_2$. It is a colorless volatile liquid. Isoprene is produced by many plants. |
| Double bond | A double bond in chemistry is a chemical bond between two chemical elements involving four bonding electrons instead of the usual two. The most common double bond, that is between two carbon atoms, can be found in alkenes. Many types of double bonds exist between two different elements. |
| Lipid | Lipids are a group of naturally occurring molecules that include fats, waxes, sterols, fat-soluble vitamins, monoglycerides, diglycerides, triglycerides, phospholipids, and others. The main biological functions of lipids include storing energy, signaling, and acting as structural components of cell membranes. Lipids have applications in the cosmetic and food industries as well as in nanotechnology. |
| Vulcanization | Vulcanization or vulcanisation is a chemical process for converting rubber or related polymers into more durable materials via the addition of sulfur or other equivalent 'curatives' or 'accelerators'. These additives modify the polymer by forming crosslinks (bridges) between individual polymer chains. Vulcanized materials are less sticky and have superior mechanical properties. |
| Quantum dot | A quantum dot is a nanocrystal made of semiconductor materials that are small enough to display quantum mechanical properties, specifically its excitons are confined in all three spatial dimensions. The electronic properties of these materials are intermediate between those of bulk semiconductors and of discrete molecules. Quantum dots were discovered in the early 1980s by Alexei Ekimov in a glass matrix and by Louis E. Brus in colloidal solutions. |
| Photoluminescence | Photoluminescence describes the phenomenon of light emission from any form of matter after the absorption of photons (electromagnetic radiation). It is one of many forms of luminescence (light emission) and is initiated by photoexcitation (excitation by photons), hence the prefix photo-. The excitation typically undergoes various relaxation processes and then photons are re-radiated. |
| Polyphosphate | Triphosphates are salts or esters of polymeric oxyanions formed from tetrahedral $PO_4$ structural units linked together by sharing oxygen atoms. When two corners are shared the polyphosphate may have a linear chain structure or a cyclic ring structure. In biology the polyphosphate esters AMP, ADP and ATP are involved in energy transfer. |
| Quantum well | A quantum well is a potential well with only discrete energy values.<br><br>One technology to create quantization is to confine particles, which were originally free to move in three dimensions, to two dimensions, forcing them to occupy a planar region. |

| | |
|---|---|
| Quantum wire | In condensed matter physics, a quantum wire is an electrically conducting wire in which quantum effects influence the transport properties. |
| Quantum | In physics, a quantum is the minimum amount of any physical entity involved in an interaction. Behind this, one finds the fundamental notion that a physical property may be 'quantized,' referred to as 'the hypothesis of quantization'. This means that the magnitude can take on only certain discrete values. |
| Carbon | Carbon fiber, alternatively graphite fiber, carbon graphite or CF, is a material consisting of fibers about 5-10 μm in diameter and composed mostly of carbon atoms. The carbon atoms are bonded together in crystals that are more or less aligned parallel to the long axis of the fiber. The crystal alignment gives the fiber high strength-to-volume ratio (making it strong for its size). |
| Carbon nanotube | Carbon nanotubes are allotropes of carbon with a cylindrical nanostructure. Nanotubes have been constructed with length-to-diameter ratio of up to 132,000,000:1, significantly larger than for any other material. These cylindrical carbon molecules have unusual properties, which are valuable for nanotechnology, electronics, optics and other fields of materials science and technology. |
| Fullerene | A fullerene is any molecule composed entirely of carbon, in the form of a hollow sphere, ellipsoid, tube, and many other shapes. Spherical fullerenes are also called buckyballs, and they resemble the balls used in football (soccer). Cylindrical ones are called carbon nanotubes or buckytubes. |
| Polyacetylene | Polyacetylene is an organic polymer with the repeating unit $(C_2H_2)_n$. The high electrical conductivity discovered for these polymers led to intense interest in the use of organic compounds in microelectronics (organic semiconductors). The discovery of the high conductivity of polyacetylene by Hideki Shirakawa, Alan J. Heeger, and Alan G MacDiarmid was recognized by the Nobel Prize in Chemistry in 2000. |
| Semimetal | A Semimetal is a material with a very small overlap between the bottom of the conduction band and the top of the valence band. According to electronic band theory, solids can be classified as insulators, semiconductors, semimetals, or metals. In insulators and semiconductors the filled valence band is separated from an empty conduction band by a band gap. |
| Rutile | Rutile is a mineral composed primarily of titanium dioxide, $TiO_2$. |
| | Rutile is the most common natural form of $TiO_2$. Two rarer polymorphs of $TiO_2$ are known:•Anatase (sometimes known by the obsolete name 'octahedrite'), a tetragonal mineral of pseudo-octahedral habit•Brookite, an orthorhombic mineral |
| | Rutile has among the highest refractive indices of any known mineral and also exhibits high dispersion. |

# 12. Solids and Modern Materials

| | |
|---|---|
| Clausthalite | Clausthalite is a lead selenide mineral, PbSe. It forms a solid solution series with galena PbS. |
| Cadmium telluride | Cadmium telluride is a crystalline compound formed from cadmium and tellurium. It is used as an infrared optical window and a solar cell material. It is usually sandwiched with cadmium sulfide to form a p-n junction photovoltaic solar cell. |
| Natural gas | Natural gas is a fossil fuel formed when layers of buried plants and animals are exposed to intense heat and pressure over thousands of years. The energy that the plants originally obtained from the sun is stored in the form of carbon in natural gas. Natural gas is a nonrenewable resource because it cannot be replenished on a human time frame. |
| Nomex | Nomex is a registered trademark for flame-resistant meta-aramid material developed in the early 1960s by DuPont and first marketed in 1967. |
| Polyacrylonitrile | Polyacrylonitrile is a synthetic, semicrystalline organic polymer resin, with the linear formula $(C_3H_3N)_n$. Though it is thermoplastic, it does not melt under normal conditions. It degrades before melting. |
| Spinel | Spinel is the magnesium aluminium member of the larger spinel group of minerals. It has the formula $MgAl_2O_4$. Balas ruby is an old name for a rose-tinted variety. |

1. _____ is one of the crystalline forms of carbon, alongside diamond, graphite, carbon nanotubes and fullerenes. In this material, carbon atoms are arranged in a regular hexagonal pattern. _____ can be described as a one-atom thick layer of the layered mineral graphite.

   a. Bamboo charcoal
   b. Benzotriyne
   c. Bilayer graphene
   d. Graphene

2. . _____ is a naturally occurring volcanic glass formed as an extrusive igneous rock.

   It is produced when felsic lava extruded from a volcano cools rapidly with minimum crystal growth. _____ is commonly found within the margins of rhyolitic lava flows known as _____ flows, where the chemical composition (high silica content) induces a high viscosity and polymerization degree of the lava.

   a. Batrachite

    b. Bisbee Blue

    c. Briolette

    d. Obsidian

3. A _____ is a nanocrystal made of semiconductor materials that are small enough to display quantum mechanical properties, specifically its excitons are confined in all three spatial dimensions. The electronic properties of these materials are intermediate between those of bulk semiconductors and of discrete molecules. _____s were discovered in the early 1980s by Alexei Ekimov in a glass matrix and by Louis E. Brus in colloidal solutions.

    a. Band bending

    b. Quantum dot

    c. Deep-level trap

    d. Depletion region

4. In physics, a _____ is the minimum amount of any physical entity involved in an interaction. Behind this, one finds the fundamental notion that a physical property may be 'quantized,' referred to as 'the hypothesis of quantization'. This means that the magnitude can take on only certain discrete values.

    a. 6-j symbol

    b. Quantum

    c. Bloch spectrum

    d. Bloch sphere

5. _____ or sulphur is a chemical element with symbol S and atomic number 16. It is an abundant, multivalent non-metal. Under normal conditions, _____ atoms form cyclic octatomic molecules with chemical formula $S_8$. Elemental _____ is a bright yellow crystalline solid when at room temperature.

    a. Baryte

    b. Sulfur

    c. Bertrandite

    d. Bismuthinite

**1.** d
**2.** d
**3.** b
**4.** b
**5.** b

---

## You can take the complete Chapter Practice Test

### for 12. Solids and Modern Materials
on all key terms, persons, places, and concepts.

## Online 99 Cents

## http://www.JustTheFacts101.com

**Use www.JustTheFacts101.com for all your study needs**

**including Facts101's online interactive problem solving labs in**

**chemistry, statistics, mathematics, and more.**

# 13. Properties of Solutions

CHAPTER OUTLINE: KEY TERMS, PEOPLE, PLACES, CONCEPTS

Aqueous solution

Solid solution

Solute

Solvent

Sterling silver

Entropy

Mole

Volume

Ideal gas

Effusion

Chloroform

Hydrogen

Sodium chloride

Solvation

Dissolution

Sodium

Ammonium nitrate

Exothermic

Ice pack

Magnesium sulfate

Hydrochloric acid

CHAPTER OUTLINE: KEY TERMS, PEOPLE, PLACES, CONCEPTS

| | Chemical reaction |
| --- | --- |
| | Crystallization |
| | Dynamic equilibrium |
| | Solubility |
| | Sodium acetate |
| | Acetone |
| | Alcohol |
| | Ascorbic acid |
| | Cyclohexane |
| | Carbon tetrachloride |
| | Ionic compound |
| | Concentration |
| | Density |
| | Arsenic |
| | Mole fraction |
| | Drinking water |
| | Lewis structure |
| | Antifreeze |
| | Ethylene glycol |
| | Osmotic pressure |
| | Toluene |

Vapor pressure

Colligative properties

Benzene

Distillation

Ideal solution

Component

Boiling-point elevation

Phase diagram

Freezing-point depression

Calcium chloride

Cellophane

Osmosis

Semipermeable membrane

Crenation

Hemolysis

Electrolyte

Colloid

Hemoglobin

Particle

Absorption

Adsorption

# 13. Properties of Solutions

CHAPTER OUTLINE: KEY TERMS, PEOPLE, PLACES, CONCEPTS

- Tyndall effect
- Sodium stearate
- Bile
- Mean free path
- Sickle
- Brownian motion
- Einstein
- Noble metal
- Ibuprofen
- Stearic acid
- Acetonitrile
- Brass
- Caffeine
- Carbon disulfide
- Radon
- Acetaldehyde
- Cyclopropane
- Ethylene oxide
- Fluorocarbon

# 13. Properties of Solutions

| | |
|---|---|
| Aqueous solution | An aqueous solution is a solution in which the solvent is water. It is usually shown in chemical equations by appending (aq) to the relevant formula. For example, a solution of ordinary table salt, or sodium chloride (NaCl), in water would be represented as NaCl(aq). |
| Solid solution | A solid solution is a solid-state solution of one or more solutes in a solvent. Such a mixture is considered a solution rather than a compound when the crystal structure of the solvent remains unchanged by addition of the solutes, and when the mixture remains in a single homogeneous phase. This often happens when the two elements (generally metals) involved are close together on the periodic table; conversely, a chemical compound is generally a result of the non-proximity of the two metals involved on the periodic table. |
| Solute | A solute is a substance that creates a solution when dissolved in a solvent. For example, when sugar (solute) is dissolved in water (solvent).Solute can change its physical state but solvent and solution are of same phase.e.g sugar is solid before getting dissolved in water, and after dissolution it changes its phase to a liquid.<br><br>Etymology: from Latin solutus, past participle of solvere, meaning to loosen. |
| Solvent | A solvent is a substance that dissolves a solute (a chemically different liquid, solid or gas), resulting in a solution. A solvent is usually a liquid but can also be a solid or a gas. The maximum quantity of solute that can dissolve in a specific volume of solvent varies with temperature. |
| Sterling silver | Sterling silver is an alloy of silver containing 92.5% by mass of silver and 7.5% by mass of other metals, usually copper. The sterling silver standard has a minimum millesimal fineness of 925.<br><br>Fine silver, for example 99.9% pure silver, is generally too soft for producing functional objects; therefore, the silver is usually alloyed with copper to give it strength while preserving the ductility and beauty of the precious metal. |
| Entropy | In thermodynamics, entropy is a measure of the number of specific ways in which a thermodynamic system may be arranged, often taken to be a measure of disorder, or a measure of progressing towards thermodynamic equilibrium. The entropy of an isolated system never decreases, because isolated systems spontaneously evolve towards thermodynamic equilibrium, which is the state of maximum entropy.<br><br>Entropy was originally defined for a thermodynamically reversible process<br><br>as $$\Delta S = \int \frac{dQ_{rev}}{T}$$<br><br>where the entropy is found from the uniform thermodynamic temperature of a closed system dividing an incremental reversible transfer of heat into that system . |

| | |
|---|---|
| Mole | Mole is a unit of measurement used in chemistry to express amounts of a chemical substance, defined as the amount of any substance that contains as many elementary entities (e.g., atoms, molecules, ions, electrons) as there are atoms in 12 grams of pure carbon-12, the isotope of carbon with relative atomic mass 12. This corresponds to the Avogadro constant, which has a value of $6.02214129(27) \times 10^{23}$ elementary entities of the substance. It is one of the base units in the International System of Units, and has the unit symbol mol and corresponds with the dimension symbol N. In honour of the unit, chemists often celebrate October 23 (a reference to the $10^{23}$ part of Avogadro's number) as 'Mole Day'.<br><br>The mole is widely used in chemistry instead of units of mass or volume as a convenient way to express amounts of reactants or of products of chemical reactions. |
| Volume | In thermodynamics, the volume of a system is an important extensive parameter for describing its thermodynamic state. The specific volume, an intensive property, is the system's volume per unit of mass. Volume is a function of state and is interdependent with other thermodynamic properties such as pressure and temperature. |
| Ideal gas | An ideal gas is a theoretical gas composed of a set of randomly moving, non-interacting point particles. The ideal gas concept is useful because it obeys the ideal gas law, a simplified equation of state, and is amenable to analysis under statistical mechanics.<br><br>At normal conditions such as standard temperature and pressure, most real gases behave qualitatively like an ideal gas. |
| Effusion | Effusion is the process in which a gas escapes through a small hole. This occurs if the diameter of the hole is considerably smaller than the mean free path of the molecules. According to Graham's law, the rate at which gases effuse (i.e., how many molecules pass through the hole per second) is dependent on their molecular weight. |
| Chloroform | Chloroform is an organic compound with formula $CHCl_3$. It is one of the four chloromethanes. The colorless, sweet-smelling, dense liquid is a trihalomethane, and is considered somewhat hazardous. |
| Hydrogen | Hydrogen is a chemical element with chemical symbol H and atomic number 1. With an atomic weight of 1.00794 u, hydrogen is the lightest element and its monatomic form (H) is the most abundant chemical substance, constituting roughly 75% of the Universe's baryonic mass. Non-remnant stars are mainly composed of hydrogen in its plasma state.<br><br>At standard temperature and pressure, hydrogen is a colorless, odorless, tasteless, non-toxic, nonmetallic, highly combustible diatomic gas with the molecular formula $H_2$. |

# 13. Properties of Solutions

| | |
|---|---|
| Sodium chloride | Sodium chloride, also known as salt, common salt, table salt or halite, is an ionic compound with the formula NaCl, representing equal proportions of sodium and chlorine. Sodium chloride is the salt most responsible for the salinity of the ocean and of the extracellular fluid of many multicellular organisms. As the major ingredient in edible salt, it is commonly used as a condiment and food preservative. |
| Solvation | Solvation, also sometimes called dissolution, is the process of attraction and association of molecules of a solvent with molecules or ions of a solute. As ions dissolve in a solvent they spread out and become surrounded by solvent molecules. |
| Dissolution | Dissolution is the process by which a solute forms a solution in a solvent. The solute, in the case of solids, has its crystalline structure disintegrated as separate ions, atoms, and molecules form. For liquids and gases, the molecules must be adaptable with those of the solvent for a solution to form. |
| Sodium | Sodium is a chemical element with the symbol Na and atomic number 11. It is a soft, silver-white, highly reactive metal and is a member of the alkali metals; its only stable isotope is $^{23}$Na. The free metal does not occur in nature, but instead must be prepared from its compounds; it was first isolated by Humphry Davy in 1807 by the electrolysis of sodium hydroxide. Sodium is the sixth most abundant element in the Earth's crust, and exists in numerous minerals such as feldspars, sodalite and rock salt. |
| Ammonium nitrate | The chemical compound ammonium nitrate, the nitrate of ammonia with the chemical formula $NH_4NO_3$, is a white crystalline solid at room temperature and standard pressure. It is commonly used in agriculture as a high-nitrogen fertilizer, and it has also been used as an oxidizing agent in explosives, including improvised explosive devices. It is the main component of ANFO, a popular explosive, which accounts for 80% explosives used in North America. It is used in instant cold packs, as hydrating the salt is an endothermic process. |
| Exothermic | In thermodynamics, the term exothermic describes a process or reaction that releases energy from the system, usually in the form of heat, but also in a form of light (e.g. a spark, flame, or flash), electricity (e.g. a battery), or sound (e.g. explosion heard when burning hydrogen). Its etymology stems from the prefix exo (derived from the Greek word ???, exo, 'outside') and the Greek word thermasi (meaning 'to heat'). The term exothermic was first coined by Marcellin Berthelot. |
| Ice pack | An ice pack or gel pack is a plastic sac of ice, or of refrigerant gel or liquid. Both the ice pack and the non-toxic gel (which is mostly water) can absorb a considerable amount of heat due to the high enthalpy of fusion of water. These packs are commonly used to keep food cool in coolers for consumption later in the day; or as a cold compress to alleviate the pain of minor injuries; or in insulated shipping containers to keep products cool during transport. |
| Magnesium sulfate | Magnesium sulfate is an inorganic salt (chemical compound) containing magnesium, sulfur and oxygen, with the formula $MgSO_4$. |

| | It is often encountered as the heptahydrate sulfate mineral epsomite ($MgSO_4 \cdot 7H_2O$), commonly called Epsom salt, taking its name from a bitter saline spring in Epsom in Surrey, England, where the salt was produced from the springs that arise where the porous chalk of the North Downs meets non-porous London clay. Epsom salt occurs naturally as a pure mineral. |
|---|---|
| Hydrochloric acid | Hydrochloric acid is a clear, colorless, highly pungent solution of hydrogen chloride in water. It is a highly corrosive, strong mineral acid with many industrial uses. Hydrochloric acid is found naturally in gastric acid. |
| Chemical reaction | A chemical reaction is a process that leads to the transformation of one set of chemical substances to another. Classically, chemical reactions encompass changes that only involve the positions of electrons in the forming and breaking of chemical bonds between atoms, with no change to the nuclei (no change to the elements present), and can often be described by a chemical equation. Nuclear chemistry is a sub-discipline of chemistry that involves the chemical reactions of unstable and radioactive elements where both electronic and nuclear changes may both occur. |
| Crystallization | Crystallization is the process of formation of solid crystals precipitating from a solution, melt or more rarely deposited directly from a gas. Crystallization is also a chemical solid-liquid separation technique, in which mass transfer of a solute from the liquid solution to a pure solid crystalline phase occurs. In chemical engineering crystallization occurs in a crystallizer. |
| Dynamic equilibrium | A dynamic equilibrium exists once a reversible reaction ceases to change its ratio of reactants/products, but substances move between the chemicals at an equal rate, meaning there is no net change. It is a particular example of a system in a steady state. In thermodynamics a closed system is in thermodynamic equilibrium when reactions occur at such rates that the composition of the mixture does not change with time. |
| Solubility | Solubility is the property of a solid, liquid, or gaseous chemical substance called solute to dissolve in a solid, liquid, or gaseous solvent to form a homogeneous solution of the solute in the solvent. The solubility of a substance fundamentally depends on the physical and chemical properties of the solute and solvent as well as on temperature, pressure and the pH of the solution. The extent of the solubility of a substance in a specific solvent is measured as the saturation concentration, where adding more solute does not increase the concentration of the solution and begin to precipitate the excess amount of solute. |
| Sodium acetate | Sodium acetate, $CH_3COONa$, also abbreviated NaOAc, also sodium ethanoate, is the sodium salt of acetic acid. This colourless salt has a wide range of uses. |
| Acetone | Acetone is the organic compound with the formula $(CH_3)_2CO$. It is a colorless, mobile, flammable liquid, and is the simplest ketone. |

# 13. Properties of Solutions

| | |
|---|---|
| | Acetone is miscible with water and serves as an important solvent in its own right, typically for cleaning purposes in the laboratory. About 6.7 million tonnes were produced worldwide in 2010, mainly for use as a solvent and production of methyl methacrylate and bisphenol A. It is a common building block in organic chemistry. |
| Alcohol | In chemistry, an alcohol is an organic compound in which the hydroxyl functional group is bound to a carbon atom. In particular, this carbon center should be saturated, having single bonds to three other atoms.<br><br>An important class of alcohols are the simple acyclic alcohols, the general formula for which is $C_nH_{2n+1}OH$. Of those, ethanol ($C_2H_5OH$) is the type of alcohol found in alcoholic beverages, and in common speech the word alcohol refers specifically to ethanol. |
| Ascorbic acid | Ascorbic acid is a naturally occurring organic compound with antioxidant properties. It is a white solid, but impure samples can appear yellowish. It dissolves well in water to give mildly acidic solutions. |
| Cyclohexane | Cyclohexane is a cycloalkane with the molecular formula $C_6H_{12}$. Cyclohexane is used as a nonpolar solvent for the chemical industry, and also as a raw material for the industrial production of adipic acid and caprolactam, both of which being intermediates used in the production of nylon. On an industrial scale, cyclohexane is produced by reacting benzene with hydrogen. |
| Carbon tetrachloride | Carbon tetrachloride, also known by many other names, is the organic compound with the formula $CCl_4$. It was formerly widely used in fire extinguishers, as a precursor to refrigerants, and as a cleaning agent. It is a colourless liquid with a 'sweet' smell that can be detected at low levels. |
| Ionic compound | In chemistry, an ionic compound is a chemical compound in which ions are held together in a lattice structure by ionic bonds. Usually, the positively charged portion consists of metal cations and the negatively charged portion is an anion or polyatomic ion. Ions in ionic compounds are held together by the electrostatic forces between oppositely charged bodies. |
| Concentration | In chemistry, concentration is the abundance of a constituent divided by the total volume of a mixture. Several types of mathematical description can be distinguished: mass concentration, molar concentration, number concentration, and volume concentration. The term concentration can be applied to any kind of chemical mixture, but most frequently it refers to solutes and solvents in solutions. |
| Density | The density, or more precisely, the volumetric mass density, of a substance is its mass per unit volume. The symbol most often used for density is ? (the lower case Greek letter rho).<br><br>Mathematically, density is defined as mass divided by volume: $\rho = \dfrac{m}{V}$, |

| Arsenic | Arsenic is a chemical element with symbol As and atomic number 33. Arsenic occurs in many minerals, usually in conjunction with sulfur and metals, and also as a pure elemental crystal. It was first documented by Albertus Magnus in 1250. Arsenic is a metalloid. It can exist in various allotropes, although only the gray form has important use in industry. |
|---|---|
| Mole fraction | In chemistry, the mole fraction $x_i$ is defined as the amount of a constituent $n_i$ divided by the total amount of all constituents in a mixture $n_{tot}$ : $$x_i = \frac{n_i}{n_{tot}}$$ The sum of all the mole fractions is equal to 1: $$\sum_{i=1}^{N} n_i = n_{tot}; \quad \sum_{i=1}^{N} x_i = 1$$ The mole fraction is also called the amount fraction. It is identical to the number fraction, which is defined as the number of molecules of a constituent $N_i$ divided by the total number of all molecules $N_{tot}$. It is one way of expressing the composition of a mixture with a dimensionless quantity (mass fraction is another). |
| Drinking water | Drinking water or potable water is water safe enough to be consumed by humans or used with low risk of immediate or long term harm. In most developed countries, the water supplied to households, commerce and industry meets drinking water standards, even though only a very small proportion is actually consumed or used in food preparation. Typical uses (for other than potable purposes) include toilet flushing, washing and landscape irrigation. |
| Lewis structure | Lewis structures are diagrams that show the bonding between atoms of a molecule and the lone pairs of electrons that may exist in the molecule. A Lewis structure can be drawn for any covalently bonded molecule, as well as coordination compounds. The Lewis structure was named after Gilbert N |
| Antifreeze | An antifreeze is a chemical additive which lowers the freezing point of a water-based liquid. An antifreeze mixture is used to achieve freezing-point depression for cold environments and also achieves boiling-point elevation ('anti-boil') to allow higher coolant temperature. Freezing and boiling points are colligative properties of a solution, which depend on the concentration of the dissolved substance. |
| Ethylene glycol | Ethylene glycol is an organic compound primarily used as a raw material in the manufacture of polyester fibers and fabric industry, and polyethylene terephthalate resins (PET) used in bottling. A small percent is also used in industrial applications like antifreeze formulations and other industrial products. It is an odorless, colorless, syrupy, sweet-tasting liquid. |

# 13. Properties of Solutions

| | |
|---|---|
| Osmotic pressure | Osmotic pressure is the pressure which needs to be applied to a solution to prevent the inward flow of water across a semipermeable membrane. It is also defined as the minimum pressure needed to nullify osmosis.<br><br>The phenomenon of osmotic pressure arises from the tendency of a pure solvent to move through a semi-permeable membrane and into a solution containing a solute to which the membrane is impermeable. |
| Toluene | Toluene, formerly known as toluol, is a clear, water-insoluble liquid with the typical smell of paint thinners. It is a mono-substituted benzene derivative, i.e., one in which a single hydrogen atom from a group of six atoms from the benzene molecule has been replaced by a univalent group, in this case $CH_3$. As such, its IUPAC systematic name is methylbenzene. |
| Vapor pressure | Vapor pressure or equilibrium vapor pressure is the pressure exerted by a vapor in thermodynamic equilibrium with its condensed phases at a given temperature in a closed system. The equilibrium vapor pressure is an indication of a liquid's evaporation rate. It relates to the tendency of particles to escape from the liquid (or a solid). |
| Colligative properties | In chemistry, colligative properties are properties of solutions that depend upon the ratio of the number of solute particles to the number of solvent molecules in a solution, and not on the type of chemical species present. This number ratio can be related to the various units for concentration of solutions. Here we shall only consider those properties which result because of the dissolution of nonvolatile solute in a volatile liquid solvent. |
| Benzene | Benzene is an organic chemical compound with the molecular formula $C_6H_6$. Its molecule is composed of 6 carbon atoms joined in a ring, with 1 hydrogen atom attached to each carbon atom. Because its molecules contain only carbon and hydrogen atoms, benzene is classed as a hydrocarbon. |
| Distillation | Distillation is a method of separating mixtures based on differences in volatility of components in a boiling liquid mixture. Distillation is a unit operation, or a physical separation process, and not a chemical reaction.<br><br>Commercially, distillation has a number of applications. |
| Ideal solution | In chemistry, an ideal solution or ideal mixture is a solution with thermodynamic properties analogous to those of a mixture of ideal gases. The enthalpy of solution (or 'enthalpy of mixing') is zero as is the volume change on mixing; the closer to zero the enthalpy of solution is, the more 'ideal' the behavior of the solution becomes. The vapour pressure of the solution obeys Raoult's law, and the activity coefficients (which measure deviation from ideality) are equal to one. |
| Component | In thermodynamics, a component is a chemically-independent constituent of a system. |

CHAPTER HIGHLIGHTS & NOTES: KEY TERMS, PEOPLE, PLACES, CONCEPTS

| | |
|---|---|
| | The number of components represents the minimum number of independent species necessary to define the composition of all phases of the system.

Calculating the number of components in a system is necessary, for example, when applying Gibbs' phase rule in determination of the number of degrees of freedom of a system. |
| Boiling-point elevation | Boiling-point elevation describes the phenomenon that the boiling point of a liquid will be higher when another compound is added, meaning that a solution has a higher boiling point than a pure solvent. This happens whenever a non-volatile solute, such as a salt, is added to a pure solvent, such as water. The boiling point can be measured accurately using an ebullioscope. |
| Phase diagram | A phase diagram in physical chemistry, engineering, mineralogy, and materials science is a type of chart used to show conditions at which thermodynamically distinct phases can occur at equilibrium. In mathematics and physics, 'phase diagram' is used with a different meaning: a synonym for a phase space. |
| Freezing-point depression | Freezing-point depression describes the process in which adding a solute to a solvent decreases the freezing point of the solvent.

Examples include salt in water, alcohol in water, or the mixing of two solids such as impurities in a finely powdered drug. In such cases, the added compound is the solute, and the original solid can be thought of as the solvent. |
| Calcium chloride | Calcium chloride, $CaCl_2$, is a salt of calcium and chlorine. It behaves as a typical ionic halide, and is solid at room temperature. Common applications include brine for refrigeration plants, ice and dust control on roads, and desiccation. |
| Cellophane | Cellophane is a thin, transparent sheet made of regenerated cellulose. Its low permeability to air, oils, greases, bacteria and water makes it useful for food packaging. Cellophane is in many countries a registered trade mark of Innovia Films Ltd based in Wigton, Cumbria, United Kingdom. |
| Osmosis | Osmosis is the spontaneous net movement of solvent molecules through a partially permeable membrane into a region of higher solute concentration, in the direction that tends to equalize the solute concentrations on the two sides. It may also be used to describe a physical process in which any solvent moves, without input of energy, across a semipermeable membrane (permeable to the solvent, but not the solute) separating two solutions of different concentrations. Although osmosis does not require input of energy, it does use kinetic energy and can be made to do work. |
| Semipermeable membrane | A semipermeable membrane, also termed a selectively permeable membrane, a partially permeable membrane or a differentially permeable membrane, is a membrane that will allow certain molecules or ions to pass through it by diffusion and occasionally specialized 'facilitated diffusion'. Prof. |

# 13. Properties of Solutions

| | |
|---|---|
| Crenation | Crenation in botany and zoology, describes an object's shape, especially a leaf or shell, as being round-toothed or having a scalloped edge.<br><br>The descriptor can apply to objects of different types, including cells, where one mechanism of crenation is the contraction of a cell after exposure to a hypertonic solution, due to the loss of water through osmosis. In a hypertonic environment, the cell has a lower concentration of solutes than the surrounding extracellular fluid, and water diffuses out of the cell by osmosis, causing the cytoplasm to decrease in volume. |
| Hemolysis | Hemolysis is the breakdown of red blood cells. The ability of bacterial colonies to induce hemolysis when grown on blood agar is used to classify certain microorganisms. This is particularly useful in classifying streptococcal species. |
| Electrolyte | An electrolyte is a compound that ionizes when dissolved in suitable ionizing solvents such as water. This includes most soluble salts, acids, and bases. Some gases, such as hydrogen chloride, under conditions of high temperature or low pressure can also function as electrolytes. |
| Colloid | A colloid is a substance microscopically dispersed throughout another substance.<br><br>The dispersed-phase particles have a diameter of between approximately 1 and 1000 nanometers. Such particles are normally invisible in an optical microscope, though their presence can be confirmed with the use of an ultramicroscope or an electron microscope. |
| Hemoglobin | Hemoglobin; also spelled haemoglobin and abbreviated Hb or Hgb, is the iron-containing oxygen-transport metalloprotein in the red blood cells of all vertebrates as well as the tissues of some invertebrates. Hemoglobin in the blood carries oxygen from the respiratory organs (lungs or gills) to the rest of the body (i.e. the tissues) where it releases the oxygen to burn nutrients to provide energy to power the functions of the organism, and collects the resultant carbon dioxide to bring it back to the respiratory organs to be dispensed from the organism.<br><br>In mammals, the protein makes up about 97% of the red blood cells' dry content (by weight), and around 35% of the total content (including water). |
| Particle | In the physical sciences, a particle is a small localized object to which can be ascribed several physical or chemical properties such as volume or mass. The word is rather general in meaning, and is refined as needed by various scientific fields. Something that is composed of particles may be referred to as particulate, although this term is generally used to refer to a suspension of unconnected particles, rather than a connected particle aggregation. |
| Absorption | In chemistry, absorption is a physical or chemical phenomenon or a process in which atoms, molecules, or ions enter some bulk phase - gas, liquid, or solid material. |

| | |
|---|---|
| | This is a different process from adsorption, since molecules undergoing absorption are taken up by the volume, not by the surface (as in the case for adsorption). A more general term is sorption, which covers absorption, adsorption, and ion exchange. |
| Adsorption | Adsorption is the adhesion of atoms, ions, or molecules from a gas, liquid, or dissolved solid to a surface. This process creates a film of the adsorbate on the surface of the adsorbent. This process differs from absorption, in which a fluid (the absorbate) permeates or is dissolved by a liquid or solid (the absorbent). |
| Tyndall effect | The Tyndall effect, also known as Tyndall scattering, is light scattering by particles in a colloid or particles in a fine suspension. It is named after the 19th century physicist John Tyndall. It is similar to Rayleigh scattering, in that the intensity of the scattered light depends on the fourth power of the frequency, so blue light is scattered much more strongly than red light. |
| Sodium stearate | Sodium stearate is the sodium salt of stearic acid. This white solid is the most common soap. It is found in many types of solid deodorants, rubbers, latex paints, and inks. |
| Bile | Bile or gall is a bitter-tasting, dark green to yellowish brown fluid, produced by the liver of most vertebrates, that aids the digestion of lipids in the small intestine. In many species, bile is stored in the gallbladder and, when the organism eats, is discharged into the duodenum. Bile is 85% water, 10% bile salts, 3% mucus and pigments, 1% fats, and 0.7% inorganic salts. |
| Mean free path | In physics, the mean free path is the average distance travelled by a moving particle between successive impacts (collisions), which modify its direction or energy or other particle properties. |
| Sickle | A sickle is a hand-held agricultural tool with a variously curved blade typically used for harvesting grain crops or cutting succulent forage chiefly for feeding livestock . <br><br> The diversity of sickles that have been used around the globe is staggering. Between the dawn of the Iron Age and present, hundreds of region-specific variants of this basic forage-cutting tool were forged of iron, later steel. |
| Brownian motion | Brownian motion or pedesis is the presumably random moving of particles suspended in a fluid (a liquid or a gas) resulting from their collision with the quick atoms or molecules in the gas or liquid. The term 'Brownian motion' can also refer to the mathematical model used to describe such random movements, which is often called a particle theory. <br><br> In 1827, the botanist Robert Brown, looking through a microscope at particles found in pollen grains in water, noted that the particles moved through the water but was not able to determine the mechanisms that caused this motion. |
| Einstein | An einstein is a unit defined as the energy in one mole of photons. Because energy is inversely proportional to wavelength, the unit is frequency dependent. |

# 13. Properties of Solutions

| | |
|---|---|
| Noble metal | The noble metals are metals that are resistant to corrosion and oxidation in moist air, unlike most base metals. They tend to be precious, often due to their rarity in the Earth's crust. The noble metals are most commonly considered to be ruthenium, rhodium, palladium, silver, osmium, iridium, platinum, and gold. |
| Ibuprofen | Ibuprofen is a nonsteroidal anti-inflammatory drug (NSAID) used for pain relief, fever reduction, and for reducing swelling.<br><br>Ibuprofen has an antiplatelet effect, though relatively mild and somewhat short-lived compared with aspirin or prescription antiplatelet drugs. In general, ibuprofen also has a vasodilation effect. |
| Stearic acid | Stearic acid is the saturated fatty acid with an 18-carbon chain and has the IUPAC name octadecanoic acid. It is a waxy solid, and its chemical formula is $CH_3(CH_2)_{16}CO_2H$. Its name comes from the Greek word st?a? 'stéar', which means tallow. The salts and esters of stearic acid are called stearates. |
| Acetonitrile | Acetonitrile is the chemical compound with the formula CH3CN. This colourless liquid is the simplest organic nitrile (hydrogen cyanide is a simpler nitrile, but the cyanide anion is not classed as organic). It is produced mainly as a byproduct of acrylonitrile manufacture. |
| Brass | Brass is an alloy made of copper and zinc; the proportions of zinc and copper can be varied to create a range of brasses with varying properties.<br><br>By comparison, bronze is principally an alloy of copper and tin. Bronze does not necessarily contain tin, and a variety of alloys of copper, including alloys with arsenic, phosphorus, aluminium, manganese, and silicon, are commonly termed 'bronze'. |
| Caffeine | Caffeine is a bitter, white crystalline xanthine alkaloid and a stimulant drug. Caffeine is found in varying quantities in the seeds, leaves, and fruit of some plants, where it acts as a natural pesticide that paralyzes and kills certain insects feeding on the plants, as well as enhancing the reward memory of pollinators. It is most commonly consumed by humans in infusions extracted from the seed of the coffee plant and the leaves of the tea bush, as well as from various foods and drinks containing products derived from the kola nut. |
| Carbon disulfide | Carbon disulfide is a colorless volatile liquid with the formula $CS_2$. The compound is used frequently as a building block in organic chemistry as well as an industrial and chemical non-polar solvent. It has an 'ether-like' odor, but commercial samples are typically contaminated with foul-smelling impurities, such as carbonyl sulfide. |
| Radon | Radon is a chemical element with symbol Rn and atomic number 86. It is a radioactive, colorless, odorless, tasteless noble gas, occurring naturally as an indirect decay product of uranium or thorium. Its most stable isotope, $^{222}Rn$, has a half-life of 3.8 days. |

| Acetaldehyde | Acetaldehyde is an organic chemical compound with the formula $CH_3CHO$, sometimes abbreviated by chemists as MeCHO (Me = methyl). It is one of the most important aldehydes, occurring widely in nature and being produced on a large scale industrially. Acetaldehyde occurs naturally in coffee, bread, and ripe fruit, and is produced by plants. |
|---|---|
| Cyclopropane | Cyclopropane is a cycloalkane molecule with the molecular formula $C_3H_6$, consisting of three carbon atoms linked to each other to form a ring, with each carbon atom bearing two hydrogen atoms resulting in $D_{3h}$ molecular symmetry. Cyclopropane and propene have the same molecular formula but have different structures, making them structural isomers.<br><br>Cyclopropane is an anaesthetic when inhaled. |
| Ethylene oxide | Ethylene oxide, also called oxirane, is the organic compound with the formula $C2H4O$. It is a cyclic ether. (A cyclic ether consists of an alkane with an oxygen atom bonded to two carbon atoms of the alkane, forming a ring). |
| Fluorocarbon | Fluorocarbons, sometimes referred to as perfluorocarbons or PFCs, are organofluorine compounds that contain only carbon and fluorine bonded together in strong carbon-fluorine bonds. Fluoroalkanes that contain only single bonds are more chemically and thermally stable than alkanes. However, fluorocarbons with double bonds (fluoroalkenes) and especially triple bonds (fluoroalkynes) are more reactive than their corresponding hydrocarbons. |

1. A _____ exists once a reversible reaction ceases to change its ratio of reactants/products, but substances move between the chemicals at an equal rate, meaning there is no net change. It is a particular example of a system in a steady state. In thermodynamics a closed system is in thermo_____ when reactions occur at such rates that the composition of the mixture does not change with time.

   a. Dynamic equilibrium
   b. Binding selectivity
   c. Bromley equation
   d. Buffer solution

2. . _____ is the pressure which needs to be applied to a solution to prevent the inward flow of water across a semipermeable membrane. It is also defined as the minimum pressure needed to nullify osmosis.

# 13. Properties of Solutions

The phenomenon of _____ arises from the tendency of a pure solvent to move through a semi-permeable membrane and into a solution containing a solute to which the membrane is impermeable.

a. Bunsen solubility coefficient
b. Osmotic pressure
c. Condosity
d. Crenation

3. _____ is the process by which a solute forms a solution in a solvent. The solute, in the case of solids, has its crystalline structure disintegrated as separate ions, atoms, and molecules form. For liquids and gases, the molecules must be adaptable with those of the solvent for a solution to form.

a. Bioaerosol
b. Bjerrum length
c. Dissolution
d. Bolaamphiphile

4. In chemistry, an _____ is a chemical compound in which ions are held together in a lattice structure by ionic bonds. Usually, the positively charged portion consists of metal cations and the negatively charged portion is an anion or polyatomic ion. Ions in _____s are held together by the electrostatic forces between oppositely charged bodies.

a. Ionic compound
b. Dication
c. Distonic ion
d. Bioasphalt

5. In chemistry, an _____ or ideal mixture is a solution with thermodynamic properties analogous to those of a mixture of ideal gases. The enthalpy of solution (or 'enthalpy of mixing') is zero as is the volume change on mixing; the closer to zero the enthalpy of solution is, the more 'ideal' the behavior of the solution becomes. The vapour pressure of the solution obeys Raoult's law, and the activity coefficients (which measure deviation from ideality) are equal to one.

a. Bunsen solubility coefficient
b. Concentrate
c. Ideal solution
d. Crenation

**1.** a
**2.** b
**3.** c
**4.** a
**5.** c

## You can take the complete Chapter Practice Test

### for 13. Properties of Solutions
on all key terms, persons, places, and concepts.

## Online 99 Cents

## http://www.JustTheFacts101.com

Use www.JustTheFacts101.com for all your study needs

including Facts101's online interactive problem solving labs in

chemistry, statistics, mathematics, and more.

# 14. Chemical Kinetics

CHAPTER OUTLINE: KEY TERMS, PEOPLE, PLACES, CONCEPTS

_____ | Chemical kinetics _____

_____ | Reaction rate _____

_____ | Reaction mechanism _____

_____ | Concentration _____

_____ | Catalysis _____

_____ | Hydrochloric acid _____

_____ | Stoichiometry _____

_____ | Spectroscopy _____

_____ | Rate constant _____

_____ | Acetonitrile _____

_____ | Nitrogen _____

_____ | Nitrogen dioxide _____

_____ | Decomposition _____

_____ | Half-life _____

_____ | Chlorofluorocarbon _____

_____ | Environment _____

_____ | Ozone _____

_____ | Ozone layer _____

_____ | Bromide _____

_____ | Molecule _____

_____ | Chemiluminescence _____

Activation energy

Activation

Activated complex

Transition state

Isomerization

Kinetic energy

Elementary reaction

Molecularity

Rate-determining step

Nitric oxide

Nitrous oxide

Bromide ion

Homogeneous catalysis

Hydrogen peroxide

Homogeneous

Absorption

Adsorption

Heterogeneous catalysis

Enzyme

Ethyl group

Air pollution

# 14. Chemical Kinetics

CHAPTER OUTLINE: KEY TERMS, PEOPLE, PLACES, CONCEPTS

_____ | Carbon monoxide

_____ | Catalase

_____ | Catalytic converter

_____ | Hydrogen

_____ | Noble metal

_____ | Unburned hydrocarbon

_____ | Active site

_____ | Enzyme inhibitor

_____ | Substrate

_____ | Turnover number

_____ | Efficiency

_____ | Nitrogen cycle

_____ | Nitrogenase

_____ | Formic acid

_____ | Carbonic anhydrase

_____ | Americium

_____ | Hydrogen sulfide

_____ | Urea

_____ | Cellulose

_____ | Cyclopentadiene

_____ | Dicyclopentadiene

# 14. Chemical Kinetics

| | Dinitrogen pentoxide |
|---|---|
| | Platinum |

| Chemical kinetics | Chemical kinetics, also known as reaction kinetics, is the study of rates of chemical processes. Chemical kinetics includes investigations of how different experimental conditions can influence the speed of a chemical reaction and yield information about the reaction's mechanism and transition states, as well as the construction of mathematical models that can describe the characteristics of a chemical reaction. In 1864, Peter Waage and Cato Guldberg pioneered the development of chemical kinetics by formulating the law of mass action, which states that the speed of a chemical reaction is proportional to the quantity of the reacting substances. |
|---|---|
| Reaction rate | The reaction rate or speed of reaction for a reactant or product in a particular reaction is intuitively defined as how fast or slow a reaction takes place. For example, the oxidative rusting of iron under Earth's atmosphere is a slow reaction that can take many years, but the combustion of cellulose in a fire is a reaction that takes place in fractions of a second.<br><br>Chemical kinetics is the part of physical chemistry that studies reaction rates. |
| Reaction mechanism | In chemistry, a reaction mechanism is the step by step sequence of elementary reactions by which overall chemical change occurs.<br><br>Although only the net chemical change is directly observable for most chemical reactions, experiments can often be designed that suggest the possible sequence of steps in a reaction mechanism. Recently, electrospray ionization mass spectrometry has been used to corroborate the mechanism of several organic reaction proposals. |
| Concentration | In chemistry, concentration is the abundance of a constituent divided by the total volume of a mixture. Several types of mathematical description can be distinguished: mass concentration, molar concentration, number concentration, and volume concentration. The term concentration can be applied to any kind of chemical mixture, but most frequently it refers to solutes and solvents in solutions. |
| Catalysis | Catalysis is the increase rate of a chemical reaction due to the participation of a substance called a catalyst. Unlike other reagents in the chemical reaction, a catalyst is not consumed. |

| | |
|---|---|
| Hydrochloric acid | Hydrochloric acid is a clear, colorless, highly pungent solution of hydrogen chloride in water. It is a highly corrosive, strong mineral acid with many industrial uses. Hydrochloric acid is found naturally in gastric acid. |
| Stoichiometry | Stoichiometry is a branch of chemistry that deals with the relative quantities of reactants and products in chemical reactions. In a balanced chemical reaction, the relations among quantities of reactants and products typically form a ratio of positive integers. For example, in a reaction that forms ammonia ($NH_3$), exactly one molecule of nitrogen gas ($N_2$) reacts with three molecules of hydrogen gas ($H_2$) to produce two molecules of $NH_3$:N2 + 3H2 ? 2NH3 |
| | This particular kind of stoichiometry - describing the quantitative relationships among substances as they participate in chemical reactions - is known as reaction stoichiometry. |
| Spectroscopy | Spectroscopy is the study of the interaction between matter and radiated energy. Historically, spectroscopy originated through the study of visible light dispersed according to its wavelength, e.g., by a prism. Later the concept was expanded greatly to comprise any interaction with radiative energy as a function of its wavelength or frequency. |
| Rate constant | In chemical kinetics a reaction rate constant, k or $\lambda$, quantifies the rate of a chemical reaction. |
| | For a reaction between reactants A and B to form product C $aA + bB \rightarrow cC$ |
| | the reaction rate is often found to have the form: $r = k(T)[A]^m [B]^n$ |
| | Here k(T) is the reaction rate constant that depends on temperature. [A] and [B] are the concentrations of substance A in moles per volume of solution assuming the reaction is taking place throughout the volume of the solution. |
| Acetonitrile | Acetonitrile is the chemical compound with the formula CH3CN. This colourless liquid is the simplest organic nitrile (hydrogen cyanide is a simpler nitrile, but the cyanide anion is not classed as organic). It is produced mainly as a byproduct of acrylonitrile manufacture. |
| Nitrogen | Nitrogen, symbol N, is the chemical element of atomic number 7. At room temperature, it is a gas of diatomic molecules and is colorless and odorless. Nitrogen is a common element in the universe, estimated at about seventh in total abundance in our galaxy and the Solar System. On Earth, the element is primarily found as the free element; it forms about 80% of the Earth's atmosphere. |
| Nitrogen dioxide | Nitrogen dioxide is the chemical compound with the formula NO2. It is one of several nitrogen oxides. NO |

# 14. Chemical Kinetics

| | |
|---|---|
| Decomposition | Decomposition is the process by which organic substances are broken down into simpler forms of matter. The process is essential for recycling the finite matter that occupies physical space in the biome. Bodies of living organisms begin to decompose shortly after death. |
| Half-life | Half-life is the amount of time required for a quantity to fall to half its value as measured at the beginning of the time period. While the term 'half-life' can be used to describe any quantity which follows an exponential decay, it is most often used within the context of nuclear physics and nuclear chemistry--that is, the time required, probabilistically, for half of the unstable, radioactive atoms in a sample to undergo radioactive decay.<br><br>The original term, dating to Ernest Rutherford's discovery of the principle in 1907, was 'half-life period', which was shortened to 'half-life' in the early 1950s. |
| Chlorofluorocarbon | A chlorofluorocarbon is an organic compound that contains only carbon, chlorine, and fluorine, produced as a volatile derivative of methane and ethane. They are also commonly known by the DuPont brand name Freon. The most common representative is dichlorodifluoromethane (R-12 or Freon-12). |
| Environment | In science and engineering, a system is the part of the universe that is being studied, while the environment is the remainder of the universe that lies outside the boundaries of the system. It is also known as the surroundings, and in thermodynamics, as the reservoir. Depending on the type of system, it may interact with the environment by exchanging mass, energy (including heat and work), linear momentum, angular momentum, electric charge, or other conserved properties. |
| Ozone | Ozone, or trioxygen, is an inorganic compound with the chemical formula $O3(\mu\text{-}O)$ (also written $[O(\mu\text{-}O)O]$ or $O3$). It is a pale blue gas with a distinctively pungent smell. It is an allotrope of oxygen that is much less stable than the diatomic allotrope $O2$, breaking down in the lower atmosphere to normal dioxygen. |
| Ozone layer | The ozone layer is a layer in Earth's atmosphere that absorbs most of the Sun's UV radiation. It contains relatively high concentrations of ozone ($O_3$), although it is still very small with regard to ordinary oxygen, and is less than ten parts per million, the average ozone concentration in Earth's atmosphere being only about 0.6 parts per million. The ozone layer is mainly found in the lower portion of the stratosphere from approximately 20 to 30 kilometres (12 to 19 mi) above Earth, though the thickness varies seasonally and geographically. |
| Bromide | A bromide is a chemical compound containing a bromide ion or ligand. This is a bromine atom with an ionic charge of -1 ($Br^-$); for example, in caesium bromide, caesium cations ($Cs^+$) are electrically attracted to bromide anions ($Br^-$) to form the electrically neutral ionic compound CsBr. The term 'bromide' can also refer to a bromine atom with an oxidation number of -1 in covalent compounds such as sulfur dibromide. |

| | |
|---|---|
| Molecule | A molecule is an electrically neutral group of two or more atoms held together by chemical bonds. Molecules are distinguished from ions by their lack of electrical charge. However, in quantum physics, organic chemistry, and biochemistry, the term molecule is often used less strictly, also being applied to polyatomic ions. |
| Chemiluminescence | Chemiluminescence is the emission of light (luminescence), as the result of a chemical reaction. There may also be limited emission of heat. Given reactants A and B, with an excited intermediate ?,[A] + [B] ? [?] ? [Products] + light <br><br> For example, if [A] is luminol and [B] is hydrogen peroxide in the presence of a suitable catalyst we have:luminol + $H_2O_2$ ? 3-APA[?] ? 3-APA + light <br><br> where:•where 3-APA is 3-aminophthalate•3-APA[?] is the vibronic excited state fluorescing as it decays to a lower energy level. <br><br> The decay of this excited state[?] to a lower energy level causes light emission. |
| Activation energy | In chemistry, activation energy is a term introduced in 1889 by the Swedish scientist Svante Arrhenius that is defined as the minimum energy that must be input to a chemical system, containing potential reactants, in order for a chemical reaction to occur. Activation energy may also be defined as the minimum energy required to start a chemical reaction. The activation energy of a reaction is usually denoted by $E_a$ and given in units of kilojoules per mole. |
| Activation | Activation in chemical sciences generally refers to the process whereby something is prepared or excited for a subsequent reaction. |
| Activated complex | In chemistry an activated complex is defined by the International Union of Pure and Applied Chemistry as 'that assembly of atoms which corresponds to an arbitrary infinitesimally small region at or near the col of a potential energy surface'. In other words, it refers to a collection of intermediate structures in a chemical reaction that persist while bonds are breaking and new bonds are forming. It therefore represents not one defined state, but rather a range of transient configurations that a collection of atoms passes through in between clearly defined products and reactants. |
| Transition state | The transition state of a chemical reaction is a particular configuration along the reaction coordinate. It is defined as the state corresponding to the highest potential energy along this reaction coordinate. At this point, assuming a perfectly irreversible reaction, colliding reactant molecules always go on to form products. |
| Isomerization | In chemistry isomerization is the process by which one molecule is transformed into another molecule which has exactly the same atoms, but the atoms have a different arrangement e.g. A-B-C ? B-A-C (these related molecules are known as isomers ). |

# 14. Chemical Kinetics

In some molecules and under some conditions, isomerization occurs spontaneously. Many isomers are equal or roughly equal in bond energy, and so exist in roughly equal amounts, provided that they can interconvert relatively freely, that is the energy barrier between the two isomers is not too high.

**Kinetic energy**

In physics, the kinetic energy of an object is the energy which it possesses due to its motion. It is defined as the work needed to accelerate a body of a given mass from rest to its stated velocity. Having gained this energy during its acceleration, the body maintains this kinetic energy unless its speed changes.

**Elementary reaction**

An elementary reaction is a chemical reaction in which one or more of the chemical species react directly to form products in a single reaction step and with a single transition state.

In a unimolecular elementary reaction, a molecule A dissociates or isomerises to form the products $A \rightarrow products.$

At constant temperature, the rate of such a reaction is proportional to the concentration of the species A $\dfrac{d[A]}{dt} = -k[A].$

In a bimolecular elementary reaction, two atoms, molecules, ions or radicals, A and B, react together to form the product(s) $A + B \rightarrow products.$

The rate of such a reaction, at constant temperature, is proportional to the product of the concentrations of the species A and B $\dfrac{d[A]}{dt} = \dfrac{d[B]}{dt} = -k[A][B].$

The rate expression for an elementary bimolecular reaction is sometimes referred to as the Law of Mass Action as it was first proposed by Guldberg and Waage in 1864. An example of this type of reaction is a cycloaddition reaction. This rate expression can be derived from first principles by using collision theory for ideal gases.

**Molecularity**

Molecularity in chemistry is the number of colliding molecular entities that are involved in a single reaction step. While the order of a reaction is derived experimentally, the molecularity is a theoretical concept and can only be applied to elementary reactions. In elementary reactions, the reaction order, the molecularity and the stoichiometric coefficient are the same, although only numerically, because they are different concepts.

**Rate-determining step**

In chemical kinetics, the rate of a reaction mechanism with several steps is often determined by the slowest step, known as the rate-determining step or rate-limiting step.

The experimental rate equation can help to identify which step is rate-determining.

In a reaction coordinate, the transition state with the highest energy is the rate-determining step of a given reaction.

| | |
|---|---|
| Nitric oxide | Nitric oxide, or nitrogen oxide, also known as nitrogen monoxide, is a molecule with chemical formula NO. It is a free radical and is an important intermediate in the chemical industry. Nitric oxide is a by-product of combustion of substances in the air, as in automobile engines, fossil fuel power plants, and is produced naturally during the electrical discharges of lightning in thunderstorms.<br><br>In mammals including humans, NO is an important cellular signaling molecule involved in many physiological and pathological processes. |
| Nitrous oxide | Nitrous oxide, commonly known as laughing gas, is a chemical compound with the formula N2O. It is an oxide of nitrogen. At room temperature, it is a colourless, non-flammable gas, with a slightly sweet odour and taste. |
| Bromide ion | A bromide is a chemical compound containing a bromide ion or ligand. This is a bromine atom with an ionic charge of -1 ($Br^-$); for example, in caesium bromide, caesium cations ($Cs^+$) are electrically attracted to bromide anions ($Br^-$) to form the electrically neutral ionic compound CsBr. The term 'bromide' can also refer to a bromine atom with an oxidation number of -1 in covalent compounds such as sulfur dibromide ($SBr_2$). |
| Homogeneous catalysis | In chemistry, homogeneous catalysis is a sequence of reactions that involve a catalyst in the same phase as the reactants. Most commonly, a homogeneous catalyst is codissolved in a solvent with the reactants. |
| Hydrogen peroxide | Hydrogen peroxide is the simplest peroxide (a compound with an oxygen-oxygen single bond). It is also a strong oxidizer. Hydrogen peroxide is a clear liquid, slightly more viscous than water. |
| Homogeneous | Homogeneous as a term in physical chemistry and material science refers to substances and mixtures which are in a single phase. This is in contrast to a substance that is heterogeneous. The definition of homogeneous strongly depends on the context used. |
| Absorption | In chemistry, absorption is a physical or chemical phenomenon or a process in which atoms, molecules, or ions enter some bulk phase - gas, liquid, or solid material. This is a different process from adsorption, since molecules undergoing absorption are taken up by the volume, not by the surface (as in the case for adsorption). A more general term is sorption, which covers absorption, adsorption, and ion exchange. |

# 14. Chemical Kinetics

| | |
|---|---|
| Adsorption | Adsorption is the adhesion of atoms, ions, or molecules from a gas, liquid, or dissolved solid to a surface. This process creates a film of the adsorbate on the surface of the adsorbent. This process differs from absorption, in which a fluid (the absorbate) permeates or is dissolved by a liquid or solid (the absorbent). |
| Heterogeneous catalysis | In chemistry, heterogeneous catalysis refers to the form of catalysis where the phase of the catalyst differs from that of the reactants. Phase here refers not only to solid, liquid, vs gas, but also immiscible liquids, e.g. oil and water. The great majority of practical heterogeneous catalysts are solids and the great majority of reactants are gases or liquids. |
| Enzyme | Enzymes are large biological molecules responsible for the thousands of metabolic processes that sustain life. They are highly selective catalysts, greatly accelerating both the rate and specificity of metabolic reactions, from the digestion of food to the synthesis of DNA. Most enzymes are proteins, although some catalytic RNA molecules have been identified. Enzymes adopt a specific three-dimensional structure, and may employ organic (e.g. biotin) and inorganic (e.g. magnesium ion) cofactors to assist in catalysis. |
| Ethyl group | In chemistry, an ethyl group is an alkyl substituent derived from ethane . It has the formula $-C_2H_5$ and is very often abbreviated Et. Ethyl is used in the IUPAC nomenclature of organic chemistry for a saturated two-carbon moiety in a molecule, whilst the prefix 'eth-' is used to indicate the presence of two carbon atoms in the molecule. |
| Air pollution | Air pollution is the introduction into the atmosphere of chemicals, particulates, or biological materials that cause discomfort, disease, or death to humans, damage other living organisms such as food crops, or damage the natural environment or built environment.

The atmosphere is a complex dynamic natural gaseous system that is essential to support life on planet Earth. Stratospheric ozone depletion due to air pollution has long been recognized as a threat to human health as well as to the Earth's ecosystems. |
| Carbon monoxide | Carbon monoxide is a colorless, odorless, and tasteless gas that is slightly less dense than air. It is toxic to humans and animals when encountered in higher concentrations, although it is also produced in normal animal metabolism in low quantities, and is thought to have some normal biological functions. In the atmosphere, it is spatially variable, short lived, having a role in the formation of ground-level ozone. |
| Catalase | Catalase is a common enzyme found in nearly all living organisms exposed to oxygen. It catalyzes the decomposition of hydrogen peroxide to water and oxygen. It is a very important enzyme in protecting the cell from oxidative damage by reactive oxygen species (ROS). |

| Catalytic converter | A catalytic converter is a vehicle emissions control device which converts toxic byproducts of combustion in the exhaust of an internal combustion engine to less toxic substances by way of catalyzed chemical reactions. The specific reactions vary with the type of catalyst installed. Most present-day vehicles that run on gasoline are fitted with a "three-way" converter, so named because it converts the three main pollutants in automobile exhaust: carbon monoxide, unburned hydrocarbon and oxides of nitrogen. |
| --- | --- |
| Hydrogen | Hydrogen is a chemical element with chemical symbol H and atomic number 1. With an atomic weight of 1.00794 u, hydrogen is the lightest element and its monatomic form (H) is the most abundant chemical substance, constituting roughly 75% of the Universe's baryonic mass. Non-remnant stars are mainly composed of hydrogen in its plasma state. <br><br> At standard temperature and pressure, hydrogen is a colorless, odorless, tasteless, non-toxic, nonmetallic, highly combustible diatomic gas with the molecular formula $H_2$. |
| Noble metal | The noble metals are metals that are resistant to corrosion and oxidation in moist air, unlike most base metals. They tend to be precious, often due to their rarity in the Earth's crust. The noble metals are most commonly considered to be ruthenium, rhodium, palladium, silver, osmium, iridium, platinum, and gold. |
| Unburned hydrocarbon | Unburned hydrocarbons are the hydrocarbons emitted after petroleum is burned in an engine. <br><br> When unburned fuel is emitted from a combustor, the emission is caused by fuel 'avoiding' the flame zones. For example, in piston engines, some of the fuel-air mixture 'hides' from the flame in the crevices provided by the piston ring grooves. |
| Active site | In biology, the active site is the small port of an enzyme where substrate molecules bind and undergo a chemical reaction. This chemical reaction occurs when a substrate collides with and slots into the active site of an enzyme. The active site is usually found in a 3-D groove or pocket of the enzyme, lined with amino acid residues (or nucleotides in RNA enzymes). |
| Enzyme inhibitor | An enzyme inhibitor is a molecule, which binds to enzymes and decreases their activity. Since blocking an enzyme's activity can kill a pathogen or correct a metabolic imbalance, many drugs are enzyme inhibitors. They are also used as herbicides and pesticides. |
| Substrate | In chemistry, a substrate is the chemical species being observed, which reacts with a reagent. This term is highly context-dependent. In particular, in biochemistry, an enzyme substrate is the material upon which an enzyme acts. |
| Turnover number | Turnover number has two related meanings: |

# 14. Chemical Kinetics

In enzymology, turnover number is defined as the maximum number of molecules of substrate that an enzyme can convert to product per catalytic site per unit of time and can be calculated as follows:

For example, carbonic anhydrase has a turnover number of 400,000 to 600,000 $s^{-1}$, which means that each carbonic anhydrase molecule can produce up to 600,000 molecules of product (bicarbonate ions) per second.

In other chemical fields, such as organometallic catalysis, turnover number is used with a slightly different meaning: the number of moles of substrate that a mole of catalyst can convert before becoming inactivated. An ideal catalyst would have an infinite turnover number in this sense, because it wouldn't ever be consumed, but in actual practice one often sees turnover numbers which go from 100 up to 40 million for Catalase.

|  |  |
|---|---|
| Efficiency | Efficiency in general, describes the extent to which time, effort or cost is well used for the intended task or purpose. It is often used with the specific purpose of relaying the capability of a specific application of effort to produce a specific outcome effectively with a minimum amount or quantity of waste, expense, or unnecessary effort. 'Efficiency' has widely varying meanings in different disciplines. |
| Nitrogen cycle | The nitrogen cycle is the process by which nitrogen is converted between its various chemical forms. This transformation can be carried out through both biological and physical processes. Important processes in the nitrogen cycle include fixation, ammonification, nitrification, and denitrification. |
| Nitrogenase | Nitrogenases are enzymes used by some organisms to fix atmospheric nitrogen gas ($N_2$). There is only one known family of enzymes that accomplishes this process. Dinitrogen is quite inert because of the strength of its N≡N triple bond. |
| Formic acid | Formic acid is the simplest carboxylic acid. Its chemical formula is $HCOOH$ or $HCO_2H$. It is an important intermediate in chemical synthesis and occurs naturally, most notably in ant venom. In fact, its name comes from the Latin word for ant, formica, referring to its early isolation by the distillation of ant bodies. |
| Carbonic anhydrase | The carbonic anhydrases form a family of enzymes that catalyze the rapid interconversion of carbon dioxide and water to bicarbonate and protons (or vice versa), a reversible reaction that occurs rather slowly in the absence of a catalyst. The active site of most carbonic anhydrases contains a zinc ion; they are therefore classified as metalloenzymes. |

| Americium | Americium is a transuranic radioactive chemical element that has the symbol Am and atomic number 95 |
|---|---|
| | Americium was first produced in 1944 by the group of Glenn T. Seaborg at the University of California, Berkeley. Although it is the third element in the transuranic series, it was discovered fourth, after the heavier curium. The discovery was kept secret and only released to the public in November 1945. Most americium is produced by bombarding uranium or plutonium with neutrons in nuclear reactors - one tonne of spent nuclear fuel contains about 100 grams of americium. |
| Hydrogen sulfide | Hydrogen sulfide is the chemical compound with the formula H2S. It is a colorless gas with the characteristic foul odor of rotten eggs; it is heavier than air, very poisonous, corrosive, flammable and explosive. |
| | Hydrogen sulfide often results from the bacterial breakdown of organic matter in the absence of oxygen, such as in swamps and sewers; this process is commonly known as anaerobic digestion. |
| Urea | Urea or carbamide is an organic compound with the chemical formula $CO_2$. The molecule has two --$NH_2$ groups joined by a carbonyl (C=O) functional group. |
| | Urea serves an important role in the metabolism of nitrogen-containing compounds by animals and is the main nitrogen-containing substance in the urine of mammals. |
| Cellulose | Cellulose is an organic compound with the formula n, a polysaccharide consisting of a linear chain of several hundred to over ten thousand ß(1?4) linked -glucose units. Cellulose is an important structural component of the primary cell wall of green plants, many forms of algae and the oomycetes. Some species of bacteria secrete it to form biofilms. |
| Cyclopentadiene | Cyclopentadiene is an organic compound with the formula $C_5H_6$. This colorless liquid has a strong and unpleasant odor. At room temperature, this cyclic diene dimerizes over the course of hours to give dicyclopentadiene via a Diels-Alder reaction. |
| Dicyclopentadiene | Dicyclopentadiene, abbreviated DCPD, is a chemical compound with formula $C_{10}H_{12}$. At room temperature, it is a white crystalline solid with a camphor-like odor. Its energy density is 10,975 Wh/l. |
| Dinitrogen pentoxide | Dinitrogen pentoxide is the chemical compound with the formula $N_2O_5$. Also known as nitrogen pentoxide, $N_2O_5$ is one of the binary nitrogen oxides, a family of compounds that only contain nitrogen and oxygen. It is an unstable and potentially dangerous oxidizer that once was used as a reagent when dissolved in chloroform for nitrations but has largely been superseded by $NO_2BF_4$ (nitronium tetrafluoroborate). |

# 14. Chemical Kinetics

| Platinum | Platinum is a chemical element with the chemical symbol Pt and an atomic number of 78. |
| | |
| | Its name is derived from the Spanish term platina, which is literally translated into 'little silver'. It is a dense, malleable, ductile, precious, gray-white transition metal. |

CHAPTER QUIZ: KEY TERMS, PEOPLE, PLACES, CONCEPTS

1. _____ is an organic compound with the formula n, a polysaccharide consisting of a linear chain of several hundred to over ten thousand ß(1?4) linked -glucose units. _____ is an important structural component of the primary cell wall of green plants, many forms of algae and the oomycetes. Some species of bacteria secrete it to form biofilms.

   a. Beta-glucan
   b. Cellulose
   c. Callose
   d. Capsulan

2. In chemistry, _____ refers to the form of catalysis where the phase of the catalyst differs from that of the reactants. Phase here refers not only to solid, liquid, vs gas, but also immiscible liquids, e.g. oil and water. The great majority of practical heterogeneous catalysts are solids and the great majority of reactants are gases or liquids.

   a. Heterogeneous catalysis
   b. Caseinase
   c. Catalase
   d. Catalyst poisoning

3. In physics, the _____ of an object is the energy which it possesses due to its motion. It is defined as the work needed to accelerate a body of a given mass from rest to its stated velocity. Having gained this energy during its acceleration, the body maintains this _____ unless its speed changes.

   a. Kinetic energy
   b. Fundamental equation of constrained motion
   c. Beat
   d. Bass trap

4. . _____ is a chemical element with the chemical symbol Pt and an atomic number of 78.

   Its name is derived from the Spanish term platina, which is literally translated into 'little silver'. It is a dense, malleable, ductile, precious, gray-white transition metal.

a. Betafite
b. Bixbyite
c. Boleite
d. Platinum

5. _____ is a branch of chemistry that deals with the relative quantities of reactants and products in chemical reactions. In a balanced chemical reaction, the relations among quantities of reactants and products typically form a ratio of positive integers. For example, in a reaction that forms ammonia ($NH_3$), exactly one molecule of nitrogen gas ($N_2$) reacts with three molecules of hydrogen gas ($H_2$) to produce two molecules of $NH_3$:N2 + 3H2 ? 2NH3

This particular kind of _____ - describing the quantitative relationships among substances as they participate in chemical reactions - is known as reaction _____.

a. Stoichiometry
b. Basic sediment and water
c. Biochemical engineering
d. Bioheat transfer

1. b
2. a
3. a
4. d
5. a

---

## You can take the complete Chapter Practice Test

**for 14. Chemical Kinetics**
on all key terms, persons, places, and concepts.

### Online 99 Cents

### http://www.JustTheFacts101.com

Use www.JustTheFacts101.com for all your study needs

including Facts101's online interactive problem solving labs in

chemistry, statistics, mathematics, and more.

# 15. Chemical Equilibrium

_____ | Crystallization

_____ | Dissolution

_____ | Dynamic equilibrium

_____ | Statics

_____ | Concentration

_____ | Equilibrium constant

_____ | Fertilizer

_____ | Dinitrogen tetroxide

_____ | Nitrogen dioxide

_____ | Thermodynamic

_____ | Phosgene

_____ | Homogeneous

_____ | Calcium

_____ | Calcium carbonate

_____ | Decomposition

_____ | Solvent

_____ | Reaction quotient

_____ | Nernst equation

_____ | Volume

_____ | Hydrochloric acid

_____ | Partial pressure

CHAPTER OUTLINE: KEY TERMS, PEOPLE, PLACES, CONCEPTS

| | Activation |
|---|---|
| | Activation energy |
| | Catalysis |
| | Nitric oxide |
| | Methanol |
| | Phosphorus pentachloride |
| | Organic acid |
| | Carbon monoxide |
| | Iron sulfide |
| | Silver chloride |
| | Dimer |
| | Hemoglobin |

CHAPTER HIGHLIGHTS & NOTES: KEY TERMS, PEOPLE, PLACES, CONCEPTS

Crystallization — Crystallization is the process of formation of solid crystals precipitating from a solution, melt or more rarely deposited directly from a gas. Crystallization is also a chemical solid-liquid separation technique, in which mass transfer of a solute from the liquid solution to a pure solid crystalline phase occurs. In chemical engineering crystallization occurs in a crystallizer.

Dissolution — Dissolution is the process by which a solute forms a solution in a solvent. The solute, in the case of solids, has its crystalline structure disintegrated as separate ions, atoms, and molecules form. For liquids and gases, the molecules must be adaptable with those of the solvent for a solution to form.

# 15. Chemical Equilibrium

| | |
|---|---|
| Dynamic equilibrium | A dynamic equilibrium exists once a reversible reaction ceases to change its ratio of reactants/products, but substances move between the chemicals at an equal rate, meaning there is no net change. It is a particular example of a system in a steady state. In thermodynamics a closed system is in thermodynamic equilibrium when reactions occur at such rates that the composition of the mixture does not change with time. |
| Statics | Statics is the branch of mechanics that is concerned with the analysis of loads on physical systems in static equilibrium, that is, in a state where the relative positions of subsystems do not vary over time, or where components and structures are at a constant velocity. When in static equilibrium, the system is either at rest, or its center of mass moves at constant velocity. <br><br> By Newton's first law, this situation implies that the net force and net torque (also known as moment of force) on every part of the system is zero. |
| Concentration | In chemistry, concentration is the abundance of a constituent divided by the total volume of a mixture. Several types of mathematical description can be distinguished: mass concentration, molar concentration, number concentration, and volume concentration. The term concentration can be applied to any kind of chemical mixture, but most frequently it refers to solutes and solvents in solutions. |
| Equilibrium constant | For a general chemical equilibrium $\alpha A + \beta B \ldots \rightleftharpoons \rho R + \sigma S \ldots$ <br><br> the thermodynamic equilibrium constant can be defined such that, at equilibrium, $$K^{\ominus} = \frac{\{R\}^{\rho}\{S\}^{\sigma}\ldots}{\{A\}^{\alpha}\{B\}^{\beta}\ldots}$$ <br><br> where curly brackets denote the thermodynamic activities of the chemical species. The logarithm of this expression appears in the formula for the Gibbs free energy change for the reaction. If deviations from ideal behaviour are neglected, the activities may be replaced by concentrations, [A], and a concentration quotient, $K_c$. |
| Fertilizer | Fertilizer is any organic or inorganic material of natural or synthetic origin (other than liming materials) that is added to a soil to supply one or more plant nutrients essential to the growth of plants. Conservative estimates report 30 to 50% of crop yields are attributed to natural or synthetic commercial fertilizer. Global market value is likely to rise to more than US$185 billion until 2019. The European fertilizer market will grow to earn revenues of approx. |
| Dinitrogen tetroxide | Dinitrogen tetroxide is the chemical compound $N_2O_4$. It is a useful reagent in chemical synthesis. It forms an equilibrium mixture with nitrogen dioxide; some call this mixture dinitrogen tetroxide, while some call it nitrogen dioxide. |

| | |
|---|---|
| Nitrogen dioxide | Nitrogen dioxide is the chemical compound with the formula $NO2$. It is one of several nitrogen oxides. $NO2$ is an intermediate in the industrial synthesis of nitric acid, millions of tons of which are produced each year. |
| Thermodynamic | Thermodynamics is a branch of natural science concerned with heat and temperature and their relation to energy and work. It defines macroscopic variables, such as internal energy, entropy, and pressure, that partly describe a body of matter or radiation. It states that the behavior of those variables is subject to general constraints, that are common to all materials, not the peculiar properties of particular materials. |
| Phosgene | Phosgene is the chemical compound with the formula $COCl_2$. This colorless gas gained infamy as a chemical weapon during World War I. It is also a valued industrial reagent and building block in synthesis of pharmaceuticals and other organic compounds. In low concentrations, its odor resembles freshly cut hay or grass. |
| Homogeneous | Homogeneous as a term in physical chemistry and material science refers to substances and mixtures which are in a single phase. This is in contrast to a substance that is heterogeneous. The definition of homogeneous strongly depends on the context used. |
| Calcium | Calcium is the chemical element with symbol Ca and atomic number 20. Calcium is a soft gray alkaline earth metal, and is the fifth-most-abundant element by mass in the Earth's crust. Calcium is also the fifth-most-abundant dissolved ion in seawater by both molarity and mass, after sodium, chloride, magnesium, and sulfate. |
| | Calcium is essential for living organisms, in particular in cell physiology, where movement of the calcium ion $Ca^{2+}$ into and out of the cytoplasm functions as a signal for many cellular processes. |
| Calcium carbonate | Calcium carbonate is a chemical compound with the formula $CaCO_3$. It is a common substance found in rocks in all parts of the world, and is the main component of shells of marine organisms, snails, coal balls, pearls, and eggshells. Calcium carbonate is the active ingredient in agricultural lime, and is created when Ca ions in hard water react with carbonate ions creating limescale. |
| Decomposition | Decomposition is the process by which organic substances are broken down into simpler forms of matter. The process is essential for recycling the finite matter that occupies physical space in the biome. Bodies of living organisms begin to decompose shortly after death. |
| Solvent | A solvent is a substance that dissolves a solute (a chemically different liquid, solid or gas), resulting in a solution. A solvent is usually a liquid but can also be a solid or a gas. The maximum quantity of solute that can dissolve in a specific volume of solvent varies with temperature. |
| Reaction quotient | In chemistry, a reaction quotient: $Q_r$ is a function of the activities or concentrations of the chemical species involved in a chemical reaction. |

# 15. Chemical Equilibrium

In the special case that the reaction is at equilibrium the reaction quotient is equal to the equilibrium constant.

A general chemical reaction in which a moles of a reactant A and ß moles of a reactant B react to give s moles of a product S and t moles of a product T can be written as aA + ßB sS + tT

The reaction is written as an equilibrium even though in many cases it may appear to have gone to completion.

**Nernst equation**

In electrochemistry, the Nernst equation is an equation that relates the equilibrium reduction potential of a half-cell in an electrochemical cell (or the total voltage for a full cell) to the standard electrode potential, temperature, activity, and reaction quotient of the underlying reactions and species used. It is named after the German physical chemist who first formulated it, Walther Nernst.

The Nernst equation gives a formula that relates the numerical values of the concentration gradient to the electric gradient that balances it.

**Volume**

In thermodynamics, the volume of a system is an important extensive parameter for describing its thermodynamic state. The specific volume, an intensive property, is the system's volume per unit of mass. Volume is a function of state and is interdependent with other thermodynamic properties such as pressure and temperature.

**Hydrochloric acid**

Hydrochloric acid is a clear, colorless, highly pungent solution of hydrogen chloride in water. It is a highly corrosive, strong mineral acid with many industrial uses. Hydrochloric acid is found naturally in gastric acid.

**Partial pressure**

In a mixture of gases, each gas has a partial pressure which is the hypothetical pressure of that gas if it alone occupied the volume of the mixture at the same temperature. The total pressure of an ideal gas mixture is the sum of the partial pressures of each individual gas in the mixture.

It relies on the following isotherm relation: $V_x \times p_{tot} = V_{tot} \times p_x$ •$V_x$ is the partial volume of any individual gas component (X)•$V_{tot}$ is the total volume in gas mixture•$p_x$ is the partial pressure of gas X•$p_{tot}$ is the total pressure of gas mixture•$n_x$ is the amount of substance of a gas (X)•$n_{tot}$ is the total amount of substance in gas mixture

The partial pressure of a gas is a measure of thermodynamic activity of the gas's molecules.

**Activation**

Activation in chemical sciences generally refers to the process whereby something is prepared or excited for a subsequent reaction.

CHAPTER HIGHLIGHTS & NOTES: KEY TERMS, PEOPLE, PLACES, CONCEPTS

| | |
|---|---|
| Activation energy | In chemistry, activation energy is a term introduced in 1889 by the Swedish scientist Svante Arrhenius that is defined as the minimum energy that must be input to a chemical system, containing potential reactants, in order for a chemical reaction to occur. Activation energy may also be defined as the minimum energy required to start a chemical reaction. The activation energy of a reaction is usually denoted by $E_a$ and given in units of kilojoules per mole. |
| Catalysis | Catalysis is the increase rate of a chemical reaction due to the participation of a substance called a catalyst. Unlike other reagents in the chemical reaction, a catalyst is not consumed. With a catalyst, less free energy is required to reach the transition state, but the total free energy from reactants to products does not change. |
| Nitric oxide | Nitric oxide, or nitrogen oxide, also known as nitrogen monoxide, is a molecule with chemical formula $NO$. It is a free radical and is an important intermediate in the chemical industry. Nitric oxide is a by-product of combustion of substances in the air, as in automobile engines, fossil fuel power plants, and is produced naturally during the electrical discharges of lightning in thunderstorms.<br><br>In mammals including humans, NO is an important cellular signaling molecule involved in many physiological and pathological processes. |
| Methanol | Methanol, also known as methyl alcohol, wood alcohol, wood naphtha or wood spirits, is a chemical with the formula $CH_3OH$. Methanol acquired the name 'wood alcohol' because it was once produced chiefly as a byproduct of the destructive distillation of wood. Modern methanol is produced in a catalytic industrial process directly from carbon monoxide, carbon dioxide, and hydrogen. |
| Phosphorus pentachloride | Phosphorus pentachloride is the chemical compound with the formula $PCl_5$. It is one of the most important phosphorus chlorides, others being $PCl_3$ and $POCl_3$. $PCl_5$ finds use as a chlorinating reagent. |
| Organic acid | An organic acid is an organic compound with acidic properties. The most common organic acids are the carboxylic acids, whose acidity is associated with their carboxyl group -COOH. Sulfonic acids, containing the group -$SO_2OH$, are relatively stronger acids. Alcohols, with -OH, can act as acids but they are usually very weak. |
| Carbon monoxide | Carbon monoxide is a colorless, odorless, and tasteless gas that is slightly less dense than air. It is toxic to humans and animals when encountered in higher concentrations, although it is also produced in normal animal metabolism in low quantities, and is thought to have some normal biological functions. In the atmosphere, it is spatially variable, short lived, having a role in the formation of ground-level ozone. |

# 15. Chemical Equilibrium

| Silver chloride | Silver chloride is a chemical compound with the chemical formula AgCl. This white crystalline solid is well known for its low solubility in water (this behavior being reminiscent of the chlorides of $Tl^+$ and $Pb^{2+}$). Upon illumination or heating, silver chloride converts to silver (and chlorine), which is signaled by greyish or purplish coloration to some samples. |
|---|---|
| Dimer | A dimer is a chemical entity consisting of two structurally similar monomers joined by bonds that can be either strong or weak, covalent or intermolecular. The term homodimer is used when the two molecules are identical (e.g. A-A) and heterodimer when they are not (e.g. A-B). The reverse of dimerisation is often called dissociation. |
| Hemoglobin | Hemoglobin; also spelled haemoglobin and abbreviated Hb or Hgb, is the iron-containing oxygen-transport metalloprotein in the red blood cells of all vertebrates as well as the tissues of some invertebrates. Hemoglobin in the blood carries oxygen from the respiratory organs (lungs or gills) to the rest of the body (i.e. the tissues) where it releases the oxygen to burn nutrients to provide energy to power the functions of the organism, and collects the resultant carbon dioxide to bring it back to the respiratory organs to be dispensed from the organism.<br><br>In mammals, the protein makes up about 97% of the red blood cells' dry content (by weight), and around 35% of the total content (including water). |

1. _____; also spelled haemoglobin and abbreviated Hb or Hgb, is the iron-containing oxygen-transport metalloprotein in the red blood cells of all vertebrates as well as the tissues of some invertebrates. _____ in the blood carries oxygen from the respiratory organs (lungs or gills) to the rest of the body (i.e. the tissues) where it releases the oxygen to burn nutrients to provide energy to power the functions of the organism, and collects the resultant carbon dioxide to bring it back to the respiratory organs to be dispensed from the organism.

   In mammals, the protein makes up about 97% of the red blood cells' dry content (by weight), and around 35% of the total content (including water).

   a. Binding constant
   b. Binding selectivity
   c. Hemoglobin
   d. Buffer solution

2. . _____ is a colorless, odorless, and tasteless gas that is slightly less dense than air.

It is toxic to humans and animals when encountered in higher concentrations, although it is also produced in normal animal metabolism in low quantities, and is thought to have some normal biological functions. In the atmosphere, it is spatially variable, short lived, having a role in the formation of ground-level ozone.

a. Carbon monoxide
b. Carbon hexoxide
c. Barium acetylacetonate
d. Cerium acetylacetonate

3. _____ is the process of formation of solid crystals precipitating from a solution, melt or more rarely deposited directly from a gas. _____ is also a chemical solid-liquid separation technique, in which mass transfer of a solute from the liquid solution to a pure solid crystalline phase occurs. In chemical engineering _____ occurs in a crystallizer.

a. Biaxial nematic
b. Crystallization
c. Borrmann effect
d. Bragg plane

4. _____ in chemical sciences generally refers to the process whereby something is prepared or excited for a subsequent reaction.

a. Detailed balance
b. Behentrimonium chloride
c. Activation
d. Cocamidopropyl hydroxysultaine

5. A _____ is a substance that dissolves a solute (a chemically different liquid, solid or gas), resulting in a solution. A _____ is usually a liquid but can also be a solid or a gas. The maximum quantity of solute that can dissolve in a specific volume of _____ varies with temperature.

a. Bioorthogonal chemistry
b. Solvent
c. Carbothermic reaction
d. Ceramide phosphoethanolamine synthase

1. c
2. a
3. b
4. c
5. b

## You can take the complete Chapter Practice Test

**for 15. Chemical Equilibrium**
on all key terms, persons, places, and concepts.

## Online 99 Cents

## http://www.JustTheFacts101.com

Use www.JustTheFacts101.com for all your study needs

including Facts101's online interactive problem solving labs in

chemistry, statistics, mathematics, and more.

# 16. Acid-Base Equilibria

CHAPTER OUTLINE: KEY TERMS, PEOPLE, PLACES, CONCEPTS

Citric acid

Malic acid

Hydrochloric acid

Hydrogen chloride

Sodium hydroxide

Chloride ion

Conjugate acid

Nitrous acid

Ammonia

Strength

Leveling effect

Autoionization

Entropy

Product

Blackbody radiation

Litmus

Petroleum

PH meter

Diprotic acid

Methyl red

Methyl violet

# 16. Acid-Base Equilibria



CHAPTER OUTLINE: KEY TERMS, PEOPLE, PLACES, CONCEPTS

- Nitric acid
- Phenolphthalein
- Strong electrolyte
- Thymol blue
- Alkali
- Alkali metal
- Hydroxide
- Acetic acid
- Benzoic acid
- Chlorous acid
- Hydrofluoric acid
- Hypochlorous acid
- Formic acid
- Niacin
- Ionization
- Dissociation constant
- Concentration
- Ascorbic acid
- Sulfuric acid
- Sulfurous acid
- Tartaric acid

Weak base

Hydroxylamine

Methylamine

Pyridine

Amine

Sodium hypochlorite

Acid salt

Cadaverine

Caffeine

Codeine

Putrescine

Quinine

Hydrolysis

Metal hydroxide

Chemical structure

Binary acid

Hypobromous acid

Hypoiodous acid

Chloric acid

Oxidation

Perchloric acid

# 16. Acid-Base Equilibria



CHAPTER OUTLINE: KEY TERMS, PEOPLE, PLACES, CONCEPTS

- Alanine
- Amino acid
- Carboxylic acid
- Electron
- Electron acceptor
- Carbonic acid
- Phosphorous acid
- Phenylacetic acid
- Absorption
- Carbon dioxide
- Dioxide
- Acetylsalicylic acid
- Aspirin
- Hydrazoic acid
- Saccharin
- Butyric acid
- Hemoglobin
- Oxalic acid
- Cocaine

# 16. Acid-Base Equilibria

| | |
|---|---|
| Citric acid | Citric acid is a weak organic acid with the formula $C_6H_8O_7$. It is a natural preservative/conservative and is also used to add an acidic or sour taste to foods and drinks. In biochemistry, the conjugate base of citric acid, citrate, is important as an intermediate in the citric acid cycle, which occurs in the metabolism of all aerobic organisms. |
| Malic acid | Malic acid is an organic compound with the formula $HO_2CCH_2CHOHCO_2H$. It is a dicarboxylic acid that is made by all living organisms, contributes to the pleasantly sour taste of fruits, and is used as a food additive. Malic acid has two stereoisomeric forms (- and -enantiomers), though only the -isomer exists naturally. The salts and esters of malic acid are known as malates. |
| Hydrochloric acid | Hydrochloric acid is a clear, colorless, highly pungent solution of hydrogen chloride in water. It is a highly corrosive, strong mineral acid with many industrial uses. Hydrochloric acid is found naturally in gastric acid. |
| Hydrogen chloride | The compound hydrogen chloride has the chemical formula HCl. At room temperature, it is a colorless gas, which forms white fumes of hydrochloric acid upon contact with atmospheric humidity. Hydrogen chloride gas and hydrochloric acid are important in technology and industry. |
| Sodium hydroxide | Sodium hydroxide, also known as caustic soda, or lye, is an inorganic compound with the chemical formula NaOH . It is a white solid, and is a highly caustic metallic base and alkali salt. It is available in pellets, flakes, granules, and as prepared solutions at a number of different concentrations. |
| Chloride ion | The chloride ion is the anion $Cl^-$. It is formed when the element chlorine (a halogen) gains an electron or when a compound such as hydrogen chloride is dissolved in water or other polar solvents. Chlorides salts such as sodium chloride are often very soluble in water. |
| Conjugate acid | A conjugate acid, within the Brønsted-Lowry theory, is a species formed by the reception of a proton, by a base - in other words, the base with a hydrogen ion added to it - while a conjugate base is formed by the removal of a proton from an acid: the conjugate base of an acid is that acid with a hydrogen ion removed. <br><br>Visually, this can be represented as:A conjugate acid of the base ? Base + H+A conjugate base of the acid ? Acid - H+ <br><br>The Brønsted-Lowry model is based on the idea that acids are proton donors and bases are proton acceptors; the conjugate base or conjugate acid is merely what is left after an acid has lost a proton or a base has gained a proton, respectively. |
| Nitrous acid | Nitrous acid is a weak and monobasic acid known only in solution and in the form of nitrite salts. <br><br>Nitrous acid is used to make diazides from amines; this occurs by nucleophilic attack of the amine onto the nitrite, reprotonation by the surrounding solvent, and double-elimination of water. |

| | |
|---|---|
| Ammonia | Ammonia or azane is a compound of nitrogen and hydrogen with the formula $NH_3$. It is a colourless gas with a characteristic pungent smell. Ammonia contributes significantly to the nutritional needs of terrestrial organisms by serving as a precursor to food and fertilizers. |
| Strength | In explosive materials, strength is the parameter determining the ability of the explosive to move the surrounding material. It is related to the total gas yield of the reaction, and the amount of heat produced. Cf. |
| Leveling effect | Leveling effect or solvent leveling refers to the effect of solvent on the properties of acids and bases. The strength of a strong acid is limited ('leveled') by the basicity of the solvent. Similarly the strength of a strong base is leveled by the acidity of the solvent. |
| Autoionization | Autoionization is a process by which atoms or molecules spontaneously emit one of the shell electrons, thus going from a state with charge Z to a state with charge Z?+?1, for example from an electrically neutral state to a singly ionized state.<br><br>Atoms can autoionize when either two or more valence electrons are excited or one or more inner-shell electrons are missing. In the latter case, it is called the Auger effect. |
| Entropy | In thermodynamics, entropy is a measure of the number of specific ways in which a thermodynamic system may be arranged, often taken to be a measure of disorder, or a measure of progressing towards thermodynamic equilibrium. The entropy of an isolated system never decreases, because isolated systems spontaneously evolve towards thermodynamic equilibrium, which is the state of maximum entropy.<br><br>Entropy was originally defined for a thermodynamically reversible process<br><br>as $$\Delta S = \int \frac{dQ_{rev}}{T}$$<br><br>where the entropy is found from the uniform thermodynamic temperature of a closed system dividing an incremental reversible transfer of heat into that system . |
| Product | Product are formed during chemical reactions as reagents are consumed. Products have lower energy than the reagents and are produced during the reaction according to the second law of thermodynamics. The released energy comes from changes in chemical bonds between atoms in reagent molecules and may be given off in the form of heat or light. |
| Blackbody radiation | Black-body radiation is the type of electromagnetic radiation within or surrounding a body in thermodynamic equilibrium with its environment, or emitted by a black body held at constant, uniform temperature. The radiation has a specific spectrum and intensity that depends only on the temperature of the body. |

# 16. Acid-Base Equilibria

| | |
|---|---|
| Litmus | Litmus is a water-soluble mixture of different dyes extracted from lichens, especially Roccella tinctoria. It is often absorbed onto filter paper to produce one of the oldest forms of pH indicator, used to test materials for acidity. Blue litmus paper turns red under acidic conditions and red litmus paper turns blue under basic (i.e. alkaline) conditions, with the color change occurring over the pH range 4.5–8.3 at 25 °C. Neutral litmus paper is purple. |
| Petroleum | Petroleum (L. petroleum, from Greek: p?t?a + Latin: oleum (oil)) is a naturally occurring, smelly, yellow-to-black liquid consisting of a complex mixture of hydrocarbons of various molecular weights and other liquid organic compounds, that are found in geologic formations beneath the Earth's surface. The name Petroleum covers both naturally occurring unprocessed crude oils and petroleum products that are made up of refined crude oil. A fossil fuel, it is formed when large quantities of dead organisms, usually zooplankton and algae, are buried underneath sedimentary rock and undergo intense heat and pressure. |
| PH meter | A pH meter is an electronic device used for measuring the pH of a liquid (though special probes are sometimes used to measure the pH of semi-solid substances). A typical pH meter consists of a special measuring probe (a glass electrode) connected to an electronic meter that measures and displays the pH reading. |
| Diprotic acid | A diprotic acid is an acid such as $H_2SO_4$ that contains within its molecular structure two hydrogen atoms per molecule capable of dissociating (i.e. ionizable) in water. The complete dissociation of diprotic acids is of the same form as sulfuric acid: $H_2SO_4 \rightleftharpoons H^+(aq) + HSO_4^-(aq)$ $K_a = 1 \times 10^3$ $HSO_4^- \rightleftharpoons H^+(aq) + SO_4^{2-}(aq)$ $K_a = 1 \times 10^{-2}$ <br><br> The dissociation does not happen all at once due to the two stages of dissociation having different $K_a$ values. The first dissociation will, in the case of sulfuric acid, occur completely, but the second one will not. |
| Methyl red | Methyl red also called C.I. Acid Red 2, is an indicator dye that turns red in acidic solutions. It is an azo dye, and is a dark red crystalline powder. <br><br> Methyl red is a pH indicator; it is red in pH under 4.4, yellow in pH over 6.2, and orange in between, with a $pK_a$ of 5.1. |
| Methyl violet | Methyl violet is a family of organic compounds that are mainly used as dyes. Depending on the amount of attached methyl groups, the color of the dye can be altered. Its main use is as a purple dye for textiles and to give deep violet colors in paint and ink. |
| Nitric acid | Nitric acid, also known as aqua fortis and spirit of niter, is a highly corrosive strong mineral acid. The pure compound is colorless, but older samples tend to acquire a yellow cast due to decomposition into oxides of nitrogen and water. |

| | |
|---|---|
| Phenolphthalein | Phenolphthalein is a chemical compound with the formula $C_{20}H_{14}O_4$ and is often written as 'HIn' or 'phph' in shorthand notation. Often used in titrations, it turns colorless in acidic solutions and pink in basic solutions. If the concentration of indicator is particularly strong, it can appear purple. |
| Strong electrolyte | A strong electrolyte is a solute that completely, or almost completely, ionizes or dissociates in a solution. These ions are good conductors of electric current in the solution.<br><br>Originally, a 'strong electrolyte' was defined as a chemical that, when in aqueous solution, is a good conductor of electricity. |
| Thymol blue | Thymol blue is a brownish-green or reddish-brown crystalline powder that is used as a pH indicator. It is insoluble in water but soluble in alcohol and dilute alkali solutions. It transitions from red to yellow at pH 1.2-2.8 and from yellow to blue at pH 8.0-9.6. It is usually a component of Universal indicator. |
| Alkali | In chemistry, an alkali is a basic, ionic salt of an alkali metal or alkaline earth metal chemical element. Some authors also define an alkali as a base that dissolves in water. A solution of a soluble base has a pH greater than 7.0. The adjective alkaline is commonly, and alkalescent less often, used in English as a synonym for basic, especially for soluble bases. |
| Alkali metal | The alkali metals are a group in the periodic table consisting of the chemical elements lithium, sodium (Na), potassium (K), rubidium (Rb), caesium (Cs), and francium (Fr). This group lies in the s-block of the periodic table as all alkali metals have their outermost electron in an s-orbital. The alkali metals provide the best example of group trends in properties in the periodic table, with elements exhibiting well-characterized homologous behaviour. |
| Hydroxide | Hydroxide is a diatomic anion with chemical formula $OH^-$. It consists of an oxygen and a hydrogen atom held together by a covalent bond, and carries a negative electric charge. It is an important but usually minor constituent of water. |
| Acetic acid | Acetic acid is an organic compound with the chemical formula $CH_3COOH$ (also written as $CH_3CO_2H$ or $C_2H_4O_2$). It is a colourless liquid that when undiluted is also called glacial acetic acid. Acetic acid is the main component of vinegar (apart from water; vinegar is roughly 8% acetic acid by volume), and has a distinctive sour taste and pungent smell. |
| Benzoic acid | Benzoic acid, $C_7H_6O_2$, is a colorless crystalline solid and a simple aromatic carboxylic acid. The name is derived from gum benzoin, which was for a long time the only source for benzoic acid. Its salts are used as food preservatives and benzoic acid is an important precursor for the synthesis of many other organic substances. |
| Chlorous acid | Chlorous acid is an inorganic compound with the formula $HClO_2$. It is a weak acid. |

# 16. Acid-Base Equilibria

| | |
|---|---|
| Hydrofluoric acid | Hydrofluoric acid is a solution of hydrogen fluoride in water. It is a valued source of fluorine and is a precursor to numerous pharmaceuticals such as fluoxetine (Prozac) and diverse materials such as PTFE (Teflon).<br><br>Hydrofluoric acid is a highly corrosive acid, capable of dissolving many materials, especially oxides. |
| Hypochlorous acid | Hypochlorous acid is a weak acid with the chemical formula HClO. It forms when chlorine dissolves in water. It cannot be isolated in pure form due to rapid equilibration with its precursor. HOCl is an oxidizer, and as its sodium salt sodium hypochlorite, $(NaClO)$, or its calcium salt calcium hypochlorite, $(Ca(ClO)_2)$ is used as a bleach, a deodorant, and a disinfectant. |
| Formic acid | Formic acid is the simplest carboxylic acid. Its chemical formula is $HCOOH$ or $HCO_2H$. It is an important intermediate in chemical synthesis and occurs naturally, most notably in ant venom. In fact, its name comes from the Latin word for ant, formica, referring to its early isolation by the distillation of ant bodies. |
| Niacin | Niacin is an organic compound with the formula C6H5NO2 and, depending on the definition used, one of the 20 to 80 essential human nutrients.<br><br>Not enough Niacin in the diet can cause nausea, skin and mouth lesions, anemia, headaches, and tiredness. Chronic Niacin deficiency leads to a disease called Pellagra. |
| ionization | Ionization is the process by which an atom or a molecule acquires a negative or positive charge by gaining or losing electrons. |
| Dissociation constant | In chemistry, biochemistry, and pharmacology, a dissociation constant is a specific type of equilibrium constant that measures the propensity of a larger object to separate (dissociate) reversibly into smaller components, as when a complex falls apart into its component molecules, or when a salt splits up into its component ions. The dissociation constant is the inverse of the association constant. In the special case of salts, the dissociation constant can also be called an ionization constant. |
| Concentration | In chemistry, concentration is the abundance of a constituent divided by the total volume of a mixture. Several types of mathematical description can be distinguished: mass concentration, molar concentration, number concentration, and volume concentration. The term concentration can be applied to any kind of chemical mixture, but most frequently it refers to solutes and solvents in solutions. |
| Ascorbic acid | Ascorbic acid is a naturally occurring organic compound with antioxidant properties. It is a white solid, but impure samples can appear yellowish. It dissolves well in water to give mildly acidic solutions. |

| | |
|---|---|
| Sulfuric acid | Sulfuric acid is a highly corrosive strong mineral acid with the molecular formula $H_2SO_4$. It is a pungent, colorless to slightly yellow viscous liquid which is soluble in water at all concentrations. Sometimes, it is dyed dark brown during production to alert people to its hazards. |
| Sulfurous acid | Sulfurous acid is the chemical compound with the formula $H_2SO_3$. There is no evidence that sulfurous acid exists in solution, but the molecule has been detected in the gas phase. The conjugate bases of this elusive acid are, however, common anions, bisulfite (or hydrogensulfite) and sulfite. |
| Tartaric acid | Tartaric acid is a white crystalline diprotic aldaric acid. It occurs naturally in many plants, particularly grapes, bananas, and tamarinds, is commonly combined with baking soda to function as a leavening agent in recipes, and is one of the main acids found in wine. It is added to other foods to give a sour taste, and is used as an antioxidant. |
| Weak base | In chemistry, a weak base is a chemical base that does not ionize fully in an aqueous solution. As Brønsted-Lowry bases are proton acceptors, a weak base may also be defined as a chemical base in which protonation is incomplete. This results in a relatively low pH compared to strong bases. |
| Hydroxylamine | Hydroxylamine is an inorganic compound with the formula $NH_2OH$. The pure material is a white, unstable crystalline, hygroscopic compound. However, hydroxylamine is almost always provided and used as an aqueous solution. It is used to prepare oximes, an important functional group. |
| Methylamine | Methylamine is the organic compound with a formula of $CH_3NH_2$. This colorless gas is a derivative of ammonia, but with one H atom replaced by a methyl group. It is the simplest primary amine. |
| Pyridine | Pyridine is a basic heterocyclic organic compound with the chemical formula $C_5H_5N$. It is structurally related to benzene, with one methine group (=CH-) replaced by a nitrogen atom. The pyridine ring occurs in many important compounds, including azines and the vitamins niacin and pyridoxal.<br><br>Pyridine was discovered in 1849 by the Scottish chemist Thomas Anderson as one of the constituents of bone oil. |
| Amine | Amines are organic compounds and functional groups that contain a basic nitrogen atom with a lone pair. Amines are derivatives of ammonia, wherein one or more hydrogen atoms have been replaced by a substituent such as an alkyl or aryl group. Important amines include amino acids, biogenic amines, trimethylamine, and aniline; see Category:Amines for a list of amines. |
| Sodium hypochlorite | Sodium hypochlorite is a chemical compound with the formula NaClO. It is composed of a sodium cation (Na+) and a hypochlorite anion (ClO-); it may also be viewed as the sodium salt of hypochlorous acid. It is commonly known as bleach or liquid bleach, is frequently used as a disinfectant or a bleaching agent. |

# 16. Acid-Base Equilibria

| | |
|---|---|
| Acid salt | Acid salt is a term for a class of salts formed by the partial neutralization of diprotic or polyprotic acids. Because the parent acid is only partially neutralized, one or more replaceable hydrogen atoms remain. Typical acid salts have one or more alkali (alkaline) metal ions as well as one or more hydrogen atoms. |
| Cadaverine | Cadaverine is a foul-smelling diamine compound produced by protein hydrolysis during putrefaction of animal tissue. Cadaverine is a toxic diamine with the formula $NH_2(CH_2)_5NH_2$, which is similar to putrescine. Cadaverine is also known by the names 1,5-pentanediamine and pentamethylenediamine. |
| Caffeine | Caffeine is a bitter, white crystalline xanthine alkaloid and a stimulant drug. Caffeine is found in varying quantities in the seeds, leaves, and fruit of some plants, where it acts as a natural pesticide that paralyzes and kills certain insects feeding on the plants, as well as enhancing the reward memory of pollinators. It is most commonly consumed by humans in infusions extracted from the seed of the coffee plant and the leaves of the tea bush, as well as from various foods and drinks containing products derived from the kola nut. |
| Codeine | Codeine or 3-methylmorphine is an opiate used for its analgesic, antitussive, antidiarrheal, antihypertensive, anxiolytic, antidepressant, sedative and hypnotic properties. It is also used to suppress premature labor contractions, myocardial infarction, and has many other potential and indicated uses. Codeine is the second-most predominant alkaloid in opium, at up to three percent. |
| Putrescine | Putrescine, or tetramethylenediamine, is a foul-smelling organic chemical compound $NH_24NH_2$ (1,4-diaminobutane or butanediamine) that is related to cadaverine; both are produced by the breakdown of amino acids in living and dead organisms and both are toxic in large doses. The two compounds are largely responsible for the foul odor of putrefying flesh, but also contribute to the odor of such processes as bad breath and bacterial vaginosis. They are also found in semen and some microalgae, together with related molecules like spermine and spermidine. |
| Quinine | Quinine is a natural white crystalline alkaloid having antipyretic (fever-reducing), antimalarial, analgesic (painkilling), and anti-inflammatory properties and a bitter taste. It is a stereoisomer of quinidine which, unlike quinine, is an antiarrhythmic. Quinine contains two major fused-ring systems: the aromatic quinoline and the bicyclic quinuclidine. |
| Hydrolysis | Hydrolysis usually means the cleavage of chemical bonds by the addition of water. Where a carbohydrate is broken into its component sugar molecules by hydrolysis this is termed saccharification. Generally, hydrolysis or saccharification is a step in the degradation of a substance. |
| Metal hydroxide | Metal hydroxide are hydroxides of metals. |

# 16. Acid-Base Equilibria

| Chemical structure | A chemical structure includes molecular geometry, electronic structure and crystal structure of molecules. Molecular geometry refers to the spatial arrangement of atoms in a molecule and the chemical bonds that hold the atoms together. Molecular geometry can range from the very simple, such as diatomic oxygen or nitrogen molecules, to the very complex, such as protein or DNA molecules. |
|---|---|
| Binary acid | Binary acids are certain molecular compounds in which hydrogen is combined with a second nonmetallic element.<br><br>Examples:•HF•HCl•HBr•HI<br><br>Their strengths depend on the solvation of the initial acid, the H-X bond energy, the electron affinity energy of X, and the solvation energy of X. Observed trends in acidity correlate with bond energies, the weaker the H-X bond, the stronger the acid. For example, there is a weak bond between hydrogen and iodine in hydroiodic acid, making it a very strong acid. |
| Hypobromous acid | Hypobromous acid is a weak, unstable acid with chemical formula HBrO. It is also called bromic(I) acid, bromanol or hydroxidobromine. It occurs only in solution and has chemical and physical properties that are very similar to those of hypochlorous acid.<br><br>In aqueous solution, hypobromous acid partially dissociates into the hypobromite anion $OBr^-$ and the cation $H^+$. |
| Hypoiodous acid | Hypoiodous acid is the inorganic compound with the chemical formula HIO. It forms when an aqueous solution of iodine is treated with mercuric or silver salts. It rapidly decomposes by disproportionation:$5\ HIO\ ?\ HIO_3 + 2I_2 + 2H_2O$<br><br>Hypoiodous acid is a weak acid with a $K_a$ of about $10^{-11}$. The conjugate base is hypoiodite ($IO^-$). |
| Chloric acid | Chloric acid, $HClO_3$, is an oxoacid of chlorine, and the formal precursor of chlorate salts. It is a strong acid ($pK_a$ ˜ -1) and oxidizing agent.<br><br>It is prepared by the reaction of sulfuric acid with barium chlorate, the insoluble barium sulfate being removed by precipitation:$Ba(ClO_3)_2 + H_2SO_4\ ?\ 2HClO_3 + BaSO_4$<br><br>Another method is the heating of hypochlorous acid, of which productions include chloric acid and hydrogen chloride:$3HClO\ ?\ HClO_3 + 2\ HCl$<br><br>It is also produced by the reaction of sulfuric acid with potassium chlorate in the combustion of sugar using potassium chlorate, sulfuric acid, and sugar. |

# 16. Acid-Base Equilibria

| | |
|---|---|
| Oxidation | Redox (reduction-oxidation) reactions include all chemical reactions in which atoms have their oxidation state changed; in general, redox reactions involve the transfer of electrons between species.<br><br>This can be either a simple redox process, such as the oxidation of carbon to yield carbon dioxide or the reduction of carbon by hydrogen to yield methane ($CH_4$), or a complex process such as the oxidation of glucose ($C_6H_{12}O_6$) in the human body through a series of complex electron transfer processes.<br><br>The term 'redox' comes from two concepts involved with electron transfer: reduction and oxidation. |
| Perchloric acid | Perchloric acid is an inorganic compound with the formula $HClO_4$. Usually found as an aqueous solution, this colorless compound is a stronger acid than sulfuric and nitric acids. It is a powerful oxidizer, but its aqueous solutions up to approximately 70% are generally safe, only showing strong acid features and no oxidizing properties. |
| Alanine | Alanine is an a-amino acid with the chemical formula $CH_3CH(NH_2)COOH$. The -isomer is one of the 20 amino acids encoded by the genetic code. Its codons are GCU, GCC, GCA, and GCG. It is classified as a nonpolar amino acid. -Alanine is second only to leucine in rate of occurrence, accounting for 7.8% of the primary structure in a sample of 1,150 proteins. |
| Amino acid | Amino acids are biologically important organic compounds made from amine ($-NH_2$) and carboxylic acid (-COOH) functional groups, along with a side-chain specific to each amino acid. The key elements of an amino acid are carbon, hydrogen, oxygen, and nitrogen, though other elements are found in the side-chains of certain amino acids. About 500 amino acids are known and can be classified in many ways. |
| Carboxylic acid | A carboxylic acid is an organic acid characterized by the presence of at least one carboxyl group. The general formula of a carboxylic acid is R-COOH, where R is some monovalent functional group. A carboxyl group (or carboxy) is a functional group consisting of a carbonyl (RR'C=O) and a hydroxyl (R-O-H), which has the formula -C(=O)OH, usually written as -COOH or $-CO_2H$.<br><br>Carboxylic acids are Brønsted-Lowry acids because they are proton ($H^+$) donors. |
| Electron | The electron is a subatomic particle with a negative elementary electric charge. Electrons belong to the first generation of the lepton particle family, and are generally thought to be elementary particles because they have no known components or substructure. The electron has a mass that is approximately 1/1836 that of the proton. |
| Electron acceptor | An electron acceptor is a chemical entity that accepts electrons transferred to it from another compound. |

|  | It is an oxidizing agent that, by virtue of its accepting electrons, is itself reduced in the process. |
|---|---|
|  | Typical oxidizing agents undergo permanent chemical alteration through covalent or ionic reaction chemistry, resulting in the complete and irreversible transfer of one or more electrons. |
| Carbonic acid | Not to be confused with carbolic acid, an antiquated name for phenol.Carbonic acid is also an archaic name for carbon dioxide. |
|  | Carbonic acid is the chemical compound with the formula $H_2CO_3$ (equivalently $OC_2$). It is also a name sometimes given to solutions of carbon dioxide in water (carbonated water), because such solutions contain small amounts of $H_2CO_3$. Carbonic acid, which is a weak acid, forms two kinds of salts, the carbonates and the bicarbonates. |
| Phosphorous acid | Phosphorous acid is the compound described by the formula $H_3PO_3$. This acid is diprotic (readily ionizes two protons), not triprotic as might be suggested by this formula. Phosphorous acid is an intermediate in the preparation of other phosphorus compounds. |
| Phenylacetic acid | Phenylacetic acid is an organic compound containing a phenyl functional group and a carboxylic acid functional group. It is a white solid with a disagreeable odour. |
| Absorption | In chemistry, absorption is a physical or chemical phenomenon or a process in which atoms, molecules, or ions enter some bulk phase - gas, liquid, or solid material. This is a different process from adsorption, since molecules undergoing absorption are taken up by the volume, not by the surface (as in the case for adsorption). A more general term is sorption, which covers absorption, adsorption, and ion exchange. |
| Carbon dioxide | Carbon dioxide is a naturally occurring chemical compound composed of two oxygen atoms each covalently double bonded to a single carbon atom. It is a gas at standard temperature and pressure and exists in Earth's atmosphere in this state, as a trace gas at a concentration of 0.039 per cent by volume. |
|  | As part of the carbon cycle, plants, algae, and cyanobacteria use light energy to photosynthesize carbohydrate from carbon dioxide and water, with oxygen produced as a waste product. |
| Dioxide | An oxide is a chemical compound that contains at least one oxygen atom and one other element in its chemical formula. Metal oxides typically contain an anion of oxygen in the oxidation state of -2. Most of the Earth's crust consists of solid oxides, the result of elements being oxidized by the oxygen in air or in water. Hydrocarbon combustion affords the two principal carbon oxides: carbon monoxide and carbon dioxide. |
| Acetylsalicylic acid | Aspirin, also known as acetylsalicylic acid (INN ( ?--?I--i- |

# 16. Acid-Base Equilibria

|  |  |
|---|---|
|  | -ik) ASA), is a salicylate drug, often used as an analgesic to relieve minor aches and pains, as an antipyretic to reduce fever, and as an anti-inflammatory medication. The active ingredient of Aspirin was first discovered from the bark of the willow tree in 1763 by Edward Stone of Wadham College, Oxford University. He had discovered salicylic acid, the active metabolite of aspirin. |
| Aspirin | Aspirin, also known as acetylsalicylic acid (INN ( ?--?l--i--ik) ASA), is a salicylate drug, often used as an analgesic to relieve minor aches and pains, as an antipyretic to reduce fever, and as an anti-inflammatory medication. Aspirin was first isolated by Felix Hoffmann, a chemist with the German company Bayer in 1897.<br><br>Salicylic acid, the main metabolite of aspirin, is an integral part of human and animal metabolism. |
| Hydrazoic acid | Hydrazoic acid, also known as hydrogen azide or azoimide, is a colorless, volatile, and explosive liquid at room temperature and pressure. It is a compound of nitrogen and hydrogen, having chemical formula $HN_3$. It was first isolated in 1890 by Theodor Curtius. |
| Saccharin | Saccharin is an artificial sweetener. The basic substance, benzoic sulfilimine, has effectively no food energy and is much sweeter than sucrose, but has a bitter or metallic aftertaste, especially at high concentrations. It is used to sweeten products such as drinks, candies, cookies, medicines, and toothpaste. |
| Butyric acid | Butyric acid, also known under the systematic name butanoic acid, is a carboxylic acid with the structural formula $CH_3CH_2CH_2-COOH$. Salts and esters of butyric acid are known as butyrates or butanoates. Butyric acid is found in milk, especially goat, sheep and buffalo's milk, butter, Parmesan cheese, and as a product of anaerobic fermentation (including in the colon and as body odor). It has an unpleasant smell and acrid taste, with a sweetish aftertaste (similar to ether). |
| Hemoglobin | Hemoglobin; also spelled haemoglobin and abbreviated Hb or Hgb, is the iron-containing oxygen-transport metalloprotein in the red blood cells of all vertebrates as well as the tissues of some invertebrates. Hemoglobin in the blood carries oxygen from the respiratory organs (lungs or gills) to the rest of the body (i.e. the tissues) where it releases the oxygen to burn nutrients to provide energy to power the functions of the organism, and collects the resultant carbon dioxide to bring it back to the respiratory organs to be dispensed from the organism.<br><br>In mammals, the protein makes up about 97% of the red blood cells' dry content (by weight), and around 35% of the total content (including water). |
| Oxalic acid | Oxalic acid is an organic compound with the formula $H_2C_2O_4$. It is a colorless crystalline solid that dissolves in water to give colorless solutions. It is classified as a dicarboxylic acid. |
| Cocaine | Cocaine is a crystalline tropane alkaloid that is obtained from the leaves of the coca plant. The name comes from 'coca' and the alkaloid suffix '-ine', forming 'cocaine'. |

1. The _____ is the anion Cl⁻. It is formed when the element chlorine (a halogen) gains an electron or when a compound such as hydrogen chloride is dissolved in water or other polar solvents. Chlorides salts such as sodium chloride are often very soluble in water.

   a. Chloride ion
   b. Barium azide
   c. Barium chlorate
   d. Barium iodate

2. _____ is a clear, colorless, highly pungent solution of hydrogen chloride in water. It is a highly corrosive, strong mineral acid with many industrial uses. _____ is found naturally in gastric acid.

   a. Boric acid
   b. Bromic acid
   c. Chloric acid
   d. Hydrochloric acid

3. _____ usually means the cleavage of chemical bonds by the addition of water. Where a carbohydrate is broken into its component sugar molecules by _____ this is termed saccharification. Generally, _____ or saccharification is a step in the degradation of a substance.

   a. Hydrolysis
   b. Binding selectivity
   c. Bromley equation
   d. Buffer solution

4. _____ is the process by which an atom or a molecule acquires a negative or positive charge by gaining or losing electrons.

   a. Berkeley Geochronology Center
   b. Ionization
   c. Calutron
   d. Canadian Penning Trap Mass Spectrometer

5. _____ is a foul-smelling diamine compound produced by protein hydrolysis during putrefaction of animal tissue. _____ is a toxic diamine with the formula $NH_2(CH_2)_5NH_2$, which is similar to putrescine. _____ is also known by the names 1,5-pentanediamine and pentamethylenediamine.

   a. Benzathine
   b. Cadaverine
   c. 1,3,5-Trioxanetrione
   d. 1,3,5-Trioxane

1. a
2. d
3. a
4. b
5. b

*You can take the complete Chapter Practice Test*

**for 16. Acid-Base Equilibria**
on all key terms, persons, places, and concepts.

**Online 99 Cents**

*http://www.JustTheFacts101.com*

**Use www.JustTheFacts101.com for all your study needs**

**including Facts101's online interactive problem solving labs in**

**chemistry, statistics, mathematics, and more.**

# 17. Additional Aspects of Aqueous Equilibria

CHAPTER OUTLINE: KEY TERMS, PEOPLE, PLACES, CONCEPTS

| | |
|---|---|
| | Calcium |
| | Calcium carbonate |
| | Coral reef |
| | Absorption |
| | Carbon dioxide |
| | Dioxide |
| | Solvent |
| | Acetic acid |
| | Sodium acetate |
| | Weak base |
| | Concentration |
| | Product |
| | Blackbody radiation |
| | Radiation |
| | Petroleum |
| | Sodium lactate |
| | Buffer |
| | Aqueous |
| | Mole |
| | Carbonic acid |
| | Hemoglobin |

Oxygen

Equivalence point

Hydrochloric acid

Titration curve

Titration

Methyl red

Phenolphthalein

Diprotic acid

Calcium fluoride

Dissolution

Ionic compound

Precipitation

Entropy

Molar solubility

Silver chromate

Solubility

Amphoterism

Calcite

Sodium fluoride

Sodium monofluorophosphate

Metal hydroxide

# 17. Additional Aspects of Aqueous Equilibria
CHAPTER OUTLINE: KEY TERMS, PEOPLE, PLACES, CONCEPTS

Alkali

Alkali metal

Bauxite

Reaction quotient

Sulfide

Chloride ion

Pyruvic acid

Quantitative analysis

Hydroxide

Lewis structure

Ammonia

Formic acid

Sodium formate

Acetylsalicylic acid

Aspirin

| Calcium | Calcium is the chemical element with symbol Ca and atomic number 20. Calcium is a soft gray alkaline earth metal, and is the fifth-most-abundant element by mass in the Earth's crust. Calcium is also the fifth-most-abundant dissolved ion in seawater by both molarity and mass, after sodium, chloride, magnesium, and sulfate.<br><br>Calcium is essential for living organisms, in particular in cell physiology, where movement of the calcium ion $Ca^{2+}$ into and out of the cytoplasm functions as a signal for many cellular processes. |
|---|---|
| Calcium carbonate | Calcium carbonate is a chemical compound with the formula $CaCO_3$. It is a common substance found in rocks in all parts of the world, and is the main component of shells of marine organisms, snails, coal balls, pearls, and eggshells. Calcium carbonate is the active ingredient in agricultural lime, and is created when Ca ions in hard water react with carbonate ions creating limescale. |
| Coral reef | Coral reefs are underwater structures made from calcium carbonate secreted by corals. Coral reefs are colonies of tiny animals found in marine waters that contain few nutrients. Most coral reefs are built from stony corals, which in turn consist of polyps that cluster in groups. |
| Absorption | In chemistry, absorption is a physical or chemical phenomenon or a process in which atoms, molecules, or ions enter some bulk phase - gas, liquid, or solid material. This is a different process from adsorption, since molecules undergoing absorption are taken up by the volume, not by the surface (as in the case for adsorption). A more general term is sorption, which covers absorption, adsorption, and ion exchange. |
| Carbon dioxide | Carbon dioxide is a naturally occurring chemical compound composed of two oxygen atoms each covalently double bonded to a single carbon atom. It is a gas at standard temperature and pressure and exists in Earth's atmosphere in this state, as a trace gas at a concentration of 0.039 per cent by volume.<br><br>As part of the carbon cycle, plants, algae, and cyanobacteria use light energy to photosynthesize carbohydrate from carbon dioxide and water, with oxygen produced as a waste product. |
| Dioxide | An oxide is a chemical compound that contains at least one oxygen atom and one other element in its chemical formula. Metal oxides typically contain an anion of oxygen in the oxidation state of -2. Most of the Earth's crust consists of solid oxides, the result of elements being oxidized by the oxygen in air or in water. Hydrocarbon combustion affords the two principal carbon oxides: carbon monoxide and carbon dioxide. |
| Solvent | A solvent is a substance that dissolves a solute (a chemically different liquid, solid or gas), resulting in a solution. A solvent is usually a liquid but can also be a solid or a gas. The maximum quantity of solute that can dissolve in a specific volume of solvent varies with temperature. |

# 17. Additional Aspects of Aqueous Equilibria

| | |
|---|---|
| Acetic acid | Acetic acid is an organic compound with the chemical formula $CH_3COOH$ (also written as $CH_3CO_2H$ or $C_2H_4O_2$). It is a colourless liquid that when undiluted is also called glacial acetic acid. Acetic acid is the main component of vinegar (apart from water; vinegar is roughly 8% acetic acid by volume), and has a distinctive sour taste and pungent smell. |
| Sodium acetate | Sodium acetate, $CH_3COONa$, also abbreviated NaOAc, also sodium ethanoate, is the sodium salt of acetic acid. This colourless salt has a wide range of uses. |
| Weak base | In chemistry, a weak base is a chemical base that does not ionize fully in an aqueous solution. As Brønsted-Lowry bases are proton acceptors, a weak base may also be defined as a chemical base in which protonation is incomplete. This results in a relatively low pH compared to strong bases. |
| Concentration | In chemistry, concentration is the abundance of a constituent divided by the total volume of a mixture. Several types of mathematical description can be distinguished: mass concentration, molar concentration, number concentration, and volume concentration. The term concentration can be applied to any kind of chemical mixture, but most frequently it refers to solutes and solvents in solutions. |
| Product | Product are formed during chemical reactions as reagents are consumed. Products have lower energy than the reagents and are produced during the reaction according to the second law of thermodynamics. The released energy comes from changes in chemical bonds between atoms in reagent molecules and may be given off in the form of heat or light. |
| Blackbody radiation | Black-body radiation is the type of electromagnetic radiation within or surrounding a body in thermodynamic equilibrium with its environment, or emitted by a black body held at constant, uniform temperature. The radiation has a specific spectrum and intensity that depends only on the temperature of the body.

The thermal radiation spontaneously emitted by many ordinary objects can be approximated as blackbody radiation. |
| Radiation | In physics, radiation is a process in which energetic particles or energetic waves travel through a vacuum, or through matter-containing media that are not required for their propagation. Waves of a mass filled medium itself, such as water waves or sound waves, are usually not considered to be forms of 'radiation' in this sense.

Radiation can be classified as either ionizing or non-ionizing according to whether it ionizes or does not ionize ordinary chemical matter. |
| Petroleum | Petroleum (L. petroleum, from Greek: p?t?a + Latin: |

oleum (oil)) is a naturally occurring, smelly, yellow-to-black liquid consisting of a complex mixture of hydrocarbons of various molecular weights and other liquid organic compounds, that are found in geologic formations beneath the Earth's surface. The name Petroleum covers both naturally occurring unprocessed crude oils and petroleum products that are made up of refined crude oil. A fossil fuel, it is formed when large quantities of dead organisms, usually zooplankton and algae, are buried underneath sedimentary rock and undergo intense heat and pressure.

| Sodium lactate | Sodium lactate is the sodium salt of lactic acid that has a mild saline taste. It is produced by fermentation of a sugar source, such as corn or beets, and then, by neutralizing the resulting lactic acid to create a compound having the formula $NaC_3H_5O_3$ |
|---|---|
| Buffer | In a fiber optic cable, a buffer is one type of component used to encapsulate one or more optical fibers for the purpose of providing such functions as mechanical isolation, protection from physical damage and fiber identification. |
| | The buffer may take the form of a miniature conduit, contained within the cable and called a 'loose buffer', or 'loose buffer tube'. A loose buffer may contain more than one fiber, and sometimes contains a lubricating gel. |
| Aqueous | An aqueous solution is a solution in which the solvent is water. It is usually shown in chemical equations by appending (aq) to the relevant formula. For example, a solution of ordinary table salt, or sodium chloride (NaCl), in water would be represented as NaCl(aq). |
| Mole | Mole is a unit of measurement used in chemistry to express amounts of a chemical substance, defined as the amount of any substance that contains as many elementary entities (e.g., atoms, molecules, ions, electrons) as there are atoms in 12 grams of pure carbon-12, the isotope of carbon with relative atomic mass 12. This corresponds to the Avogadro constant, which has a value of $6.02214129(27) \times 10^{23}$ elementary entities of the substance. It is one of the base units in the International System of Units, and has the unit symbol mol and corresponds with the dimension symbol N. In honour of the unit, chemists often celebrate October 23 (a reference to the $10^{23}$ part of Avogadro's number) as 'Mole Day'. |
| | The mole is widely used in chemistry instead of units of mass or volume as a convenient way to express amounts of reactants or of products of chemical reactions. |
| Carbonic acid | Not to be confused with carbolic acid, an antiquated name for phenol. Carbonic acid is also an archaic name for carbon dioxide. |
| | Carbonic acid is the chemical compound with the formula $H_2CO_3$ (equivalently $OC_2$). It is also a name sometimes given to solutions of carbon dioxide in water (carbonated water), because such solutions contain small amounts of $H_2CO_3$. |

# 17. Additional Aspects of Aqueous Equilibria

| | |
|---|---|
| Hemoglobin | Hemoglobin; also spelled haemoglobin and abbreviated Hb or Hgb, is the iron-containing oxygen-transport metalloprotein in the red blood cells of all vertebrates as well as the tissues of some invertebrates. Hemoglobin in the blood carries oxygen from the respiratory organs (lungs or gills) to the rest of the body (i.e. the tissues) where it releases the oxygen to burn nutrients to provide energy to power the functions of the organism, and collects the resultant carbon dioxide to bring it back to the respiratory organs to be dispensed from the organism.<br><br>In mammals, the protein makes up about 97% of the red blood cells' dry content (by weight), and around 35% of the total content (including water). |
| Oxygen | Oxygen is a chemical element with symbol O and atomic number 8. It is a member of the chalcogen group on the periodic table and is a highly reactive nonmetallic element and oxidizing agent that readily forms compounds (notably oxides) with most elements. By mass, oxygen is the third-most abundant element in the universe, after hydrogen and helium At STP, two atoms of the element bind to form dioxygen, a diatomic gas that is colorless, odorless, and tasteless; with the formula $O_2$.<br><br>Many major classes of organic molecules in living organisms, such as proteins, nucleic acids, carbohydrates, and fats, contain oxygen, as do the major inorganic compounds that are constituents of animal shells, teeth, and bone. |
| Equivalence point | The equivalence point, or stoichiometric point, of a chemical reaction is the point at which an added titrant is stoichiometrically equal to the number of moles of substance present in the sample: the smallest amount of titrant that is sufficient to fully neutralize or react with the analyte. In some cases there are multiple equivalence points, which are multiples of the first equivalence point, such as in the titration of a diprotic acid.<br><br>Acid-Base Equivalence Point - the point at which chemically equivalent quantities of acid and base have been mixed, can be found by means of an indicator<br><br>In a reaction, the equivalence of the reactants as well as products is conserved. |
| Hydrochloric acid | Hydrochloric acid is a clear, colorless, highly pungent solution of hydrogen chloride in water. It is a highly corrosive, strong mineral acid with many industrial uses. Hydrochloric acid is found naturally in gastric acid. |
| Titration curve | Titrations are often recorded on graphs called titration curves, which generally contain the volume of the titrant as the independent variable and the pH of the solution as the dependent variable.<br><br>The equivalence point on the graph is where all of the starting solution (usually an acid) has been neutralized by the titrant (usually a base). |

| Titration | Titration, also known as titrimetry, is a common laboratory method of quantitative chemical analysis that is used to determine the unknown concentration of an identified analyte. Since volume measurements play a key role in titration, it is also known as volumetric analysis. A reagent, called the titrant or titrator is prepared as a standard solution. |
|---|---|
| Methyl red | Methyl red also called C.I. Acid Red 2, is an indicator dye that turns red in acidic solutions. It is an azo dye, and is a dark red crystalline powder.<br><br>Methyl red is a pH indicator; it is red in pH under 4.4, yellow in pH over 6.2, and orange in between, with a $pK_a$ of 5.1. |
| Phenolphthalein | Phenolphthalein is a chemical compound with the formula $C_{20}H_{14}O_4$ and is often written as 'HIn' or 'phph' in shorthand notation. Often used in titrations, it turns colorless in acidic solutions and pink in basic solutions. If the concentration of indicator is particularly strong, it can appear purple. |
| Diprotic acid | A diprotic acid is an acid such as $H_2SO_4$ that contains within its molecular structure two hydrogen atoms per molecule capable of dissociating (i.e. ionizable) in water. The complete dissociation of diprotic acids is of the same form as sulfuric acid: $H_2SO_4$ ? $H^+(aq) + HSO_4^-(aq)$ $K_a = 1 \times 10^3 HSO_4^-$ ? $H^+(aq) + SO_4^{2-}(aq)$ $K_a = 1 \times 10^{-2}$<br><br>The dissociation does not happen all at once due to the two stages of dissociation having different $K_a$ values. The first dissociation will, in the case of sulfuric acid, occur completely, but the second one will not. |
| Calcium fluoride | Calcium fluoride is the inorganic compound with the formula $CaF_2$. This ionic compound of calcium and fluorine occurs naturally as the mineral fluorite (also called fluorspar). It is the source of most of the world's fluorine. |
| Dissolution | Dissolution is the process by which a solute forms a solution in a solvent. The solute, in the case of solids, has its crystalline structure disintegrated as separate ions, atoms, and molecules form. For liquids and gases, the molecules must be adaptable with those of the solvent for a solution to form. |
| Ionic compound | In chemistry, an ionic compound is a chemical compound in which ions are held together in a lattice structure by ionic bonds. Usually, the positively charged portion consists of metal cations and the negatively charged portion is an anion or polyatomic ion. Ions in ionic compounds are held together by the electrostatic forces between oppositely charged bodies. |
| Precipitation | Precipitation is the formation of a solid in a solution or inside another solid during a chemical reaction or by diffusion in a solid. When the reaction occurs in a liquid solution, the solid formed is called the precipitate. The chemical that causes the solid to form is called the precipitant. |

# 17. Additional Aspects of Aqueous Equilibria

| | |
|---|---|
| Entropy | In thermodynamics, entropy is a measure of the number of specific ways in which a thermodynamic system may be arranged, often taken to be a measure of disorder, or a measure of progressing towards thermodynamic equilibrium. The entropy of an isolated system never decreases, because isolated systems spontaneously evolve towards thermodynamic equilibrium, which is the state of maximum entropy.<br><br>Entropy was originally defined for a thermodynamically reversible process $$\Delta S = \int \frac{dQ_{rev}}{T}$$ as<br><br>where the entropy is found from the uniform thermodynamic temperature of a closed system dividing an incremental reversible transfer of heat into that system . |
| Molar solubility | Molar solubility is the number of moles of a substance that can be dissolved per liter of solution before the solution becomes saturated. It can be calculated from a substance's solubility product constant ($K_{sp}$) and stoichiometry. The units are mol/L, sometimes written as M. |
| Silver chromate | Silver chromate is a brown-red monoclinic crystal and is a chemical precursor to modern photography. It can be formed by combining silver nitrate ($AgNO_3$) and potassium chromate ($K_2CrO_4$) or sodium chromate ($Na_2CrO_4$). This reaction has been important in neuroscience, as it is used in the 'Golgi method' of staining neurons for microscopy: the silver chromate produced precipitates inside neurons and makes their morphology visible. |
| Solubility | Solubility is the property of a solid, liquid, or gaseous chemical substance called solute to dissolve in a solid, liquid, or gaseous solvent to form a homogeneous solution of the solute in the solvent. The solubility of a substance fundamentally depends on the physical and chemical properties of the solute and solvent as well as on temperature, pressure and the pH of the solution. The extent of the solubility of a substance in a specific solvent is measured as the saturation concentration, where adding more solute does not increase the concentration of the solution and begin to precipitate the excess amount of solute. |
| Amphoterism | In chemistry, an amphoteric species is a molecule or ion that can react as an acid as well as a base. Many metals (such as zinc, tin, lead, aluminium, and beryllium) and most metalloids form amphoteric oxides or hydroxides. Amphoterism depends on the oxidation state of the oxide. |
| Calcite | Calcite is a carbonate mineral and the most stable polymorph of calcium carbonate . The other polymorphs are the minerals aragonite and vaterite. Aragonite will change to calcite at 380-470°C, and vaterite is even less stable. |
| Sodium fluoride | Sodium fluoride is an inorganic chemical compound with the formula NaF. A colorless solid, it is a source of the fluoride ion in diverse applications. |

| | |
|---|---|
| Sodium monofluorophosphate | Sodium monofluorophosphate, commonly abbreviated MFP, is the inorganic compound with the formula $Na_2PO_3F$. Typical for a salt, MFP is odourless, colourless, and water-soluble. This salt is an ingredient in some toothpastes. |
| Metal hydroxide | Metal hydroxide are hydroxides of metals. |
| Alkali | In chemistry, an alkali is a basic, ionic salt of an alkali metal or alkaline earth metal chemical element. Some authors also define an alkali as a base that dissolves in water. A solution of a soluble base has a pH greater than 7.0. The adjective alkaline is commonly, and alkalescent less often, used in English as a synonym for basic, especially for soluble bases. |
| Alkali metal | The alkali metals are a group in the periodic table consisting of the chemical elements lithium, sodium (Na), potassium (K), rubidium (Rb), caesium (Cs), and francium (Fr). This group lies in the s-block of the periodic table as all alkali metals have their outermost electron in an s-orbital. The alkali metals provide the best example of group trends in properties in the periodic table, with elements exhibiting well-characterized homologous behaviour. |
| Bauxite | Bauxite is an aluminium ore and is the main source of aluminium. This form of rock consists mostly of the minerals gibbsite $Al(OH)_3$, boehmite ?-AlO(OH), and diaspore a-AlO(OH), in a mixture with the two iron oxides goethite and haematite, the clay mineral kaolinite, and small amounts of anatase $TiO_2$. Bauxite was named after the village Les Baux in southern France, where it was first recognized as containing aluminium and named by the French geologist Pierre Berthier in 1821. |
| Reaction quotient | In chemistry, a reaction quotient: $Q_r$ is a function of the activities or concentrations of the chemical species involved in a chemical reaction. In the special case that the reaction is at equilibrium the reaction quotient is equal to the equilibrium constant. |
| | A general chemical reaction in which a moles of a reactant A and ß moles of a reactant B react to give s moles of a product S and t moles of a product T can be written asaA + ßB sS + tT |
| | The reaction is written as an equilibrium even though in many cases it may appear to have gone to completion. |
| Sulfide | Sulfide is an inorganic anion with the chemical formula $S^{2-}$. It contributes no color to sulfide salts. Sulfide is the main component of niningerite (niningerite is roughly 47% sulfide by mass), and contributes no odor to sulfide salts. |
| Chloride ion | The chloride ion is the anion $Cl^-$. It is formed when the element chlorine (a halogen) gains an electron or when a compound such as hydrogen chloride is dissolved in water or other polar solvents. Chlorides salts such as sodium chloride are often very soluble in water. |

# 17. Additional Aspects of Aqueous Equilibria

| | |
|---|---|
| Pyruvic acid | Pyruvic acid is an organic acid, a ketone, as well as the simplest of the alpha-keto acids. The carboxylate ($COO^-$) anion of pyruvic acid, its Brønsted-Lowry conjugate base, $CH_3COCOO^-$, is known as pyruvate, and is a key intersection in several metabolic pathways.<br><br>Pyruvic acid can be made from glucose through glycolysis, converted back to carbohydrates (such as glucose) via gluconeogenesis, or to fatty acids through acetyl-CoA. It can also be used to construct the amino acid alanine and be converted into ethanol. |
| Quantitative analysis | In chemistry, quantitative analysis is the determination of the absolute or relative abundance of one, several or all particular substance(s) present in a sample. |
| Hydroxide | Hydroxide is a diatomic anion with chemical formula $OH^-$. It consists of an oxygen and a hydrogen atom held together by a covalent bond, and carries a negative electric charge. It is an important but usually minor constituent of water. |
| Lewis structure | Lewis structures are diagrams that show the bonding between atoms of a molecule and the lone pairs of electrons that may exist in the molecule. A Lewis structure can be drawn for any covalently bonded molecule, as well as coordination compounds. The Lewis structure was named after Gilbert N |
| Ammonia | Ammonia or azane is a compound of nitrogen and hydrogen with the formula $NH_3$. It is a colourless gas with a characteristic pungent smell. Ammonia contributes significantly to the nutritional needs of terrestrial organisms by serving as a precursor to food and fertilizers. |
| Formic acid | Formic acid is the simplest carboxylic acid. Its chemical formula is $HCOOH$ or $HCO_2H$. It is an important intermediate in chemical synthesis and occurs naturally, most notably in ant venom. In fact, its name comes from the Latin word for ant, formica, referring to its early isolation by the distillation of ant bodies. |
| Sodium formate | Sodium formate, $HCOONa$, is the sodium salt of formic acid, $HCOOH$. It usually appears as a white deliquescent powder. |
| Acetylsalicylic acid | Aspirin, also known as acetylsalicylic acid (INN ( ?--?I--i--ik) ASA), is a salicylate drug, often used as an analgesic to relieve minor aches and pains, as an antipyretic to reduce fever, and as an anti-inflammatory medication. The active ingredient of Aspirin was first discovered from the bark of the willow tree in 1763 by Edward Stone of Wadham College, Oxford University. He had discovered salicylic acid, the active metabolite of aspirin. |
| Aspirin | Aspirin, also known as acetylsalicylic acid (INN ( ?--?I--i--ik) ASA), is a salicylate drug, often used as an analgesic to relieve minor aches and pains, as an antipyretic to reduce fever, and as an anti-inflammatory medication. Aspirin was first isolated by Felix Hoffmann, a chemist with the German company Bayer in 1897. |

1. _____s are diagrams that show the bonding between atoms of a molecule and the lone pairs of electrons that may exist in the molecule. A _____ can be drawn for any covalently bonded molecule, as well as coordination compounds. The _____ was named after Gilbert N

   a. Bond energy
   b. Lewis structure
   c. Double bond
   d. Formal charge

2. Aspirin, also known as _____ (INN ( ?--?I--i--ik) ASA), is a salicylate drug, often used as an analgesic to relieve minor aches and pains, as an antipyretic to reduce fever, and as an anti-inflammatory medication. The active ingredient of Aspirin was first discovered from the bark of the willow tree in 1763 by Edward Stone of Wadham College, Oxford University. He had discovered salicylic acid, the active metabolite of aspirin.

   a. Acetylsalicylic acid
   b. Calcium iodide
   c. Choleretic
   d. Hydrocholeretic

3. _____ is the chemical element with symbol Ca and atomic number 20. _____ is a soft gray alkaline earth metal, and is the fifth-most-abundant element by mass in the Earth's crust. _____ is also the fifth-most-abundant dissolved ion in seawater by both molarity and mass, after sodium, chloride, magnesium, and sulfate.

   _____ is essential for living organisms, in particular in cell physiology, where movement of the _____ ion $Ca^{2+}$ into and out of the cytoplasm functions as a signal for many cellular processes.

   a. Barium
   b. Calcium
   c. Beryllium
   d. Bismuth

4. A _____ is a substance that dissolves a solute (a chemically different liquid, solid or gas), resulting in a solution. A _____ is usually a liquid but can also be a solid or a gas. The maximum quantity of solute that can dissolve in a specific volume of _____ varies with temperature.

   a. Bioorthogonal chemistry
   b. Solvent
   c. Carbothermic reaction
   d. Ceramide phosphoethanolamine synthase

5. . In chemistry, an amphoteric species is a molecule or ion that can react as an acid as well as a base. Many metals (such as zinc, tin, lead, aluminium, and beryllium) and most metalloids form amphoteric oxides or hydroxides. _____ depends on the oxidation state of the oxide.

a. Amphoterism
b. GeSbTe
c. Liquidmetal
d. Magnesium aluminide

**1.** b
**2.** a
**3.** b
**4.** b
**5.** a

## You can take the complete Chapter Practice Test

**for 17. Additional Aspects of Aqueous Equilibria**
on all key terms, persons, places, and concepts.

### Online 99 Cents

### http://www.JustTheFacts101.com

**Use www.JustTheFacts101.com for all your study needs**

**including Facts101's online interactive problem solving labs in**

**chemistry, statistics, mathematics, and more.**

CHAPTER OUTLINE: KEY TERMS, PEOPLE, PLACES, CONCEPTS

| | |
|---|---|
| | Environment |
| | Atmosphere |
| | Mesosphere |
| | Stratosphere |
| | Tellurium |
| | Thermosphere |
| | Tropopause |
| | Troposphere |
| | Argon |
| | Bond energy |
| | Carbon monoxide |
| | Helium |
| | Hydrogen |
| | Krypton |
| | Lewis structure |
| | Methane |
| | Neon |
| | Nitric oxide |
| | Nitrogen |
| | Nitrous oxide |
| | Oxygen |

# 18. Chemistry of the Environment

CHAPTER OUTLINE: KEY TERMS, PEOPLE, PLACES, CONCEPTS

- Ozone
- Sulfur dioxide
- Xenon
- Absorption
- Component
- Dioxide
- Effusion
- Photodissociation
- Photochemical reactions
- Dissociation
- Ozone layer
- Chlorine monoxide
- Chlorofluorocarbon
- Curie
- Dobson unit
- Bromine
- Bromide
- Carbonic acid
- Hydrocarbon
- Polar molecules
- Sulfur

CHAPTER OUTLINE: KEY TERMS, PEOPLE, PLACES, CONCEPTS

| | Sulfuric acid |
| --- | --- |
| | Combustion |
| | Calcium carbonate |
| | Corrosion |
| | Calcium oxide |
| | Catalytic converter |
| | Nitrogen dioxide |
| | Unburned hydrocarbon |
| | Fossil fuel |
| | Greenhouse effect |
| | Natural gas |
| | Carbon dioxide |
| | Extraction |
| | Greenhouse gas |
| | Half-life |
| | Oxidation |
| | Water cycle |
| | Boric acid |
| | Calcium |
| | Chloride ion |
| | Fluoride |

Potassium

Strontium

Groundwater

Arsenic

Water quality

Dissolution

Desalination

Distillation

Reverse osmosis

Water purification

Sewage

LifeStraw

Hydraulic fracturing

Trihalomethane

Water chlorination

Atom economy

Chlorine dioxide

Closed system

Green chemistry

Atom

Absorption spectrum

# 18. Chemistry of the Environment



CHAPTER OUTLINE: KEY TERMS, PEOPLE, PLACES, CONCEPTS

- Benzene
- Catalysis
- Styrene
- Efficiency
- Acetic acid
- Hydroquinone
- Organic compound
- Supercritical fluid
- Terephthalic acid
- Toluene
- Volatile organic compound
- Solvent
- Alkyne
- Azide
- Air pollution
- Hard water
- Formaldehyde
- Gold
- Chloromethane
- Ketone
- Lactone

# 18. Chemistry of the Environment
### CHAPTER OUTLINE: KEY TERMS, PEOPLE, PLACES, CONCEPTS

| | Water softening |
|---|---|
| | Hydroxyl radical |
| | Bioremediation |
| | Polyurethane |

**Environment**

In science and engineering, a system is the part of the universe that is being studied, while the environment is the remainder of the universe that lies outside the boundaries of the system. It is also known as the surroundings, and in thermodynamics, as the reservoir. Depending on the type of system, it may interact with the environment by exchanging mass, energy (including heat and work), linear momentum, angular momentum, electric charge, or other conserved properties.

**Atmosphere**

The standard atmosphere is an international reference pressure defined as 101325 Pa and used as a unit of pressure.

**Mesosphere**

The mesosphere is the layer of the Earth's atmosphere that is directly above the stratopause and directly below the mesopause. In the mesosphere temperature decreases with increasing height. The upper boundary of the mesosphere is the mesopause, which can be the coldest naturally occurring place on Earth with temperatures below 130 K (-226 °F; -143 °C).

**Stratosphere**

The stratosphere is the second major layer of Earth's atmosphere, just above the troposphere, and below the mesosphere. It is stratified in temperature, with warmer layers higher up and cooler layers farther down. This is in contrast to the troposphere near the Earth's surface, which is cooler higher up and warmer farther down.

**Tellurium**

Tellurium is a chemical element with symbol Te and atomic number 52. A brittle, mildly toxic, rare, silver-white metalloid which looks similar to tin, tellurium is chemically related to selenium and sulfur. It is occasionally found in native form, as elemental crystals. Tellurium is far more common in the universe as a whole than it is on Earth.

**Thermosphere**

The thermosphere is the layer of the Earth's atmosphere directly above the mesosphere and directly below the exosphere. Within this layer, ultraviolet radiation (UV) causes ionization.

| Tropopause | The tropopause is the boundary in the Earth's atmosphere between the troposphere and the stratosphere. |
|---|---|
| Troposphere | The troposphere is the lowest portion of Earth's atmosphere. It contains approximately 80% of the atmosphere's mass and 99% of its water vapour and aerosols. The average depth of the troposphere is approximately 17 km (11 mi) in the middle latitudes. |
| Argon | Argon is a chemical element with symbol Ar and atomic number 18. It is in group 18 of the periodic table and is a noble gas. Argon is the third most common gas in the Earth's atmosphere, at 0.93% (9,300 ppm), making it approximately 23.8 times as abundant as the next most common atmospheric gas, carbon dioxide (390 ppm), and more than 500 times as abundant as the next most common noble gas, neon (18 ppm). Nearly all of this argon is radiogenic argon-40 derived from the decay of potassium-40 in the Earth's crust. |
| Bond energy | In chemistry, bond energy is the measure of bond strength in a chemical bond. It is the heat required to break one mole of molecules into their individual atoms. For example, the carbon-hydrogen bond energy in methane E(C-H) is the enthalpy change involved with breaking up one molecule of methane into a carbon atom and 4 hydrogen radicals divided by 4. Bond energy should not be confused with bond-dissociation energy. |
| Carbon monoxide | Carbon monoxide is a colorless, odorless, and tasteless gas that is slightly less dense than air. It is toxic to humans and animals when encountered in higher concentrations, although it is also produced in normal animal metabolism in low quantities, and is thought to have some normal biological functions. In the atmosphere, it is spatially variable, short lived, having a role in the formation of ground-level ozone. |
| Helium | Helium is a chemical element with symbol He and atomic number 2. It is a colorless, odorless, tasteless, non-toxic, inert, monatomic gas that heads the noble gas group in the periodic table. Its boiling and melting points are the lowest among the elements and it exists only as a gas except in extreme conditions.<br><br>Helium is the second lightest element and is the second most abundant element in the observable universe, being present at about 24% of the total elemental mass, which is more than 12 times the mass of all the heavier elements combined. |
| Hydrogen | Hydrogen is a chemical element with chemical symbol H and atomic number 1. With an atomic weight of 1.00794 u, hydrogen is the lightest element and its monatomic form (H) is the most abundant chemical substance, constituting roughly 75% of the Universe's baryonic mass. Non-remnant stars are mainly composed of hydrogen in its plasma state. |

# 18. Chemistry of the Environment

| | |
|---|---|
| Krypton | Krypton is a chemical element with symbol Kr and atomic number 36. It is a member of group 18 (noble gases) elements. A colorless, odorless, tasteless noble gas, krypton occurs in trace amounts in the atmosphere, is isolated by fractionally distilling liquified air, and is often used with other rare gases in fluorescent lamps. Krypton is inert for most practical purposes. |
| Lewis structure | Lewis structures are diagrams that show the bonding between atoms of a molecule and the lone pairs of electrons that may exist in the molecule. A Lewis structure can be drawn for any covalently bonded molecule, as well as coordination compounds. The Lewis structure was named after Gilbert N |
| Methane | Methane is a chemical compound with the chemical formula $CH_4$ (one atom of carbon and four atoms of hydrogen). It is the simplest alkane and the main component of natural gas. The relative abundance of methane makes it an attractive fuel. |
| Neon | Neon is a chemical element with symbol Ne and atomic number 10. It is in group 18 (noble gases) of the periodic table. Neon is a colorless, odorless, inert monatomic gas under standard conditions, with about two-thirds the density of air. It was discovered (along with krypton and xenon) in 1898 as one of the three residual rare inert elements remaining in dry air, after nitrogen, oxygen, argon and carbon dioxide are removed. |
| Nitric oxide | Nitric oxide, or nitrogen oxide, also known as nitrogen monoxide, is a molecule with chemical formula NO. It is a free radical and is an important intermediate in the chemical industry. Nitric oxide is a by-product of combustion of substances in the air, as in automobile engines, fossil fuel power plants, and is produced naturally during the electrical discharges of lightning in thunderstorms.

In mammals including humans, NO is an important cellular signaling molecule involved in many physiological and pathological processes. |
| Nitrogen | Nitrogen, symbol N, is the chemical element of atomic number 7. At room temperature, it is a gas of diatomic molecules and is colorless and odorless. Nitrogen is a common element in the universe, estimated at about seventh in total abundance in our galaxy and the Solar System. On Earth, the element is primarily found as the free element; it forms about 80% of the Earth's atmosphere. |
| Nitrous oxide | Nitrous oxide, commonly known as laughing gas, is a chemical compound with the formula $N_2O$. It is an oxide of nitrogen. At room temperature, it is a colourless, non-flammable gas, with a slightly sweet odour and taste. |
| Oxygen | Oxygen is a chemical element with symbol O and atomic number 8. It is a member of the chalcogen group on the periodic table and is a highly reactive nonmetallic element and oxidizing agent that readily forms compounds (notably oxides) with most elements. |

By mass, oxygen is the third-most abundant element in the universe, after hydrogen and helium At STP, two atoms of the element bind to form dioxygen, a diatomic gas that is colorless, odorless, and tasteless; with the formula O2.

Many major classes of organic molecules in living organisms, such as proteins, nucleic acids, carbohydrates, and fats, contain oxygen, as do the major inorganic compounds that are constituents of animal shells, teeth, and bone.

| | |
|---|---|
| Ozone | Ozone, or trioxygen, is an inorganic compound with the chemical formula O3(μ-O) (also written [O (μ-O)O] or O3). It is a pale blue gas with a distinctively pungent smell. It is an allotrope of oxygen that is much less stable than the diatomic allotrope O2, breaking down in the lower atmosphere to normal dioxygen. |
| Sulfur dioxide | Sulfur dioxide is the chemical compound with the formula SO2. At standard atmosphere it is a toxic gas with a pungent, irritating and rotten smell. The triple point is 197.69 K and 1.67Kpa. |
| Xenon | Xenon is a chemical element with the symbol Xe and atomic number 54. It is a colorless, heavy, odorless noble gas, that occurs in the Earth's atmosphere in trace amounts. Although generally unreactive, xenon can undergo a few chemical reactions such as the formation of xenon hexafluoroplatinate, the first noble gas compound to be synthesized.

Naturally occurring xenon consists of eight stable isotopes. |
| Absorption | In chemistry, absorption is a physical or chemical phenomenon or a process in which atoms, molecules, or ions enter some bulk phase - gas, liquid, or solid material. This is a different process from adsorption, since molecules undergoing absorption are taken up by the volume, not by the surface (as in the case for adsorption). A more general term is sorption, which covers absorption, adsorption, and ion exchange. |
| Component | In thermodynamics, a component is a chemically-independent constituent of a system. The number of components represents the minimum number of independent species necessary to define the composition of all phases of the system.

Calculating the number of components in a system is necessary, for example, when applying Gibbs' phase rule in determination of the number of degrees of freedom of a system. |
| Dioxide | An oxide is a chemical compound that contains at least one oxygen atom and one other element in its chemical formula. Metal oxides typically contain an anion of oxygen in the oxidation state of -2. Most of the Earth's crust consists of solid oxides, the result of elements being oxidized by the oxygen in air or in water. Hydrocarbon combustion affords the two principal carbon oxides: carbon monoxide and carbon dioxide. |

# 18. Chemistry of the Environment

| | |
|---|---|
| Effusion | Effusion is the process in which a gas escapes through a small hole. This occurs if the diameter of the hole is considerably smaller than the mean free path of the molecules. According to Graham's law, the rate at which gases effuse (i.e., how many molecules pass through the hole per second) is dependent on their molecular weight. |
| Photodissociation | Photodissociation, photolysis, or photodecomposition is a chemical reaction in which a chemical compound is broken down by photons. It is defined as the interaction of one or more photons with one target molecule.<br><br>Photodissociation is not limited to visible light. |
| Photochemical reactions | Mechanistic organic photochemistry is that aspect of organic photochemistry which seeks to explain the mechanisms of organic photochemical reactions. The absorption of ultraviolet light by organic molecules very often leads to reactions. In the earliest days sunlight was employed while in more modern times ultraviolet lamps are employed. |
| Dissociation | Dissociation in chemistry and biochemistry is a general process in which ionic compounds separate or split into smaller particles, ions, or radicals, usually in a reversible manner. For instance, when a Brønsted-Lowry acid is put in water, a covalent bond between an electronegative atom and a hydrogen atom is broken by heterolytic fission, which gives a proton and a negative ion. Dissociation is the opposite of association and recombination. |
| Ozone layer | The ozone layer is a layer in Earth's atmosphere that absorbs most of the Sun's UV radiation. It contains relatively high concentrations of ozone ($O_3$), although it is still very small with regard to ordinary oxygen, and is less than ten parts per million, the average ozone concentration in Earth's atmosphere being only about 0.6 parts per million. The ozone layer is mainly found in the lower portion of the stratosphere from approximately 20 to 30 kilometres (12 to 19 mi) above Earth, though the thickness varies seasonally and geographically. |
| Chlorine monoxide | Chlorine monoxide is a chemical radical with the formula ClO. It plays an important role in the process of ozone depletion. In the stratosphere, chlorine atoms react with ozone molecules to form chlorine monoxide and oxygen. $Cl\cdot + O3 ? ClO\cdot + O2$<br><br>This reaction causes the depletion of the ozone layer. |
| Chlorofluorocarbon | A chlorofluorocarbon is an organic compound that contains only carbon, chlorine, and fluorine, produced as a volatile derivative of methane and ethane. They are also commonly known by the DuPont brand name Freon. The most common representative is dichlorodifluoromethane (R-12 or Freon-12). |
| Curie | The curie is a non-SI unit of radioactivity the curie is widely used throughout the US government and industry. |

One curie is roughly the activity of 1 gram of the radium isotope $^{226}Ra$, a substance studied by the Curies.

The SI derived unit of radioactivity is the becquerel (Bq), which equates to one decay per second.

**Dobson unit**

The Dobson unit is a unit of measurement of the columnar density of a trace gas in the Earth's atmosphere. It originated, and continues to be widely used, as a measure of total-column ozone, which is dominated by ozone in the stratospheric ozone layer. One Dobson unit refers to a layer of gas that would be 10 μm thick under standard temperature and pressure, sometimes referred to as a 'milli-atmo-centimeter.' For example, 300 DU of ozone brought down to the surface of the Earth at 0 °C would occupy a layer only 3 mm thick.

**Bromine**

Bromine is a chemical element with the symbol Br, and atomic number of 35. It is in the halogen group (17). The element was isolated independently by two chemists, Carl Jacob Löwig and Antoine Jerome Balard, in 1825-1826. Elemental bromine is a fuming red-brown liquid at room temperature, corrosive and toxic, with properties between those of chlorine and iodine. Free bromine does not occur in nature, but occurs as colorless soluble crystalline mineral halide salts, analogous to table salt.

**Bromide**

A bromide is a chemical compound containing a bromide ion or ligand. This is a bromine atom with an ionic charge of -1 (Br⁻); for example, in caesium bromide, caesium cations (Cs⁺) are electrically attracted to bromide anions (Br⁻) to form the electrically neutral ionic compound CsBr. The term 'bromide' can also refer to a bromine atom with an oxidation number of -1 in covalent compounds such as sulfur dibromide.

**Carbonic acid**

Not to be confused with carbolic acid, an antiquated name for phenol. Carbonic acid is also an archaic name for carbon dioxide.

Carbonic acid is the chemical compound with the formula $H_2CO_3$ (equivalently $OC_2$). It is also a name sometimes given to solutions of carbon dioxide in water (carbonated water), because such solutions contain small amounts of $H_2CO_3$. Carbonic acid, which is a weak acid, forms two kinds of salts, the carbonates and the bicarbonates.

**Hydrocarbon**

In organic chemistry, a hydrocarbon is an organic compound consisting entirely of hydrogen and carbon. Hydrocarbons from which one hydrogen atom has been removed are functional groups, called hydrocarbyls. Aromatic hydrocarbons (arenes), alkanes, alkenes, cycloalkanes and alkyne-based compounds are different types of hydrocarbons.

**Polar molecules**

In chemistry, polarity refers to a separation of electric charge leading to a molecule or its chemical groups having an electric dipole or multipole moment.

# 18. Chemistry of the Environment

|  |  |
|---|---|
| | Polar molecules interact through dipole-dipole intermolecular forces and hydrogen bonds. Molecular polarity is dependent on the difference in electronegativity between atoms in a compound and the asymmetry of the compound's structure. |
| Sulfur | Sulfur or sulphur is a chemical element with symbol S and atomic number 16. It is an abundant, multivalent non-metal. Under normal conditions, sulfur atoms form cyclic octatomic molecules with chemical formula $S_8$. Elemental sulfur is a bright yellow crystalline solid when at room temperature. |
| Sulfuric acid | Sulfuric acid is a highly corrosive strong mineral acid with the molecular formula $H_2SO_4$. It is a pungent, colorless to slightly yellow viscous liquid which is soluble in water at all concentrations. Sometimes, it is dyed dark brown during production to alert people to its hazards. |
| Combustion | Combustion or burning is the sequence of exothermic chemical reactions between a fuel and an oxidant accompanied by the production of heat and conversion of chemical species. The release of heat can produce light in the form of either glowing or a flame.<br><br>In a complete combustion reaction, a compound reacts with an oxidizing element, such as oxygen or fluorine, and the products are compounds of each element in the fuel with the oxidizing element. |
| Calcium carbonate | Calcium carbonate is a chemical compound with the formula $CaCO_3$. It is a common substance found in rocks in all parts of the world, and is the main component of shells of marine organisms, snails, coal balls, pearls, and eggshells. Calcium carbonate is the active ingredient in agricultural lime, and is created when Ca ions in hard water react with carbonate ions creating limescale. |
| Corrosion | Corrosion is the gradual destruction of materials by chemical reaction with its environment.<br><br>In the most common use of the word, this means electrochemical oxidation of metals in reaction with an oxidant such as oxygen. Rusting, the formation of iron oxides, is a well-known example of electrochemical corrosion. |
| Calcium oxide | Calcium oxide, commonly known as quicklime or burnt lime, is a widely used chemical compound. It is a white, caustic, alkaline crystalline solid at room temperature. The broadly used term 'lime' connotes calcium-containing inorganic materials, which include carbonates, oxides and hydroxides of calcium, silicon, magnesium, aluminium, and iron predominate, such as limestone. |
| Catalytic converter | A catalytic converter is a vehicle emissions control device which converts toxic byproducts of combustion in the exhaust of an internal combustion engine to less toxic substances by way of catalyzed chemical reactions. The specific reactions vary with the type of catalyst installed. Most present-day vehicles that run on gasoline are fitted with a "three-way" converter, so named because it converts the three main pollutants in automobile exhaust: carbon monoxide, unburned hydrocarbon and oxides of nitrogen. |

| Nitrogen dioxide | Nitrogen dioxide is the chemical compound with the formula $NO_2$. It is one of several nitrogen oxides. $NO_2$ is an intermediate in the industrial synthesis of nitric acid, millions of tons of which are produced each year. |
|---|---|
| Unburned hydrocarbon | Unburned hydrocarbons are the hydrocarbons emitted after petroleum is burned in an engine.<br><br>When unburned fuel is emitted from a combustor, the emission is caused by fuel 'avoiding' the flame zones. For example, in piston engines, some of the fuel-air mixture 'hides' from the flame in the crevices provided by the piston ring grooves. |
| Fossil fuel | Fossil fuels are fuels formed by natural processes such as anaerobic decomposition of buried dead organisms. The age of the organisms and their resulting fossil fuels is typically millions of years, and sometimes exceeds 650 million years. Fossil fuels contain high percentages of carbon and include coal, petroleum, and natural gas. |
| Greenhouse effect | The greenhouse effect is a process by which thermal radiation from a planetary surface is absorbed by atmospheric greenhouse gases, and is re-radiated in all directions. Since part of this re-radiation is back towards the surface and the lower atmosphere, it results in an elevation of the average surface temperature above what it would be in the absence of the gases.<br><br>Solar radiation at the frequencies of visible light largely passes through the atmosphere to warm the planetary surface, which then emits this energy at the lower frequencies of infrared thermal radiation. |
| Natural gas | Natural gas is a fossil fuel formed when layers of buried plants and animals are exposed to intense heat and pressure over thousands of years. The energy that the plants originally obtained from the sun is stored in the form of carbon in natural gas. Natural gas is a nonrenewable resource because it cannot be replenished on a human time frame. |
| Carbon dioxide | Carbon dioxide is a naturally occurring chemical compound composed of two oxygen atoms each covalently double bonded to a single carbon atom. It is a gas at standard temperature and pressure and exists in Earth's atmosphere in this state, as a trace gas at a concentration of 0.039 per cent by volume.<br><br>As part of the carbon cycle, plants, algae, and cyanobacteria use light energy to photosynthesize carbohydrate from carbon dioxide and water, with oxygen produced as a waste product. |
| Extraction | Extraction in chemistry is a separation process consisting in the separation of a substance from a matrix. It may refer to Liquid-liquid extraction, and Solid phase extraction. |

# 18. Chemistry of the Environment

| | |
|---|---|
| Greenhouse gas | A greenhouse gas is a gas in an atmosphere that absorbs and emits radiation within the thermal infrared range. This process is the fundamental cause of the greenhouse effect. The primary greenhouse gases in the Earth's atmosphere are water vapor, carbon dioxide, methane, nitrous oxide, and ozone. |
| Half-life | Half-life is the amount of time required for a quantity to fall to half its value as measured at the beginning of the time period. While the term 'half-life' can be used to describe any quantity which follows an exponential decay, it is most often used within the context of nuclear physics and nuclear chemistry--that is, the time required, probabilistically, for half of the unstable, radioactive atoms in a sample to undergo radioactive decay. |
| | The original term, dating to Ernest Rutherford's discovery of the principle in 1907, was 'half-life period', which was shortened to 'half-life' in the early 1950s. |
| Oxidation | Redox (reduction-oxidation) reactions include all chemical reactions in which atoms have their oxidation state changed; in general, redox reactions involve the transfer of electrons between species. |
| | This can be either a simple redox process, such as the oxidation of carbon to yield carbon dioxide or the reduction of carbon by hydrogen to yield methane ($CH_4$), or a complex process such as the oxidation of glucose ($C_6H_{12}O_6$) in the human body through a series of complex electron transfer processes. |
| | The term 'redox' comes from two concepts involved with electron transfer: reduction and oxidation. |
| Water cycle | The water cycle, also known as the hydrologic cycle or the $H_2O$ cycle, describes the continuous movement of water on, above and below the surface of the Earth. The mass water on Earth remains fairly constant over time but the partitioning of the water into the major reservoirs of ice, fresh water, saline water and atmospheric water is variable depending on a wide range of climatic variables. The water moves from one reservoir to another, such as from river to ocean, or from the ocean to the atmosphere, by the physical processes of evaporation, condensation, precipitation, infiltration, runoff, and subsurface flow. |
| Boric acid | Boric acid, also called hydrogen borate, boracic acid, orthoboric acid and acidum boricum, is a weak acid of boron often used as an antiseptic, insecticide, flame retardant, neutron absorber, or precursor to other chemical compounds. It has the chemical formula $H_3BO_3$ (sometimes written B(OH)$_3$), and exists in the form of colorless crystals or a white powder that dissolves in water. When occurring as a mineral, it is called sassolite. |
| Calcium | Calcium is the chemical element with symbol Ca and atomic number 20. Calcium is a soft gray alkaline earth metal, and is the fifth-most-abundant element by mass in the Earth's crust. |

Calcium is also the fifth-most-abundant dissolved ion in seawater by both molarity and mass, after sodium, chloride, magnesium, and sulfate.

Calcium is essential for living organisms, in particular in cell physiology, where movement of the calcium ion $Ca^{2+}$ into and out of the cytoplasm functions as a signal for many cellular processes.

Chloride ion

The chloride ion is the anion $Cl^-$. It is formed when the element chlorine (a halogen) gains an electron or when a compound such as hydrogen chloride is dissolved in water or other polar solvents. Chlorides salts such as sodium chloride are often very soluble in water.

Fluoride

Fluoride is an inorganic anion of fluorine with the chemical formula F-. It contributes no color to fluoride salts. Fluoride is the main component of fluorite (apart from calcium ions; fluorite is roughly 49% fluoride by mass), and contributes a distinctive bitter taste, but no odor to fluoride salts.

Potassium

Potassium is a chemical element with symbol K and atomic number 19. Elemental potassium is a soft silvery-white alkali metal that oxidizes rapidly in air and is very reactive with water, generating sufficient heat to ignite the hydrogen emitted in the reaction and burning with a lilac flame.

Because potassium and sodium are chemically very similar, their salts were not at first differentiated. The existence of multiple elements in their salts was suspected from 1702, and this was proven in 1807 when potassium and sodium were individually isolated from different salts by electrolysis.

Strontium

Strontium is a chemical element with symbol Sr and atomic number 38. An alkaline earth metal, strontium is a soft silver-white or yellowish metallic element that is highly reactive chemically. The metal turns yellow when it is exposed to air. Strontium has physical and chemical properties similar to those of its two neighbors calcium and barium.

Groundwater

Groundwater is the water located beneath the earth's surface in soil pore spaces and in the fractures of rock formations. A unit of rock or an unconsolidated deposit is called an aquifer when it can yield a usable quantity of water. The depth at which soil pore spaces or fractures and voids in rock become completely saturated with water is called the water table.

Arsenic

Arsenic is a chemical element with symbol As and atomic number 33. Arsenic occurs in many minerals, usually in conjunction with sulfur and metals, and also as a pure elemental crystal. It was first documented by Albertus Magnus in 1250. Arsenic is a metalloid. It can exist in various allotropes, although only the gray form has important use in industry.

Water quality

Water quality refers to the chemical, physical and biological characteristics of water. It is a measure of the condition of water relative to the requirements of one or more biotic species and or to any human need or purpose.

# 18. Chemistry of the Environment

| | |
|---|---|
| Dissolution | Dissolution is the process by which a solute forms a solution in a solvent. The solute, in the case of solids, has its crystalline structure disintegrated as separate ions, atoms, and molecules form. For liquids and gases, the molecules must be adaptable with those of the solvent for a solution to form. |
| Desalination | Desalination, desalinization, desalinisation or desalting refers to any of several processes that remove some amount of salt and other minerals from saline water. More generally, desalination may also refer to the removal of salts and minerals, as in soil desalination.<br><br>Salt water is desalinated to produce fresh water suitable for human consumption or irrigation. |
| Distillation | Distillation is a method of separating mixtures based on differences in volatility of components in a boiling liquid mixture. Distillation is a unit operation, or a physical separation process, and not a chemical reaction.<br><br>Commercially, distillation has a number of applications. |
| Reverse osmosis | Reverse osmosis is a water purification technology that uses a semipermeable membrane. This membrane-technology is not properly a filtration method. In RO, an applied pressure is used to overcome osmotic pressure, a colligative property, that is driven by chemical potential, a thermodynamic parameter. |
| Water purification | Water purification is the process of removing undesirable chemicals, biological contaminants, suspended solids and gases from contaminated water. The goal is to produce water fit for a specific purpose. Most water is purified for human consumption (drinking water), but water purification may also be designed for a variety of other purposes, including meeting the requirements of medical, pharmacological, chemical and industrial applications. |
| Sewage | Sewage is a water-carried waste, in solution or suspension, that is intended to be removed from a community. Also known as wastewater, it is more than 99% water and is characterized by volume or rate of flow, physical condition, chemical constituents and the bacteriological organisms that it contains. In loose American English usage, the terms 'sewage' and 'sewerage' are sometimes interchanged. |
| LifeStraw | LifeStraw is a water filter designed to be used by one person to filter water so that they may safely drink it. It filters a maximum of 1000 litres of water, enough for one person for one year. It removes 99.9999% of waterborne bacteria and 99.9% of parasites. |
| Hydraulic fracturing | Hydraulic fracturing is the fracturing of rock by a pressurized liquid. Some hydraulic fractures form naturally--certain veins or dikes are examples. |

| Trihalomethane | Trihalomethanes are chemical compounds in which three of the four hydrogen atoms of methane ($CH_4$) are replaced by halogen atoms. Many trihalomethanes find uses in industry as solvents or refrigerants. THMs are also environmental pollutants, and many are considered carcinogenic. |
| --- | --- |
| Water chlorination | Water chlorination is the process of adding chlorine to water as a method of water purification to make it fit for human consumption as drinking water. Water that has been treated with chlorine is effective in preventing the spread of waterborne disease. |
| Atom economy | Atom economy describes the conversion efficiency of a chemical process in terms of all atoms involved (desired products produced). In an ideal chemical process, the amount of starting materials or reactants equals the amount of all products generated and no atom is wasted. Recent developments like high raw material (such as petrochemicals) costs and increased sensitivity to environmental concerns have made atom economical approaches more popular. |
| Chlorine dioxide | Chlorine dioxide is a chemical compound with the formula $ClO_2$. This yellowish-green gas crystallizes as bright orange crystals at -59 °C. As one of several oxides of chlorine, it is a potent and useful oxidizing agent used in water treatment and in bleaching. |
| Closed system | The term closed system refers to a physical system that is closed to certain types of transfers in or out of the system. The specification of what types of transfers are excluded, is different in different contexts. |
| Green chemistry | Green chemistry, also called sustainable chemistry, is a philosophy of chemical research and engineering that encourages the design of products and processes that minimize the use and generation of hazardous substances. Whereas environmental chemistry is the chemistry of the natural environment, and of pollutant chemicals in nature, green chemistry seeks to reduce and prevent pollution at its source.<br><br>As a chemical philosophy, green chemistry applies to organic chemistry, inorganic chemistry, biochemistry, analytical chemistry, and even physical chemistry. |
| Atom | The atom is a basic unit of matter that consists of a dense central nucleus surrounded by a cloud of negatively charged electrons. The atomic nucleus contains a mix of positively charged protons and electrically neutral neutrons, which means 'uncuttable' or 'the smallest indivisible particle of matter'. Although the Indian and Greek concepts of the atom were based purely on philosophy, modern science has retained the name coined by Democritus. |
| Absorption spectrum | Absorption spectroscopy refers to spectroscopic techniques that measure the absorption of radiation, as a function of frequency or wavelength, due to its interaction with a sample. The sample absorbs energy, i.e., photons, from the radiating field. The intensity of the absorption varies as a function of frequency, and this variation is the absorption spectrum. |

# 18. Chemistry of the Environment

| | |
|---|---|
| Benzene | Benzene is an organic chemical compound with the molecular formula $C_6H_6$. Its molecule is composed of 6 carbon atoms joined in a ring, with 1 hydrogen atom attached to each carbon atom. Because its molecules contain only carbon and hydrogen atoms, benzene is classed as a hydrocarbon. |
| Catalysis | Catalysis is the increase rate of a chemical reaction due to the participation of a substance called a catalyst. Unlike other reagents in the chemical reaction, a catalyst is not consumed. With a catalyst, less free energy is required to reach the transition state, but the total free energy from reactants to products does not change. |
| Styrene | Styrene, also known as vinyl benzene and phenyl ethene, is an organic compound with the chemical formula $C_6H_5CH=CH_2$. This derivative of benzene is a colorless oily liquid that evaporates easily and has a sweet smell, although high concentrations confer a less pleasant odor. Styrene is the precursor to polystyrene and several copolymers. |
| Efficiency | Efficiency in general, describes the extent to which time, effort or cost is well used for the intended task or purpose. It is often used with the specific purpose of relaying the capability of a specific application of effort to produce a specific outcome effectively with a minimum amount or quantity of waste, expense, or unnecessary effort. 'Efficiency' has widely varying meanings in different disciplines. |
| Acetic acid | Acetic acid is an organic compound with the chemical formula $CH_3COOH$ (also written as $CH_3CO_2H$ or $C_2H_4O_2$). It is a colourless liquid that when undiluted is also called glacial acetic acid. Acetic acid is the main component of vinegar (apart from water; vinegar is roughly 8% acetic acid by volume), and has a distinctive sour taste and pungent smell. |
| Hydroquinone | Hydroquinone, also benzene-1,4-diol or quinol, is an aromatic organic compound that is a type of phenol, having the chemical formula $C_6H_{42}$. Its chemical structure, shown in the table at right, features two hydroxyl groups bonded to a benzene ring in a para position. It is a white granular solid. |
| Organic compound | An organic compound is any member of a large class of gaseous, liquid, or solid chemical compounds whose molecules contain carbon. For historical reasons discussed below, a few types of carbon-containing compounds such as carbides, carbonates, simple oxides of carbon (such as CO and $CO_2$), and cyanides are considered inorganic. The distinction between 'organic' and 'inorganic' carbon compounds, while 'useful in organizing the vast subject of chemistry... is somewhat arbitrary'. |
| Supercritical fluid | A supercritical fluid is any substance at a temperature and pressure above its critical point, where distinct liquid and gas phases do not exist. It can effuse through solids like a gas, and dissolve materials like a liquid. |

CHAPTER HIGHLIGHTS & NOTES: KEY TERMS, PEOPLE, PLACES, CONCEPTS

| | |
|---|---|
| Terephthalic acid | Terephthalic acid is the organic compound with formula $C_6H_{42}$. This colourless solid is a commodity chemical, used principally as a precursor to the polyester PET, used to make clothing and plastic bottles. Several million tonnes are produced annually. |
| Toluene | Toluene, formerly known as toluol, is a clear, water-insoluble liquid with the typical smell of paint thinners. It is a mono-substituted benzene derivative, i.e., one in which a single hydrogen atom from a group of six atoms from the benzene molecule has been replaced by a univalent group, in this case $CH_3$. As such, its IUPAC systematic name is methylbenzene. |
| Volatile organic compound | Volatile organic compounds are organic chemicals that have a high vapor pressure at ordinary, room-temperature conditions. Their high vapor pressure results from a low boiling point, which causes large numbers of molecules to evaporate or sublimate from the liquid or solid form of the compound and enter the surrounding air. An example is formaldehyde, with a boiling point of -19 ° C (-2 °F), slowly exiting paint and getting into the air. |
| Solvent | A solvent is a substance that dissolves a solute (a chemically different liquid, solid or gas), resulting in a solution. A solvent is usually a liquid but can also be a solid or a gas. The maximum quantity of solute that can dissolve in a specific volume of solvent varies with temperature. |
| Alkyne | In organic chemistry, an alkyne is an unsaturated hydrocarbon which has at least one carbon-- carbon triple bond between two carbon atoms. The simplest acyclic alkynes with only one triple bond and no other functional groups form a homologous series with the general chemical formula $C_nH_{2n-2}$. Alkynes are traditionally known as acetylenes, although the name acetylene also refers specifically to $C_2H_2$, known formally as ethyne using IUPAC nomenclature. |
| Azide | Azide is the anion with the formula $N_3^-$. It is the conjugate base of hydrazoic acid $(HN_3)$. $N_3^-$ is a linear anion that is isoelectronic with $CO_2$ and $N_2O$. Per valence bond theory, azide can be described by several resonance structures, an important one being $N^-=N^+=N^-$. |
| Air pollution | Air pollution is the introduction into the atmosphere of chemicals, particulates, or biological materials that cause discomfort, disease, or death to humans, damage other living organisms such as food crops, or damage the natural environment or built environment.<br><br>The atmosphere is a complex dynamic natural gaseous system that is essential to support life on planet Earth. Stratospheric ozone depletion due to air pollution has long been recognized as a threat to human health as well as to the Earth's ecosystems. |
| Hard water | Hard water is water that has high mineral content . |

Hard drinking water is generally not harmful to one's health, but can pose serious problems in industrial settings, where water hardness is monitored to avoid costly breakdowns in boilers, cooling towers, and other equipment that handles water. In domestic settings, hard water is often indicated by a lack of suds formation when soap is agitated in water, and by the formation of limescale in kettles and water heaters.

| | |
|---|---|
| Formaldehyde | Formaldehyde is an organic compound with the formula $CH_2O$ or HCHO. It is the simplest aldehyde, hence its systematic name methanal. The common name of the substance comes from its similarity and relation to formic acid.<br><br>A gas at room temperature, formaldehyde is colorless and has a characteristic pungent, irritating odor. |
| Gold | Gold is a chemical element with the symbol Au and atomic number 79. It is a dense, soft, malleable, and ductile metal with an attractive, bright yellow color and luster that is maintained without tarnishing in air or water. Chemically, gold is a transition metal and a group 11 element. It is one of the least reactive chemical elements, solid under standard conditions. |
| Chloromethane | Chloromethane, also called methyl chloride, R-40 or HCC 40, is a chemical compound of the group of organic compounds called haloalkanes. It was once widely used as a refrigerant. It is a colorless extremely flammable gas with a mildly sweet odor, which is, however, detected at possibly toxic levels. |
| Ketone | In chemistry, a ketone is an organic compound with the structure RC(=O)R', where R and R' can be a variety of carbon-containing substituents. Ketones feature a carbonyl group (C=O) bonded to two other carbon atoms. Many ketones are known and many are of great importance in industry and in biology. |
| Lactone | In chemistry, a lactone is a cyclic ester which can be seen as the condensation product of an alcohol group -OH and a carboxylic acid group -COOH in the same molecule. It is characterized by a closed ring consisting of two or more carbon atoms, and a single endocyclic oxygen coupled with an adjacent ketone (typical ester type functional group). |
| Water softening | Water softening is the removal of calcium, magnesium, and certain other metal cations in hard water. The resulting soft water is more compatible with soap and extends the lifetime of plumbing. Water softening is usually achieved using lime softening or ion-exchange resins. |
| Hydroxyl radical | The hydroxyl radical, ˙HO, is the neutral form of the hydroxide ion . Hydroxyl radicals are highly reactive and consequently short-lived; however, they form an important part of radical chemistry. |

# 18. Chemistry of the Environment

CHAPTER HIGHLIGHTS & NOTES: KEY TERMS, PEOPLE, PLACES, CONCEPTS

| Bioremediation | Bioremediation is the use of any organism metabolism to remove pollutants. Technologies can be generally classified as in situ or ex situ. In situ bioremediation involves treating the contaminated material at the site, while ex siti involves the removal of the contaminated material to be treated elsewhere. |
| --- | --- |
| Polyurethane | Polyurethane is a polymer composed of a chain of organic units joined by carbamate (urethane) links. While most polyurethanes are thermosetting polymers that do not melt when heated, thermoplastic polyurethanes are also available.

Polyurethane polymers are formed by reacting an isocyanate with a polyol. |

CHAPTER QUIZ: KEY TERMS, PEOPLE, PLACES, CONCEPTS

1. _____ is a chemical radical with the formula ClO. It plays an important role in the process of ozone depletion. In the stratosphere, chlorine atoms react with ozone molecules to form _____ and oxygen. $Cl\cdot + O_3 ? ClO\cdot + O_2$

This reaction causes the depletion of the ozone layer.

   a. Chlorine dioxide
   b. Chlorine fluoride
   c. Chlorine monoxide
   d. Barium acetylacetonate

2. _____, also known as vinyl benzene and phenyl ethene, is an organic compound with the chemical formula $C_6H_5CH=CH_2$. This derivative of benzene is a colorless oily liquid that evaporates easily and has a sweet smell, although high concentrations confer a less pleasant odor. _____ is the precursor to poly_____ and several copolymers.

   a. 1,2,4-Butanetriol
   b. Styrene
   c. 2,5-Diaminotoluene
   d. 2-Acrylamido-2-methylpropane sulfonic acid

3. The _____ is the boundary in the Earth's atmosphere between the troposphere and the stratosphere.

   a. Balanced flow
   b. Barometric formula
   c. Carbon respiration
   d. Tropopause

# 18. Chemistry of the Environment

4. The _____ is a non-SI unit of radioactivity the _____ is widely used throughout the US government and industry.

   One _____ is roughly the activity of 1 gram of the radium isotope $^{226}$Ra, a substance studied by the _____s.

   The SI derived unit of radioactivity is the becquerel (Bq), which equates to one decay per second.

   a. Curie
   b. Background radiation
   c. Background radiation equivalent time
   d. Bateman Equation

5. The standard _____ is an international reference pressure defined as 101325 Pa and used as a unit of pressure.

   a. 4A Molecular Sieve
   b. Chemical engineering
   c. Atmosphere
   d. Barium acetylacetonate

**ANSWER KEY**
18. Chemistry of the Environment

**1.** c
**2.** b
**3.** d
**4.** a
**5.** c

## You can take the complete Chapter Practice Test

**for 18. Chemistry of the Environment**
on all key terms, persons, places, and concepts.

### Online 99 Cents

### http://www.JustTheFacts101.com

Use www.JustTheFacts101.com for all your study needs

including Facts101's online interactive problem solving labs in

chemistry, statistics, mathematics, and more.

CHAPTER OUTLINE: KEY TERMS, PEOPLE, PLACES, CONCEPTS

_____ | Thermodynamic

_____ | Conservation of energy

_____ | Entropy

_____ | Equilibrium constant

_____ | Boiling-point elevation

_____ | Oxidation

_____ | Reversible process

_____ | State function

_____ | Isothermal process

_____ | Heat transfer

_____ | Ideal gas

_____ | Second law of thermodynamics

_____ | Effusion

_____ | Ethanol

_____ | Probability

_____ | Boltzmann constant

_____ | Rotational motion

_____ | Degree

_____ | Lewis structure

_____ | Nitric oxide

_____ | Third law of thermodynamics

Natural gas

Absolute value

Standard molar entropy

Gibbs free energy

Potential energy

Ammonia

Hydrogen

Nitrogen

Concentration

Combustion

Benzene

Adenosine

Adenosine diphosphate

Adenosine triphosphate

Adipic acid

Chalcocite

Isomer

Neopentane

Acetic acid

Acetylene

Methanol

# 19. Chemical Thermodynamics

CHAPTER OUTLINE: KEY TERMS, PEOPLE, PLACES, CONCEPTS

Octane

Strontium oxide

Sulfur dioxide

Methane

Carbonylation

Refrigerant

Activation

Entropy of activation

Carbon disulfide

Elastomer

CHAPTER HIGHLIGHTS & NOTES: KEY TERMS, PEOPLE, PLACES, CONCEPTS

| | |
|---|---|
| Thermodynamic | Thermodynamics is a branch of natural science concerned with heat and temperature and their relation to energy and work. It defines macroscopic variables, such as internal energy, entropy, and pressure, that partly describe a body of matter or radiation. It states that the behavior of those variables is subject to general constraints, that are common to all materials, not the peculiar properties of particular materials. |
| Conservation of energy | In physics, the law of conservation of energy states that the total energy of an isolated system cannot change--it is said to be conserved over time. Energy can be neither created nor destroyed, but can change form, for instance chemical energy can be converted to kinetic energy in the explosion of a stick of dynamite.<br><br>A consequence of the law of conservation of energy is that a perpetual motion machine of the first kind cannot exist. |

# 19. Chemical Thermodynamics

| | |
|---|---|
| Entropy | In thermodynamics, entropy is a measure of the number of specific ways in which a thermodynamic system may be arranged, often taken to be a measure of disorder, or a measure of progressing towards thermodynamic equilibrium. The entropy of an isolated system never decreases, because isolated systems spontaneously evolve towards thermodynamic equilibrium, which is the state of maximum entropy. |

Entropy was originally defined for a thermodynamically reversible process

$$\Delta S = \int \frac{dQ_{rev}}{T}$$

as

where the entropy is found from the uniform thermodynamic temperature of a closed system dividing an incremental reversible transfer of heat into that system .

| | |
|---|---|
| Equilibrium constant | For a general chemical equilibrium $\alpha A + \beta B... \rightleftharpoons \rho R + \sigma S...$ |

the thermodynamic equilibrium constant can be defined such that, at

$$K^{\ominus} = \frac{\{R\}^{\rho}\{S\}^{\sigma}...}{\{A\}^{\alpha}\{B\}^{\beta}...}$$

equilibrium,

where curly brackets denote the thermodynamic activities of the chemical species. The logarithm of this expression appears in the formula for the Gibbs free energy change for the reaction. If deviations from ideal behaviour are neglected, the activities may be replaced by concentrations, [A], and a concentration quotient, $K_c$.

| | |
|---|---|
| Boiling-point elevation | Boiling-point elevation describes the phenomenon that the boiling point of a liquid will be higher when another compound is added, meaning that a solution has a higher boiling point than a pure solvent. This happens whenever a non-volatile solute, such as a salt, is added to a pure solvent, such as water. The boiling point can be measured accurately using an ebullioscope. |
| Oxidation | Redox (reduction-oxidation) reactions include all chemical reactions in which atoms have their oxidation state changed; in general, redox reactions involve the transfer of electrons between species.<br><br>This can be either a simple redox process, such as the oxidation of carbon to yield carbon dioxide or the reduction of carbon by hydrogen to yield methane ($CH_4$), or a complex process such as the oxidation of glucose ($C_6H_{12}O_6$) in the human body through a series of complex electron transfer processes.<br><br>The term 'redox' comes from two concepts involved with electron transfer: reduction and oxidation. |

# 19. Chemical Thermodynamics

CHAPTER HIGHLIGHTS & NOTES: KEY TERMS, PEOPLE, PLACES, CONCEPTS

| Reversible process | In thermodynamics, a reversible process, or reversible cycle if the process is cyclic, is a process that can be 'reversed' by means of infinitesimal changes in some property of the system without entropy production . Due to these infinitesimal changes, the system is in thermodynamic equilibrium throughout the entire process. Since it would take an infinite amount of time for the reversible process to finish, perfectly reversible processes are impossible. |
| --- | --- |
| State function | In thermodynamics, a state function, function of state, state quantity, or state variable is a property of a system that depends only on the current state of the system, not on the way in which the system acquired that state . A state function describes the equilibrium state of a system. For example, internal energy, enthalpy, and entropy are state quantities because they describe quantitatively an equilibrium state of a thermodynamic system, irrespective of how the system arrived in that state. |
| Isothermal process | An isothermal process is a change of a system, in which the temperature remains constant: $?T = 0$. This typically occurs when a system is in contact with an outside thermal reservoir (heat bath), and the change occurs slowly enough to allow the system to continually adjust to the temperature of the reservoir through heat exchange. In contrast, an adiabatic process is where a system exchanges no heat with its surroundings ($Q = 0$). In other words, in an isothermal process, the value $?T = 0$ but $Q ? 0$, while in an adiabatic process, $?T ? 0$ but $Q = 0$. |
| Heat transfer | Heat transfer is a discipline of thermal engineering that concerns the generation, use, conversion, and exchange of thermal energy and heat between physical systems. As such, heat transfer is involved in almost every sector of the economy. Heat transfer is classified into various mechanisms, such as thermal conduction, thermal convection, thermal radiation, and transfer of energy by phase changes. |
| Ideal gas | An ideal gas is a theoretical gas composed of a set of randomly moving, non-interacting point particles. The ideal gas concept is useful because it obeys the ideal gas law, a simplified equation of state, and is amenable to analysis under statistical mechanics.<br><br>At normal conditions such as standard temperature and pressure, most real gases behave qualitatively like an ideal gas. |
| Second law of thermodynamics | The second law of thermodynamics states that the entropy of an isolated system never decreases, because isolated systems spontaneously evolve toward thermodynamic equilibrium--the state of maximum entropy. Equivalently, perpetual motion machines of the second kind are impossible. |

# 19. Chemical Thermodynamics

| | |
|---|---|
| Effusion | Effusion is the process in which a gas escapes through a small hole. This occurs if the diameter of the hole is considerably smaller than the mean free path of the molecules. According to Graham's law, the rate at which gases effuse (i.e., how many molecules pass through the hole per second) is dependent on their molecular weight. |
| Ethanol | Ethanol, also called ethyl alcohol, pure alcohol, grain alcohol, or drinking alcohol, is a volatile, flammable, colorless liquid with the structural formula $CH_3CH_2OH$, often abbreviated as $C_2H_5OH$ or $C_2H_6O$. A psychoactive drug and one of the oldest recreational drugs, ethanol can cause alcohol intoxication when consumed. Best known as the type of alcohol found in alcoholic beverages, it is also used in thermometers, as a solvent, and as a fuel. In common usage, it is often referred to simply as alcohol or spirits. |
| Probability | Probability is a measure of the likeliness that an event will occur.<br><br>Probability is used to quantify an attitude of mind towards some proposition of whose truth we are not certain. The proposition of interest is usually of the form 'Will a specific event occur?' The attitude of mind is of the form 'How certain are we that the event will occur?' The certainty we adopt can be described in terms of a numerical measure and this number, between 0 and 1 (where 0 indicates impossibility and 1 indicates certainty), we call probability. |
| Boltzmann constant | The Boltzmann constant is a physical constant relating energy at the individual particle level with temperature. It is the gas constant R divided by the Avogadro constant $N_A$: $$k = \frac{R}{N_A}.$$<br><br>It has the same dimension . Introducing the Boltzmann constant transforms the ideal gas law into an alternative form: $PV = NkT$<br><br>where N is the number of molecules of gas. |
| Rotational motion | Rotation around a fixed axis is a special case of rotational motion. The fixed axis hypothesis excludes the possibility of an axis changing its orientation, and cannot describe such phenomena as wobbling or precession. According to Euler's rotation theorem, simultaneous rotation along a number of stationary axes at the same time is impossible. |
| Degree | The term degree is used in several scales of temperature. The symbol ° is usually used, followed by the initial letter of the unit, for example "°C" for degree(s) Celsius. A degree can be defined as a set change in temperature measured against a given scale, for example, one degree Celsius is one hundredth of the temperature change between the point at which water starts to change state from Solid to liquid state and the point at which it starts to change from its gaseous state to liquid. |

| | |
|---|---|
| Lewis structure | Lewis structures are diagrams that show the bonding between atoms of a molecule and the lone pairs of electrons that may exist in the molecule. A Lewis structure can be drawn for any covalently bonded molecule, as well as coordination compounds. The Lewis structure was named after Gilbert N |
| Nitric oxide | Nitric oxide, or nitrogen oxide, also known as nitrogen monoxide, is a molecule with chemical formula NO. It is a free radical and is an important intermediate in the chemical industry. Nitric oxide is a by-product of combustion of substances in the air, as in automobile engines, fossil fuel power plants, and is produced naturally during the electrical discharges of lightning in thunderstorms.<br><br>In mammals including humans, NO is an important cellular signaling molecule involved in many physiological and pathological processes. |
| Third law of thermodynamics | The third law of thermodynamics is sometimes stated as follows:'<br><br>The entropy of a perfect crystal, at absolute zero kelvin, is exactly equal to zero. '<br><br>At zero kelvin the system must be in a state with the minimum possible energy, and this statement of the third law holds true if the perfect crystal has only one minimum energy state. Entropy is related to the number of possible microstates, and with only one microstate available at zero kelvin, the entropy is exactly zero. |
| Natural gas | Natural gas is a fossil fuel formed when layers of buried plants and animals are exposed to intense heat and pressure over thousands of years. The energy that the plants originally obtained from the sun is stored in the form of carbon in natural gas. Natural gas is a nonrenewable resource because it cannot be replenished on a human time frame. |
| Absolute value | In mathematics, the absolute value ?x? of a real number x is the non-negative value of x without regard to its sign. Namely, ?x? = x for a positive x, ?x? = -x for a negative x, and ?0? = 0. For example, the absolute value of 3 is 3, and the absolute value of -3 is also 3. The absolute value of a number may be thought of as its distance from zero. |
| Standard molar entropy | In chemistry, the standard molar entropy is the entropy content of one mole of substance, under standard conditions .<br><br>The standard molar entropy is usually given the symbol S°, and has units of joules per mole kelvin (J mol$^{-1}$ K$^{-1}$). Unlike standard enthalpies of formation, the value of S° is an absolute. |
| Gibbs free energy | In thermodynamics, the Gibbs free energy is a thermodynamic potential that measures the 'usefulness' or process-initiating work obtainable from a thermodynamic system at a constant temperature and pressure (isothermal, isobaric). |

# 19. Chemical Thermodynamics

Just as in mechanics, where potential energy is defined as capacity to do work, similarly different potentials have different meanings. The Gibbs free energy is the maximum amount of non-expansion work that can be extracted from a closed system; this maximum can be attained only in a completely reversible process.

**Potential energy**

In physics, potential energy is energy stored in a system of forcefully interacting physical entities. The SI unit for measuring work and energy is the joule (symbol J).

The term potential energy was introduced by the 19th century Scottish engineer and physicist William Rankine, although it has links to Greek philosopher Aristotle's concept of potentiality.

**Ammonia**

Ammonia or azane is a compound of nitrogen and hydrogen with the formula $NH_3$. It is a colourless gas with a characteristic pungent smell. Ammonia contributes significantly to the nutritional needs of terrestrial organisms by serving as a precursor to food and fertilizers.

**Hydrogen**

Hydrogen is a chemical element with chemical symbol H and atomic number 1. With an atomic weight of 1.00794 u, hydrogen is the lightest element and its monatomic form (H) is the most abundant chemical substance, constituting roughly 75% of the Universe's baryonic mass. Non-remnant stars are mainly composed of hydrogen in its plasma state.

At standard temperature and pressure, hydrogen is a colorless, odorless, tasteless, non-toxic, nonmetallic, highly combustible diatomic gas with the molecular formula $H_2$.

**Nitrogen**

Nitrogen, symbol N, is the chemical element of atomic number 7. At room temperature, it is a gas of diatomic molecules and is colorless and odorless. Nitrogen is a common element in the universe, estimated at about seventh in total abundance in our galaxy and the Solar System. On Earth, the element is primarily found as the free element; it forms about 80% of the Earth's atmosphere.

**Concentration**

In chemistry, concentration is the abundance of a constituent divided by the total volume of a mixture. Several types of mathematical description can be distinguished: mass concentration, molar concentration, number concentration, and volume concentration. The term concentration can be applied to any kind of chemical mixture, but most frequently it refers to solutes and solvents in solutions.

**Combustion**

Combustion or burning is the sequence of exothermic chemical reactions between a fuel and an oxidant accompanied by the production of heat and conversion of chemical species. The release of heat can produce light in the form of either glowing or a flame.

In a complete combustion reaction, a compound reacts with an oxidizing element, such as oxygen or fluorine, and the products are compounds of each element in the fuel with the oxidizing element.

| | |
|---|---|
| Benzene | Benzene is an organic chemical compound with the molecular formula $C_6H_6$. Its molecule is composed of 6 carbon atoms joined in a ring, with 1 hydrogen atom attached to each carbon atom. Because its molecules contain only carbon and hydrogen atoms, benzene is classed as a hydrocarbon. |
| Adenosine | Adenosine is a purine nucleoside comprising a molecule of adenine attached to a ribose sugar molecule (ribofuranose) moiety via a ß-$N_9$-glycosidic bond.<br><br>Adenosine plays an important role in biochemical processes, such as energy transfer--as adenosine triphosphate (ATP) and adenosine diphosphate (ADP)--as well as in signal transduction as cyclic adenosine monophosphate, cAMP. It is also an inhibitory neurotransmitter, believed to play a role in promoting sleep and suppressing arousal. |
| Adenosine diphosphate | Adenosine diphosphate, abbreviated ADP, is an important organic compound in metabolism and is essential to the flow of energy in living cells. A molecule of ADP consists of three important structural components: a sugar backbone attached to a molecule of adenine and two phosphate groups bonded to the 5' carbon atom of ribose. The carbon molecules that make up the ring structure of a sugar can be named in a way that more specifically designates the location of the phosphate and adenosine attachments: The sugar backbone of ADP is known as a pentose sugar and consists of five carbon molecules. |
| Adenosine triphosphate | Adenosine triphosphate is a nucleoside triphosphate used in cells as a coenzyme. It is often called the 'molecular unit of currency' of intracellular energy transfer. ATP transports chemical energy within cells for metabolism. |
| Adipic acid | Adipic acid is the organic compound with the formula $(CH_2)_4(COOH)_2$. From an industrial perspective, it is the most important dicarboxylic acid: About 2.5 billion kilograms of this white crystalline powder are produced annually, mainly as a precursor for the production of nylon. Adipic acid otherwise rarely occurs in nature. |
| Chalcocite | Chalcocite, copper sulfide ($Cu_2S$), is an important copper ore mineral. It is opaque, being colored dark-gray to black with a metallic luster. It has a hardness of 2½ - 3 on the Mohs scale. |
| Isomer | In chemistry, isomers (; from Greek ?s?µe???, isomerès; isos = 'equal', méros = 'part') are molecules with the same molecular formula but different chemical structures. That is, isomers contain the same number of atoms of each element, but have different arrangements of their atoms in space. Isomers do not necessarily share similar properties, unless they also have the same functional groups. |
| Neopentane | Neopentane, also called 2,2-dimethylpropane, is a double-branched-chain alkane with five carbon atoms. |

# 19. Chemical Thermodynamics

Neopentane is an extremely flammable gas at room temperature and pressure which can condense into a highly volatile liquid on a cold day, in an ice bath, or when compressed to a higher pressure.

Neopentane is the simplest alkane with a quaternary carbon.

| | |
|---|---|
| Acetic acid | Acetic acid is an organic compound with the chemical formula $CH_3COOH$ (also written as $CH_3CO_2H$ or $C_2H_4O_2$). It is a colourless liquid that when undiluted is also called glacial acetic acid. Acetic acid is the main component of vinegar (apart from water; vinegar is roughly 8% acetic acid by volume), and has a distinctive sour taste and pungent smell. |
| Acetylene | Acetylene is the chemical compound with the formula $C_2H_2$. It is a hydrocarbon and the simplest alkyne. This colorless gas is widely used as a fuel and a chemical building block. |
| Methanol | Methanol, also known as methyl alcohol, wood alcohol, wood naphtha or wood spirits, is a chemical with the formula $CH_3OH$. Methanol acquired the name 'wood alcohol' because it was once produced chiefly as a byproduct of the destructive distillation of wood. Modern methanol is produced in a catalytic industrial process directly from carbon monoxide, carbon dioxide, and hydrogen. |
| Octane | Octane is a hydrocarbon and an alkane with the chemical formula $C_8H_{18}$, and the condensed structural formula $CH_{36}CH_3$. Octane has many structural isomers that differ by the amount and location of branching in the carbon chain. One of these isomers, 2,2,4-trimethylpentane (isooctane) is used as one of the standard values in the octane rating scale. |
| Strontium oxide | Strontium oxide or strontia, SrO, is formed when strontium reacts with oxygen. Burning strontium in air results in a mixture of strontium oxide and strontium nitride. It also forms from the decomposition of strontium carbonate $SrCO_3$. |
| Sulfur dioxide | Sulfur dioxide is the chemical compound with the formula SO2. At standard atmosphere it is a toxic gas with a pungent, irritating and rotten smell. The triple point is 197.69 K and 1.67Kpa. |
| Methane | Methane is a chemical compound with the chemical formula CH4 (one atom of carbon and four atoms of hydrogen). It is the simplest alkane and the main component of natural gas. The relative abundance of methane makes it an attractive fuel. |
| Carbonylation | Carbonylation refers to reactions that introduce carbon monoxide into organic and inorganic substrates. Carbon monoxide is abundantly available and conveniently reactive, so it is widely used as a reactant in industrial chemistry. The term carbonylation also refers to oxidation of protein side chains. |

| Refrigerant | A refrigerant is a substance used in a heat cycle usually including, for enhanced efficiency, a reversible phase transition from a liquid to a gas. Traditionally, fluorocarbons, especially chlorofluorocarbons, were used as refrigerants, but they are being phased out because of their ozone depletion effects. Other common refrigerants used in various applications are ammonia, sulfur dioxide, and non-halogenated hydrocarbons such as propane. |
|---|---|
| Activation | Activation in chemical sciences generally refers to the process whereby something is prepared or excited for a subsequent reaction. |
| Entropy of activation | The entropy of activation is one of the two parameters typically obtained from the temperature dependence of a reaction rate, when these data are analysed using the Eyring equation. Symbolized $?S^{\ddagger}$, the entropy of activation provides clues about the molecularity of the rate determining step in a reaction, i.e. whether the reactants are bonded to each other, or not. Positive values suggest that entropy increases upon achieving the transition state, which often indicates a dissociative mechanism. |
| Carbon disulfide | Carbon disulfide is a colorless volatile liquid with the formula $CS_2$. The compound is used frequently as a building block in organic chemistry as well as an industrial and chemical non-polar solvent. It has an 'ether-like' odor, but commercial samples are typically contaminated with foul-smelling impurities, such as carbonyl sulfide. |
| Elastomer | An elastomer is a polymer with viscoelasticity, generally having low Young's modulus and high failure strain compared with other materials. The term, which is derived from elastic polymer, is often used interchangeably with the term rubber, although the latter is preferred when referring to vulcanisates. Each of the monomers which link to form the polymer is usually made of carbon, hydrogen, oxygen and/or silicon. |

# 19. Chemical Thermodynamics

1. A _____ is a substance used in a heat cycle usually including, for enhanced efficiency, a reversible phase transition from a liquid to a gas. Traditionally, fluorocarbons, especially chlorofluorocarbons, were used as _____s, but they are being phased out because of their ozone depletion effects. Other common _____s used in various applications are ammonia, sulfur dioxide, and non-halogenated hydrocarbons such as propane.

    a. Back boiler
    b. Refrigerant
    c. Barrier pipe
    d. BE-Bridge

2. Rotation around a fixed axis is a special case of _____. The fixed axis hypothesis excludes the possibility of an axis changing its orientation, and cannot describe such phenomena as wobbling or precession. According to Euler's rotation theorem, simultaneous rotation along a number of stationary axes at the same time is impossible.

    a. Merck Index
    b. Batteryless radio
    c. Binodal
    d. Rotational motion

3. _____, copper sulfide ($Cu_2S$), is an important copper ore mineral. It is opaque, being colored dark-gray to black with a metallic luster. It has a hardness of 2½ - 3 on the Mohs scale.

    a. Chalcocite
    b. Berthierite
    c. Bertrandite
    d. Bismuthinite

4. _____ is the chemical compound with the formula SO2. At standard atmosphere it is a toxic gas with a pungent, irritating and rotten smell. The triple point is 197.69 K and 1.67Kpa.

    a. Barium oxide
    b. Boron trioxide
    c. Calcium oxide
    d. Sulfur dioxide

5. . The _____ is sometimes stated as follows:'

    The entropy of a perfect crystal, at absolute zero kelvin, is exactly equal to zero. '

    At zero kelvin the system must be in a state with the minimum possible energy, and this statement of the third law holds true if the perfect crystal has only one minimum energy state. Entropy is related to the number of possible microstates, and with only one microstate available at zero kelvin, the entropy is exactly zero.

    a. CrystaSulf

b. Third law of thermodynamics
c. Rectisol
d. Scrubber

1. b
2. d
3. a
4. d
5. b

---

## You can take the complete Chapter Practice Test

**for 19. Chemical Thermodynamics**
on all key terms, persons, places, and concepts.

## Online 99 Cents

### http://www.JustTheFacts101.com

**Use www.JustTheFacts101.com for all your study needs**

**including Facts101's online interactive problem solving labs in**

**chemistry, statistics, mathematics, and more.**

# 20. Electrochemistry

CHAPTER OUTLINE: KEY TERMS, PEOPLE, PLACES, CONCEPTS

Battery

Electrochemistry

Hydrochloric acid

Oxidation state

Oxidizing agent

Reducing agent

Half-reaction

Galvanic cell

Anode

Cathode

Electrode

Salt bridge

Electrolyte

Electron

Standard hydrogen electrode

Alkali

Halogen

Lewis structure

Oxyanion

Zinc

Strength

Niacin

Nernst equation

PH meter

Semipermeable membrane

Concentration

Graphite

Fuel cell

Hydrogen fuel

Methanol fuel

Corrosion

Stainless steel

Oxidation

Cathodic protection

Aqueous

Electrolytic cell

Electroplating

Sodium chloride

Electrolysis

Stoichiometry

Bauxite

Charged particle

# 20. Electrochemistry

CHAPTER OUTLINE: KEY TERMS, PEOPLE, PLACES, CONCEPTS

| | |
|---|---|
| | Electrometallurgy |
| | Cryolite |
| | Dinitrogen tetroxide |
| | Hydrazine |
| | Titanium tetrachloride |
| | Disproportionation |
| | Ammeter |

CHAPTER HIGHLIGHTS & NOTES: KEY TERMS, PEOPLE, PLACES, CONCEPTS

| | |
|---|---|
| Battery | An electric battery is a device consisting of one or more electrochemical cells that convert stored chemical energy into electrical energy. Each battery consists of a negative electrode material, a positive electrode material, an electrolyte that allows ions to move between the electrodes, and terminals that allow current to flow out of the battery to perform work.<br><br>Primary (single-use or 'disposable') batteries are used once and discarded; the electrode materials are irrevesibly changed during discharge. |
| Electrochemistry | Electrochemistry is a branch of chemistry that studies chemical reactions which take place in a solution at the interface of an electron conductor and an ionic conductor (the electrolyte). These reactions involve electron transfer between the electrode and the electrolyte or species in solution.<br><br>If a chemical reaction is driven by an externally applied voltage, as in electrolysis, or if a voltage is created by a chemical reaction as in a battery, it is an electrochemical reaction. |
| Hydrochloric acid | Hydrochloric acid is a clear, colorless, highly pungent solution of hydrogen chloride in water. It is a highly corrosive, strong mineral acid with many industrial uses. Hydrochloric acid is found naturally in gastric acid. |
| Oxidation state | The oxidation state, often called the oxidation number, is an indicator of the degree of oxidation of an atom in a chemical compound. |

# 20. Electrochemistry

|  | The formal oxidation state is the hypothetical charge that an atom would have if all bonds to atoms of different elements were 100% ionic. Oxidation states are typically represented by integers, which can be positive, negative, or zero. |
|---|---|
| Oxidizing agent | An oxidizing agent is the element or compound in an oxidation-reduction (redox) reaction that accepts an electron from another species. Because the oxidizing agent is gaining electrons, it is said to have been reduced. |
|  | The oxidizing agent itself is reduced, as it is taking electrons onto itself, but the reactant is oxidized by having its electrons taken away by the oxidizing agent. |
| Reducing agent | A reducing agent is the element or compound in an oxidation-reduction reaction that donates an electron to another species. Because the reducing agent is losing electrons, we say it has been oxidized. |
|  | This means that there must be an 'oxidizer'; because if any chemical is an electron donor (reducer), another must be an electron recipient (oxidizer). |
| Half-reaction | A half reaction is either the oxidation or reduction reaction component of a redox reaction. A half reaction is obtained by considering the change in oxidation states of individual substances involved in the redox reaction. |
|  | Often, the concept of half-reactions is used to describe what occurs in an electrochemical cell, such as a Galvanic cell battery. |
| Galvanic cell | A galvanic cell, or voltaic cell or Alessandro Volta respectively, is an electrochemical cell that derives electrical energy from spontaneous redox reactions taking place within the cell. It generally consists of two different metals connected by a salt bridge, or individual half-cells separated by a porous membrane. |
|  | Volta was the inventor of the voltaic pile, the first electrical battery. |
| Anode | An anode is an electrode through which electric current flows into a polarized electrical device. The direction of electric current is, by convention, opposite to the direction of electron flow. In other words, the electrons flow from the anode into, for example, an electrical circuit. |
| Cathode | A cathode is an electrode through which electric current flows out of a polarized electrical device. The direction of electric current is, by convention, opposite to the direction of electron flow--thus, electrons are considered to flow toward the cathode electrode while current flows away from it. This convention is sometimes remembered using the mnemonic CCD for cathode current departs. |
| Electrode | An electrode is an electrical conductor used to make contact with a nonmetallic part of a circuit . |

CHAPTER HIGHLIGHTS & NOTES: KEY TERMS, PEOPLE, PLACES, CONCEPTS

| | |
|---|---|
| | The word was coined by the scientist Michael Faraday from the Greek words elektron (meaning amber, from which the word electricity is derived) and hodos, a way. |
| Salt bridge | A salt bridge, in electrochemistry, is a laboratory device used to connect the oxidation and reduction half-cells of a galvanic cell, a type of electrochemical cell. Salt bridges usually come in two types: glass tube and filter paper. |
| Electrolyte | An electrolyte is a compound that ionizes when dissolved in suitable ionizing solvents such as water. This includes most soluble salts, acids, and bases. Some gases, such as hydrogen chloride, under conditions of high temperature or low pressure can also function as electrolytes. |
| Electron | The electron is a subatomic particle with a negative elementary electric charge. Electrons belong to the first generation of the lepton particle family, and are generally thought to be elementary particles because they have no known components or substructure. The electron has a mass that is approximately 1/1836 that of the proton. |
| Standard hydrogen electrode | The standard hydrogen electrode, is a redox electrode which forms the basis of the thermodynamic scale of oxidation-reduction potentials. Its absolute electrode potential is estimated to be 4.44 ± 0.02 V at 25 °C, but to form a basis for comparison with all other electrode reactions, hydrogen's standard electrode potential ($E^0$) is declared to be zero at all temperatures. Potentials of any other electrodes are compared with that of the standard hydrogen electrode at the same temperature. |
| Alkali | In chemistry, an alkali is a basic, ionic salt of an alkali metal or alkaline earth metal chemical element. Some authors also define an alkali as a base that dissolves in water. A solution of a soluble base has a pH greater than 7.0. The adjective alkaline is commonly, and alkalescent less often, used in English as a synonym for basic, especially for soluble bases. |
| Halogen | The halogens or halogen elements are a group in the periodic table consisting of five chemically related elements, fluorine, chlorine (Cl), bromine (Br), iodine (I), and astatine (At). The artificially created element 117 (ununseptium) may also be a halogen. In the modern IUPAC nomenclature, this group is known as group 17. |
| Lewis structure | Lewis structures are diagrams that show the bonding between atoms of a molecule and the lone pairs of electrons that may exist in the molecule. A Lewis structure can be drawn for any covalently bonded molecule, as well as coordination compounds. The Lewis structure was named after Gilbert N |
| Oxyanion | An oxyanion or oxoanion is a chemical compound with the generic formula $A_xO_y^{z-}$. Oxoanions are formed by a large majority of the chemical elements. The formulae of simple oxoanions are determined by the octet rule. |

# 20. Electrochemistry

| | |
|---|---|
| Zinc | Zinc, in commerce also spelter, is a metallic chemical element; it has the symbol Zn and atomic number 30. It is the first element of group 12 of the periodic table. Zinc is, in some respects, chemically similar to magnesium, because its ion is of similar size and its only common oxidation state is +2. Zinc is the 24th most abundant element in the Earth's crust and has five stable isotopes. The most common zinc ore is sphalerite (zinc blende), a zinc sulfide mineral. |
| Strength | In explosive materials, strength is the parameter determining the ability of the explosive to move the surrounding material. It is related to the total gas yield of the reaction, and the amount of heat produced. Cf. |
| Niacin | Niacin is an organic compound with the formula $C_6H_5NO_2$ and, depending on the definition used, one of the 20 to 80 essential human nutrients.<br><br>Not enough Niacin in the diet can cause nausea, skin and mouth lesions, anemia, headaches, and tiredness. Chronic Niacin deficiency leads to a disease called Pellagra. |
| Nernst equation | In electrochemistry, the Nernst equation is an equation that relates the equilibrium reduction potential of a half-cell in an electrochemical cell (or the total voltage for a full cell) to the standard electrode potential, temperature, activity, and reaction quotient of the underlying reactions and species used. It is named after the German physical chemist who first formulated it, Walther Nernst.<br><br>The Nernst equation gives a formula that relates the numerical values of the concentration gradient to the electric gradient that balances it. |
| PH meter | A pH meter is an electronic device used for measuring the pH of a liquid (though special probes are sometimes used to measure the pH of semi-solid substances). A typical pH meter consists of a special measuring probe (a glass electrode) connected to an electronic meter that measures and displays the pH reading. |
| Semipermeable membrane | A semipermeable membrane, also termed a selectively permeable membrane, a partially permeable membrane or a differentially permeable membrane, is a membrane that will allow certain molecules or ions to pass through it by diffusion and occasionally specialized 'facilitated diffusion'. Prof. Sidney Loeb and Srinivasa Sourirajan invented the first practical synthetic semi-permeable membrane. |
| Concentration | In chemistry, concentration is the abundance of a constituent divided by the total volume of a mixture. Several types of mathematical description can be distinguished: mass concentration, molar concentration, number concentration, and volume concentration. The term concentration can be applied to any kind of chemical mixture, but most frequently it refers to solutes and solvents in solutions. |

# 20. Electrochemistry

| | |
|---|---|
| Graphite | The mineral graphite is an allotrope of carbon. It was named by Abraham Gottlob Werner in 1789 from the Ancient Greek ???f? (grapho), 'to draw/write', for its use in pencils, where it is commonly called lead (not to be confused with the metallic element lead). Unlike diamond (another carbon allotrope), graphite is an electrical conductor, a semimetal. |
| Fuel cell | A fuel cell is a device that converts the chemical energy from a fuel into electricity through a chemical reaction with oxygen or another oxidizing agent. Hydrogen is the most common fuel, but hydrocarbons such as natural gas and alcohols like methanol are sometimes used. Fuel cells are different from batteries in that they require a constant source of fuel and oxygen/air to sustain the chemical reaction; however, fuel cells can produce electricity continually for as long as these inputs are supplied. |
| Hydrogen fuel | Hydrogen fuel is a zero-emission fuel which uses electrochemical cells, or combustion in internal engines, to power vehicles and electric devices. It is also used in the propulsion of spacecraft and can potentially be mass-produced and commercialized for passenger vehicles and aircraft.<br><br>Hydrogen is the first element on the periodic table, making it the lightest element on earth. |
| Methanol fuel | Methanol is an alternative fuel for internal combustion and other engines, either in combination with gasoline or directly . It is used in racing cars in many countries and in China. In the U.S., methanol fuel has received less attention than ethanol fuel as an alternative to petroleum-based fuels, because in the 2000s particularly, the support of corn-based ethanol offered certain political advantages. |
| Corrosion | Corrosion is the gradual destruction of materials by chemical reaction with its environment.<br><br>In the most common use of the word, this means electrochemical oxidation of metals in reaction with an oxidant such as oxygen. Rusting, the formation of iron oxides, is a well-known example of electrochemical corrosion. |
| Stainless steel | In metallurgy, stainless steel, also known as inox steel or inox from French 'inoxydable', is a steel alloy with a minimum of 10.5% chromium content by mass.<br><br>Stainless steel does not readily corrode, rust or stain with water as ordinary steel does, but despite the name it is not fully stain-proof, most notably under low oxygen, high salinity, or poor circulation environments. There are different grades and surface finishes of stainless steel to suit the environment the alloy must endure. |
| Oxidation | Redox (reduction-oxidation) reactions include all chemical reactions in which atoms have their oxidation state changed; in general, redox reactions involve the transfer of electrons between species. |

# 20. Electrochemistry

|  |  |
|---|---|
|  | This can be either a simple redox process, such as the oxidation of carbon to yield carbon dioxide or the reduction of carbon by hydrogen to yield methane ($CH_4$), or a complex process such as the oxidation of glucose ($C_6H_{12}O_6$) in the human body through a series of complex electron transfer processes.<br><br>The term 'redox' comes from two concepts involved with electron transfer: reduction and oxidation. |
| Cathodic protection | Cathodic Protection is a technique used to control the corrosion of a metal surface by making it the cathode of an electrochemical cell. A simple method of protection connects protected metal to a more easily corroded 'sacrificial metal' to act as the anode. The sacrificial metal then corrodes instead of the protected metal. |
| Aqueous | An aqueous solution is a solution in which the solvent is water. It is usually shown in chemical equations by appending (aq) to the relevant formula. For example, a solution of ordinary table salt, or sodium chloride (NaCl), in water would be represented as NaCl(aq). |
| Electrolytic cell | An electrolytic cell is an electrochemical cell that undergoes a redox reaction when electrical energy is applied. It is most often used to decompose chemical compounds, in a process called electrolysis--the Greek word lysis means to break up. When electrical energy is added to the system, the chemical energy is increased. |
| Electroplating | Electroplating is a process that uses electrical current to reduce dissolved metal cations so that they form a coherent metal coating on an electrode. The term is also used for electrical oxidation of anions onto a solid substrate, as in the formation silver chloride on silver wire to make silver/silver-chloride electrodes. Electroplating is primarily used to change the surface properties of an object (e.g. abrasion and wear resistance, corrosion protection, lubricity, aesthetic qualities, etc)., but may also be used to build up thickness on undersized parts or to form objects by electroforming. |
| Sodium chloride | Sodium chloride, also known as salt, common salt, table salt or halite, is an ionic compound with the formula NaCl, representing equal proportions of sodium and chlorine. Sodium chloride is the salt most responsible for the salinity of the ocean and of the extracellular fluid of many multicellular organisms. As the major ingredient in edible salt, it is commonly used as a condiment and food preservative. |
| Electrolysis | In chemistry and manufacturing, electrolysis is a method of using a direct electric current to drive an otherwise non-spontaneous chemical reaction. Electrolysis is commercially highly important as a stage in the separation of elements from naturally occurring sources such as ores using an electrolytic cell. |
| Stoichiometry | Stoichiometry is a branch of chemistry that deals with the relative quantities of reactants and products in chemical reactions. |

In a balanced chemical reaction, the relations among quantities of reactants and products typically form a ratio of positive integers. For example, in a reaction that forms ammonia ($NH_3$), exactly one molecule of nitrogen gas ($N_2$) reacts with three molecules of hydrogen gas ($H_2$) to produce two molecules of $NH_3$:N2 + 3H2 ? 2NH3

This particular kind of stoichiometry - describing the quantitative relationships among substances as they participate in chemical reactions - is known as reaction stoichiometry.

| Bauxite | Bauxite is an aluminium ore and is the main source of aluminium. This form of rock consists mostly of the minerals gibbsite $Al(OH)_3$, boehmite ?-AlO(OH), and diaspore a-AlO(OH), in a mixture with the two iron oxides goethite and haematite, the clay mineral kaolinite, and small amounts of anatase $TiO_2$. Bauxite was named after the village Les Baux in southern France, where it was first recognized as containing aluminium and named by the French geologist Pierre Berthier in 1821. |

| Charged particle | In physics, a charged particle is a particle with an electric charge. It may be either a subatomic particle or an ion. A collection of charged particles, or even a gas containing a proportion of charged particles, is called a plasma, which is called the fourth state of matter because its properties are quite different from solids, liquids and gases (plasma is the most common state of matter in the universe). |

| Electrometallurgy | Electrometallurgy is the field concerned with the processes of metal electrodeposition. There are four categories of these processes:•Electrowinning, the extraction of metal from ores•Electrorefining, the purification of metals. Metal powder production by electrodeposition is included in this category, or sometimes electrowinning, or a separate category depending on application.•Electroplating, the deposition of a layer of one metal on another•Electroforming, the manufacture of, usually thin, metal parts through electroplating. |

| Cryolite | Cryolite is an uncommon mineral identified with the once large deposit at Ivigtût on the west coast of Greenland, depleted by 1987.

It was historically used as an ore of aluminium and later in the electrolytic processing of the aluminium-rich oxide ore bauxite (itself a combination of aluminium oxide minerals such as gibbsite, boehmite and diaspore). The difficulty of separating aluminium from oxygen in the oxide ores was overcome by the use of cryolite as a flux to dissolve the oxide mineral(s). |

| Dinitrogen tetroxide | Dinitrogen tetroxide is the chemical compound $N_2O_4$. It is a useful reagent in chemical synthesis. It forms an equilibrium mixture with nitrogen dioxide; some call this mixture dinitrogen tetroxide, while some call it nitrogen dioxide. |

| Hydrazine | Hydrazine is an inorganic compound with the formula $N_2H_4$. It is a colourless flammable liquid with an ammonia-like odor. |

# 20. Electrochemistry

| Titanium tetrachloride | Titanium tetrachloride is the inorganic compound with the formula $TiCl_4$. It is an important intermediate in the production of titanium metal and the pigment titanium dioxide. $TiCl_4$ is an unusual example of a metal halide that is highly volatile. |
|---|---|
| Disproportionation | Disproportionation is a specific type of redox reaction in which a species is simultaneously reduced and oxidized to form two different products. |
| | For example: the UV photolysis of mercury chloride $Hg_2Cl_2$ ? $Hg + HgCl_2$ is a disproportionation. Mercury (I) is a diatomic dication $Hg2+2$. |
| Ammeter | An ammeter is a measuring instrument used to measure the electric current in a circuit. Electric currents are measured in amperes (A), hence the name. Instruments used to measure smaller currents, in the milliampere or microampere range, are designated as milliammeters or microammeters. |

1. A _____, also termed a selectively permeable membrane, a partially permeable membrane or a differentially permeable membrane, is a membrane that will allow certain molecules or ions to pass through it by diffusion and occasionally specialized 'facilitated diffusion'. Prof. Sidney Loeb and Srinivasa Sourirajan invented the first practical synthetic semi-permeable membrane.

   a. Semipermeable membrane
   b. Diafiltration
   c. Dialysis tubing
   d. Diffuser

2. A _____ is an electronic device used for measuring the pH of a liquid (though special probes are sometimes used to measure the pH of semi-solid substances). A typical _____ consists of a special measuring probe (a glass electrode) connected to an electronic meter that measures and displays the pH reading.

   a. Bisulfide
   b. Buffering agent
   c. PH meter
   d. Charlot equation

3. . _____ is an aluminium ore and is the main source of aluminium. This form of rock consists mostly of the minerals gibbsite $Al(OH)_3$, boehmite ?-AlO(OH), and diaspore a-AlO(OH), in a mixture with the two iron oxides goethite and haematite, the clay mineral kaolinite, and small amounts of anatase $TiO_2$.

_____ was named after the village Les Baux in southern France, where it was first recognized as containing aluminium and named by the French geologist Pierre Berthier in 1821.

a. Crown gold
b. Bauxite
c. Liquidmetal
d. Magnesium aluminide

4. The _____ is a subatomic particle with a negative elementary electric charge. _____s belong to the first generation of the lepton particle family, and are generally thought to be elementary particles because they have no known components or substructure. The _____ has a mass that is approximately 1/1836 that of the proton.

a. Electron
b. Compton scattering
c. Bohr model
d. Bohr magneton

5. A half reaction is either the oxidation or reduction reaction component of a redox reaction. A half reaction is obtained by considering the change in oxidation states of individual substances involved in the redox reaction.

Often, the concept of _____s is used to describe what occurs in an electrochemical cell, such as a Galvanic cell battery.

a. Biophotovoltaic
b. Bipolar electrochemistry
c. Camille Alphonse Faure
d. Half-reaction

**1.** a
**2.** c
**3.** b
**4.** a
**5.** d

---

## You can take the complete Chapter Practice Test

### for 20. Electrochemistry
on all key terms, persons, places, and concepts.

### Online 99 Cents

### http://www.JustTheFacts101.com

Use www.JustTheFacts101.com for all your study needs

including Facts101's online interactive problem solving labs in

chemistry, statistics, mathematics, and more.

# 21. Nuclear Chemistry

CHAPTER OUTLINE: KEY TERMS, PEOPLE, PLACES, CONCEPTS

Isotope

Nuclear chemistry

Nuclear reaction

Neutron

Nucleon

Proton

Atomic number

Mass number

Nuclide

Radiant energy

Radioactive decay

Radionuclide

Thorium

Uranium

Radium

Electron capture

Positron

Positron emission

Nuclear force

Magic number

Charged particle

CHAPTER OUTLINE: KEY TERMS, PEOPLE, PLACES, CONCEPTS

Cyclotron

Nuclear transmutation

Particle

Cobalt

Relativistic Heavy Ion Collider

Radiation therapy

Copernicium

Curium

Darmstadtium

Fermium

Half-life

Neptunium

Plutonium

Strontium

Transuranium element

Carbon

Radiocarbon dating

Nitrogen

Curie

Scintillation counter

Zinc sulfide

# 21. Nuclear Chemistry

_____ Fluorine

_____ Iodine

_____ Medical imaging

_____ Phosphorus

_____ Sodium

_____ Technetium

_____ Thallium

_____ Radiation

_____ Helium

_____ Nuclear binding energy

_____ Binding energy

_____ Nuclear fusion

_____ Chain reaction

_____ Critical mass

_____ Einstein

_____ Nuclear fission

_____ Nuclear reactor

_____ Heavy water

_____ Nuclear power

_____ Equilibrium constant

_____ Environment

# 21. Nuclear Chemistry



CHAPTER OUTLINE: KEY TERMS, PEOPLE, PLACES, CONCEPTS

| | |
|---|---|
| | Ionizing radiation |
| | Rubidium |
| | Tokamak |
| | Abundance |
| | Beryllium |
| | Boron |
| | Deuterium |
| | Triple-alpha process |
| | Hydroxyl radical |
| | Radical |
| | Relative biological effectiveness |
| | Background radiation |
| | Polonium |
| | Radon |
| | Potassium |
| | Methyl acetate |
| | Chlorine |
| | Sodium perchlorate |

# 21. Nuclear Chemistry

| | |
|---|---|
| Isotope | Isotopes are variants of a particular chemical element such that, while all isotopes of a given element have the same number of protons in each atom, they differ in neutron number. The term isotope is formed from the Greek roots isos (?s?? 'equal') and topos (t?p?? 'place'), meaning 'the same place'. Thus, different isotopes of a single element occupy the same position on the periodic table. |
| Nuclear chemistry | Nuclear chemistry is the subfield of chemistry dealing with radioactivity, nuclear processes and nuclear properties. |
| | It is the chemistry of radioactive elements such as the actinides, radium and radon together with the chemistry associated with equipment which are designed to perform nuclear processes. This includes the corrosion of surfaces and the behavior under conditions of both normal and abnormal operation (such as during an accident). |
| Nuclear reaction | In nuclear physics and nuclear chemistry, a nuclear reaction is semantically considered to be the process in which two nuclei, or else a nucleus of an atom and a subatomic particle from outside the atom, collide to produce one or more nuclides that are different from the nuclide(s) that began the process. Thus, a nuclear reaction must cause a transformation of at least one nuclide to another. If a nucleus interacts with another nucleus or particle and they then separate without changing the nature of any nuclide, the process is simply referred to as a type of nuclear scattering, rather than a nuclear reaction. |
| Neutron | The neutron is a subatomic hadron particle that has the symbol n or n0, no net electric charge and a mass slightly larger than that of a proton. With the exception of hydrogen-1, nuclei of atoms consist of protons and neutrons, which are therefore collectively referred to as nucleons. The number of protons in a nucleus is the atomic number and defines the type of element the atom forms. |
| Nucleon | In chemistry and physics, a nucleon is one of the particles that makes up the atomic nucleus. Each atomic nucleus consists of one or more nucleons, and each atom in turn consists of a cluster of nucleons surrounded by one or more electrons. There are two known kinds of nucleon: the neutron and the proton. |
| Proton | The proton is a subatomic particle with the symbol p or p+ and a positive electric charge of 1 elementary charge. One or more protons are present in the nucleus of each atom. The number of protons in each atom is its atomic number. |
| Atomic number | In chemistry and physics, the atomic number is the number of protons found in the nucleus of an atom and therefore identical to the charge number of the nucleus. It is conventionally represented by the symbol Z. The atomic number uniquely identifies a chemical element. In an atom of neutral charge, the atomic number is also equal to the number of electrons. |

| | |
|---|---|
| Mass number | The mass number, also called atomic mass number or nucleon number, is the total number of protons and neutrons (together known as nucleons) in an atomic nucleus. Because protons and neutrons both are baryons, the mass number A is identical with the baryon number B as of the nucleus as of the whole atom or ion. The mass number is different for each different isotope of a chemical element. |
| Nuclide | A nuclide is an atomic species characterized by the specific constitution of its nucleus, i.e., by its number of protons Z, its number of neutrons N, and its nuclear energy state.<br><br>The word nuclide was proposed by Truman P. Kohman in 1947. Doctor Kohman originally suggested nuclide as referring to a 'species of nucleus' defined by containing a certain number of neutrons and protons. The word thus was originally intended to focus on the nucleus. |
| Radiant energy | Radiant energy is the energy of electromagnetic waves. The quantity of radiant energy may be calculated by integrating radiant flux (or power) with respect to time and, like all forms of energy, its SI unit is the joule. The term is used particularly when radiation is emitted by a source into the surrounding environment. |
| Radioactive decay | Radioactive decay, also known as nuclear decay or radioactivity, is the process by which a nucleus of an unstable atom loses energy by emitting particles of ionizing radiation. A material that spontaneously emits this kind of radiation--which includes the emission of energetic alpha particles, beta particles, and gamma rays--is considered radioactive.<br><br>Radioactive decay is a stochastic (i.e., random) process at the level of single atoms, in that, according to quantum theory, it is impossible to predict when a particular atom will decay. |
| Radionuclide | A radionuclide, or a radioactive nuclide, is an atom with an unstable nucleus, characterized by excess energy available to be imparted either to a newly created radiation particle within the nucleus or via internal conversion. During this process, the radionuclide is said to undergo radioactive decay, resulting in the emission of gamma ray(s) and/or subatomic particles such as alpha or beta particles. These emissions constitute ionizing radiation. |
| Thorium | Thorium is a naturally occurring radioactive chemical element with the symbol Th and atomic number 90. It was discovered in 1828 by the Norwegian mineralogist Morten Thrane Esmark and identified by the Swedish chemist Jöns Jakob Berzelius and named after Thor, the Norse god of thunder.<br><br>Thorium produces a radioactive gas, radon-220, as one of its decay products. Secondary decay products of thorium include radium and actinium. |
| Uranium | Uranium is a silvery-white metallic chemical element in the actinide series of the periodic table, with symbol U and atomic number 92. |

# 21. Nuclear Chemistry

A uranium atom has 92 protons and 92 electrons, of which 6 are valence electrons. Uranium is weakly radioactive because all its isotopes are unstable. The most common isotopes of uranium are uranium-238 (which has 146 neutrons) and uranium-235 (which has 143 neutrons).

| | |
|---|---|
| Radium | Radium is a chemical element with symbol Ra and atomic number 88. Radium is an almost pure-white alkaline earth metal, but it readily oxidizes on exposure to air, becoming black in color. All isotopes of radium are highly radioactive, with the most stable isotope being radium-226, which has a half-life of 1601 years and decays into radon gas. Because of such instability, radium is luminescent, glowing a faint blue. |
| Electron capture | Electron capture is a process in which a proton-rich nuclide absorbs an inner atomic electron, thereby changing a nuclear proton to a neutron and simultaneously causing the emission of an electron neutrino. Various photon emissions follow, as the energy of the atom falls to the ground state of the new nuclide. <br><br> Electron capture is the primary decay mode for isotopes with a relative superabundance of protons in the nucleus, but with insufficient energy difference between the isotope and its prospective daughter (the isobar with one less positive charge) for the nuclide to decay by emitting a positron. |
| Positron | The positron or antielectron is the antiparticle or the antimatter counterpart of the electron. The positron has an electric charge of $+1e$, a spin of ½, and has the same mass as an electron. When a low-energy positron collides with a low-energy electron, annihilation occurs, resulting in the production of two or more gamma ray photons . |
| Positron emission | Positron emission or beta plus decay is a particular type of radioactive decay and a subtype of beta decay, in which a proton inside a radionuclide nucleus is converted into a neutron while releasing a positron and an electron neutrino ($?_e$). Positron emission is mediated by the weak force. The positron is a type of beta particle ($\beta^+$), the other beta particle being the electron ($\beta^-$) emitted from the $\beta^-$ decay of a nucleus. |
| Nuclear force | The nuclear force is the force between two or more nucleons. Its fundamental laws and constants are unknown unlike the Coulomb and Newton laws. It is responsible for binding protons and neutrons into atomic nuclei. |
| Magic number | In nuclear physics, a magic number is a number of nucleons such that they are arranged into complete shells within the atomic nucleus. The seven most widely recognised magic numbers as of 2007 are 2, 8, 20, 28, 50, 82, and 126 (sequence A018226 in OEIS). Recently, another magic number 34 has been predicted and experimentally confirmed. |
| Charged particle | In physics, a charged particle is a particle with an electric charge. It may be either a subatomic particle or an ion. |

| | |
|---|---|
| Cyclotron | A cyclotron is a type of particle accelerator in which charged particles accelerate outwards from the center along a spiral path. The particles are held to a spiral trajectory by a static magnetic field and accelerated by a rapidly varying (radio frequency) electric field. |
| Nuclear transmutation | Nuclear transmutation is the conversion of one chemical element or isotope into another. In other words, atoms of one element can be changed into atoms of other element by 'transmutation'. This occurs either through nuclear reactions (in which an outside particle reacts with a nucleus), or through radioactive decay (where no outside particle is needed). |
| Particle | In the physical sciences, a particle is a small localized object to which can be ascribed several physical or chemical properties such as volume or mass. The word is rather general in meaning, and is refined as needed by various scientific fields. Something that is composed of particles may be referred to as particulate, although this term is generally used to refer to a suspension of unconnected particles, rather than a connected particle aggregation. |
| Cobalt | Cobalt is a chemical element with symbol Co and atomic number 27. Like nickel, cobalt in the Earth's crust is found only in chemically combined form, save for small deposits found in alloys of natural meteoric iron. The free element, produced by reductive smelting, is a hard, lustrous, silver-gray metal.<br><br>Cobalt-based blue pigments (cobalt blue) have been used since ancient times for jewelry and paints, and to impart a distinctive blue tint to glass, but the color was later thought by alchemists to be due to the known metal bismuth. |
| Relativistic Heavy Ion Collider | The Relativistic Heavy Ion Collider is one of only two operating heavy-ion colliders, and the only spin-polarized proton collider ever built. Located at Brookhaven National Laboratory (BNL) in Upton, New York, and used by an international team of researchers, it is the only operating particle collider in the US. By using Relativistic Heavy Ion Collider to collide ions traveling at relativistic speeds, physicists study the primordial form of matter that existed in the universe shortly after the Big Bang. By colliding spin-polarized protons, the spin structure of the proton is explored. |
| Radiation therapy | Radiation therapy, radiation oncology, or radiotherapy (in the UK, and Australia), sometimes abbreviated to XRT or DXT, is the medical use of ionizing radiation, generally as part of cancer treatment to control or kill malignant cells. Radiation therapy may be curative in a number of types of cancer if they are localized to one area of the body. It may also be used as part of adjuvant therapy, to prevent tumor recurrence after surgery to remove a primary malignant tumor (for example, early stages of breast cancer). |
| Copernicium | Copernicium is a chemical element with symbol Cn and atomic number 112. It is an extremely radioactive synthetic element that can only be created in a laboratory. The most stable known isotope, copernicium-285, has a half-life of approximately 29 seconds, but it is possible that this copernicium isotope may have a nuclear isomer with a longer half-life, 8.9 min. |

# 21. Nuclear Chemistry

| | |
|---|---|
| Curium | Curium is a transuranic radioactive chemical element with the symbol Cm and atomic number 96. This element of the actinide series was named after Marie Sklodowska-Curie and Pierre Curie - both were known for their research on radioactivity. Curium was first intentionally produced and identified in July 1944 by the group of Glenn T. Seaborg at the University of California, Berkeley. The discovery was kept secret and only released to the public in November 1945. Most curium is produced by bombarding uranium or plutonium with neutrons in nuclear reactors - one tonne of spent nuclear fuel contains about 20 grams of curium. |
| Darmstadtium | Darmstadtium is a chemical element with the symbol Ds and atomic number 110. It is an extremely radioactive synthetic element. The most stable known isotope, darmstadtium-281, has a half-life of approximately 11 seconds, but it is possible that this darmstadtium isotope may have an isomer with a longer half-life, 3.7 minutes. Darmstadtium was first created in 1994 by the GSI Helmholtz Centre for Heavy Ion Research in Darmstadt-Wixhausen part of Darmstadt, Germany. |
| Fermium | Fermium is a synthetic element with symbol Fm and atomic number 100. It is a member of the actinide series. It is the heaviest element that can be formed by neutron bombardment of lighter elements, and hence the last element that can be prepared in macroscopic quantities, although pure fermium metal has not yet been prepared. A total of 19 isotopes are known, with $^{257}$Fm being the longest-lived with a half-life of 100.5 days. |
| Half-life | Half-life is the amount of time required for a quantity to fall to half its value as measured at the beginning of the time period. While the term 'half-life' can be used to describe any quantity which follows an exponential decay, it is most often used within the context of nuclear physics and nuclear chemistry--that is, the time required, probabilistically, for half of the unstable, radioactive atoms in a sample to undergo radioactive decay. <br><br> The original term, dating to Ernest Rutherford's discovery of the principle in 1907, was 'half-life period', which was shortened to 'half-life' in the early 1950s. |
| Neptunium | Neptunium is a chemical element with the symbol Np and atomic number 93. A radioactive actinide metal, neptunium is the first transuranic element. Its position in the periodic table just after uranium led to its being named after Neptune, the next planet beyond Uranus. A neptunium atom has 93 protons and 93 electrons, of which seven are valence electrons. |
| Plutonium | Plutonium is a transuranic radioactive chemical element with the symbol Pu and atomic number 94. It is an actinide metal of silvery-gray appearance that tarnishes when exposed to air, and forms a dull coating when oxidized. The element normally exhibits six allotropes and four oxidation states. It reacts with carbon, halogens, nitrogen, silicon and hydrogen. |
| Strontium | Strontium is a chemical element with symbol Sr and atomic number 38. An alkaline earth metal, strontium is a soft silver-white or yellowish metallic element that is highly reactive chemically. The metal turns yellow when it is exposed to air. |

# 21. Nuclear Chemistry

CHAPTER HIGHLIGHTS & NOTES: KEY TERMS, PEOPLE, PLACES, CONCEPTS

| | |
|---|---|
| Transuranium element | The transuranium elements are the chemical elements with atomic numbers greater than 92 (the atomic number of uranium). All of these elements are unstable and decay radioactively into other elements. |
| Carbon | Carbon fiber, alternatively graphite fiber, carbon graphite or CF, is a material consisting of fibers about 5-10 μm in diameter and composed mostly of carbon atoms. The carbon atoms are bonded together in crystals that are more or less aligned parallel to the long axis of the fiber. The crystal alignment gives the fiber high strength-to-volume ratio (making it strong for its size). |
| Radiocarbon dating | Radiocarbon dating is a radiometric dating technique that uses the decay of carbon-14 ($14C$) to estimate the age of organic materials, such as wood and leather, up to about 58,000 to 62,000 years Before Present (BP, present defined as 1950). Carbon dating was presented to the world by Willard Libby in 1949, for which he was awarded the Nobel Prize in Chemistry.<br><br>Since the introduction of carbon dating, the method has been used to date many items, including samples of the Dead Sea Scrolls, the Shroud of Turin, enough Egyptian artifacts to supply a chronology of Dynastic Egypt, and Ötzi the Iceman. |
| Nitrogen | Nitrogen, symbol N, is the chemical element of atomic number 7. At room temperature, it is a gas of diatomic molecules and is colorless and odorless. Nitrogen is a common element in the universe, estimated at about seventh in total abundance in our galaxy and the Solar System. On Earth, the element is primarily found as the free element; it forms about 80% of the Earth's atmosphere. |
| Curie | The curie is a non-SI unit of radioactivity the curie is widely used throughout the US government and industry.<br><br>One curie is roughly the activity of 1 gram of the radium isotope $^{226}Ra$, a substance studied by the Curies.<br><br>The SI derived unit of radioactivity is the becquerel (Bq), which equates to one decay per second. |
| Scintillation counter | A scintillation counter is an instrument for detecting and measuring ionizing radiation.<br><br>It consists of a scintillator which generates photons of light in response to incident radiation, a sensitive photomultiplier tube which converts the light to an electrical signal, and the necessary electronics to process the photomultiplier tube output.<br><br>Scintillation counters are widely used because they can be made inexpensively yet with good quantum efficiency and can measure both the intensity and the energy of incident radiation. |
| Zinc sulfide | Zinc sulfide is an inorganic compound with the chemical formula of ZnS. |

# 21. Nuclear Chemistry

This is the main form of zinc found in nature, where it mainly occurs as the mineral sphalerite. Although this mineral is usually black because of various impurities, the pure material is white, and it is widely used as a pigment. In its dense synthetic form, zinc sulfide can be transparent, and it is used as a window for visible optics and infrared optics.

**Fluorine**

Fluorine is the chemical element with symbol F and atomic number 9. At room temperature, the element is a pale yellow gas composed of diatomic molecules, F2. Fluorine is the lightest halogen and the most electronegative element. It requires great care in handling as it is extremely reactive and poisonous.

**Iodine**

Iodine is a chemical element with symbol I and atomic number 53. The name is from Greek ??e? d?? ioeides, meaning violet or purple, due to the color of elemental iodine vapor.

Iodine and its compounds are primarily used in nutrition, and industrially in the production of acetic acid and certain polymers. Iodine's relatively high atomic number, low toxicity, and ease of attachment to organic compounds have made it a part of many X-ray contrast materials in modern medicine.

**Medical imaging**

Medical imaging is the technique and process used to create images of the human body for clinical purposes (medical procedures seeking to reveal, diagnose, or examine disease) or medical science (including the study of normal anatomy and physiology). Although imaging of removed organs and tissues can be performed for medical reasons, such procedures are not usually referred to as medical imaging, but rather are a part of pathology.

As a discipline and in its widest sense, it is part of biological imaging and incorporates Radiology, Magnetic Resonance Imaging, Nuclear medicine, medical Ultrasonography or Ultrasound, Endoscopy, Elastography, Tactile Imaging, Thermography and medical photography.

**Phosphorus**

Phosphorus is a nonmetallic chemical element with symbol P and atomic number 15. A multivalent pnictogen, phosphorus as a mineral is almost always present in its maximally oxidised state, as inorganic phosphate rocks. Elemental phosphorus exists in two major forms--white phosphorus and red phosphorus--but due to its high reactivity, phosphorus is never found as a free element on Earth.

The first form of elemental phosphorus to be produced (white phosphorus, in 1669) emits a faint glow upon exposure to oxygen - hence its name given from Greek mythology, F?sf???? meaning 'light-bearer' (Latin Lucifer), referring to the 'Morning Star', the planet Venus.

**Sodium**

Sodium is a chemical element with the symbol Na and atomic number 11. It is a soft, silver-white, highly reactive metal and is a member of the alkali metals; its only stable isotope is $^{23}$Na. The free metal does not occur in nature, but instead must be prepared from its compounds; it was first isolated by Humphry Davy in 1807 by the electrolysis of sodium hydroxide.

| | |
|---|---|
| Technetium | Technetium is the chemical element with atomic number 43 and the symbol Tc. It is the lowest atomic number element without any stable isotopes; every form of it is radioactive. Nearly all technetium is produced synthetically, and only minute amounts are found in nature. |
| Thallium | Thallium is a chemical element with symbol Tl and atomic number 81. This soft gray poor metal is not found free in nature. When isolated, it resembles tin, but discolors when exposed to air. Chemists William Crookes and Claude-Auguste Lamy discovered thallium independently in 1861, in residues of sulfuric acid production. |
| Radiation | In physics, radiation is a process in which energetic particles or energetic waves travel through a vacuum, or through matter-containing media that are not required for their propagation. Waves of a mass filled medium itself, such as water waves or sound waves, are usually not considered to be forms of 'radiation' in this sense.<br><br>Radiation can be classified as either ionizing or non-ionizing according to whether it ionizes or does not ionize ordinary chemical matter. |
| Helium | Helium is a chemical element with symbol He and atomic number 2. It is a colorless, odorless, tasteless, non-toxic, inert, monatomic gas that heads the noble gas group in the periodic table. Its boiling and melting points are the lowest among the elements and it exists only as a gas except in extreme conditions.<br><br>Helium is the second lightest element and is the second most abundant element in the observable universe, being present at about 24% of the total elemental mass, which is more than 12 times the mass of all the heavier elements combined. |
| Nuclear binding energy | Nuclear binding energy is the energy required to split a nucleus of an atom into its component parts. The component parts are neutrons and protons, which are collectively called nucleons. The binding energy of nuclei is always a positive number, since all nuclei require net energy to separate them into individual protons and neutrons. |
| Binding energy | Binding energy is the mechanical energy required to disassemble a whole into separate parts. A bound system typically has a lower potential energy than the sum of its constituent parts -- this is what keeps the system together. Often this means that energy is released upon the creation of a bound state. |
| Nuclear fusion | In nuclear physics, nuclear fusion is a nuclear reaction in which two or more atomic nuclei collide at a very high speed and join to form a new type of atomic nucleus. During this process, matter is not conserved because some of the mass of the fusing nuclei is converted to photons (energy). Fusion is the process that powers active or 'main sequence' stars. |

# 21. Nuclear Chemistry

CHAPTER HIGHLIGHTS & NOTES: KEY TERMS, PEOPLE, PLACES, CONCEPTS

|  |  |
|---|---|
| Chain reaction | A chain reaction is a sequence of reactions where a reactive product or by-product causes additional reactions to take place. In a chain reaction, positive feedback leads to a self-amplifying chain of events.<br><br>Chain reactions are one way in which systems which are in thermodynamic non-equilibrium can release energy or increase entropy in order to reach a state of higher entropy. |
| Critical mass | A critical mass is the smallest amount of fissile material needed for a sustained nuclear chain reaction. The critical mass of a fissionable material depends upon its nuclear properties (specifically, the nuclear fission cross-section), its density, its shape, its enrichment, its purity, its temperature, and its surroundings. The concept is important in nuclear weapon design. |
| Einstein | An einstein is a unit defined as the energy in one mole of photons. Because energy is inversely proportional to wavelength, the unit is frequency dependent. This unit is not part of the International System of Units and is redundant with the joule. |
| Nuclear fission | In nuclear physics and nuclear chemistry, nuclear fission is either a nuclear reaction or a radioactive decay process in which the nucleus of a particle splits into smaller parts . The fission process often produces free neutrons and photons (in the form of gamma rays), and releases a very large amount of energy even by the energetic standards of radioactive decay.<br><br>Nuclear fission of heavy elements was discovered on December 17, 1938 by Otto Hahn and his assistant Fritz Strassmann, and explained theoretically in January 1939 by Lise Meitner and her nephew Otto Robert Frisch. |
| Nuclear reactor | A nuclear reactor is a device to initiate and control a sustained nuclear chain reaction. Nuclear reactors are used at nuclear power plants for electricity generation and in propulsion of ships. Heat from nuclear fission is passed to a working fluid (water or gas), which runs through turbines. |
| Heavy water | Heavy water, formally called deuterium oxide or 2H2O or $D_2O$, is a form of water that contains a larger than normal amount of the hydrogen isotope deuterium, rather than the common hydrogen-1 isotope that makes up most of the hydrogen in normal water. |
| Nuclear power | Nuclear power, or nuclear energy, is the use of exothermic nuclear processes, to generate useful heat and electricity. The term includes nuclear fission, nuclear decay and nuclear fusion. Presently the nuclear fission of elements in the actinide series of the periodic table produce the vast majority of nuclear energy in the direct service of humankind, with nuclear decay processes, primarily in the form of geothermal energy, and radioisotope thermoelectric generators, in niche uses making up the rest. |
| Equilibrium constant | For a general chemical equilibrium $\alpha A + \beta B... \rightleftharpoons \rho R + \sigma S...$ |

the thermodynamic equilibrium constant can be defined such that, at

equilibrium,

$$K^\ominus = \frac{\{R\}^\rho \{S\}^\sigma \ldots}{\{A\}^\alpha \{B\}^\beta \ldots}$$

where curly brackets denote the thermodynamic activities of the chemical species. The logarithm of this expression appears in the formula for the Gibbs free energy change for the reaction. If deviations from ideal behaviour are neglected, the activities may be replaced by concentrations, $[A]$, and a concentration quotient, $K_c$.

**Environment**

In science and engineering, a system is the part of the universe that is being studied, while the environment is the remainder of the universe that lies outside the boundaries of the system. It is also known as the surroundings, and in thermodynamics, as the reservoir. Depending on the type of system, it may interact with the environment by exchanging mass, energy (including heat and work), linear momentum, angular momentum, electric charge, or other conserved properties.

**Ionizing radiation**

Ionizing radiation is radiation composed of particles that individually carry enough kinetic energy to liberate an electron from an atom or molecule, ionizing it. Ionizing radiation is generated through nuclear reactions, either artificial or natural, by very high temperature (e.g. plasma discharge or the corona of the Sun), via production of high energy particles in particle accelerators, or due to acceleration of charged particles by the electromagnetic fields produced by natural processes, from lightning to supernova explosions.

When ionizing radiation is emitted by or absorbed by an atom, it can liberate an atomic particle (typically an electron, proton, or neutron, but sometimes an entire nucleus) from the atom.

**Rubidium**

Rubidium is a chemical element with the symbol Rb and atomic number 37. Rubidium is a soft, silvery-white metallic element of the alkali metal group, with an atomic mass of 85.4678. Elemental rubidium is highly reactive, with properties similar to those of other alkali metals, such as very rapid oxidation in air. Natural rubidium is a mix of two isotopes: $^{85}$Rb, the only stable one, constitutes 72% of it, and 28% is accounted for slightly radioactive $^{87}$Rb with a half-life of 49 billion years--more than three times longer than the estimated age of the universe.

German chemists Robert Bunsen and Gustav Kirchhoff discovered rubidium in 1861 by the newly developed method of flame spectroscopy.

**Tokamak**

A tokamak is a device using a magnetic field to confine a plasma in the shape of a torus. Achieving a stable plasma equilibrium requires magnetic field lines that move around the torus in a helical shape. Such a helical field can be generated by adding a toroidal field (traveling around the torus in circles) and a poloidal field (traveling in circles orthogonal to the toroidal field).

# 21. Nuclear Chemistry

| | |
|---|---|
| Abundance | In a chemical reaction, a reactant is considered to be in abundance if the quantity of that substance is high and virtually unchanged by the reaction. Abundance differs from excess in that a reactant in excess is simply any reactant other than the limiting reagent; the amount by which a reactant is in excess is often specified, such as with terms like 'twofold excess', indicating that there is twice the amount of reactant necessary for the limiting reagent to be completely reacted. In this case, should the reaction go to completion, the quantity of the reactant in excess will have halved. |
| Beryllium | Beryllium is the chemical element with the symbol Be and atomic number 4. Because any beryllium synthesized in stars is short-lived, it is a relatively rare element in both the universe and in the crust of the Earth. It is a divalent element which occurs naturally only in combination with other elements in minerals. Notable gemstones which contain beryllium include beryl (aquamarine, emerald) and chrysoberyl. |
| Boron | Boron is a chemical element with symbol B and atomic number 5. Because boron is produced entirely by cosmic ray spallation and not by stellar nucleosynthesis, it is a low-abundance element in both the solar system and the Earth's crust. Boron is concentrated on Earth by the water-solubility of its more common naturally occurring compounds, the borate minerals. These are mined industrially as evaporites, such as borax and kernite. |
| Deuterium | Deuterium is one of two stable isotopes of hydrogen. It has a natural abundance in Earth's oceans of about one atom in 6,420 of hydrogen. Thus deuterium accounts for approximately 0.0156% (or on a mass basis: 0.0312%) of all the naturally occurring hydrogen in the oceans, while the most common isotope (hydrogen-1 or protium) accounts for more than 99.98%. |
| Triple-alpha process | The triple-alpha process is a set of nuclear fusion reactions by which three helium-4 nuclei are transformed into carbon.

Older stars start to accumulate helium produced by the proton-proton chain reaction and the carbon-nitrogen-oxygen cycle in their cores. The products of further nuclear fusion reactions of helium with hydrogen or another helium nucleus produce lithium-5 and beryllium-8 respectively, both of which are highly unstable and decay almost instantly back into smaller nuclei. |
| Hydroxyl radical | The hydroxyl radical, ·HO, is the neutral form of the hydroxide ion . Hydroxyl radicals are highly reactive and consequently short-lived; however, they form an important part of radical chemistry. Most notably hydroxyl radicals are produced from the decomposition of hydroperoxides (ROHO) or, in atmospheric chemistry, by the reaction of excited atomic oxygen with water. |
| Radical | In chemistry, a radical is an atom, molecule, or ion that has unpaired valence electrons or an open electron shell, and therefore may be seen as having one or more 'dangling' covalent bonds. |

With some exceptions, these 'dangling' bonds make free radicals highly chemically reactive towards other substances, or even towards themselves: their molecules will often spontaneously dimerize or polymerize if they come in contact with each other. Most radicals are reasonably stable only at very low concentrations in inert media or in vacuum.

| | |
|---|---|
| Relative biological effectiveness | In radiology, the relative biological effectiveness is the ratio of biological effectiveness of one type of ionizing radiation relative to another, given the same amount of absorbed energy. The Relative biological effectiveness is an empirical value that varies depending on the particles, energies involved, and which biological effects are deemed relevant. It is a set of experimental measurements. |
| Background radiation | Background radiation is the ubiquitous ionizing radiation that people on the planet Earth are exposed to, including natural and artificial sources.<br><br>Both natural and artificial background radiation varies by location. |
| Polonium | Polonium is a chemical element with the symbol Po and atomic number 84, discovered in 1898 by Marie Curie and Pierre Curie. A rare and highly radioactive element with no stable isotopes, polonium is chemically similar to bismuth and tellurium, and it occurs in uranium ores. Applications of polonium are few, and include heaters in space probes, antistatic devices, and sources of neutrons and alpha particles. |
| Radon | Radon is a chemical element with symbol Rn and atomic number 86. It is a radioactive, colorless, odorless, tasteless noble gas, occurring naturally as an indirect decay product of uranium or thorium. Its most stable isotope, $^{222}$Rn, has a half-life of 3.8 days. Radon is one of the densest substances that remains a gas under normal conditions. |
| Potassium | Potassium is a chemical element with symbol K and atomic number 19. Elemental potassium is a soft silvery-white alkali metal that oxidizes rapidly in air and is very reactive with water, generating sufficient heat to ignite the hydrogen emitted in the reaction and burning with a lilac flame.<br><br>Because potassium and sodium are chemically very similar, their salts were not at first differentiated. The existence of multiple elements in their salts was suspected from 1702, and this was proven in 1807 when potassium and sodium were individually isolated from different salts by electrolysis. |
| Methyl acetate | Methyl acetate, also known as MeOAc, acetic acid methyl ester or methyl ethanoate, is a carboxylate ester with the formula $CH_3COOCH_3$. It is a flammable liquid with a characteristically pleasant smell reminiscent of some glues and nail polish removers. |

# 21. Nuclear Chemistry

| Chlorine | Chlorine is a chemical element with symbol Cl and atomic number 17. Chlorine is in the halogen group (17) and is the second lightest halogen after fluorine. The element is a yellow-green gas under standard conditions, where it forms diatomic molecules. It has the highest electron affinity and the fourth highest electronegativity of all the reactive elements; for this reason, chlorine is a strong oxidizing agent. |
|---|---|
| Sodium perchlorate | Sodium perchlorate is the inorganic compound with the chemical formula $NaClO_4$. It is the most soluble of the common perchlorate salts. It is a white crystalline, hygroscopic solid that is highly soluble in water and in alcohol. |

1. _____ is a chemical element with symbol Cn and atomic number 112. It is an extremely radioactive synthetic element that can only be created in a laboratory. The most stable known isotope, _____-285, has a half-life of approximately 29 seconds, but it is possible that this _____ isotope may have a nuclear isomer with a longer half-life, 8.9 min. _____ was first created in 1996 by the GSI Helmholtz Centre for Heavy Ion Research near Darmstadt, Germany.

   a. Baryon number
   b. Beta decay
   c. Copernicium
   d. Binding energy

2. _____ is a chemical element with the symbol Np and atomic number 93. A radioactive actinide metal, _____ is the first transuranic element. Its position in the periodic table just after uranium led to its being named after Neptune, the next planet beyond Uranus. A _____ atom has 93 protons and 93 electrons, of which seven are valence electrons.

   a. Barium
   b. Berkelium
   c. Neptunium
   d. Bismuth

3. . _____ is the conversion of one chemical element or isotope into another. In other words, atoms of one element can be changed into atoms of other element by 'transmutation'. This occurs either through nuclear reactions (in which an outside particle reacts with a nucleus), or through radioactive decay (where no outside particle is needed).

   a. Baryon number
   b. Nuclear transmutation
   c. Binary collision approximation

4. A _____ is a device using a magnetic field to confine a plasma in the shape of a torus. Achieving a stable plasma equilibrium requires magnetic field lines that move around the torus in a helical shape. Such a helical field can be generated by adding a toroidal field (traveling around the torus in circles) and a poloidal field (traveling in circles orthogonal to the toroidal field).

a. Bootstrap current
b. Cadarache
c. Tokamak
d. DEMO

5. A _____ is an instrument for detecting and measuring ionizing radiation.

It consists of a scintillator which generates photons of light in response to incident radiation, a sensitive photomultiplier tube which converts the light to an electrical signal, and the necessary electronics to process the photomultiplier tube output.

_____s are widely used because they can be made inexpensively yet with good quantum efficiency and can measure both the intensity and the energy of incident radiation.

a. Scintillation counter
b. Clover
c. Computed tomography imaging spectrometer
d. CRISM

**1.** c
**2.** c
**3.** b
**4.** c
**5.** a

---

*You can take the complete Chapter Practice Test*

**for 21. Nuclear Chemistry**
on all key terms, persons, places, and concepts.

*Online 99 Cents*

*http://www.JustTheFacts101.com*

Use www.JustTheFacts101.com for all your study needs

including Facts101's online interactive problem solving labs in

chemistry, statistics, mathematics, and more.

# 22. Chemistry of the Nonmetals

CHAPTER OUTLINE: KEY TERMS, PEOPLE, PLACES, CONCEPTS

_____ Nonmetal

_____ Periodic trends

_____ Silicon dioxide

_____ Hydrogen

_____ Double bond

_____ Absorption

_____ Combustion

_____ Deuterium

_____ Heavy water

_____ Isotope

_____ Tritium

_____ Water gas

_____ Effusion

_____ Alkali

_____ Calcium hydride

_____ Cracking

_____ Binary compound

_____ Oxide

_____ Oxyanion

_____ Sulfur

_____ Argon

CHAPTER OUTLINE: KEY TERMS, PEOPLE, PLACES, CONCEPTS

| | Fluorine |
|---|---|
| | Helium |
| | Oxygen |
| | Radon |
| | Bromine |
| | Chlorine |
| | Cryolite |
| | Halogen |
| | Iodine |
| | Isotopes of astatine |
| | Carbon tetrachloride |
| | Sodium hypochlorite |
| | Vinyl chloride |
| | Hexafluorosilicic acid |
| | Hydrofluoric acid |
| | Phosphoric acid |
| | Sodium bromide |
| | Ammonium perchlorate |
| | Lewis structure |
| | Perchlorate |
| | Perchloric acid |

Chlorate

Hypochlorite

Oxidizing agent

Formaldehyde

Ozone

Sulfuric acid

Angular momentum

Barium hydroxide

Barium oxide

Sulfur dioxide

Acidic oxide

Atmosphere

Quantum number

Potassium superoxide

Superoxide

Catalase

Chalcogen

Hydrogen peroxide

Peroxidase

Polonium

Selenium

# 22. Chemistry of the Nonmetals



CHAPTER OUTLINE: KEY TERMS, PEOPLE, PLACES, CONCEPTS

| | |
|---|---|
| | Tellurium |
| | Product |
| | Dimethyl sulfide |
| | Galena |
| | Hydrogen sulfide |
| | Iron sulfide |
| | Pyrite |
| | Sulfide |
| | Vulcanization |
| | Bisulfite |
| | Dehydration |
| | Sulfite |
| | Ammonia |
| | Hydrogen chloride |
| | Nitrogen |
| | Oxidation |
| | Oxidation state |
| | Chloramine |
| | Hydrazine |
| | Hydroxylamine |
| | Dinitrogen pentoxide |

# 22. Chemistry of the Nonmetals

CHAPTER OUTLINE: KEY TERMS, PEOPLE, PLACES, CONCEPTS

| | |
|---|---|
| | Dinitrogen trioxide |
| | Nitric oxide |
| | Nitrous oxide |
| | Ostwald process |
| | Nitrocellulose |
| | Nitroglycerin |
| | Nitrous acid |
| | Disproportionation |
| | Antimony |
| | Arsenic |
| | Phosphorus halide |
| | Phosphorus trichloride |
| | Halide |
| | Phosphorus |
| | Adenosine diphosphate |
| | Adenosine triphosphate |
| | Condensation reaction |
| | Detergent |
| | Phosphorous acid |
| | Condensation |
| | Carbon |

CHAPTER OUTLINE: KEY TERMS, PEOPLE, PLACES, CONCEPTS

| | Carbon nanotube |
| --- | --- |
| | Fullerene |
| | Graphite |
| | Drinking water |
| | Carbon black |
| | Carbon monoxide |
| | Charcoal |
| | Synthetic diamond |
| | Carbon dioxide |
| | Dry ice |
| | Fiber |
| | Acetylene |
| | Calcite |
| | Calcium carbide |
| | Calcium oxide |
| | Carbide |
| | Carbonic acid |
| | Dolomite |
| | Magnesite |
| | Siderite |
| | Inorganic compound |

## 22. Chemistry of the Nonmetals

CHAPTER OUTLINE: KEY TERMS, PEOPLE, PLACES, CONCEPTS

| | |
|---|---|
| | Limestone |
| | Germanium |
| | Semiconductor |
| | Silicon |
| | Silicon carbide |
| | Tungsten carbide |
| | Enstatite |
| | Silicate |
| | Asbestos |
| | Chrysotile |
| | Quartz |
| | Boron |
| | Cobalt glass |
| | Diborane |
| | Pyrex |
| | Silicone |
| | Soda-lime glass |
| | Borax |
| | Boric acid |
| | Sodium borohydride |
| | Hydrogen cyanide |

CHAPTER HIGHLIGHTS & NOTES: KEY TERMS, PEOPLE, PLACES, CONCEPTS

| Nonmetal | In chemistry, a nonmetal or non-metal is a chemical element which mostly lacks metallic attributes. Physically, nonmetals tend to be highly volatile (easily vaporised), have low elasticity, and are good insulators of heat and electricity; chemically, they tend to have high ionisation energy and electronegativity values, and gain or share electrons when they react with other elements or compounds. Seventeen elements are generally classified as nonmetals; most are gases (hydrogen, helium, nitrogen, oxygen, fluorine, neon, chlorine, argon, krypton, xenon and radon); one is a liquid (bromine); and a few are solids (carbon, phosphorus, sulfur, selenium, and iodine). |
|---|---|
| Periodic trends | In chemistry, periodic trends are the tendencies of certain elemental characteristics to increase or decrease as one progresses along a row or column of the periodic table of elements. All periodic trends of the chemicals are based on Coulomb's law $F_C = \dfrac{kq_1q_2}{d^2}$ . As distance from the protons in the nucleus to the valence electrons increases values associated with attributes such as electron affinity, ionization energy, and electronegativity decrease. |
| Silicon dioxide | Silicon dioxide, also known as silica, is a chemical compound that is a dioxide of silicon with the chemical formula $SiO_2$. It has been known since ancient times. Silica is most commonly found in nature as quartz, as well as in various living organisms, Silica is one of the most complex and most abundant families of materials, existing both as several minerals and being produced synthetically. |
| Hydrogen | Hydrogen is a chemical element with chemical symbol H and atomic number 1. With an atomic weight of 1.00794 u, hydrogen is the lightest element and its monatomic form (H) is the most abundant chemical substance, constituting roughly 75% of the Universe's baryonic mass. Non-remnant stars are mainly composed of hydrogen in its plasma state. |

# 22. Chemistry of the Nonmetals

| | |
|---|---|
| Double bond | A double bond in chemistry is a chemical bond between two chemical elements involving four bonding electrons instead of the usual two. The most common double bond, that is between two carbon atoms, can be found in alkenes. Many types of double bonds exist between two different elements. |
| Absorption | In chemistry, absorption is a physical or chemical phenomenon or a process in which atoms, molecules, or ions enter some bulk phase - gas, liquid, or solid material. This is a different process from adsorption, since molecules undergoing absorption are taken up by the volume, not by the surface (as in the case for adsorption). A more general term is sorption, which covers absorption, adsorption, and ion exchange. |
| Combustion | Combustion or burning is the sequence of exothermic chemical reactions between a fuel and an oxidant accompanied by the production of heat and conversion of chemical species. The release of heat can produce light in the form of either glowing or a flame. |
| | In a complete combustion reaction, a compound reacts with an oxidizing element, such as oxygen or fluorine, and the products are compounds of each element in the fuel with the oxidizing element. |
| Deuterium | Deuterium is one of two stable isotopes of hydrogen. It has a natural abundance in Earth's oceans of about one atom in 6,420 of hydrogen. Thus deuterium accounts for approximately 0.0156% (or on a mass basis: 0.0312%) of all the naturally occurring hydrogen in the oceans, while the most common isotope (hydrogen-1 or protium) accounts for more than 99.98%. |
| Heavy water | Heavy water, formally called deuterium oxide or $2H2O$ or $D_2O$, is a form of water that contains a larger than normal amount of the hydrogen isotope deuterium, rather than the common hydrogen-1 isotope that makes up most of the hydrogen in normal water. |
| Isotope | Isotopes are variants of a particular chemical element such that, while all isotopes of a given element have the same number of protons in each atom, they differ in neutron number. The term isotope is formed from the Greek roots isos (?s?? 'equal') and topos (t?p?? 'place'), meaning 'the same place'. Thus, different isotopes of a single element occupy the same position on the periodic table. |
| Tritium | Tritium is a radioactive isotope of hydrogen. The nucleus of tritium contains one proton and two neutrons, whereas the nucleus of protium (by far the most abundant hydrogen isotope) contains one proton and no neutrons. Naturally occurring tritium is extremely rare on Earth, where trace amounts are formed by the interaction of the atmosphere with cosmic rays. |
| Water gas | Water gas is a synthesis gas, containing carbon monoxide and hydrogen. It is a useful product but requires careful handling because of the risk of carbon monoxide poisoning. The gas is made by passing steam over a red-hot carbon fuel such as coke: $H_2O + C$ ? $H_2 + CO$ ($?H$ = +131 kJ/mol) |

| | |
|---|---|
| Effusion | Effusion is the process in which a gas escapes through a small hole. This occurs if the diameter of the hole is considerably smaller than the mean free path of the molecules. According to Graham's law, the rate at which gases effuse (i.e., how many molecules pass through the hole per second) is dependent on their molecular weight. |
| Alkali | In chemistry, an alkali is a basic, ionic salt of an alkali metal or alkaline earth metal chemical element. Some authors also define an alkali as a base that dissolves in water. A solution of a soluble base has a pH greater than 7.0. The adjective alkaline is commonly, and alkalescent less often, used in English as a synonym for basic, especially for soluble bases. |
| Calcium hydride | Calcium hydride is the chemical compound with the formula $CaH_2$. This grey powder (white if pure, which is rare) reacts vigorously with water liberating hydrogen gas. $CaH_2$ is thus used as a drying agent, i.e. a desiccant. |
| Cracking | In petroleum geology and chemistry, cracking is the process whereby complex organic molecules such as kerogens or heavy hydrocarbons are broken down into simpler molecules such as light hydrocarbons, by the breaking of carbon-carbon bonds in the precursors. The rate of cracking and the end products are strongly dependent on the temperature and presence of catalysts. Cracking is the breakdown of a large alkane into smaller, more useful alkanes and alkenes. |
| Binary compound | A binary compound is a chemical compound that contains exactly two different elements. Examples of binary ionic compounds include calcium chloride ($CaCl_2$), sodium fluoride (NaF), and magnesium oxide (MgO), whilst examples of a binary covalent compounds include water ($H_2O$), carbon monoxide (CO), and sulfur hexafluoride ($SF_6$). |
| Oxide | An oxide is a chemical compound that contains at least one oxygen atom and one other element in its chemical formula. Metal oxides typically contain an anion of oxygen in the oxidation state of -2. Most of the Earth's crust consists of solid oxides, the result of elements being oxidized by the oxygen in air or in water. Hydrocarbon combustion affords the two principal carbon oxides: carbon monoxide and carbon dioxide. |
| Oxyanion | An oxyanion or oxoanion is a chemical compound with the generic formula $A_xO_y^{z-}$. Oxoanions are formed by a large majority of the chemical elements. The formulae of simple oxoanions are determined by the octet rule. |
| Sulfur | Sulfur or sulphur is a chemical element with symbol S and atomic number 16. It is an abundant, multivalent non-metal. Under normal conditions, sulfur atoms form cyclic octatomic molecules with chemical formula $S_8$. Elemental sulfur is a bright yellow crystalline solid when at room temperature. |
| Argon | Argon is a chemical element with symbol Ar and atomic number 18. It is in group 18 of the periodic table and is a noble gas. |

Argon is the third most common gas in the Earth's atmosphere, at 0.93% (9,300 ppm), making it approximately 23.8 times as abundant as the next most common atmospheric gas, carbon dioxide (390 ppm) and more than 500 times as abundant as the next most common noble gas, neon (18 ppm). Nearly all of this argon is radiogenic argon-40 derived from the decay of potassium-40 in the Earth's crust.

| | |
|---|---|
| Fluorine | Fluorine is the chemical element with symbol F and atomic number 9. At room temperature, the element is a pale yellow gas composed of diatomic molecules, $F_2$. Fluorine is the lightest halogen and the most electronegative element. It requires great care in handling as it is extremely reactive and poisonous. |
| Helium | Helium is a chemical element with symbol He and atomic number 2. It is a colorless, odorless, tasteless, non-toxic, inert, monatomic gas that heads the noble gas group in the periodic table. Its boiling and melting points are the lowest among the elements and it exists only as a gas except in extreme conditions. |
| | Helium is the second lightest element and is the second most abundant element in the observable universe, being present at about 24% of the total elemental mass, which is more than 12 times the mass of all the heavier elements combined. |
| Oxygen | Oxygen is a chemical element with symbol O and atomic number 8. It is a member of the chalcogen group on the periodic table and is a highly reactive nonmetallic element and oxidizing agent that readily forms compounds (notably oxides) with most elements. By mass, oxygen is the third-most abundant element in the universe, after hydrogen and helium At STP, two atoms of the element bind to form dioxygen, a diatomic gas that is colorless, odorless, and tasteless; with the formula $O_2$. |
| | Many major classes of organic molecules in living organisms, such as proteins, nucleic acids, carbohydrates, and fats, contain oxygen, as do the major inorganic compounds that are constituents of animal shells, teeth, and bone. |
| Radon | Radon is a chemical element with symbol Rn and atomic number 86. It is a radioactive, colorless, odorless, tasteless noble gas, occurring naturally as an indirect decay product of uranium or thorium. Its most stable isotope, $^{222}Rn$, has a half-life of 3.8 days. Radon is one of the densest substances that remains a gas under normal conditions. |
| Bromine | Bromine is a chemical element with the symbol Br, and atomic number of 35. It is in the halogen group (17). The element was isolated independently by two chemists, Carl Jacob Löwig and Antoine Jerome Balard, in 1825-1826. Elemental bromine is a fuming red-brown liquid at room temperature, corrosive and toxic, with properties between those of chlorine and iodine. |

| | |
|---|---|
| Chlorine | Chlorine is a chemical element with symbol Cl and atomic number 17. Chlorine is in the halogen group (17) and is the second lightest halogen after fluorine. The element is a yellow-green gas under standard conditions, where it forms diatomic molecules. It has the highest electron affinity and the fourth highest electronegativity of all the reactive elements; for this reason, chlorine is a strong oxidizing agent. |
| Cryolite | Cryolite is an uncommon mineral identified with the once large deposit at Ivigtût on the west coast of Greenland, depleted by 1987. |
| | It was historically used as an ore of aluminium and later in the electrolytic processing of the aluminium-rich oxide ore bauxite (itself a combination of aluminium oxide minerals such as gibbsite, boehmite and diaspore). The difficulty of separating aluminium from oxygen in the oxide ores was overcome by the use of cryolite as a flux to dissolve the oxide mineral(s). |
| Halogen | The halogens or halogen elements are a group in the periodic table consisting of five chemically related elements, fluorine, chlorine (Cl), bromine (Br), iodine (I), and astatine (At). The artificially created element 117 (ununseptium) may also be a halogen. In the modern IUPAC nomenclature, this group is known as group 17. |
| Iodine | Iodine is a chemical element with symbol I and atomic number 53. The name is from Greek ??e? d?? ioeides, meaning violet or purple, due to the color of elemental iodine vapor. |
| | Iodine and its compounds are primarily used in nutrition, and industrially in the production of acetic acid and certain polymers. Iodine's relatively high atomic number, low toxicity, and ease of attachment to organic compounds have made it a part of many X-ray contrast materials in modern medicine. |
| Isotopes of astatine | Astatine has 37 known isotopes, all of which are radioactive; the range of their mass numbers is from 191 to 229. There exist also 23 metastable excited states. The longest-lived isotope is $^{210}At$, which has a half-life of 8.1 hours; the longest-lived isotope existing in naturally occurring decay chains is $^{219}At$ with a half-life of 56 seconds. |
| | There are 32 known isotopes of astatine, with atomic masses (mass numbers) of 191 and 193-223. No stable or even long-lived astatine isotope is known, and no such isotope is expected to exist. |
| Carbon tetrachloride | Carbon tetrachloride, also known by many other names, is the organic compound with the formula $CCl_4$. It was formerly widely used in fire extinguishers, as a precursor to refrigerants, and as a cleaning agent. It is a colourless liquid with a 'sweet' smell that can be detected at low levels. |
| Sodium hypochlorite | Sodium hypochlorite is a chemical compound with the formula NaClO. It is composed of a sodium cation (Na+) and a hypochlorite anion (ClO-); it may also be viewed as the sodium salt of hypochlorous acid. |

| | |
|---|---|
| | It is commonly known as bleach or liquid bleach, is frequently used as a disinfectant or a bleaching agent. |
| Vinyl chloride | Vinyl chloride is the organochloride with the formula $H_2C=CHCl$. It is also called vinyl chloride monomer, VCM or chloroethene. This colorless compound is an important industrial chemical chiefly used to produce the polymer polyvinyl chloride. |
| Hexafluorosilicic acid | Hexafluorosilicic acid is an inorganic compound with the chemical formula $(H_3O)2SiF6$ (also written $(H_3O)2[SiF6]$ or $SiH6O2F6$). It is commonly used as a source of fluoride for water fluoridation. |
| Hydrofluoric acid | Hydrofluoric acid is a solution of hydrogen fluoride in water. It is a valued source of fluorine and is a precursor to numerous pharmaceuticals such as fluoxetine (Prozac) and diverse materials such as PTFE (Teflon). |
| | Hydrofluoric acid is a highly corrosive acid, capable of dissolving many materials, especially oxides. |
| Phosphoric acid | Phosphoric acid is a mineral (inorganic) acid having the chemical formula $H_3PO_4$. Orthophosphoric acid molecules can combine with themselves to form a variety of compounds which are also referred to as phosphoric acids, but in a more general way. The term phosphoric acid can also refer to a chemical or reagent consisting of phosphoric acids, such as pyrophosphoric acid or triphosphoric acid, but usually orthophosphoric acid. |
| Sodium bromide | Sodium bromide is an inorganic compound with the formula NaBr. It is a high-melting white, crystalline solid that resembles sodium chloride. It is a widely used source of the bromide ion and has many applications. |
| Ammonium perchlorate | Ammonium perchlorate is an inorganic compound with the formula $NH_4ClO_4$. It is the salt of perchloric acid and ammonia. It is a powerful oxidizer, which is why its main use is in solid propellants. |
| Lewis structure | Lewis structures are diagrams that show the bonding between atoms of a molecule and the lone pairs of electrons that may exist in the molecule. A Lewis structure can be drawn for any covalently bonded molecule, as well as coordination compounds. The Lewis structure was named after Gilbert N |
| Perchlorate | Perchlorates are the salts derived from perchloric acid--in particular when referencing the polyatomic anions found in solution, perchlorate is often written with the formula $ClO_4^-$. Perchlorates are often produced by natural processes but can also be produced artificially. They have been used for more than fifty years to treat thyroid disorders. |
| Perchloric acid | Perchloric acid is an inorganic compound with the formula $HClO_4$. Usually found as an aqueous solution, this colorless compound is a stronger acid than sulfuric and nitric acids. |

| | |
|---|---|
| Chlorate | The chlorate anion has the formula $ClO_3^-$. In this case, the chlorine atom is in the +5 oxidation state. 'Chlorate' can also refer to chemical compounds containing this anion; chlorates are the salts of chloric acid. |
| Hypochlorite | In chemistry, hypochlorite is an ion composed of chlorine and oxygen, with the chemical formula $ClO^-$. It can combine with a number of counter ions to form hypochlorites, which may also be regarded as the salts of hypochlorous acid. Common examples include sodium hypochlorite and calcium hypochlorite. |
| Oxidizing agent | An oxidizing agent is the element or compound in an oxidation-reduction (redox) reaction that accepts an electron from another species. Because the oxidizing agent is gaining electrons, it is said to have been reduced.<br><br>The oxidizing agent itself is reduced, as it is taking electrons onto itself, but the reactant is oxidized by having its electrons taken away by the oxidizing agent. |
| Formaldehyde | Formaldehyde is an organic compound with the formula $CH_2O$ or HCHO. It is the simplest aldehyde, hence its systematic name methanal. The common name of the substance comes from its similarity and relation to formic acid.<br><br>A gas at room temperature, formaldehyde is colorless and has a characteristic pungent, irritating odor. |
| Ozone | Ozone, or trioxygen, is an inorganic compound with the chemical formula O3(μ-O) (also written [O(μ-O)O] or O3). It is a pale blue gas with a distinctively pungent smell. It is an allotrope of oxygen that is much less stable than the diatomic allotrope O2, breaking down in the lower atmosphere to normal dioxygen. |
| Sulfuric acid | Sulfuric acid is a highly corrosive strong mineral acid with the molecular formula $H_2SO_4$. It is a pungent, colorless to slightly yellow viscous liquid which is soluble in water at all concentrations. Sometimes, it is dyed dark brown during production to alert people to its hazards. |
| Angular momentum | In physics, angular momentum, moment of momentum, or rotational momentum is a measure of the amount of rotation an object has, taking into account its mass, shape and speed. It is a vector quantity that represents the product of a body's rotational inertia and rotational velocity about a particular axis. The angular momentum of a system of particles (e.g. a rigid body) is the sum of angular momenta of the individual particles. |
| Barium hydroxide | Barium hydroxide is the chemical compound with the formula $Ba_2$. Also known as baryta, it is one of the principal compounds of barium. |

# 22. Chemistry of the Nonmetals

| | |
|---|---|
| Barium oxide | Barium oxide, BaO, is a white hygroscopic compound formed by the burning of barium in oxygen, although it is often formed through the decomposition of other barium salts. $2Ba + O_2$ ? $2BaO BaCO_3$ ? $BaO + CO_2$ |
| | It reacts with water to form barium hydroxide. $BaO + H_2O$ ? $Ba_2$ |
| | It readily oxidises to $BaO_{1+x}$ by formation of a peroxide ion. |
| Sulfur dioxide | Sulfur dioxide is the chemical compound with the formula SO2. At standard atmosphere it is a toxic gas with a pungent, irritating and rotten smell. The triple point is 197.69 K and 1.67Kpa. |
| Acidic oxide | An acidic oxide is an oxide that either |
| | Examples include:•Carbon dioxide which reacts with water to produce carbonic acid.•Sulfur dioxide, which does not form the non-existent sulfurous acid but does react with bases to form sulfites.•Silicon dioxide, which does not react with water but will react with bases to form silicates•Chromium trioxide, which reacts with water to form chromic acid. Chromic acid is a hypothetical acid. The monomer and dimer would respectively have structures similar to sulfuric and disulfuric acids.•Phosphorus pentoxide ($P_2O_5$) reacts with water and forms phosphoric acid ($H_3PO_4$) |
| | Acidic oxides are oxides of either nonmetals or of metals in high oxidation states. |
| Atmosphere | The standard atmosphere is an international reference pressure defined as 101325 Pa and used as a unit of pressure. |
| Quantum number | Quantum numbers describe values of conserved quantities in the dynamics of a quantum system. Perhaps the most peculiar aspect of quantum mechanics is the quantization of observable quantities, since quantum numbers are discrete sets of integers or half-integers. This is distinguished from classical mechanics where the values can range continuously. |
| Potassium superoxide | Potassium superoxide is the inorganic compound with the formula $KO_2$. It is a yellow solid that decomposes in moist air. It is a rare example of a stable salt of the superoxide ion. |
| Superoxide | A superoxide, also known by the obsolete name hyperoxide, is a compound that contains the superoxide anion with the chemical formula $O_2^-$. The systematic name of the anion is dioxide(1-). Superoxide anion is particularly important as the product of the one-electron reduction of dioxygen $O_2$, which occurs widely in nature. |
| Catalase | Catalase is a common enzyme found in nearly all living organisms exposed to oxygen. It catalyzes the decomposition of hydrogen peroxide to water and oxygen. |

| Chalcogen | The chalcogens are the chemical elements in group 16 of the periodic table. This group is also known as the oxygen family. It consists of the elements oxygen (O), sulfur (S), selenium (Se), tellurium (Te), and the radioactive element polonium (Po). |
| --- | --- |
| Hydrogen peroxide | Hydrogen peroxide is the simplest peroxide (a compound with an oxygen-oxygen single bond). It is also a strong oxidizer. Hydrogen peroxide is a clear liquid, slightly more viscous than water. |
| Peroxidase | Peroxidases are a large family of enzymes that typically catalyze a reaction of the form:ROOR' + electron donor (2 e⁻) + 2H⁺ ? ROH + R'OH<br><br>For many of these enzymes the optimal substrate is hydrogen peroxide, but others are more active with organic hydroperoxides such as lipid peroxides. Peroxidases can contain a heme cofactor in their active sites, or alternately redox-active cysteine or selenocysteine residues.<br><br>The nature of the electron donor is very dependent on the structure of the enzyme. |
| Polonium | Polonium is a chemical element with the symbol Po and atomic number 84, discovered in 1898 by Marie Curie and Pierre Curie. A rare and highly radioactive element with no stable isotopes, polonium is chemically similar to bismuth and tellurium, and it occurs in uranium ores. Applications of polonium are few, and include heaters in space probes, antistatic devices, and sources of neutrons and alpha particles. |
| Selenium | Selenium is a chemical element with symbol Se and atomic number 34. It is a nonmetal with properties that are intermediate between those of its periodic table column-adjacent chalcogen elements sulfur and tellurium. It rarely occurs in its elemental state in nature, or as pure ore compounds. Selenium was discovered in 1817 by Jöns Jacob Berzelius, who noted the similarity of the new element to the previously known tellurium (named for the Earth). |
| Tellurium | Tellurium is a chemical element with symbol Te and atomic number 52. A brittle, mildly toxic, rare, silver-white metalloid which looks similar to tin, tellurium is chemically related to selenium and sulfur. It is occasionally found in native form, as elemental crystals. Tellurium is far more common in the universe as a whole than it is on Earth. |
| Product | Product are formed during chemical reactions as reagents are consumed. Products have lower energy than the reagents and are produced during the reaction according to the second law of thermodynamics. The released energy comes from changes in chemical bonds between atoms in reagent molecules and may be given off in the form of heat or light. |
| Dimethyl sulfide | Dimethyl sulfide or methylthiomethane is an organosulfur compound with the formula $(CH_3)_2S$. Dimethyl sulfide is a water-insoluble flammable liquid that boils at 37 °C (99 °F) and has a characteristic disagreeable odor. It is a component of the smell produced from cooking of certain vegetables, notably maize, cabbage, beetroot and seafoods. |

# 22. Chemistry of the Nonmetals

| | |
|---|---|
| Galena | Galena is the natural mineral form of lead sulfide. It is the most important lead ore mineral. <br><br> Galena is one of the most abundant and widely distributed sulfide minerals. |
| Hydrogen sulfide | Hydrogen sulfide is the chemical compound with the formula H2S. It is a colorless gas with the characteristic foul odor of rotten eggs; it is heavier than air, very poisonous, corrosive, flammable and explosive. <br><br> Hydrogen sulfide often results from the bacterial breakdown of organic matter in the absence of oxygen, such as in swamps and sewers; this process is commonly known as anaerobic digestion. |
| Iron sulfide | Iron sulfide or Iron sulphide refers to a chemical compound of iron and sulfur with a wide range of stoichiometric formulae and different crystalline structures. |
| Pyrite | The mineral pyrite, or iron pyrite, also known as fool's gold, is an iron sulfide with the formula $FeS_2$. This mineral's metallic luster and pale brass-yellow hue give it a superficial resemblance to gold, hence the nickname fool's gold. The color has also led to the nicknames brass, brazzle and Brazil, primarily used to refer to pyrite found in coal. |
| Sulfide | Sulfide is an inorganic anion with the chemical formula $S^{2-}$. It contributes no color to sulfide salts. Sulfide is the main component of niningerite (niningerite is roughly 47% sulfide by mass), and contributes no odor to sulfide salts. |
| Vulcanization | Vulcanization or vulcanisation is a chemical process for converting rubber or related polymers into more durable materials via the addition of sulfur or other equivalent 'curatives' or 'accelerators'. These additives modify the polymer by forming crosslinks (bridges) between individual polymer chains. Vulcanized materials are less sticky and have superior mechanical properties. |
| B sulfite | Bisulfite ion is the ion $HSO_3^-$. Salts containing the $HSO_3^-$ ion are termed bisulfites also known as sulfite lyes. For example, sodium bisulfite is $NaHSO_3$. |
| Dehydration | In physiology and medicine, dehydration is the excessive loss of body water, with an accompanying disruption of metabolic processes. It is literally the removal of water (Ancient Greek: ?d?? hýdor) from an object; however, in physiological terms, it entails a deficiency of fluid within an organism. Dehydration of skin and mucous membranes can be called medical dryness. |
| Sulfite | Sulfites or sulphites are compounds that contain the sulfite ion SO2-3. The sulfite ion is the conjugate base of bisulfite. Although its acid (sulfurous acid) is elusive, its salts are widely used. |
| Ammonia | Ammonia or azane is a compound of nitrogen and hydrogen with the formula $NH_3$. It is a colourless gas with a characteristic pungent smell. |

| | |
|---|---|
| Hydrogen chloride | The compound hydrogen chloride has the chemical formula HCl. At room temperature, it is a colorless gas, which forms white fumes of hydrochloric acid upon contact with atmospheric humidity. Hydrogen chloride gas and hydrochloric acid are important in technology and industry. |
| Nitrogen | Nitrogen, symbol N, is the chemical element of atomic number 7. At room temperature, it is a gas of diatomic molecules and is colorless and odorless. Nitrogen is a common element in the universe, estimated at about seventh in total abundance in our galaxy and the Solar System. On Earth, the element is primarily found as the free element; it forms about 80% of the Earth's atmosphere. |
| Oxidation | Redox (reduction-oxidation) reactions include all chemical reactions in which atoms have their oxidation state changed; in general, redox reactions involve the transfer of electrons between species. |
| | This can be either a simple redox process, such as the oxidation of carbon to yield carbon dioxide or the reduction of carbon by hydrogen to yield methane ($CH_4$), or a complex process such as the oxidation of glucose ($C_6H_{12}O_6$) in the human body through a series of complex electron transfer processes. |
| | The term 'redox' comes from two concepts involved with electron transfer: reduction and oxidation. |
| Oxidation state | The oxidation state, often called the oxidation number, is an indicator of the degree of oxidation of an atom in a chemical compound. The formal oxidation state is the hypothetical charge that an atom would have if all bonds to atoms of different elements were 100% ionic. Oxidation states are typically represented by integers, which can be positive, negative, or zero. |
| Chloramine | Chloramines are derivatives of ammonia by substitution of one, two or three hydrogen atoms with chlorine atoms. Monochloramine is an inorganic compound with the formula $NH_2Cl$. It is an unstable colourless liquid at its melting point of -66 °C, but it is usually handled as a dilute aqueous solution, wherein it is used as a disinfectant. |
| Hydrazine | Hydrazine is an inorganic compound with the formula $N_2H_4$. It is a colourless flammable liquid with an ammonia-like odor. Hydrazine is highly toxic and dangerously unstable unless handled in solution. |
| Hydroxylamine | Hydroxylamine is an inorganic compound with the formula $NH_2OH$. The pure material is a white, unstable crystalline, hygroscopic compound. However, hydroxylamine is almost always provided and used as an aqueous solution. It is used to prepare oximes, an important functional group. |
| Dinitrogen pentoxide | Dinitrogen pentoxide is the chemical compound with the formula $N_2O_5$. |

Also known as nitrogen pentoxide, $N_2O_5$ is one of the binary nitrogen oxides, a family of compounds that only contain nitrogen and oxygen. It is an unstable and potentially dangerous oxidizer that once was used as a reagent when dissolved in chloroform for nitrations but has largely been superseded by $NO_2BF_4$ (nitronium tetrafluoroborate).

| | |
|---|---|
| Dinitrogen trioxide | Dinitrogen trioxide is the chemical compound with the formula $N_2O_3$. This deep blue liquid is one of the binary nitrogen oxides. It forms upon mixing equal parts of nitric oxide and nitrogen dioxide and cooling the mixture below -21 °C (-6 °F):$NO + NO_2\ N_2O_3$<br><br>Dinitrogen trioxide is only isolable at low temperatures, i.e. in the liquid and solid phases. |
| Nitric oxide | Nitric oxide, or nitrogen oxide, also known as nitrogen monoxide, is a molecule with chemical formula NO. It is a free radical and is an important intermediate in the chemical industry. Nitric oxide is a by-product of combustion of substances in the air, as in automobile engines, fossil fuel power plants, and is produced naturally during the electrical discharges of lightning in thunderstorms.<br><br>In mammals including humans, NO is an important cellular signaling molecule involved in many physiological and pathological processes. |
| Nitrous oxide | Nitrous oxide, commonly known as laughing gas, is a chemical compound with the formula N2O. It is an oxide of nitrogen. At room temperature, it is a colourless, non-flammable gas, with a slightly sweet odour and taste. |
| Ostwald process | The Ostwald process is a chemical process for making nitric acid. Wilhelm Ostwald developed the process, and he patented it in 1902. The Ostwald process is a mainstay of the modern chemical industry, and it provides the main raw material for the most common type of fertilizer production. Historically and practically, the Ostwald process is closely associated with the Haber process, which provides the requisite raw material, ammonia ($NH_3$). |
| Nitrocellulose | Nitrocellulose is a highly flammable compound formed by nitrating cellulose through exposure to nitric acid or another powerful nitrating agent. When used as a propellant or low-order explosive, it was originally known as guncotton. Nitrocellulose plasticized by camphor was used by Kodak, and other suppliers, from the late 1880s as a film base in photography, X-ray films and motion picture films; and was known as nitrate film. |
| Nitroglycerin | Nitroglycerin, also known as nitroglycerine, trinitroglycerin, trinitroglycerine, or nitro, is more correctly known as glyceryl trinitrate or more formally: 1,2,3-trinitroxypropane. It is a heavy, colorless, oily, explosive liquid most commonly produced by treating glycerol with white fuming nitric acid under conditions appropriate to the formation of the nitric acid ester. |

| Nitrous acid | Nitrous acid is a weak and monobasic acid known only in solution and in the form of nitrite salts. |
| | |
| | Nitrous acid is used to make diazides from amines; this occurs by nucleophilic attack of the amine onto the nitrite, reprotonation by the surrounding solvent, and double-elimination of water. The diazide can then be liberated to give a carbene or carbenoid. |
| Disproportionation | Disproportionation is a specific type of redox reaction in which a species is simultaneously reduced and oxidized to form two different products. |
| | |
| | For example: the UV photolysis of mercury chloride $Hg_2Cl_2$ ? $Hg + HgCl_2$ is a disproportionation. Mercury (I) is a diatomic dication $Hg2+2$. |
| Antimony | Antimony is a chemical element with symbol Sb and atomic number 51. A lustrous gray metalloid, it is found in nature mainly as the sulfide mineral stibnite ($Sb_2S_3$). Antimony compounds have been known since ancient times and were used for cosmetics; metallic antimony was also known, but it was erroneously identified as lead. It was established to be an element around the 17th century. |
| Arsenic | Arsenic is a chemical element with symbol As and atomic number 33. Arsenic occurs in many minerals, usually in conjunction with sulfur and metals, and also as a pure elemental crystal. It was first documented by Albertus Magnus in 1250. Arsenic is a metalloid. It can exist in various allotropes, although only the gray form has important use in industry. |
| Phosphorus halide | There are three series of binary phosphorus halides, containing phosphorus in the oxidation states +5, +3 and +2. All compounds have been described, in varying degrees of detail, although serious doubts have been cast on the existence of $PI_5$. Mixed chalcogen halides also exist. |
| Phosphorus trichloride | Phosphorus trichloride is a chemical compound of phosphorus and chlorine, having chemical formula $PCl_3$. It has a trigonal pyramidal shape. It is the most important of the three phosphorus chlorides. |
| Halide | A halide is a binary compound, of which one part is a halogen atom and the other part is an element or radical that is less electronegative than the halogen, to make a fluoride, chloride, bromide, iodide, or astatide compound. Many salts are halides. All Group 1 metals form halides which are white solids at room temperature. |
| Phosphorus | Phosphorus is a nonmetallic chemical element with symbol P and atomic number 15. A multivalent pnictogen, phosphorus as a mineral is almost always present in its maximally oxidised state, as inorganic phosphate rocks. Elemental phosphorus exists in two major forms--white phosphorus and red phosphorus--but due to its high reactivity, phosphorus is never found as a free element on Earth. |

# 22. Chemistry of the Nonmetals

The first form of elemental phosphorus to be produced (white phosphorus, in 1669) emits a faint glow upon exposure to oxygen - hence its name given from Greek mythology, F?sf???? meaning 'light-bearer' (Latin Lucifer), referring to the 'Morning Star', the planet Venus.

| | |
|---|---|
| Adenosine diphosphate | Adenosine diphosphate, abbreviated ADP, is an important organic compound in metabolism and is essential to the flow of energy in living cells. A molecule of ADP consists of three important structural components: a sugar backbone attached to a molecule of adenine and two phosphate groups bonded to the 5' carbon atom of ribose. The carbon molecules that make up the ring structure of a sugar can be named in a way that more specifically designates the location of the phosphate and adenosine attachments: The sugar backbone of ADP is known as a pentose sugar and consists of five carbon molecules. |
| Adenosine triphosphate | Adenosine triphosphate is a nucleoside triphosphate used in cells as a coenzyme. It is often called the 'molecular unit of currency' of intracellular energy transfer. ATP transports chemical energy within cells for metabolism. |
| Condensation reaction | A condensation reaction, also commonly referred to as dehydration synthesis, is a chemical reaction in which two molecules or moieties combine to form a larger molecule, together with the loss of a small molecule. Possible small molecules lost are water, hydrogen chloride, methanol, or acetic acid. The word 'condensation' suggests a process in which two or more things are brought 'together' (Latin 'con') to form something 'dense', like in condensation from gaseous to liquid state of matter; this does not imply, however, that condensation reaction products have greater density than reactants. |
| Detergent | A detergent is a surfactant or a mixture of surfactants with 'cleaning properties in dilute solutions.' These substances are usually alkylbenzenesulfonates, a family of compounds that are similar to soap but are more soluble in hard water, because the polar sulfonate (of detergents) is less likely than the polar carboxyl to bind to calcium and other ions found in hard water. In most household contexts, the term detergent by itself refers specifically to laundry detergent or dish detergent, as opposed to hand soap or other types of cleaning agents. Detergents are commonly available as powders or concentrated solutions. |
| Phosphorous acid | Phosphorous acid is the compound described by the formula $H_3PO_3$. This acid is diprotic (readily ionizes two protons), not triprotic as might be suggested by this formula. Phosphorous acid is an intermediate in the preparation of other phosphorus compounds. |
| Condensation | Condensation is the change of the physical state of matter from gas phase into liquid phase, and is the reverse of vaporization. It can also be defined as the change in the state of water vapor to water/any liquid when in contact with any surface. When the transition happens from the gaseous phase into the solid phase directly, the change is called deposition. |

CHAPTER HIGHLIGHTS & NOTES: KEY TERMS, PEOPLE, PLACES, CONCEPTS

| | |
|---|---|
| Carbon | Carbon fiber, alternatively graphite fiber, carbon graphite or CF, is a material consisting of fibers about 5-10 μm in diameter and composed mostly of carbon atoms. The carbon atoms are bonded together in crystals that are more or less aligned parallel to the long axis of the fiber. The crystal alignment gives the fiber high strength-to-volume ratio (making it strong for its size). |
| Carbon nanotube | Carbon nanotubes are allotropes of carbon with a cylindrical nanostructure. Nanotubes have been constructed with length-to-diameter ratio of up to 132,000,000:1, significantly larger than for any other material. These cylindrical carbon molecules have unusual properties, which are valuable for nanotechnology, electronics, optics and other fields of materials science and technology. |
| Fullerene | A fullerene is any molecule composed entirely of carbon, in the form of a hollow sphere, ellipsoid, tube, and many other shapes. Spherical fullerenes are also called buckyballs, and they resemble the balls used in football (soccer). Cylindrical ones are called carbon nanotubes or buckytubes. |
| Graphite | The mineral graphite is an allotrope of carbon. It was named by Abraham Gottlob Werner in 1789 from the Ancient Greek ???f? (grapho), 'to draw/write', for its use in pencils, where it is commonly called lead (not to be confused with the metallic element lead). Unlike diamond (another carbon allotrope), graphite is an electrical conductor, a semimetal. |
| Drinking water | Drinking water or potable water is water safe enough to be consumed by humans or used with low risk of immediate or long term harm. In most developed countries, the water supplied to households, commerce and industry meets drinking water standards, even though only a very small proportion is actually consumed or used in food preparation. Typical uses (for other than potable purposes) include toilet flushing, washing and landscape irrigation. |
| Carbon black | Carbon black is a material produced by the incomplete combustion of heavy petroleum products such as FCC tar, coal tar, ethylene cracking tar, and a small amount from vegetable oil. Carbon black is a form of paracrystalline carbon that has a high surface-area-to-volume ratio, albeit lower than that of activated carbon. It is dissimilar to soot in its much higher surface-area-to-volume ratio and significantly lower (negligible and non-bioavailable) PAH (polycyclic aromatic hydrocarbon) content. |
| Carbon monoxide | Carbon monoxide is a colorless, odorless, and tasteless gas that is slightly less dense than air. It is toxic to humans and animals when encountered in higher concentrations, although it is also produced in normal animal metabolism in low quantities, and is thought to have some normal biological functions. In the atmosphere, it is spatially variable, short lived, having a role in the formation of ground-level ozone. |
| Charcoal | Charcoal is a light black residue consisting of carbon, and any remaining ash, obtained by removing water and other volatile constituents from animal and vegetation substances. Charcoal is usually produced by slow pyrolysis, the heating of wood or other substances in the absence of oxygen . |

# 22. Chemistry of the Nonmetals

| | |
|---|---|
| Synthetic diamond | Synthetic diamond is diamond produced in an artificial process, as opposed to natural diamonds, which are created by geological processes. Synthetic diamond is also widely known as HPHT diamond or CVD diamond after the two common production methods (referring to the high-pressure high-temperature and chemical vapor deposition crystal formation methods, respectively).<br><br>Although often referred to as synthetic, this term has been considered somewhat problematic. |
| Carbon dioxide | Carbon dioxide is a naturally occurring chemical compound composed of two oxygen atoms each covalently double bonded to a single carbon atom. It is a gas at standard temperature and pressure and exists in Earth's atmosphere in this state, as a trace gas at a concentration of 0.039 per cent by volume.<br><br>As part of the carbon cycle, plants, algae, and cyanobacteria use light energy to photosynthesize carbohydrate from carbon dioxide and water, with oxygen produced as a waste product. |
| Dry ice | Dry ice, sometimes referred to as 'cardice' or as 'card ice', is the solid form of carbon dioxide. It is used primarily as a cooling agent. Its advantages include lower temperature than that of water ice and not leaving any residue (other than incidental frost from moisture in the atmosphere). |
| Fiber | Fiber or fibre (from the French fibre) is a rope or string used as a component of composite materials, or matted into sheets to make products such as paper or felt. Fibers are often used in the manufacture of other materials. The strongest engineering materials are generally made as fibers, for example carbon fiber and Ultra-high-molecular-weight polyethylene. |
| Acetylene | Acetylene is the chemical compound with the formula $C_2H_2$. It is a hydrocarbon and the simplest alkyne. This colorless gas is widely used as a fuel and a chemical building block. |
| Calcite | Calcite is a carbonate mineral and the most stable polymorph of calcium carbonate . The other polymorphs are the minerals aragonite and vaterite. Aragonite will change to calcite at 380-470°C, and vaterite is even less stable. |
| Calcium carbide | Calcium carbide is a chemical compound with the chemical formula of $CaC_2$. Its main use industrially is in the production of acetylene and calcium cyanamide.<br><br>The pure material is colorless, however pieces of technical-grade calcium carbide are grey or brown and consist of about 80-85% of $CaC_2$ (the rest is CaO (calcium oxide), $Ca_3P_2$ (calcium phosphide), CaS (calcium sulfide), $Ca_3N_2$ (calcium nitride), SiC (silicon carbide), etc).. |
| Calcium oxide | Calcium oxide, commonly known as quicklime or burnt lime, is a widely used chemical compound. It is a white, caustic, alkaline crystalline solid at room temperature. |

| Carbide | In chemistry, a carbide is a compound composed of carbon and a less electronegative element. Carbides can be generally classified by chemical bonding type as follows: (i) salt-like, (ii) covalent compounds, (iii) interstitial compounds, and (iv) 'intermediate' transition metal carbides. Examples include calcium carbide, silicon carbide, tungsten carbide and cementite, each used in key industrial applications. |
|---|---|
| Carbonic acid | Not to be confused with carbolic acid, an antiquated name for phenol.Carbonic acid is also an archaic name for carbon dioxide. |
| | Carbonic acid is the chemical compound with the formula $H_2CO_3$ (equivalently $OC_2$). It is also a name sometimes given to solutions of carbon dioxide in water (carbonated water), because such solutions contain small amounts of $H_2CO_3$. Carbonic acid, which is a weak acid, forms two kinds of salts, the carbonates and the bicarbonates. |
| Dolomite | Dolomite is a carbonate mineral composed of calcium magnesium carbonate $CaMg_2$. The word dolomite is also used to describe the sedimentary carbonate rock, which is composed predominantly of the mineral dolomite. |
| Magnesite | Magnesite is a mineral with the chemical formula $MgCO_3$ . It occupies one end of a solid solution series with siderite ($FeCO_3$), as the iron ion $Fe^{2+}$ substitutes for the magnesium ion $Mg^{2+}$. Calcium, manganese, cobalt and nickel may also occur in small amounts. |
| Siderite | Siderite is also the name of a type of iron meteorite. |
| | Siderite is a mineral composed of iron carbonate ($FeCO_3$). It takes its name from the Greek word s?d???? sideros, "iron". It is a valuable iron mineral, since it is 48% iron and contains no sulfur or phosphorus. |
| Inorganic compound | Inorganic compounds are those that lack carbon and hydrogen atoms. Inorganic compounds are traditionally viewed as being synthesized by the agency of geological systems. In contrast, organic compounds are found in biological systems. |
| Limestone | Limestone is a sedimentary rock composed largely of the minerals calcite and aragonite, which are different crystal forms of calcium carbonate . Many limestones are composed from skeletal fragments of marine organisms such as coral or foraminifera. |
| | Limestone makes up about 10% of the total volume of all sedimentary rocks. |
| Germanium | Germanium is a chemical element with symbol Ge and atomic number 32. It is a lustrous, hard, grayish-white metalloid in the carbon group, chemically similar to its group neighbors tin and silicon. |

Purified germanium is a semiconductor, with an appearance most similar to elemental silicon. Like silicon, germanium naturally reacts and forms complexes with oxygen in nature.

**Semiconductor**

A semiconductor is a material which has electrical conductivity to a degree between that of a metal and that of an insulator (such as glass). Semiconductors are the foundation of modern electronics, including transistors, solar cells, light-emitting diodes (LEDs), quantum dots and digital and analog integrated circuits.

A semiconductor may have a number of unique properties, one of which is the ability to change conductivity by the addition of impurities ('doping') or by interaction with another phenomenon, such as an electric field or light; this ability makes a semiconductor very useful for constructing a device that can amplify, switch, or convert an energy input.

**Silicon**

Silicon, a tetravalent metalloid, is a chemical element with the symbol Si and atomic number 14. It is less reactive than its chemical analog carbon, the nonmetal directly above it in the periodic table, but more reactive than germanium, the metalloid directly below it in the table. Controversy about silicon's character dates to its discovery; it was first prepared and characterized in pure form in 1823. In 1808, it was given the name silicium (from Latin: silex, hard stone or flint), with an -ium word-ending to suggest a metal, a name which the element retains in several non-English languages. However, its final English name, first suggested in 1817, reflects the more physically similar elements carbon and boron.

**Silicon carbide**

Silicon carbide, also known as carborundum, is a compound of silicon and carbon with chemical formula SiC. It occurs in nature as the extremely rare mineral moissanite. Silicon carbide powder has been mass-produced since 1893 for use as an abrasive. Grains of silicon carbide can be bonded together by sintering to form very hard ceramics that are widely used in applications requiring high endurance, such as car brakes, car clutches and ceramic plates in bulletproof vests.

**Tungsten carbide**

Tungsten carbide is an inorganic chemical compound (specifically, a carbide) containing equal parts of tungsten and carbon atoms. In its most basic form, tungsten carbide is a fine gray powder, but it can be pressed and formed into shapes for use in industrial machinery, cutting tools, abrasives, other tools and instruments, and jewelry.

Tungsten carbide is approximately two times stiffer than steel, with a Young's modulus of approximately 550 GPa, and is much denser than steel or titanium.

**Enstatite**

Enstatite is the magnesium endmember of the pyroxene silicate mineral series enstatite - ferrosilite ($FeSiO_3$). The magnesium rich members of the solid solution series are common rock-forming minerals found in igneous and metamorphic rocks. The intermediate composition, $(Mg,Fe)SiO_3$, has historically been known as hypersthene, although this name has been formally abandoned and replaced by orthopyroxene.

| Silicate | Silicate compounds, including the minerals, consist of silicate anions whose charge is balanced by various cations. Myriad silicate anions can exist, and each can form compounds with many different cations. Hence this class of compounds is very large. |
| --- | --- |
| Asbestos | Asbestos is a set of six naturally occurring silicate minerals used commercially for their desirable physical properties. They all have in common their eponymous asbestiform habit: long (roughly 1:20 aspect ratio), thin fibrous crystals. The prolonged inhalation of asbestos fibers can cause serious illnesses including malignant lung cancer, mesothelioma, and asbestosis (a type of pneumoconiosis). |
| Chrysotile | Chrysotile or white asbestos is the most commonly encountered form of asbestos, accounting for approximately 95% of the asbestos in place in the United States and a similar proportion in other countries. It is a soft, fibrous silicate mineral in the serpentine group of phyllosilicates; as such, it is distinct from other asbestiform minerals in the amphibole group. Its idealized chemical formula is $Mg_3(Si_2O_5)(OH)_4$. |
| Quartz | Quartz is the second most abundant mineral in the Earth's continental crust, after feldspar. It is made up of a continuous framework of $SiO_4$ silicon-oxygen tetrahedra, with each oxygen being shared between two tetrahedra, giving an overall formula $SiO_2$.<br><br>There are many different varieties of quartz, several of which are semi-precious gemstones. |
| Boron | Boron is a chemical element with symbol B and atomic number 5. Because boron is produced entirely by cosmic ray spallation and not by stellar nucleosynthesis, it is a low-abundance element in both the solar system and the Earth's crust. Boron is concentrated on Earth by the water-solubility of its more common naturally occurring compounds, the borate minerals. These are mined industrially as evaporites, such as borax and kernite. |
| Cobalt glass | Cobalt glass is a deep blue colored glass prepared by adding cobalt salts of alumina to the molten glass. It is appreciated for its attractive color. It is also used as an optical filter in flame tests to filter out the yellow flame caused by the contamination of sodium, and expand the ability to see violet and blue hues. |
| Diborane | Diborane is the chemical compound consisting of boron and hydrogen with the formula $B_2H_6$. It is a colorless gas at room temperature with a repulsively sweet odor. Diborane mixes well with air, easily forming explosive mixtures. |
| Pyrex | Pyrex is a brand which was introduced by Corning Incorporated in 1915 for a line of clear, low-thermal-expansion borosilicate glass used for laboratory glassware and kitchenware. |
| Silicone | Silicones are inert, synthetic compounds with a variety of forms and uses. |

|  | Typically heat-resistant and rubber-like, they are used in sealants, adhesives, lubricants, medical applications, cooking utensils, and insulation. |
|---|---|
|  | Silicones are polymers that include silicon together with carbon, hydrogen, oxygen, and sometimes other elements. |
| Soda-lime glass | Soda-lime glass, also called soda-lime-silica glass, is the most prevalent type of glass, used for windowpanes, and glass containers for beverages, food, and some commodity items. Glass bakeware is often made of tempered soda-lime glass. |
|  | Soda-lime glass is relatively inexpensive, chemically stable, reasonably hard, and extremely workable, because it is capable of being re-softened and re-melted numerous times, is ideal for recycling. |
| Borax | Borax, also known as sodium borate, sodium tetraborate, or disodium tetraborate, is an important boron compound, a mineral, and a salt of boric acid. Powdered borax is white, consisting of soft colorless crystals that dissolve easily in water. |
|  | Borax has a wide variety of uses. |
| Boric acid | Boric acid, also called hydrogen borate, boracic acid, orthoboric acid and acidum boricum, is a weak acid of boron often used as an antiseptic, insecticide, flame retardant, neutron absorber, or precursor to other chemical compounds. It has the chemical formula $H_3BO_3$ (sometimes written $B(OH)_3$), and exists in the form of colorless crystals or a white powder that dissolves in water. When occurring as a mineral, it is called sassolite. |
| Sodium borohydride | Sodium borohydride, also known as sodium tetrahydridoborate, is an inorganic compound with the formula $NaBH_4$. This white solid, usually encountered as a powder, is a versatile reducing agent that finds wide application in chemistry, both in the laboratory and on a technical scale. Large amounts are used for bleaching wood pulp. |
| Hydrogen cyanide | Hydrogen cyanide, sometimes called prussic acid, is an inorganic compound with chemical formula HCN. It is a colorless, extremely poisonous liquid that boils slightly above room temperature, at 26 °C (79 °F). HCN is produced on an industrial scale and is a highly valuable precursor to many chemical compounds ranging from polymers to pharmaceuticals. |
| Borazine | Borazine is an inorganic compound with the chemical formula $(BH)_3(NH)_3$. In this cyclic compound, the three BH units and three NH units alternate. The compound is isoelectronic and isostructural with benzene. |
| Carbon suboxide | Carbon suboxide, or tricarbon dioxide, is an oxide of carbon with chemical formula $C_3O_2$ or O=C=C=C=O. Its four cumulative double bonds make it a cumulene. |

|  | It is one of the stable members of the series of linear oxocarbons $O=C_n=O$, which also includes carbon dioxide ($CO_2$) and pentacarbon dioxide ($C_5O_2$).<br><br>The substance was discovered in 1873 by Benjamin Brodie by submitting carbon monoxide to an electric current. |
|---|---|
| Dimethylhydrazine | Dimethylhydrazine is the name of two compounds with the molecular formula $C_2H_8N_2$. These are:•unsymmetrical dimethylhydrazine with both methyl groups are bonded to the same nitrogen atom•symmetrical dimethylhydrazine with one methyl group is bonded to each of the two nitrogen atoms. |

CHAPTER QUIZ: KEY TERMS, PEOPLE, PLACES, CONCEPTS

1. An _____ is the element or compound in an oxidation-reduction (redox) reaction that accepts an electron from another species. Because the _____ is gaining electrons, it is said to have been reduced.

   The _____ itself is reduced, as it is taking electrons onto itself, but the reactant is oxidized by having its electrons taken away by the _____.

   a. Binder
   b. Bioadhesive
   c. Blu-Tack
   d. Oxidizing agent

2. _____ is the chemical compound with the formula $CaH_2$. This grey powder (white if pure, which is rare) reacts vigorously with water liberating hydrogen gas. $CaH_2$ is thus used as a drying agent, i.e. a desiccant.

   a. Beryllium hydride
   b. Beryllium monohydride
   c. Bismuthine
   d. Calcium hydride

3. . _____ is one of two stable isotopes of hydrogen. It has a natural abundance in Earth's oceans of about one atom in 6,420 of hydrogen. Thus _____ accounts for approximately 0.0156% (or on a mass basis: 0.0312%) of all the naturally occurring hydrogen in the oceans, while the most common isotope (hydrogen-1 or protium) accounts for more than 99.98%.

   a. Beryllium
   b. CANFLEX
   c. Deuterium

4. _____ is an inorganic compound with the formula $NH_4ClO_4$. It is the salt of perchloric acid and ammonia. It is a powerful oxidizer, which is why its main use is in solid propellants.

    a. Binder
    b. Bioadhesive
    c. Blu-Tack
    d. Ammonium perchlorate

5. A _____ in chemistry is a chemical bond between two chemical elements involving four bonding electrons instead of the usual two. The most common _____, that is between two carbon atoms, can be found in alkenes. Many types of _____s exist between two different elements.

    a. Formal charge
    b. Triple bond
    c. Merck Index
    d. Double bond

**ANSWER KEY**
22. Chemistry of the Nonmetals

1. d
2. d
3. c
4. d
5. d

---

*You can take the complete Chapter Practice Test*

**for 22. Chemistry of the Nonmetals**
on all key terms, persons, places, and concepts.

*Online 99 Cents*

*http://www.JustTheFacts101.com*

**Use www.JustTheFacts101.com for all your study needs**

**including Facts101's online interactive problem solving labs in**

**chemistry, statistics, mathematics, and more.**

# 23. Transition Metals and Coordination Chemistry

CHAPTER OUTLINE: KEY TERMS, PEOPLE, PLACES, CONCEPTS

| | Metalloid |
|---|---|
| | Transition metal |
| | Periodic table |
| | Physical properties |
| | Doping |
| | Hafnium |
| | Lanthanide contraction |
| | Zirconium |
| | Oxidation state |
| | Aqueous solution |
| | Antiferromagnetism |
| | Ferromagnetism |
| | Magnetic moment |
| | Paramagnetism |
| | Chromium |
| | Curie |
| | Curie temperature |
| | Ferrimagnetism |
| | Ligand |
| | Product |
| | Coordination number |

Coordination sphere

Metal hydroxide

Charged particle

Particle

Cobalt

Gold

Molecular geometry

Platinum

Square planar

Donor

Bipyridine

Diethylenetriamine

Ethylenediamine

Chlorophyll

Heme

Hemoglobin

Lewis structure

Medical imaging

Myoglobin

Porphyrin

Ferrichrome

# 23. Transition Metals and Coordination Chemistry



CHAPTER OUTLINE: KEY TERMS, PEOPLE, PLACES, CONCEPTS

Photosynthesis

Siderophore

Linkage isomerism

Cisplatin

Enantiomer

Chiral

Racemic mixture

Absorption spectrum

Color wheel

Atomic orbital

Spectrochemical series

Molecular orbital

Orbital theory

Chrome yellow

Pyridine

Blackbody radiation

Carbonic anhydrase

Carbon

Carbon monoxide

Methylamine

# 23. Transition Metals and Coordination Chemistry

| | |
|---|---|
| Metalloid | A metalloid is a chemical element that has properties that are in between or a mixture of those of metals and nonmetals and is consequently difficult to classify unambiguously as either a metal or a nonmetal. There is no standard definition of a metalloid, nor is there agreement as to which elements are appropriately classified as such. Despite this lack of specificity the term remains in use in chemistry literature. |
| Transition metal | In chemistry, the term transition metal has two possible meanings:•Most scientists describe a 'transition metal' as any element in the d-block of the periodic table (all are metals), which includes groups 3 to 12 on the periodic table. In actual practice, the f-block lanthanide and actinide series are also considered transition metals and are called 'inner transition metals'.<br><br>Jensen reviews the history of the terms 'transition element' (or 'metal') and 'd-block'. The word transition was first used to describe the elements now known as the d-block by the English chemist Charles Bury in 1921, who referred to a transition series of elements during the change of an inner layer of electrons (for example n=3 in the 4th row of the periodic table) from a stable group of 8 to one of 18, or from 18 to 32. |
| Periodic table | The periodic table is a tabular arrangement of the chemical elements, organized on the basis of their atomic numbers, electron configurations, and recurring chemical properties. Elements are presented in order of increasing atomic number (the number of protons in the nucleus). The standard form of the table consists of a grid of elements laid out in 18 columns and 7 rows, with a double row of elements below that. |
| Physical properties | A physical property is any property that is measurable whose value describes a state of a physical system. The changes in the physical properties of a system can be used to describe its transformations or evolutions between its momentary states. Physical properties are often referred to as observables. |
| Doping | In semiconductor production, doping intentionally introduces impurities into an extremely pure semiconductor for the purpose of modulating its electrical properties. The impurities are dependent upon the type of semiconductor. Lightly and moderately doped semiconductors are referred to as extrinsic. |
| Hafnium | Hafnium is a chemical element with the symbol Hf and atomic number 72. A lustrous, silvery gray, tetravalent transition metal, hafnium chemically resembles zirconium and is found in zirconium minerals. Its existence was predicted by Dmitri Mendeleev in 1869. Hafnium was the penultimate stable isotope element to be discovered (rhenium was identified two years later). Hafnium is named after Hafnia, the Latin name for Copenhagen, where it was discovered. |

| Lanthanide contraction | Lanthanide contraction is a term used in chemistry to describe the greater than expected decrease in ionic radii of the elements in the lanthanide series from atomic number 57, lanthanum, to 71, lutetium, which results in smaller than otherwise expected ionic radii for the subsequent elements starting with 72, hafnium. The term was coined by the Norwegian geochemist Victor Goldschmidt in his series 'Geochemische Verteilungsgesetze Der Elemente'. |
|---|---|
| Zirconium | Zirconium is a chemical element with the symbol Zr, atomic number 40 and atomic mass of 91.224. The name of zirconium is taken from the mineral zircon, the most important source of zirconium, and from the Persian word 'zargun - ?????', meaning 'gold colored'. It is a lustrous, grey-white, strong transition metal that resembles titanium. Zirconium is mainly used as a refractory and opacifier, although it is used in small amounts as an alloying agent for its strong resistance to corrosion. |
| Oxidation state | The oxidation state, often called the oxidation number, is an indicator of the degree of oxidation of an atom in a chemical compound. The formal oxidation state is the hypothetical charge that an atom would have if all bonds to atoms of different elements were 100% ionic. Oxidation states are typically represented by integers, which can be positive, negative, or zero. |
| Aqueous solution | An aqueous solution is a solution in which the solvent is water. It is usually shown in chemical equations by appending (aq) to the relevant formula. For example, a solution of ordinary table salt, or sodium chloride (NaCl), in water would be represented as NaCl(aq). |
| Antiferromagnetism | In materials that exhibit antiferromagnetism, the magnetic moments of atoms or molecules, usually related to the spins of electrons, align in a regular pattern with neighboring spins pointing in opposite directions. This is, like ferromagnetism and ferrimagnetism, a manifestation of ordered magnetism. Generally, antiferromagnetic order may exist at sufficiently low temperatures, vanishing at and above a certain temperature, the Néel temperature (named after Louis Néel, who had first identified this type of magnetic ordering). |
| Ferromagnetism | Ferromagnetism is the basic mechanism by which certain materials form permanent magnets, or are attracted to magnets. In physics, several different types of magnetism are distinguished. Ferromagnetism is the strongest type; it is the only type that creates forces strong enough to be felt, and is responsible for the common phenomena of magnetism encountered in everyday life. |
| Magnetic moment | The magnetic moment of a magnet is a quantity that determines the force that the magnet can exert on electric currents and the torque that a magnetic field will exert on it. A loop of electric current, a bar magnet, an electron, a molecule, and a planet all have magnetic moments.

Both the magnetic moment and magnetic field may be considered to be vectors having a magnitude and direction. |

# 23. Transition Metals and Coordination Chemistry

| | |
|---|---|
| Paramagnetism | Paramagnetism is a form of magnetism whereby certain materials are attracted by an externally applied magnetic field. In contrast with this behavior, diamagnetic materials are repelled by magnetic fields. Paramagnetic materials include most chemical elements and some compounds; they have a relative magnetic permeability greater than or equal to 1 (i.e., a positive magnetic susceptibility) and hence are attracted to magnetic fields. |
| Chromium | Chromium is a chemical element which has the symbol Cr and atomic number 24. It is the first element in Group 6. It is a steely-gray, lustrous, hard and brittle metal which takes a high polish, resists tarnishing, and has a high melting point. The name of the element is derived from the Greek word 'chroma' (???μα), meaning colour, because many of its compounds are intensely coloured. |
| | Chromium oxide was used by the Chinese in the Qin dynasty over 2,000 years ago to coat metal weapons found with the Terracotta Army. |
| Curie | The curie is a non-SI unit of radioactivity the curie is widely used throughout the US government and industry. |
| | One curie is roughly the activity of 1 gram of the radium isotope $^{226}$Ra, a substance studied by the Curies. |
| | The SI derived unit of radioactivity is the becquerel (Bq), which equates to one decay per second. |
| Curie temperature | In physics and materials science, the Curie temperature, or Curie point, is the temperature where a material's permanent magnetism changes to induced magnetism. The force of magnetism is determined by magnetic moments. |
| | The Curie Temperature is the critical point where a material's intrinsic magnetic moments change direction. |
| Ferrimagnetism | In physics, a ferrimagnetic material is one that has populations of atoms with opposing magnetic moments, as in antiferromagnetism; however, in ferrimagnetic materials, the opposing moments are unequal and a spontaneous magnetization remains. This happens when the populations consist of different materials or ions (such as $Fe^{2+}$ and $Fe^{3+}$). |
| | Ferrimagnetism is exhibited by ferrites and magnetic garnets. |
| Ligand | In coordination chemistry, a ligand is an ion or molecule that binds to a central metal atom to form a coordination complex. The bonding between metal and ligand generally involves formal donation of one or more of the ligand's electron pairs. The nature of metal-ligand bonding can range from covalent to ionic. |
| Product | Product are formed during chemical reactions as reagents are consumed. |

Products have lower energy than the reagents and are produced during the reaction according to the second law of thermodynamics. The released energy comes from changes in chemical bonds between atoms in reagent molecules and may be given off in the form of heat or light.

| | |
|---|---|
| Coordination number | In chemistry and crystallography, the coordination number of a central atom in a molecule or crystal is the number of its nearest neighbours. This number is determined somewhat differently for molecules than for crystals. |

In chemistry, the emphasis is on bonding structure in molecules or ions and the coordination number of an atom is determined by simply counting the other atoms to which it is bonded (by either single or multiple bonds).

| | |
|---|---|
| Coordination sphere | In coordination chemistry, the coordination sphere refers to a central atom or ion and an array of molecules or anions, the ligands, around. Molecules that are attached noncovalently to the ligands are called the second coordination sphere. |
| Metal hydroxide | Metal hydroxide are hydroxides of metals. |
| Charged particle | In physics, a charged particle is a particle with an electric charge. It may be either a subatomic particle or an ion. A collection of charged particles, or even a gas containing a proportion of charged particles, is called a plasma, which is called the fourth state of matter because its properties are quite different from solids, liquids and gases (plasma is the most common state of matter in the universe). |
| Particle | In the physical sciences, a particle is a small localized object to which can be ascribed several physical or chemical properties such as volume or mass. The word is rather general in meaning, and is refined as needed by various scientific fields. Something that is composed of particles may be referred to as particulate, although this term is generally used to refer to a suspension of unconnected particles, rather than a connected particle aggregation. |
| Cobalt | Cobalt is a chemical element with symbol Co and atomic number 27. Like nickel, cobalt in the Earth's crust is found only in chemically combined form, save for small deposits found in alloys of natural meteoric iron. The free element, produced by reductive smelting, is a hard, lustrous, silver-gray metal. |

Cobalt-based blue pigments (cobalt blue) have been used since ancient times for jewelry and paints, and to impart a distinctive blue tint to glass, but the color was later thought by alchemists to be due to the known metal bismuth.

| | |
|---|---|
| Gold | Gold is a chemical element with the symbol Au and atomic number 79. It is a dense, soft, malleable, and ductile metal with an attractive, bright yellow color and luster that is maintained without tarnishing in air or water. Chemically, gold is a transition metal and a group 11 element. |

# 23. Transition Metals and Coordination Chemistry

| | |
|---|---|
| Molecular geometry | Molecular geometry is the three-dimensional arrangement of the atoms that constitute a molecule. It determines several properties of a substance including its reactivity, polarity, phase of matter, color, magnetism, and biological activity. The angles between bonds that an atom forms depend only weakly on the rest of molecule, i.e. they can be understood as approximately local and hence transferable properties. |
| Platinum | Platinum is a chemical element with the chemical symbol Pt and an atomic number of 78.<br><br>Its name is derived from the Spanish term platina, which is literally translated into 'little silver'. It is a dense, malleable, ductile, precious, gray-white transition metal. |
| Square planar | The square planar molecular geometry in chemistry describes the stereochemistry that is adopted by certain chemical compounds. As the name suggests, molecules of this geometry have their atoms positioned at the corners of a square on the same plane about a central atom. |
| Donor | In semiconductor physics, a donor is a dopant atom that, when added to a semiconductor, can form a n-type region.<br><br>For example, when silicon, having four valence electrons, needs to be doped as an n-type semiconductor, elements from group V like phosphorus (P) or arsenic (As) can be used because they have five valence electrons. A dopant with five valence electrons is also called a pentavalent impurity. |
| Bipyridine | Bipyridines are a family of chemical compounds with the formula $(C_5H_4N)_2$, which are formed by the coupling of two pyridine rings. Six isomers of bipyridine exist, but two isomers are prominent: 2,2'-bipyridine is a popular ligand in coordination chemistry and 4,4'-bipyridine is a precursor to the herbicide paraquat. The bipyridines are colourless solids, which are soluble in organic solvents and slightly soluble in water. |
| Diethylenetriamine | Diethylenetriamine is an organic compound with the formula $HN(CH_2CH_2NH_2)_2$. This colourless hygroscopic liquid is soluble in water and polar organic solvents, but not simple hydrocarbons. Diethylenetriamine is structural analogue of diethylene glycol. |
| Ethylenediamine | Ethylenediamine is the organic compound with the formula $C_2H_4(NH_2)_2$. This colorless liquid with an ammonia-like odor is a strongly basic amine. It is a widely used building block in chemical synthesis, with approximately 500000000 kg being produced in 1998. Ethylenediamine readily reacts with moisture in humid air to produce a corrosive, toxic and irritating mist, to which even short exposures can cause serious damage to health . |
| Chlorophyll | Chlorophyll is a green pigment found in cyanobacteria and the chloroplasts of algae and plants. Its name is derived from the Greek words ??????, chloros ('green') and f?????, phyllon ('leaf'). |

| | |
|---|---|
| Heme | A haem or heme is a chemical compound of a type known as a prosthetic group consisting of an $Fe^{2+}$ (ferrous) ion contained in the centre of a large heterocyclic organic ring called a porphyrin, made up of four pyrrolic groups joined together by methine bridges. Not all porphyrins contain iron, but a substantial fraction of porphyrin-containing metalloproteins have heme as their prosthetic group; these are known as hemoproteins. Hemes are most commonly recognized in their presence as components of hemoglobin, the red pigment in blood, but they are also components of a number of other hemo-proteins such as myoglobin, cytochrome, endothelial nitric oxide synthase, catalase, etc. |
| Hemoglobin | Hemoglobin; also spelled haemoglobin and abbreviated Hb or Hgb, is the iron-containing oxygen-transport metalloprotein in the red blood cells of all vertebrates as well as the tissues of some invertebrates. Hemoglobin in the blood carries oxygen from the respiratory organs (lungs or gills) to the rest of the body (i.e. the tissues) where it releases the oxygen to burn nutrients to provide energy to power the functions of the organism, and collects the resultant carbon dioxide to bring it back to the respiratory organs to be dispensed from the organism.<br><br>In mammals, the protein makes up about 97% of the red blood cells' dry content (by weight), and around 35% of the total content (including water). |
| Lewis structure | Lewis structures are diagrams that show the bonding between atoms of a molecule and the lone pairs of electrons that may exist in the molecule. A Lewis structure can be drawn for any covalently bonded molecule, as well as coordination compounds. The Lewis structure was named after Gilbert N |
| Medical imaging | Medical imaging is the technique and process used to create images of the human body for clinical purposes (medical procedures seeking to reveal, diagnose, or examine disease) or medical science (including the study of normal anatomy and physiology). Although imaging of removed organs and tissues can be performed for medical reasons, such procedures are not usually referred to as medical imaging, but rather are a part of pathology.<br><br>As a discipline and in its widest sense, it is part of biological imaging and incorporates Radiology, Magnetic Resonance Imaging, Nuclear medicine, medical Ultrasonography or Ultrasound, Endoscopy, Elastography, Tactile Imaging, Thermography and medical photography. |
| Myoglobin | Myoglobin is an iron- and oxygen-binding protein found in the muscle tissue of vertebrates in general and in almost all mammals. It is related to hemoglobin, which is the iron- and oxygen-binding protein in blood, specifically in the red blood cells. Myoglobin is only found in the bloodstream after muscle injury. |
| Porphyrin | Porphyrins are a group of organic compounds, many naturally occurring. One of the best-known porphyrins is heme, the pigment in red blood cells; heme is a cofactor of the protein hemoglobin. |

# 23. Transition Metals and Coordination Chemistry

| | |
|---|---|
| Ferrichrome | Ferrichrome is a cyclic hexa-peptide that forms a complex with iron atoms. It is a siderophore composed of three glycine and three modified ornithine residues with hydroxamate groups [-N(OH)C(=O)C-]. The 6 oxygen atoms from the three hydroxamate groups bind Fe(III) in near perfect octahedral coordination. |
| Photosynthesis | Photosynthesis is a process used by plants and other organisms to convert light energy, normally from the sun, into chemical energy that can be later released to fuel the organisms' activities. This chemical energy is stored in carbohydrate molecules, such as sugars, which are synthesized from carbon dioxide and water - hence the name photosynthesis, from the Greek f??, phos, 'light', and s???es??, synthesis, 'putting together'. In most cases, oxygen is also released as a waste product. |
| Siderophore | Siderophores are small, high-affinity iron chelating compounds secreted by microorganisms such as bacteria, fungi and grasses. Siderophores are amongst the strongest soluble $Fe^{3+}$ binding agents known. |
| Linkage isomerism | Linkage isomerism is the existence of coordination compounds that have the same composition differing with the connectivity of the metal to a ligand.<br><br>Typical ligands that give rise to linkage isomers are:•thiocyanate, $SCN^-$ - isothiocyanate, $NCS^-$ •selenocyanate, $SeCN^-$ - isoselenocyanate, $NCSe^-$•nitrite, $NO_2^-$•sulfite, $SO_3^{2-}$<br><br>Examples of linkage isomers are violet-colored $[_5Co\text{-}SCN]^{2+}$ and orange-colored $[(NH_3)_5Co\text{-}NCS]^{2+}$. The isomerization of the S-bonded isomer to the N-bonded isomer occurs intramolecularly. |
| Cisplatin | Cisplatin, cisplatinum, or cis-diamminedichloridoplatinum (CDDP) is a chemotherapy drug. It was the first member of a class of platinum-containing anti-cancer drugs, which now also includes carboplatin and oxaliplatin. These platinum complexes react in vivo, binding to and causing crosslinking of DNA, which ultimately triggers apoptosis (programmed cell death). |
| Enantiomer | In chemistry, an enantiomer is one of two stereoisomers that are mirror images of each other that are non-superposable (not identical), much as one's left and right hands are the same except for opposite orientation.<br><br>Organic compounds that contain a chiral carbon usually have two non-superposable structures. These two structures are mirror images of each other and are, thus, commonly called enantiomorphs (enantio = opposite ; morph = form), hence this structural property is now commonly referred to as enantiomerism. |
| Chiral | Chirality is a property of asymmetry important in several branches of science. The word chirality is derived from the Greek, ?e?? (kheir), 'hand', a familiar chiral object. |

| | |
|---|---|
| Racemic mixture | In chemistry, a racemic mixture, or racemate, is one that has equal amounts of left- and right-handed enantiomers of a chiral molecule. The first known racemic mixture was 'racemic acid', which Louis Pasteur found to be a mixture of the two enantiomeric isomers of tartaric acid. A mixture with only a single enantiomers is an enantiomerically pure or enantiopure mixture. |
| Absorption spectrum | Absorption spectroscopy refers to spectroscopic techniques that measure the absorption of radiation, as a function of frequency or wavelength, due to its interaction with a sample. The sample absorbs energy, i.e., photons, from the radiating field. The intensity of the absorption varies as a function of frequency, and this variation is the absorption spectrum. |
| Color wheel | A color wheel or other switch for changing a projected hue is a device that uses different optics filters within a light beam. Common usage includes continuously-rotating wheels for seasonal home displays (e.g., at Christmas) and controllable color wheels for a particular instrument (e.g., SeaChanger Color Engine for stage lighting), while non-wheel devices include scrollers and semaphore types with lever arms (e.g., on the 1897-1917 Grand Army Plaza fountain). |
| Atomic orbital | An atomic orbital is a mathematical function that describes the wave-like behavior of either one electron or a pair of electrons in an atom. This function can be used to calculate the probability of finding any electron of an atom in any specific region around the atom's nucleus. The term may also refer to the physical region or space where the electron can be calculated to be present, as defined by the particular mathematical form of the orbital. |
| Spectrochemical series | A spectrochemical series is a list of ligands ordered on ligand strength and a list of metal ions based on oxidation number, group and its identity. In crystal field theory, ligands modify the difference in energy between the d orbitals (?) called the ligand-field splitting parameter for ligands or the crystal-field splitting parameter, which is mainly reflected in differences in color of similar metal-ligand complexes. |
| Molecular orbital | In chemistry, a molecular orbital is a mathematical function describing the wave-like behavior of an electron in a molecule. This function can be used to calculate chemical and physical properties such as the probability of finding an electron in any specific region. The term orbital was introduced by Robert S. Mulliken in 1932 as an abbreviation for one-electron orbital wave function. |
| Orbital theory | In chemistry, molecular orbital theory is a method for determining molecular structure in which electrons are not assigned to individual bonds between atoms, but are treated as moving under the influence of the nuclei in the whole molecule. Because electrons are the fundamental constituents of matter involved in bonding, their involvement in bonding has been studied exhaustively by chemists. Electrons are shared among individual atoms in a molecule to form covalent chemical bonds. |
| Chrome yellow | Chrome Yellow is a natural yellow pigment made of lead chromate ($PbCrO_4$). It was first extracted from the mineral crocoite by the French chemist Louis Vauquelin in 1797. |

# 23. Transition Metals and Coordination Chemistry

| | |
|---|---|
| Pyridine | Pyridine is a basic heterocyclic organic compound with the chemical formula $C_5H_5N$. It is structurally related to benzene, with one methine group (=CH-) replaced by a nitrogen atom. The pyridine ring occurs in many important compounds, including azines and the vitamins niacin and pyridoxal.<br><br>Pyridine was discovered in 1849 by the Scottish chemist Thomas Anderson as one of the constituents of bone oil. |
| Blackbody radiation | Black-body radiation is the type of electromagnetic radiation within or surrounding a body in thermodynamic equilibrium with its environment, or emitted by a black body held at constant, uniform temperature. The radiation has a specific spectrum and intensity that depends only on the temperature of the body.<br><br>The thermal radiation spontaneously emitted by many ordinary objects can be approximated as blackbody radiation. |
| Carbonic anhydrase | The carbonic anhydrases form a family of enzymes that catalyze the rapid interconversion of carbon dioxide and water to bicarbonate and protons (or vice versa), a reversible reaction that occurs rather slowly in the absence of a catalyst. The active site of most carbonic anhydrases contains a zinc ion; they are therefore classified as metalloenzymes.<br><br>One of the functions of the enzyme in animals is to interconvert carbon dioxide and bicarbonate to maintain acid-base balance in blood and other tissues, and to help transport carbon dioxide out of tissues. |
| Carbon | Carbon fiber, alternatively graphite fiber, carbon graphite or CF, is a material consisting of fibers about 5-10 μm in diameter and composed mostly of carbon atoms. The carbon atoms are bonded together in crystals that are more or less aligned parallel to the long axis of the fiber. The crystal alignment gives the fiber high strength-to-volume ratio (making it strong for its size). |
| Carbon monoxide | Carbon monoxide is a colorless, odorless, and tasteless gas that is slightly less dense than air. It is toxic to humans and animals when encountered in higher concentrations, although it is also produced in normal animal metabolism in low quantities, and is thought to have some normal biological functions. In the atmosphere, it is spatially variable, short lived, having a role in the formation of ground-level ozone. |
| Methylamine | Methylamine is the organic compound with a formula of $CH_3NH_2$. This colorless gas is a derivative of ammonia, but with one H atom replaced by a methyl group. It is the simplest primary amine. |

1. A _____ is a chemical element that has properties that are in between or a mixture of those of metals and nonmetals and is consequently difficult to classify unambiguously as either a metal or a nonmetal. There is no standard definition of a _____, nor is there agreement as to which elements are appropriately classified as such. Despite this lack of specificity the term remains in use in chemistry literature.

    a. Chemical Galaxy
    b. Goldschmidt classification
    c. History of the periodic table
    d. Metalloid

2. The _____ is a tabular arrangement of the chemical elements, organized on the basis of their atomic numbers, electron configurations, and recurring chemical properties. Elements are presented in order of increasing atomic number (the number of protons in the nucleus). The standard form of the table consists of a grid of elements laid out in 18 columns and 7 rows, with a double row of elements below that.

    a. Periodic table
    b. Carbonic acid
    c. Chiral Lewis acid
    d. Chloroauric acid

3. _____ is a green pigment found in cyanobacteria and the chloroplasts of algae and plants. Its name is derived from the Greek words ??????, chloros ('green') and f?????, phyllon ('leaf'). _____ is an extremely important biomolecule, critical in photosynthesis, which allows plants to absorb energy from light.

    a. Bilirubin
    b. Biliverdin
    c. Tetrapyrrole
    d. Chlorophyll

4. _____ is a chemical element with symbol Co and atomic number 27. Like nickel, _____ in the Earth's crust is found only in chemically combined form, save for small deposits found in alloys of natural meteoric iron. The free element, produced by reductive smelting, is a hard, lustrous, silver-gray metal.

    _____-based blue pigments (_____ blue) have been used since ancient times for jewelry and paints, and to impart a distinctive blue tint to glass, but the color was later thought by alchemists to be due to the known metal bismuth.

    a. Crown gold
    b. Cobalt
    c. Liquidmetal
    d. Magnesium aluminide

5. . In chemistry, the term _____ has two possible meanings:•Most scientists describe a '_____' as any element in the d-block of the periodic table (all are metals), which includes groups 3 to 12 on the periodic table.

## 23. Transition Metals and Coordination Chemistry

In actual practice, the f-block lanthanide and actinide series are also considered _____s and are called 'inner _____s'.

Jensen reviews the history of the terms 'transition element' (or 'metal') and 'd-block'. The word transition was first used to describe the elements now known as the d-block by the English chemist Charles Bury in 1921, who referred to a transition series of elements during the change of an inner layer of electrons (for example n=3 in the 4th row of the periodic table) from a stable group of 8 to one of 18, or from 18 to 32.

a. Transition metal
b. Carbon group
c. Chalcogen
d. D-block

430

**ANSWER KEY**
23. Transition Metals and Coordination Chemistry

1. d
2. a
3. d
4. b
5. a

---

## You can take the complete Chapter Practice Test

**for 23. Transition Metals and Coordination Chemistry**
on all key terms, persons, places, and concepts.

### Online 99 Cents

### http://www.JustTheFacts101.com

Use www.JustTheFacts101.com for all your study needs

including Facts101's online interactive problem solving labs in

chemistry, statistics, mathematics, and more.

| | Urea |
| --- | --- |
| | Acetonitrile |
| | Double bond |
| | Formaldehyde |
| | Linear molecular geometry |
| | Methane |
| | Organic chemistry |
| | Triple bond |
| | Molecule |
| | Amine |
| | Ascorbic acid |
| | Detergent |
| | Functional group |
| | Glucose |
| | Solubility |
| | Stearate |
| | Surfactant |
| | Acetylene |
| | Alkane |
| | Alkene |
| | Alkyne |

# 24. The Chemistry of Life: Organic and Biological Chemistry

CHAPTER OUTLINE: KEY TERMS, PEOPLE, PLACES, CONCEPTS

- ______ Aromatic hydrocarbon
- ______ Benzene
- ______ Butane
- ______ Ethane
- ______ Hydrocarbon
- ______ Propane
- ______ Unsaturated hydrocarbon
- ______ Combustion
- ______ Decane
- ______ Heptane
- ______ Hexane
- ______ Lewis structure
- ______ Nonane
- ______ Octane
- ______ Pentane
- ______ Side chain
- ______ Amino acid
- ______ Carbon
- ______ Enthalpy
- ______ Isomer
- ______ Isobutane

# 24. The Chemistry of Life: Organic and Biological Chemistry

CHAPTER OUTLINE: KEY TERMS, PEOPLE, PLACES, CONCEPTS

- Isopentane
- Neopentane
- Ethyl group
- Methyl group
- Alkyl
- Cycloalkane
- Cyclohexane
- Cyclopentane
- Cyclopropane
- Asphalt
- Cracking
- Ethanol
- Fractional distillation
- Fuel oil
- Hydrobromic acid
- Kerosene
- Octane rating
- Petroleum
- Propene
- 1-Butene
- 2-Butene

| | Butene |
| | Pentene |
| | Lipid |
| | Addition polymer |
| | Hydrogenation |
| | Addition reaction |
| | Polymer |
| | Reaction mechanism |
| | Anthracene |
| | Naphthalene |
| | Toluene |
| | Dinitrobenzene |
| | Nitrobenzene |
| | Substitution reaction |
| | Alcohol |
| | Acetaldehyde |
| | Acetic acid |
| | Acetone |
| | Dimethyl ether |
| | Ethylamine |
| | Methanol |

# 24. The Chemistry of Life: Organic and Biological Chemistry

CHAPTER OUTLINE: KEY TERMS, PEOPLE, PLACES, CONCEPTS

- Cholesterol
- Ethylene glycol
- Glycerol
- Isopropyl alcohol
- Methyl orange
- Phenol
- Aldehyde
- Butanol
- Carbonyl
- Condensation reaction
- Diethyl ether
- Ether
- Ketone
- Tetrahydrofuran
- Condensation
- Acetylsalicylic acid
- Alcohol oxidation
- Aspirin
- Benzoic acid
- Carboxylic acid
- Carvone

# 24. The Chemistry of Life: Organic and Biological Chemistry

CHAPTER OUTLINE: KEY TERMS, PEOPLE, PLACES, CONCEPTS

Citric acid

Formic acid

Oxidation

Carbonylation

Ethyl acetate

Hydrogen peroxide

Ozone

Potassium dichromate

Butyric acid

Hydrolysis

Methyl propionate

Saponification

Sodium propionate

Amide

Aniline

Benzamide

Bromobenzene

Chiral

Enantiomer

Medical imaging

Racemic mixture

# 24. The Chemistry of Life: Organic and Biological Chemistry

CHAPTER OUTLINE: KEY TERMS, PEOPLE, PLACES, CONCEPTS

- ____________ Chirality
- ____________ Biopolymer
- ____________ Entropy
- ____________ Alanine
- ____________ Arginine
- ____________ Asparagine
- ____________ Aspartic acid
- ____________ Cysteine
- ____________ Essential amino acid
- ____________ Glutamic acid
- ____________ Glutamine
- ____________ Histidine
- ____________ Isoleucine
- ____________ Leucine
- ____________ Lysine
- ____________ Methionine
- ____________ Phenylalanine
- ____________ Proline
- ____________ Serine
- ____________ Threonine
- ____________ Tryptophan

Tyrosine

Valine

Aspartame

Peptide

Folding

Myoglobin

Carbohydrate

Fructose

Disaccharide

Lactose

Monosaccharide

Sucrose

Enzyme

Glycogen

Polysaccharide

Cellulose

Fatty acid

Oleic acid

Polyunsaturated fatty acid

Trace element

Trans fat

Essential fatty acid

Nucleic acid

Phospholipid

Membrane

Adenine

Cytosine

Deoxyribose

Guanine

Nucleotide

Polynucleotide

Ribose

Thymine

Uracil

Base pair

Replication

Pyruvic acid

Acetic anhydride

Purine

Pyrimidine

Glutathione

Indole

# 24. The Chemistry of Life: Organic and Biological Chemistry
CHAPTER OUTLINE: KEY TERMS, PEOPLE, PLACES, CONCEPTS

| | Quinine |
|---|---|
| | Adenosine monophosphate |
| | Ribonuclease |

CHAPTER HIGHLIGHTS & NOTES: KEY TERMS, PEOPLE, PLACES, CONCEPTS

| | |
|---|---|
| Urea | Urea or carbamide is an organic compound with the chemical formula $CO_2$. The molecule has two --$NH_2$ groups joined by a carbonyl (C=O) functional group. |
| | Urea serves an important role in the metabolism of nitrogen-containing compounds by animals and is the main nitrogen-containing substance in the urine of mammals. |
| Acetonitrile | Acetonitrile is the chemical compound with the formula CH3CN. This colourless liquid is the simplest organic nitrile (hydrogen cyanide is a simpler nitrile, but the cyanide anion is not classed as organic). It is produced mainly as a byproduct of acrylonitrile manufacture. |
| Double bond | A double bond in chemistry is a chemical bond between two chemical elements involving four bonding electrons instead of the usual two. The most common double bond, that is between two carbon atoms, can be found in alkenes. Many types of double bonds exist between two different elements. |
| Formaldehyde | Formaldehyde is an organic compound with the formula $CH_2O$ or HCHO. It is the simplest aldehyde, hence its systematic name methanal. The common name of the substance comes from its similarity and relation to formic acid. |
| | A gas at room temperature, formaldehyde is colorless and has a characteristic pungent, irritating odor. |
| Linear molecular geometry | In chemistry, the Linear molecular geometry describes the arrangement of three or more atoms placed at an expected bond angle of 180°. Linear organic molecules, e.g. acetylene, are often described by invoking sp orbital hybridization for the carbon centers. Many linear molecules exist, prominent examples include $CO_2$, HCN, and xenon difluoride. |
| Methane | Methane is a chemical compound with the chemical formula CH |

4 (one atom of carbon and four atoms of hydrogen). It is the simplest alkane and the main component of natural gas. The relative abundance of methane makes it an attractive fuel.

| | |
|---|---|
| Organic chemistry | Organic chemistry is a chemistry subdiscipline involving the scientific study of the structure, properties, and reactions of organic compounds and organic materials, i.e., matter in its various forms that contain carbon atoms. Study of structure includes using spectroscopy and other physical and chemical methods to determine the chemical composition and constitution of organic compounds and materials. Study of properties includes both physical properties and chemical properties, and uses similar methods as well as methods to evaluate chemical reactivity, with the aim to understand the behavior of the organic matter in its pure form (when possible), but also in solutions, mixtures, and fabricated forms. |
| Triple bond | A triple bond in chemistry is a chemical bond between two atoms involving six bonding electrons instead of the usual two in a covalent single bond. The most common triple bond, that between two carbon atoms, can be found in alkynes. Other functional groups containing a triple bond are cyanides and isocyanides. |
| Molecule | A molecule is an electrically neutral group of two or more atoms held together by chemical bonds. Molecules are distinguished from ions by their lack of electrical charge. However, in quantum physics, organic chemistry, and biochemistry, the term molecule is often used less strictly, also being applied to polyatomic ions. |
| Amine | Amines are organic compounds and functional groups that contain a basic nitrogen atom with a lone pair. Amines are derivatives of ammonia, wherein one or more hydrogen atoms have been replaced by a substituent such as an alkyl or aryl group. Important amines include amino acids, biogenic amines, trimethylamine, and aniline; see Category:Amines for a list of amines. |
| Ascorbic acid | Ascorbic acid is a naturally occurring organic compound with antioxidant properties. It is a white solid, but impure samples can appear yellowish. It dissolves well in water to give mildly acidic solutions. |
| Detergent | A detergent is a surfactant or a mixture of surfactants with 'cleaning properties in dilute solutions.' These substances are usually alkylbenzenesulfonates, a family of compounds that are similar to soap but are more soluble in hard water, because the polar sulfonate (of detergents) is less likely than the polar carboxyl to bind to calcium and other ions found in hard water. In most household contexts, the term detergent by itself refers specifically to laundry detergent or dish detergent, as opposed to hand soap or other types of cleaning agents. Detergents are commonly available as powders or concentrated solutions. |
| Functional group | In organic chemistry, functional groups are lexicon-specific groups of atoms or bonds within molecules that are responsible for the characteristic chemical reactions of those molecules. |

| | |
|---|---|
| | The same functional group will undergo the same or similar chemical reaction(s) regardless of the size of the molecule it is a part of. However, its relative reactivity can be modified by nearby functional groups. |
| Glucose | Glucose, meaning 'sweet'. The suffix '-ose' denotes a sugar. |
| Solubility | Solubility is the property of a solid, liquid, or gaseous chemical substance called solute to dissolve in a solid, liquid, or gaseous solvent to form a homogeneous solution of the solute in the solvent. The solubility of a substance fundamentally depends on the physical and chemical properties of the solute and solvent as well as on temperature, pressure and the pH of the solution. The extent of the solubility of a substance in a specific solvent is measured as the saturation concentration, where adding more solute does not increase the concentration of the solution and begin to precipitate the excess amount of solute. |
| Stearate | Stearate is the anion form of stearic acid. Formula is $C_{17}H_{35}COO^-$. |
| Surfactant | Surfactants are compounds that lower the surface tension between two liquids or between a liquid and a solid. Surfactants may act as detergents, wetting agents, emulsifiers, foaming agents, and dispersants. |
| Acetylene | Acetylene is the chemical compound with the formula $C_2H_2$. It is a hydrocarbon and the simplest alkyne. This colorless gas is widely used as a fuel and a chemical building block. |
| Alkane | In organic chemistry, an alkane, or paraffin, is a saturated hydrocarbon. Alkanes consist only of hydrogen and carbon atoms, all bonds are single bonds, and the carbon atoms are not joined in cyclic structures but instead form an open chain. They have the general chemical formula $C_nH_{2n+2}$. |
| Alkene | In organic chemistry, an alkene, olefin, or olefine is an unsaturated chemical compound containing at least one carbon-carbon double bond. The simplest acyclic alkenes, with only one double bond and no other functional groups, known as mono-enes, form a homologous series of hydrocarbons with the general formula $C_nH_{2n}$. They have two hydrogen atoms less than the corresponding alkane (with the same number of carbon atoms). |
| Alkyne | In organic chemistry, an alkyne is an unsaturated hydrocarbon which has at least one carbon-carbon triple bond between two carbon atoms. The simplest acyclic alkynes with only one triple bond and no other functional groups form a homologous series with the general chemical formula $C_nH_{2n-2}$. Alkynes are traditionally known as acetylenes, although the name acetylene also refers specifically to $C_2H_2$, known formally as ethyne using IUPAC nomenclature. |
| Aromatic hydrocarbon | An aromatic hydrocarbon or arene is a hydrocarbon with alternating double and single bonds between carbon atoms forming rings. |

The term 'aromatic' was assigned before the physical mechanism determining aromaticity was discovered, and was derived from the fact that many of the compounds have a sweet scent. The configuration of six carbon atoms in aromatic compounds is known as a benzene ring, after the simplest possible such hydrocarbon, benzene.

| | |
|---|---|
| Benzene | Benzene is an organic chemical compound with the molecular formula $C_6H_6$. Its molecule is composed of 6 carbon atoms joined in a ring, with 1 hydrogen atom attached to each carbon atom. Because its molecules contain only carbon and hydrogen atoms, benzene is classed as a hydrocarbon. |
| Butane | Butane is an organic compound with the formula $C_4H_{10}$ that is an alkane with four carbon atoms. Butane is a gas at room temperature and atmospheric pressure. The term may refer to either of two structural isomers, n-butane or isobutane or to a mixture of these isomers. |
| Ethane | Ethane is a chemical compound with chemical formula $C_2H_6$. At standard temperature and pressure, ethane is a colorless, odorless gas. Ethane is isolated on an industrial scale from natural gas, and as a byproduct of petroleum refining. |
| Hydrocarbon | In organic chemistry, a hydrocarbon is an organic compound consisting entirely of hydrogen and carbon. Hydrocarbons from which one hydrogen atom has been removed are functional groups, called hydrocarbyls. Aromatic hydrocarbons (arenes), alkanes, alkenes, cycloalkanes and alkyne-based compounds are different types of hydrocarbons. |
| Propane | Propane is a three-carbon alkane with the molecular formula C3H8, normally a gas, but compressible to a transportable liquid. A by-product of natural gas processing and petroleum refining, it is commonly used as a fuel for engines, oxy-gas torches, barbecues, portable stoves, and residential central heating. Propane is one of a group of liquefied petroleum gases. |
| Unsaturated hydrocarbon | Unsaturated hydrocarbons are hydrocarbons that have double or triple covalent bonds between adjacent carbon atoms. Those with at least one carbon to carbon double bond are called alkenes and those with at least one carbon to carbon triple bond are called alkynes. The position of the double or triple bond is shown by a number written either at the start of the name, or just before the -ene or -yne suffix (e.g. pent-2-ene and 2-butyne). |
| Combustion | Combustion or burning is the sequence of exothermic chemical reactions between a fuel and an oxidant accompanied by the production of heat and conversion of chemical species. The release of heat can produce light in the form of either glowing or a flame. |
| | In a complete combustion reaction, a compound reacts with an oxidizing element, such as oxygen or fluorine, and the products are compounds of each element in the fuel with the oxidizing element. |
| Decane | Decane is an alkane hydrocarbon with the chemical formula $C_{10}H_{22}$ with 75 structural isomers. |

These isomers are flammable liquids. Decane is a component of gasoline (petrol).

| | |
|---|---|
| Heptane | N-Heptane is the straight-chain alkane with the chemical formula $H_3C_5CH_3$ or $C_7H_{16}$. When used as a test fuel component in anti-knock test engines, a 100% heptane fuel is the zero point of the octane rating scale (the 100 point is a 100% iso-octane). Octane number equates to the anti-knock qualities of a comparison mixture of heptane and isooctane which is expressed as the percentage of isooctane in heptane and is listed on pumps for gasoline dispensed in the United States and internationally. |
| Hexane | Hexane is an alkane of six carbon atoms, with the chemical formula $C_6H_{14}$.<br><br>The term may refer to any of the five structural isomers with that formula, or to a mixture of them. In IUPAC nomenclature, however, hexane is the unbranched isomer (n-hexane); the other four structures are named as methylated derivatives of pentane and butane. |
| Lewis structure | Lewis structures are diagrams that show the bonding between atoms of a molecule and the lone pairs of electrons that may exist in the molecule. A Lewis structure can be drawn for any covalently bonded molecule, as well as coordination compounds. The Lewis structure was named after Gilbert N |
| Nonane | Nonane is a linear alkane hydrocarbon with the chemical formula $C_9H_{20}$.<br><br>Nonane has 35 structural isomers. Tripropylene is a mixture of three specific isomers of nonane. |
| Octane | Octane is a hydrocarbon and an alkane with the chemical formula $C_8H_{18}$, and the condensed structural formula $CH_{36}CH_3$. Octane has many structural isomers that differ by the amount and location of branching in the carbon chain. One of these isomers, 2,2,4-trimethylpentane (isooctane) is used as one of the standard values in the octane rating scale. |
| Pentane | Pentane is an organic compound with the formula $C_5H_{12}$ -- that is, an alkane with five carbon atoms. The term may refer to any of three structural isomers, or to a mixture of them: in the IUPAC nomenclature, however, pentane means exclusively the n-pentane isomer; the other two being called 'methylbutane' and 'dimethylpropane'. Cyclopentane is not an isomer of pentane. |
| Side chain | In organic chemistry and biochemistry, a side chain is a chemical group that is attached to a core part of the molecule called 'main chain' or backbone. The placeholder R is often used as a generic placeholder for alkyl (saturated hydrocarbon) group side chains in chemical structure diagrams. To indicate other non-carbon groups in structure diagrams, X, Y, or Z is often used. |
| Amino acid | Amino acids are biologically important organic compounds made from amine (-$NH_2$) and carboxylic acid (-COOH) functional groups, along with a side-chain specific to each amino acid. |

The key elements of an amino acid are carbon, hydrogen, oxygen, and nitrogen, though other elements are found in the side-chains of certain amino acids. About 500 amino acids are known and can be classified in many ways.

| | |
|---|---|
| Carbon | Carbon fiber, alternatively graphite fiber, carbon graphite or CF, is a material consisting of fibers about 5-10 µm in diameter and composed mostly of carbon atoms. The carbon atoms are bonded together in crystals that are more or less aligned parallel to the long axis of the fiber. The crystal alignment gives the fiber high strength-to-volume ratio (making it strong for its size). |
| Enthalpy | Enthalpy is a measure of the total energy of a thermodynamic system. It includes the system's internal energy and thermodynamic potential (a state function), as well as its volume and pressure (the energy required to 'make room for it' by displacing its environment, which is an extensive quantity). The unit of measurement for enthalpy in the International System of Units (SI) is the joule, but other historical, conventional units are still in use, such as the British thermal unit and the calorie. |
| Isomer | In chemistry, isomers (; from Greek ?s?µe???, isomerès; isos = 'equal', méros = 'part') are molecules with the same molecular formula but different chemical structures. That is, isomers contain the same number of atoms of each element, but have different arrangements of their atoms in space. Isomers do not necessarily share similar properties, unless they also have the same functional groups. |
| Isobutane | Isobutane, also known as methylpropane, is an isomer of butane. It is the simplest alkane with a tertiary carbon. Concerns with depletion of the ozone layer by freon gases have led to increased use of isobutane as a gas for refrigeration systems, especially in domestic refrigerators and freezers, and as a propellant in aerosol sprays. |
| Isopentane | Isopentane, $C_5H_{12}$, also called methylbutane or 2-methylbutane, is a branched-chain alkane with five carbon atoms. Isopentane is an extremely volatile and extremely flammable liquid at room temperature and pressure. The normal boiling point is just a few degrees above room temperature and isopentane will readily boil and evaporate away on a warm day. |
| Neopentane | Neopentane, also called 2,2-dimethylpropane, is a double-branched-chain alkane with five carbon atoms. Neopentane is an extremely flammable gas at room temperature and pressure which can condense into a highly volatile liquid on a cold day, in an ice bath, or when compressed to a higher pressure. Neopentane is the simplest alkane with a quaternary carbon. |
| Ethyl group | In chemistry, an ethyl group is an alkyl substituent derived from ethane . It has the formula $-C_2H_5$ and is very often abbreviated Et. |

# 24. The Chemistry of Life: Organic and Biological Chemistry

| | |
|---|---|
| Methyl group | A methyl group is an alkyl derived from methane, containing one carbon atom bonded to three hydrogen atoms -- $CH_3$. The group is often abbreviated Me. Such hydrocarbon groups occur in many organic compounds. |
| Alkyl | In chemistry, an alkyl substituent is an alkane missing one hydrogen. An acyclic alkyl has the general formula $C_nH_{2n+1}$. A cycloalkyl is derived from a cycloalkane by removal of a hydrogen atom from a ring and has the general formula $C_nH_{2n-1}$. |
| Cycloalkane | Cycloalkanes are types of hydrocarbon compounds that have one or more rings of carbon atoms in the chemical structure of their molecules. Alkanes are types of organic hydrocarbon compounds that have only single chemical bonds in their chemical structure. Cycloalkanes consist of only carbon (C) and hydrogen (H) atoms and are saturated because there are no multiple C-C bonds to hydrogenate (add more hydrogen to). |
| Cyclohexane | Cyclohexane is a cycloalkane with the molecular formula $C_6H_{12}$. Cyclohexane is used as a nonpolar solvent for the chemical industry, and also as a raw material for the industrial production of adipic acid and caprolactam, both of which being intermediates used in the production of nylon. On an industrial scale, cyclohexane is produced by reacting benzene with hydrogen. |
| Cyclopentane | Cyclopentane is a highly flammable alicyclic hydrocarbon with chemical formula $C_5H_{10}$ and CAS number 287-92-3, consisting of a ring of five carbon atoms each bonded with two hydrogen atoms above and below the plane. It occurs as a colorless liquid with a petrol-like odor. Its melting point is -94 °C and its boiling point is 49 °C. Cyclopentane is in the class of cycloalkanes, being alkanes that have one or more rings of carbon atoms. |
| Cyclopropane | Cyclopropane is a cycloalkane molecule with the molecular formula $C_3H_6$, consisting of three carbon atoms linked to each other to form a ring, with each carbon atom bearing two hydrogen atoms resulting in $D_{3h}$ molecular symmetry. Cyclopropane and propene have the same molecular formula but have different structures, making them structural isomers.<br><br>Cyclopropane is an anaesthetic when inhaled. |
| Asphalt | Asphalt or , also known as bitumen, is a sticky, black and highly viscous liquid or semi-solid form of petroleum. It may be found in natural deposits or may be a refined product; it is a substance classed as a pitch. Until the 20th century, the term asphaltum was also used. |
| Cracking | In petroleum geology and chemistry, cracking is the process whereby complex organic molecules such as kerogens or heavy hydrocarbons are broken down into simpler molecules such as light hydrocarbons, by the breaking of carbon-carbon bonds in the precursors. The rate of cracking and the end products are strongly dependent on the temperature and presence of catalysts. |

| | |
|---|---|
| Ethanol | Ethanol, also called ethyl alcohol, pure alcohol, grain alcohol, or drinking alcohol, is a volatile, flammable, colorless liquid with the structural formula $CH_3CH_2OH$, often abbreviated as $C_2H_5OH$ or $C_2H_6O$. A psychoactive drug and one of the oldest recreational drugs, ethanol can cause alcohol intoxication when consumed. Best known as the type of alcohol found in alcoholic beverages, it is also used in thermometers, as a solvent, and as a fuel. In common usage, it is often referred to simply as alcohol or spirits. |
| Fractional distillation | Fractional distillation is the separation of a mixture into its component parts, or fractions, such as in separating chemical compounds by their boiling point by heating them to a temperature at which one or more fractions of the compound will vaporize. It is a special type of distillation. Generally the component parts boil at less than 25 °C from each other under a pressure of one atmosphere (atm). |
| Fuel oil | Fuel oil is a fraction obtained from petroleum distillation, either as a distillate or a residue. Broadly speaking fuel oil is any liquid petroleum product that is burned in a furnace or boiler for the generation of heat or used in an engine for the generation of power, except oils having a flash point of approximately 40 °C (104 °F) and oils burned in cotton or wool-wick burners. In this sense, diesel is a type of fuel oil. |
| Hydrobromic acid | Hydrobromic acid is a strong acid formed by dissolving the diatomic molecule hydrogen bromide in water. 'Constant boiling' hydrobromic acid is an aqueous solution that distills at 124.3 °C and contains 47.6% HBr by weight, which is 8.89 mol/L. Hydrobromic acid has a $pK_a$ of -9, making it a stronger acid than hydrochloric acid, but not as strong as hydroiodic acid. Hydrobromic acid is one of the strongest mineral acids known. |
| Kerosene | Kerosene is a combustible hydrocarbon liquid. The name is derived from Greek: ????? (keros) meaning wax. The word 'Kerosene' was registered as a trademark by Abraham Gesner in 1854, and for several years, only the North American Gas Light Company and the Downer Company (to which Gesner had granted the right) were allowed to call their lamp oil 'Kerosene' in the United States. |
| Octane rating | Octane rating or octane number is a standard measure of the performance of a motor or aviation fuel. The higher the octane number, the more compression the fuel can withstand before detonating. In broad terms, fuels with a higher octane rating are used in high-compression engines that generally have higher performance. |
| Petroleum | Petroleum (L. petroleum, from Greek: p?t?a + Latin: oleum (oil)) is a naturally occurring, smelly, yellow-to-black liquid consisting of a complex mixture of hydrocarbons of various molecular weights and other liquid organic compounds, that are found in geologic formations beneath the Earth's surface. The name Petroleum covers both naturally occurring unprocessed crude oils and petroleum products that are made up of refined crude oil. |

# 24. The Chemistry of Life: Organic and Biological Chemistry

| | |
|---|---|
| Propene | Propene, also known as propylene or methylethylene, is an unsaturated organic compound having the chemical formula $C_3H_6$. It has one double bond, and is the second simplest member of the alkene class of hydrocarbons. |
| 1-Butene | 1-Butene is an organic chemical compound, linear alpha-olefin, and one of the isomers of butene. The formula is C4H8. |
| 2-Butene | 2-Butene is an acyclic alkene with four carbon atoms. It is the simplest alkene exhibiting cis/trans-isomerism (also known as (E/Z)-isomerism); that is, it exists as two geometrical isomers cis-2-butene ((Z)-2-butene) and trans-2-butene ((E)-2-butene). <br><br> It is a petrochemical, produced by the catalytic cracking of crude oil or the dimerization of ethylene. |
| Butene | Butene, also known as butylene, is an alkene with the formula $C_4H_8$. It is a colourless gas that is present in crude oil as a minor constituent in quantities that are too small for viable extraction. It is therefore obtained by catalytic cracking of long chain hydrocarbons left during refining of crude oil. |
| Pentene | Pentene refers to all the alkenes with chemical formula C5H10. Each contains one double bond within its molecular structure. There are a total of six different compounds in this class, differing from each other by whether the carbon atoms are attached linearly or in a branched structure, and whether the double bond has a cis or trans form. |
| Lipid | Lipids are a group of naturally occurring molecules that include fats, waxes, sterols, fat-soluble vitamins, monoglycerides, diglycerides, triglycerides, phospholipids, and others. The main biological functions of lipids include storing energy, signaling, and acting as structural components of cell membranes. Lipids have applications in the cosmetic and food industries as well as in nanotechnology. |
| Addition polymer | An addition polymer is a polymer which is formed by an addition reaction, where many monomers bond together via rearrangement of bonds without the loss of any atom or molecule. This is in contrast to a condensation polymer which is formed by a condensation reaction where a molecule, usually water, is lost during the formation. |
| Hydrogenation | Hydrogenation - to treat with hydrogen - is a chemical reaction between molecular hydrogen and another compound or element, usually in the presence of a catalyst. The process is commonly employed to reduce or saturate organic compounds. Hydrogenation typically constitutes the addition of pairs of hydrogen atoms to a molecule, generally an alkene. |
| Addition reaction | An addition reaction, in organic chemistry, is in its simplest terms an organic reaction where two or more molecules combine to form a larger one. |

|  | Addition reactions are limited to chemical compounds that have multiple bonds, such as molecules with carbon-carbon double bonds, or with triple bonds (alkynes). Molecules containing carbon-hetero double bonds like carbonyl (C=O) groups, or imine (C=N) groups, can undergo addition as they too have double bond character. |
|---|---|
| Polymer | A polymer is a large molecule composed of many repeated subunits, known as monomers. Because of their broad range of properties, both synthetic and natural polymers play an essential and ubiquitous role in everyday life. Polymers range from familiar synthetic plastics such as polystyrene (or styrofoam) to natural biopolymers such as DNA and proteins that are fundamental to biological structure and function. |
| Reaction mechanism | In chemistry, a reaction mechanism is the step by step sequence of elementary reactions by which overall chemical change occurs.<br><br>Although only the net chemical change is directly observable for most chemical reactions, experiments can often be designed that suggest the possible sequence of steps in a reaction mechanism. Recently, electrospray ionization mass spectrometry has been used to corroborate the mechanism of several organic reaction proposals. |
| Anthracene | Anthracene is a solid polycyclic aromatic hydrocarbon of formula $C_{14}H_{10}$, consisting of three fused benzene rings. It is a component of coal tar. Anthracene is used in the production of the red dye alizarin and other dyes. |
| Naphthalene | Naphthalene is an organic compound with formula C10H8. It is the simplest polycyclic aromatic hydrocarbon, and is a white crystalline solid with a characteristic odor that is detectable at concentrations as low as 0.08 ppm by mass. As an aromatic hydrocarbon, naphthalene's structure consists of a fused pair of benzene rings. |
| Toluene | Toluene, formerly known as toluol, is a clear, water-insoluble liquid with the typical smell of paint thinners. It is a mono-substituted benzene derivative, i.e., one in which a single hydrogen atom from a group of six atoms from the benzene molecule has been replaced by a univalent group, in this case $CH_3$. As such, its IUPAC systematic name is methylbenzene. |
| Dinitrobenzene | Dinitrobenzenes are chemical compounds composed of a benzene ring and two nitro group substituents. The three possible arrangements of the nitro groups afford three isomers, 1,2-dinitrobenzene, 1,3-dinitrobenzene, and 1,4-dinitrobenzene. Each isomer has the chemical formula $C_6H_4N_2O_4$. |
| Nitrobenzene | Nitrobenzene is an organic compound with the chemical formula $C_6H_5NO_2$. It is a water-insoluble pale yellow oil with an almond-like odor. It freezes to give greenish-yellow crystals. |

# 24. The Chemistry of Life: Organic and Biological Chemistry

| | |
|---|---|
| Substitution reaction | Substitution reaction is also known as single displacement reaction and single replacement reaction. In a substitution reaction, a functional group in a particular chemical compound is replaced by another group. In organic chemistry, the electrophilic and nucleophilic substitution reactions are of prime importance. |
| Alcohol | In chemistry, an alcohol is an organic compound in which the hydroxyl functional group is bound to a carbon atom. In particular, this carbon center should be saturated, having single bonds to three other atoms.<br><br>An important class of alcohols are the simple acyclic alcohols, the general formula for which is $C_nH_{2n+1}OH$. Of those, ethanol ($C_2H_5OH$) is the type of alcohol found in alcoholic beverages, and in common speech the word alcohol refers specifically to ethanol. |
| Acetaldehyde | Acetaldehyde is an organic chemical compound with the formula $CH_3CHO$, sometimes abbreviated by chemists as MeCHO (Me = methyl). It is one of the most important aldehydes, occurring widely in nature and being produced on a large scale industrially. Acetaldehyde occurs naturally in coffee, bread, and ripe fruit, and is produced by plants. |
| Acetic acid | Acetic acid is an organic compound with the chemical formula $CH_3COOH$ (also written as $CH_3CO_2H$ or $C_2H_4O_2$). It is a colourless liquid that when undiluted is also called glacial acetic acid. Acetic acid is the main component of vinegar (apart from water; vinegar is roughly 8% acetic acid by volume), and has a distinctive sour taste and pungent smell. |
| Acetone | Acetone is the organic compound with the formula $(CH_3)_2CO$. It is a colorless, mobile, flammable liquid, and is the simplest ketone.<br><br>Acetone is miscible with water and serves as an important solvent in its own right, typically for cleaning purposes in the laboratory. About 6.7 million tonnes were produced worldwide in 2010, mainly for use as a solvent and production of methyl methacrylate and bisphenol A. It is a common building block in organic chemistry. |
| Dimethyl ether | Dimethyl ether, also known as methoxymethane, is the organic compound with the formula $CH3OCH3$. The simplest ether, it is a colourless gas that is a useful precursor to other organic compounds and an aerosol propellant. |
| Ethylamine | Ethylamine is an organic compound with the formula $CH_3CH_2NH_2$. This colourless gas has a strong ammonia-like odor. It is miscible with virtually all solvents and is a weak base, as is typical for amines. |
| Methanol | Methanol, also known as methyl alcohol, wood alcohol, wood naphtha or wood spirits, is a chemical with the formula $CH_3OH$ . |

Methanol acquired the name 'wood alcohol' because it was once produced chiefly as a byproduct of the destructive distillation of wood. Modern methanol is produced in a catalytic industrial process directly from carbon monoxide, carbon dioxide, and hydrogen.

| | |
|---|---|
| Cholesterol | Cholesterol, from the Ancient Greek chole- and stereos (solid) followed by the chemical suffix -ol for an alcohol, is an organic molecule. It is a sterol (or modified steroid), and an essential structural component of animal cell membranes that is required to establish proper membrane permeability and fluidity. Cholesterol is thus considered within the class of lipid molecules. |
| Ethylene glycol | Ethylene glycol is an organic compound primarily used as a raw material in the manufacture of polyester fibers and fabric industry, and polyethylene terephthalate resins (PET) used in bottling. A small percent is also used in industrial applications like antifreeze formulations and other industrial products. It is an odorless, colorless, syrupy, sweet-tasting liquid. |
| Glycerol | Glycerol is a simple polyol (sugar alcohol) compound. It is a colorless, odorless, viscous liquid that is widely used in pharmaceutical formulations. Glycerol has three hydroxyl groups that are responsible for its solubility in water and its hygroscopic nature. |
| Isopropyl alcohol | Isopropyl alcohol is a common name for a chemical compound with the molecular formula $C_3H_8O$ or $C_3H_7OH$. It is a colorless, flammable chemical compound with a strong odor. It is the simplest example of a secondary alcohol, where the alcohol carbon atom is attached to two other carbon atoms sometimes shown as $(CH_3)_2CHOH$. It is a structural isomer of propanol. Isopropyl alcohol is denatured for certain uses, in which case the NFPA 704 rating is changed to 2,3,1. |
| Methyl orange | Methyl orange is a pH indicator frequently used in titrations.<br><br>It is often used in titrations because of its clear and distinct colour change. Because it changes colour at the pH of a mid-strength acid, it is usually used in titrations for acids. |
| Phenol | Phenol -- also known as carbolic acid -- is an aromatic organic compound with the molecular formula $C_6H_5OH$. It is a white crystalline solid that is volatile. The molecule consists of a phenyl group ($-C_6H_5$) bonded to a hydroxyl group ($-OH$). It is mildly acidic, but requires careful handling due to its propensity to cause burns. |
| Aldehyde | An aldehyde is an organic compound containing a formyl group. This functional group, with the structure R-CHO, consists of a carbonyl center (a carbon double bonded to oxygen) bonded to hydrogen and an R group, which is any generic alkyl or side chain. The group without R is called the aldehyde group or formyl group. |
| Butanol | Butanol refers to a four-carbon alcohol, with a formula of $C_4H_9OH$. There are four possible isomeric structures for butanol, from a straight-chain primary alcohol to a branched-chain tertiary alcohol. It is primarily used as a solvent, as an intermediate in chemical synthesis, and as a fuel. |

# 24. The Chemistry of Life: Organic and Biological Chemistry

| | |
|---|---|
| Carbonyl | In organic chemistry, a carbonyl group is a functional group composed of a carbon atom double-bonded to an oxygen atom: C=O. It is common to several classes of organic compounds, as part of many larger functional groups.<br><br>The term carbonyl can also refer to carbon monoxide as a ligand in an inorganic or organometallic complex (a metal carbonyl, e.g. nickel carbonyl). |
| Condensation reaction | A condensation reaction, also commonly referred to as dehydration synthesis, is a chemical reaction in which two molecules or moieties combine to form a larger molecule, together with the loss of a small molecule. Possible small molecules lost are water, hydrogen chloride, methanol, or acetic acid. The word 'condensation' suggests a process in which two or more things are brought 'together' (Latin 'con') to form something 'dense', like in condensation from gaseous to liquid state of matter; this does not imply, however, that condensation reaction products have greater density than reactants. |
| Diethyl ether | Diethyl ether, also known as ethyl ether, sulfuric ether, simply ether, or ethoxyethane, is an organic compound in the ether class with the formula 2O. It is a colorless, highly volatile flammable liquid. It is commonly used as a solvent and was once used as a general anesthetic. |
| Ether | Ethers are a class of organic compounds that contain an ether group -- an oxygen atom connected to two alkyl or aryl groups -- of general formula R-O-R'. A typical example is the solvent and anesthetic diethyl ether, commonly referred to simply as 'ether' ($CH_3$-$CH_2$-O-$CH_2$-$CH_3$). Ethers are common in organic chemistry and pervasive in biochemistry, as they are common linkages in carbohydrates and lignin. |
| Ketone | In chemistry, a ketone is an organic compound with the structure RC(=O)R', where R and R' can be a variety of carbon-containing substituents. Ketones feature a carbonyl group (C=O) bonded to two other carbon atoms. Many ketones are known and many are of great importance in industry and in biology. |
| Tetrahydrofuran | Tetrahydrofuran is an organic compound with the formula $(CH_2)_4O$. It is a colorless, water-miscible organic liquid with low viscosity at standard temperature and pressure. The compound is heterocyclic. As one of the most polar ethers with a wide liquid range, it is a useful solvent. |
| Condensation | Condensation is the change of the physical state of matter from gas phase into liquid phase, and is the reverse of vaporization. It can also be defined as the change in the state of water vapor to water/any liquid when in contact with any surface. When the transition happens from the gaseous phase into the solid phase directly, the change is called deposition. |
| Acetylsalicylic acid | Aspirin, also known as acetylsalicylic acid (INN ( ?--?l--i--ik) ASA), is a salicylate drug, often used as an analgesic to relieve minor aches and pains, as an antipyretic to reduce fever, and as an anti-inflammatory medication. |

The active ingredient of Aspirin was first discovered from the bark of the willow tree in 1763 by Edward Stone of Wadham College, Oxford University. He had discovered salicylic acid, the active metabolite of aspirin.

| | |
|---|---|
| Alcohol oxidation | Alcohol oxidation is an important organic reaction. Primary alcohols ($R-CH_2-OH$) can be oxidized either to aldehydes ($R-CHO$) or to carboxylic acids ($R-CO_2H$), while the oxidation of secondary alcohols ($R^1R^2CH-OH$) normally terminates at the ketone ($R^1R^2C=O$) stage. Tertiary alcohols ($R^1R^2R^3C-OH$) are resistant to oxidation. |
| Aspirin | Aspirin, also known as acetylsalicylic acid (INN ( ?--?l--i--ik) ASA), is a salicylate drug, often used as an analgesic to relieve minor aches and pains, as an antipyretic to reduce fever, and as an anti-inflammatory medication. Aspirin was first isolated by Felix Hoffmann, a chemist with the German company Bayer in 1897. |
| | Salicylic acid, the main metabolite of aspirin, is an integral part of human and animal metabolism. |
| Benzoic acid | Benzoic acid, $C_7H_6O_2$, is a colorless crystalline solid and a simple aromatic carboxylic acid. The name is derived from gum benzoin, which was for a long time the only source for benzoic acid. Its salts are used as food preservatives and benzoic acid is an important precursor for the synthesis of many other organic substances. |
| Carboxylic acid | A carboxylic acid is an organic acid characterized by the presence of at least one carboxyl group. The general formula of a carboxylic acid is R-COOH, where R is some monovalent functional group. A carboxyl group (or carboxy) is a functional group consisting of a carbonyl (RR'C=O) and a hydroxyl (R-O-H), which has the formula -C(=O)OH, usually written as -COOH or $-CO_2H$. |
| | Carboxylic acids are Brønsted-Lowry acids because they are proton ($H^+$) donors. |
| Carvone | Carvone is a member of a family of chemicals called terpenoids. Carvone is found naturally in many essential oils, but is most abundant in the oils from seeds of caraway (Carum carvi) and dill. |
| Citric acid | Citric acid is a weak organic acid with the formula $C_6H_8O_7$. It is a natural preservative/conservative and is also used to add an acidic or sour taste to foods and drinks. In biochemistry, the conjugate base of citric acid, citrate, is important as an intermediate in the citric acid cycle, which occurs in the metabolism of all aerobic organisms. |
| Formic acid | Formic acid is the simplest carboxylic acid. Its chemical formula is HCOOH or $HCO_2H$. It is an important intermediate in chemical synthesis and occurs naturally, most notably in ant venom. In fact, its name comes from the Latin word for ant, formica, referring to its early isolation by the distillation of ant bodies. |

# 24. The Chemistry of Life: Organic and Biological Chemistry

| | |
|---|---|
| Oxidation | Redox (reduction-oxidation) reactions include all chemical reactions in which atoms have their oxidation state changed; in general, redox reactions involve the transfer of electrons between species. |
| | This can be either a simple redox process, such as the oxidation of carbon to yield carbon dioxide or the reduction of carbon by hydrogen to yield methane ($CH_4$), or a complex process such as the oxidation of glucose ($C_6H_{12}O_6$) in the human body through a series of complex electron transfer processes. |
| | The term 'redox' comes from two concepts involved with electron transfer: reduction and oxidation. |
| Carbonylation | Carbonylation refers to reactions that introduce carbon monoxide into organic and inorganic substrates. Carbon monoxide is abundantly available and conveniently reactive, so it is widely used as a reactant in industrial chemistry. The term carbonylation also refers to oxidation of protein side chains. |
| Ethyl acetate | Ethyl acetate is the organic compound with the formula $CH_3$-COO-$CH_2$-$CH_3$. This colorless liquid has a characteristic sweet smell (similar to pear drops) and is used in glues, nail polish removers, decaffeinating tea and coffee, and cigarettes . Ethyl acetate is the ester of ethanol and acetic acid; it is manufactured on a large scale for use as a solvent. |
| Hydrogen peroxide | Hydrogen peroxide is the simplest peroxide (a compound with an oxygen-oxygen single bond). It is also a strong oxidizer. Hydrogen peroxide is a clear liquid, slightly more viscous than water. |
| Ozone | Ozone, or trioxygen, is an inorganic compound with the chemical formula O3($\mu$-O) (also written [O($\mu$-O)O] or O3). It is a pale blue gas with a distinctively pungent smell. It is an allotrope of oxygen that is much less stable than the diatomic allotrope O2, breaking down in the lower atmosphere to normal dioxygen. |
| Potassium dichromate | Potassium dichromate, $K_2Cr_2O_7$, is a common inorganic chemical reagent, most commonly used as an oxidizing agent in various laboratory and industrial applications. As with all hexavalent chromium compounds, it is acutely and chronically harmful to health and must be handled and disposed of appropriately. It is a crystalline ionic solid with a very bright, red-orange color. |
| Butyric acid | Butyric acid, also known under the systematic name butanoic acid, is a carboxylic acid with the structural formula $CH_3CH_2CH_2$-COOH. Salts and esters of butyric acid are known as butyrates or butanoates. Butyric acid is found in milk, especially goat, sheep and buffalo's milk, butter, Parmesan cheese, and as a product of anaerobic fermentation (including in the colon and as body odor). It has an unpleasant smell and acrid taste, with a sweetish aftertaste (similar to ether). |
| Hydrolysis | Hydrolysis usually means the cleavage of chemical bonds by the addition of water. |

| | Where a carbohydrate is broken into its component sugar molecules by hydrolysis this is termed saccharification. Generally, hydrolysis or saccharification is a step in the degradation of a substance. |
|---|---|
| Methyl propionate | Methyl propionate, also known as methyl propanoate, is a chemical compound with the molecular formula $C_4H_8O_2$. It is a volatile ester with a sweet, fruity, rum-like odor. |
| Saponification | Saponification is a process that produces soap, usually from fats and lye. In technical terms, saponification involves base (usually caustic soda NaOH) hydrolysis of triglycerides, which are esters of fatty acids, to form the sodium salt of a carboxylate. In addition to soap, such traditional saponification processes produce glycerol. |
| Sodium propionate | Sodium propanoate or sodium propionate is the sodium salt of propionic acid which has the chemical formula Na. |
| Amide | An amide, also known as an '-acid amide', is a compound with the functional group $R_nE_xNR'_2$ (R and R' refer to H or organic groups). Most common are 'organic amides' (n = 1, E = C, x = 1), but many other important types of amides are known including phosphor amides (n = 2, E = P, x = 1 and many related formulas) and sulfonamides (E = S, x= 2). The term amide refers both to classes of compounds and to the functional group $(R_nE(O)_xNR'_2)$ within those compounds. |
| Aniline | Aniline, phenylamine or aminobenzene is an organic compound with the formula $C_6H_5NH_2$. Consisting of a phenyl group attached to an amino group, aniline is the prototypical aromatic amine. Being a precursor to many industrial chemicals, its main use is in the manufacture of precursors to polyurethane. |
| Benzamide | Benzamide is an off-white solid with the chemical formula of $C_6H_5CONH_2$. It is a derivative of benzoic acid. It is slightly soluble in water, and soluble in many organic solvents. |
| Bromobenzene | Bromobenzene is an aryl halide, $C_6H_5Br$, which can be formed by electrophilic aromatic substitution of benzene using bromine. It is a clear, colourless or pale yellow liquid. It is soluble in methanol and diethyl ether, and very slightly soluble in cold water. |
| Chiral | Chirality is a property of asymmetry important in several branches of science. The word chirality is derived from the Greek, ?e?? (kheir), 'hand', a familiar chiral object. An object or a system is chiral if it is not identical to its mirror image, that is, it cannot be superposed onto it. |
| Enantiomer | In chemistry, an enantiomer is one of two stereoisomers that are mirror images of each other that are non-superposable (not identical), much as one's left and right hands are the same except for opposite orientation. |

Organic compounds that contain a chiral carbon usually have two non-superposable structures. These two structures are mirror images of each other and are, thus, commonly called enantiomorphs (enantio = opposite ; morph = form), hence this structural property is now commonly referred to as enantiomerism.

| | |
|---|---|
| **Medical imaging** | Medical imaging is the technique and process used to create images of the human body for clinical purposes (medical procedures seeking to reveal, diagnose, or examine disease) or medical science (including the study of normal anatomy and physiology). Although imaging of removed organs and tissues can be performed for medical reasons, such procedures are not usually referred to as medical imaging, but rather are a part of pathology. |
| | As a discipline and in its widest sense, it is part of biological imaging and incorporates Radiology, Magnetic Resonance Imaging, Nuclear medicine, medical Ultrasonography or Ultrasound, Endoscopy, Elastography, Tactile Imaging, Thermography and medical photography. |
| **Racemic mixture** | In chemistry, a racemic mixture, or racemate, is one that has equal amounts of left- and right-handed enantiomers of a chiral molecule. The first known racemic mixture was 'racemic acid', which Louis Pasteur found to be a mixture of the two enantiomeric isomers of tartaric acid. A mixture with only a single enantiomers is an enantiomerically pure or enantiopure mixture. |
| **Chirality** | The term chiral describes an object, especially a molecule, which has or produces a non-superimposeable mirror image of itself. In chemistry, such a molecule is called an enantiomer or is said to exhibit chirality or enantiomerism. The term 'chiral' comes from the Greek word for the human hand, which itself exhibits such non-superimposeability of the left hand precisely over the right. |
| **Biopolymer** | Biopolymers are polymers produced by living organisms. Since they are polymers, biopolymers contain monomeric units that are covalently bonded to form larger structures. There are three main classes of biopolymers, classified according to the monomeric units used and the structure of the biopolymer formed: polynucleotides (RNA and DNA), which are long polymers composed of 13 or more nucleotide monomers; polypeptides, which are short polymers of amino acids; and polysaccharides, which are often linear bonded polymeric carbohydrate structures. |
| **Entropy** | In thermodynamics, entropy is a measure of the number of specific ways in which a thermodynamic system may be arranged, often taken to be a measure of disorder, or a measure of progressing towards thermodynamic equilibrium. The entropy of an isolated system never decreases, because isolated systems spontaneously evolve towards thermodynamic equilibrium, which is the state of maximum entropy. |
| | Entropy was originally defined for a thermodynamically reversible process as |

$$\Delta S = \int \frac{dQ_{rev}}{T}$$

where the entropy is found from the uniform thermodynamic temperature of a closed system dividing an incremental reversible transfer of heat into that system .

| | |
|---|---|
| Alanine | Alanine is an a-amino acid with the chemical formula $CH_3CH(NH_2)COOH$. The -isomer is one of the 20 amino acids encoded by the genetic code. Its codons are GCU, GCC, GCA, and GCG. It is classified as a nonpolar amino acid. -Alanine is second only to leucine in rate of occurrence, accounting for 7.8% of the primary structure in a sample of 1,150 proteins. |
| Arginine | Arginine is an a-amino acid. It was first isolated in 1886. The -form is one of the 20 most common natural amino acids. At the level of molecular genetics, in the structure of the messenger ribonucleic acid mRNA, CGU, CGC, CGA, CGG, AGA, and AGG, are the triplets of nucleotide bases or codons that code for arginine during protein synthesis. |
| Asparagine | Asparagine is one of the 20 most common natural amino acids on Earth. It has carboxamide as the side-chain's functional group. It is not an essential amino acid. |
| Aspartic acid | Aspartic acid is an a-amino acid with the chemical formula $HOOCCH(NH_2)CH_2COOH$. The carboxylate anion, salt, or ester of aspartic acid is known as aspartate. The -isomer of aspartate is one of the 22 proteinogenic amino acids, i.e., the building blocks of proteins. Its codons are GAU and GAC.<br><br>Aspartic acid is, together with glutamic acid, classified as an acidic amino acid with a $pK_a$ of 3.9, however in a peptide the $pK_a$ is highly dependent on the local environment. |
| Cysteine | Cysteine is an a-amino acid with the chemical formula $HO_2CCH(NH_2)CH_2SH$. It is a semi-essential amino acid, which means that it can be biosynthesized in humans. The thiol side chain in cysteine often participates in enzymatic reactions, serving as a nucleophile. The thiol is susceptible to oxidization to give the disulfide derivative cystine, which serves an important structural role in many proteins. |
| Essential amino acid | An essential amino acid or indispensable amino acid is an amino acid that cannot be synthesized natively by the organism being considered, and therefore must be supplied in its diet. |
| Glutamic acid | Glutamic acid is one of the 20-22 proteinogenic amino acids, and its codons are GAA and GAG. It is a non-essential amino acid. The carboxylate anions and salts of glutamic acid are known as glutamates. In neuroscience, glutamate is an important neurotransmitter that plays a key role in long-term potentiation and is important for learning and memory. |

# 24. The Chemistry of Life: Organic and Biological Chemistry

| | |
|---|---|
| Glutamine | Glutamine is one of the 20 amino acids encoded by the standard genetic code. It is not recognized as an essential amino acid, but may become conditionally essential in certain situations, including intensive athletic training or certain gastrointestinal disorders. Its side-chain is an amide formed by replacing the side-chain hydroxyl of glutamic acid with an amine functional group, making it the amide of glutamic acid. |
| Histidine | Histidine is an a-amino acid with an imidazole functional group. It is one of the 22 proteinogenic amino acids. Its codons are CAU and CAC. Histidine was first isolated by German physician Albrecht Kossel in 1896. Histidine is an essential amino acid in humans and other mammals. |
| Isoleucine | Isoleucine is an a-amino acid with the chemical formula $HO_2CCH(NH_2)CH(CH_3)CH_2CH_3$. It is an essential amino acid, which means that humans cannot synthesize it, so it must be ingested. Its codons are AUU, AUC and AUA. |
| | With a hydrocarbon side chain, isoleucine is classified as a hydrophobic amino acid. |
| Leucine | Leucine is a branched-chain a-amino acid with the chemical formula $HO_2CCH(NH_2)CH_2CH(CH_3)_2$. Leucine is classified as a hydrophobic amino acid due to its aliphatic isobutyl side chain. It is encoded by six codons (UUA, UUG, CUU, CUC, CUA, and CUG) and s a major component of the subunits in ferritin, astacin and other 'buffer' proteins. |
| Lysine | Lysine is an a-amino acid with the chemical formula $HO_2CCH(NH_2)(CH_2)_4NH_2$. It is an essential amino acid for humans. Lysine's codons are AAA and AAG. |
| | Lysine is a base, as are arginine and histidine. |
| Methionine | Methionine is an a-amino acid with the chemical formula $HO_2CCH(NH_2)CH_2CH_2SCH_3$. This essential amino acid is classified as nonpolar. This amino-acid is coded by the initiation codon AUG which indicates mRNA's coding region where translation into protein begins. |
| Phenylalanine | Phenylalanine is an a-amino acid with the formula $C_6H_5CH_2CH(NH_2)COOH$. This essential amino acid is classified as nonpolar because of the hydrophobic nature of the benzyl side chain. -Phenylalanine is an electrically neutral amino acid, one of the twenty common amino acids used to biochemically form proteins, coded for by DNA. The codons for -phenylalanine are UUU and UUC. Phenylalanine is a precursor for tyrosine, the monoamine signaling molecules dopamine, norepinephrine (noradrenaline), and epinephrine (adrenaline), and the skin pigment melanin. |
| | Phenylalanine is found naturally in the breast milk of mammals. |
| Proline | Proline is an a-amino acid, one of the twenty DNA-encoded amino acids. Its codons are CCU, CCC, CCA, and CCG. It is not an essential amino acid, which means that the human body can synthesize it. |

| | |
|---|---|
| Serine | Serine is an amino acid with the formula $HO_2CCH(NH_2)CH_2OH$. It is one of the proteinogenic amino acids. Its codons in the genetic code are UCU, UCC, UCA, UCG, AGU and AGC. By virtue of the hydroxyl group, serine is classified as a polar amino acid. |
| Threonine | Threonine is an a-amino acid with the chemical formula $HO_2CCH(NH_2)CH(OH)CH_3$. Its codons are ACU, ACA, ACC, and ACG. This essential amino acid is classified as polar. Together with serine, threonine is one of two proteinogenic amino acids bearing an alcohol group (tyrosine is not an alcohol but a phenol, since its hydroxyl group is bonded directly to an aromatic ring, giving it different acid/base and oxidative properties). |
| Tryptophan | Tryptophan is one of the 22 standard amino acids and an essential amino acid in the human diet. It is encoded in the standard genetic code as the codon UGG. Only the L-stereoisomer of tryptophan is used in structural or enzyme proteins, but the R -stereoisomer is occasionally found in naturally produced peptides (for example, the marine venom peptide contryphan). The distinguishing structural characteristic of tryptophan is that it contains an indole functional group. |
| Tyrosine | Tyrosine or 4-hydroxyphenylalanine, is one of the 20 amino acids that are used by cells to synthesize proteins. Its codons are UAC and UAU. It is a non-essential amino acid with a polar side group. The word 'tyrosine' is from the Greek tyri, meaning cheese, as it was first discovered in 1846 by German chemist Justus von Liebig in the protein casein from cheese. |
| Valine | Valine is an a-amino acid with the chemical formula $HO_2CCH(NH_2)CH(CH_3)_2$. -Valine is one of 20 proteinogenic amino acids. Its codons are GUU, GUC, GUA, and GUG. This essential amino acid is classified as nonpolar. |
| Aspartame | Aspartame is an artificial, non-saccharide sweetener used as a sugar substitute in some foods and beverages. In the European Union, it is codified as E951. Aspartame is a methyl ester of the aspartic acid/phenylalanine dipeptide. It was first sold under the brand name NutraSweet; since 2009 it also has been sold under the brand name AminoSweet. |
| Peptide | Peptides are short chains of amino acid monomers linked by peptide bonds. The covalent chemical bonds are formed when the carboxyl group of one amino acid reacts with the amino group of another. The shortest peptides are dipeptides, consisting of 2 amino acids joined by a single peptide bond, followed by tripeptides, tetrapeptides, etc. |
| Folding | In chemistry, folding is the process by which a molecule assumes its shape or conformation. The process can also be described as intramolecular self-assembly, a type of molecular self-assembly, where the molecule is directed to form a specific shape through noncovalent interactions, such as hydrogen bonding, metal coordination, hydrophobic forces, van der Waals forces, pi-pi interactions, and/or electrostatic effects. |

# 24. The Chemistry of Life: Organic and Biological Chemistry

| | |
|---|---|
| Myoglobin | Myoglobin is an iron- and oxygen-binding protein found in the muscle tissue of vertebrates in general and in almost all mammals. It is related to hemoglobin, which is the iron- and oxygen-binding protein in blood, specifically in the red blood cells. Myoglobin is only found in the bloodstream after muscle injury. |
| Carbohydrate | A carbohydrate is a large biological molecule, or macromolecule, consisting only of carbon, hydrogen (H), and oxygen (O), usually with a hydrogen:oxygen atom ratio of 2:1 (as in water); in other words, with the empirical formula $C_m(H_2O)_n$ (where m could be different from n). Some exceptions exist; for example, deoxyribose, a sugar component of DNA, has the empirical formula $C_5H_{10}O_4$. Carbohydrates are technically hydrates of carbon; structurally it is more accurate to view them as polyhydroxy aldehydes and ketones. |
| Fructose | Fructose, or fruit sugar, is a simple monosaccharide found in many plants, where it is often bonded to glucose to form the disaccharide sucrose. It is one of the three dietary monosaccharides, along with glucose and galactose, that are absorbed directly into the bloodstream during digestion. Fructose was discovered by French chemist Augustin-Pierre Dubrunfaut in 1847. Pure, dry fructose is a very sweet, white, odorless, crystalline solid and is the most water-soluble of all the sugars. |
| Disaccharide | A disaccharide or biose is the carbohydrate formed when two monosaccharides undergo a condensation reaction which involves the elimination of a small molecule, such as water, from the functional groups only. Like monosaccharides, disaccharides form an aqueous solution when dissolved in water. Three common examples are sucrose, lactose, and maltose. |
| Lactose | Lactose is a disaccharide sugar derived from galactose and glucose that is found in milk. Lactose makes up around 0-8% of milk (by weight), although the amount varies among species and individuals. It is extracted from sweet or sour whey. |
| Monosaccharide | Monosaccharides are the most basic units of carbohydrates. They are the simplest form of sugar and are usually colorless, water-soluble, crystalline solids. Some monosaccharides have a sweet taste. |
| Sucrose | Sucrose is the organic compound commonly known as table sugar and sometimes called saccharose. A white, odorless, crystalline powder with a sweet taste, it is best known for its role in food. The molecule is a disaccharide composed of the monosaccharides glucose and fructose with the molecular formula $C_{12}H_{22}O_{11}$. |
| Enzyme | Enzymes are large biological molecules responsible for the thousands of metabolic processes that sustain life. They are highly selective catalysts, greatly accelerating both the rate and specificity of metabolic reactions, from the digestion of food to the synthesis of DNA. Most enzymes are proteins, although some catalytic RNA molecules have been identified. Enzymes adopt a specific three-dimensional structure, and may employ organic (e.g. biotin) and inorganic (e.g. |

| | |
|---|---|
| Glycogen | Glycogen is a multibranched polysaccharide of glucose that serves as a form of energy storage in animals and fungi. The polysaccharide structure represents the main storage form of glucose in the body.<br><br>In humans, glycogen is made and stored primarily in the cells of the liver and the muscles, and functions as the secondary long-term energy storage (with the primary energy stores being fats held in adipose tissue). |
| Polysaccharide | Polysaccharides are polymeric carbohydrate molecules composed of long chains of monosaccharide units bound together by glycosidic bonds. They range in structure from linear to highly branched. Examples include storage polysaccharides such as starch and glycogen, and structural polysaccharides such as cellulose and chitin. |
| Cellulose | Cellulose is an organic compound with the formula n, a polysaccharide consisting of a linear chain of several hundred to over ten thousand ß(1?4) linked -glucose units. Cellulose is an important structural component of the primary cell wall of green plants, many forms of algae and the oomycetes. Some species of bacteria secrete it to form biofilms. |
| Fatty acid | In chemistry, and especially in biochemistry, a fatty acid is a carboxylic acid with a long aliphatic tail, which is either saturated or unsaturated. Most naturally occurring fatty acids have a chain of an even number of carbon atoms, from 4 to 28. Fatty acids are usually derived from triglycerides or phospholipids. When they are not attached to other molecules, they are known as 'free' fatty acids. |
| Oleic acid | Oleic acid is a fatty acid that occurs naturally in various animal and vegetable fats and oils. It is an odorless, colourless oil, although commercial samples may be yellowish. In chemical terms, oleic acid is classified as a monounsaturated omega-9 fatty acid, abbreviated with a lipid number of 18:1 cis-9. It has the formula $CH_3(CH_2)_7CH=CH(CH_2)_7COOH$. The term 'oleic' means related to, or derived from, oil or olive, the oil that is predominantly composed of oleic acid. |
| Polyunsaturated fatty acid | Polyunsaturated fatty acids are fatty acids that contain more than one double bond in their backbone. This class includes many important compounds, such as essential fatty acids and those that give drying oils their characteristic property.<br><br>Polyunsaturated fatty acids can be classified in various groups by their chemical structure: |
| Trace element | In analytical chemistry, a trace element is an element in a sample that has an average concentration of less than 100 parts per million measured in atomic count or less than 100 micrograms per gram.<br><br>In biochemistry, a trace element is a dietary mineral that is needed in very minute quantities for the proper growth, development, and physiology of the organism. |

# 24. The Chemistry of Life: Organic and Biological Chemistry

| | |
|---|---|
| Trans fat | Trans fats are a type of unsaturated fat, which is uncommon in nature but can be created artificially. In the hydrocarbon chain of fatty acid, a double carbon-carbon bond can be either across (trans) or bent (cis). In the vegetable and animal kingdoms, fatty acids generally have cis (as opposed to trans) unsaturations. |
| Essential fatty acid | Essential fatty acids, or Essential fatty acids, are fatty acids that humans and other animals must ingest because the body requires them for good health but cannot synthesize them. The term 'essential fatty acid' refers to fatty acids required for biological processes but does not include the fats that only act as fuel.<br><br>Only two fatty acids are known to be essential for humans: alpha-linolenic acid (an omega-3 fatty acid) and linoleic acid (an omega-6 fatty acid). |
| Nucleic acid | Nucleic acids are polymeric macromolecules, or large biological molecules, essential for all known forms of life. Nucleic acids, which include DNA (deoxyribonucleic acid) and RNA (ribonucleic acid), are made from monomers known as nucleotides. Each nucleotide has three components: a 5-carbon sugar, a phosphate group, and a nitrogenous base. |
| Phospholipid | Phospholipids are a class of lipids that are a major component of all cell membranes as they can form lipid bilayers. Most phospholipids contain a diglyceride, a phosphate group, and a simple organic molecule such as choline; one exception to this rule is sphingomyelin, which is derived from sphingosine instead of glycerol. The first phospholipid identified as such in biological tissues was lecithin, or phosphatidylcholine, in the egg yolk, by Theodore Nicolas Gobley, a French chemist and pharmacist, in 1847. The structure of the phospholipid molecule generally consists of hydrophobic tails and a hydrophilic head. |
| Membrane | A membrane is a thin, film-like structure that separates two fluids. It acts as a selective barrier, allowing some particles or chemicals to pass through, but not others. In some cases, especially in anatomy, membrane may refer to a thin film that is primarily a separating structure rather than a selective barrier. |
| Adenine | Adenine is a nucleobase (a purine derivative) with a variety of roles in biochemistry including cellular respiration, in the form of both the energy-rich adenosine triphosphate (ATP) and the cofactors nicotinamide adenine dinucleotide (NAD) and flavin adenine dinucleotide (FAD), and protein synthesis, as a chemical component of DNA and RNA. The shape of adenine is complementary to either thymine in DNA or uracil in RNA. |
| Cytosine | Cytosine is one of the four main bases found in DNA and RNA, along with adenine, guanine, and thymine (uracil in RNA). It is a pyrimidine derivative, with a heterocyclic aromatic ring and two substituents attached (an amine group at position 4 and a keto group at position 2). The nucleoside of cytosine is cytidine. |

| | |
|---|---|
| Deoxyribose | Deoxyribose, or more precisely 2-deoxyribose, is a monosaccharide with idealized formula H--$(CH_2)$-$(CHOH)_3$-H. Its name indicates that it is a deoxy sugar, meaning that it is derived from the sugar ribose by loss of an oxygen atom. Since the pentose sugars arabinose and ribose only differ by the stereochemistry at C2', 2-deoxyribose and 2-deoxyarabinose are equivalent, although the latter term is rarely used because ribose, not arabinose, is the precursor to deoxyribose. |
| Guanine | Guanine is one of the four main nucleobases found in the nucleic acids DNA and RNA, the others being adenine, cytosine, and thymine (uracil in RNA). In DNA, guanine is paired with cytosine. With the formula $C_5H_5N_5O$, guanine is a derivative of purine, consisting of a fused pyrimidine-imidazole ring system with conjugated double bonds. |
| Nucleotide | Nucleotides are organic molecules that serve as the monomers, or subunits, of nucleic acids like DNA and RNA. The building blocks of nucleic acids, nucleotides are composed of a nitrogenous base, a five-carbon sugar (ribose or deoxyribose), and at least one phosphate group.<br><br>Nucleotides serve to carry packets of energy within the cell (ATP). In the form of the nucleoside triphosphates (ATP, GTP, CTP and UTP), nucleotides play central roles in metabolism. |
| Polynucleotide | A polynucleotide molecule is a biopolymer composed of 13 or more nucleotide monomers covalently bonded in a chain. DNA (deoxyribonucleic acid) and RNA (ribonucleic acid) are examples of polynucleotides with distinct biological function. The prefix poly comes from the ancient Greek p???? (polys, many). |
| Ribose | Ribose is an organic compound with the formula $C_5H_{10}O_5$; specifically, a monosaccharide with linear form H-(C=O)-$(CHOH)_4$-H, which has all the hydroxyl groups on the same side in the Fischer projection.<br><br>The term may refer to either of two enantiomers. The term usually indicates -ribose, which occurs widely in nature and is discussed here. |
| Thymine | Thymine is one of the four nucleobases in the nucleic acid of DNA that are represented by the letters G-C-A-T. The others are adenine, guanine, and cytosine. Thymine is also known as 5-methyluracil, a pyrimidine nucleobase. |
| Uracil | Uracil is one of the four nucleobases in the nucleic acid of RNA that are represented by the letters A, G, C and U. The others are adenine (A), cytosine, and guanine. In RNA, uracil binds to adenine via two hydrogen bonds. In DNA, the uracil nucleobase is replaced by thymine. |
| Base pair | Base pairs are the building blocks of the DNA double helix, and contribute to the folded structure of both DNA and RNA. Dictated by specific hydrogen bonding patterns, Watson-Crick base pairs (guanine-cytosine and adenine-thymine) allow the DNA helix to maintain a regular helical structure that is independent of its nucleotide sequence. |

The complementary nature of this based-paired structure provides a backup copy of all genetic information encoded within double-stranded DNA. The regular structure and data redundancy provided by the DNA double helix make DNA well suited to the storage of genetic information, while base-pairing between DNA and incoming nucleotides provides the mechanism through which DNA polymerase replicates DNA, and RNA polymerase transcribes DNA into RNA. Many DNA-binding proteins can recognize specific base pairing patterns that identify particular regulatory regions of genes.

Intramolecular base pairs can occur within single-stranded nucleic acids.

**Replication**

Replication, in metallography, is the use of thin plastic films to nondestructively duplicate the microstructure of a component. The film is then examined at high magnifications.

Replication is a method of copying the topography of a surface by casting or impressing material onto the surface.

**Pyruvic acid**

Pyruvic acid is an organic acid, a ketone, as well as the simplest of the alpha-keto acids. The carboxylate ($COO^-$) anion of pyruvic acid, its Brønsted-Lowry conjugate base, $CH_3COCOO^-$, is known as pyruvate, and is a key intersection in several metabolic pathways.

Pyruvic acid can be made from glucose through glycolysis, converted back to carbohydrates (such as glucose) via gluconeogenesis, or to fatty acids through acetyl-CoA. It can also be used to construct the amino acid alanine and be converted into ethanol.

**Acetic anhydride**

Acetic anhydride, or ethanoic anhydride, is the chemical compound with the formula $(CH_3CO)_2O$. Commonly abbreviated $Ac_2O$, it is the simplest isolatable acid anhydride and is a widely used reagent in organic synthesis. It is a colorless liquid that smells strongly of acetic acid, formed by its reaction with the moisture in the air.

Formic anhydride is an even simpler acid anhydride, but it spontaneously decomposes, especially once removed from solution.

**Purine**

A purine is a heterocyclic aromatic organic compound. It consists of a pyrimidine ring fused to an imidazole ring. Purines, including substituted purines and their tautomers, are the most widely occurring nitrogen-containing heterocycle in nature.

**Pyrimidine**

Pyrimidine is an aromatic heterocyclic organic compound similar to pyridine. One of the three diazines (six-membered heterocyclics with two nitrogen atoms in the ring), it has the nitrogens at positions 1 and 3 in the ring. The other diazines are pyrazine (nitrogens 1 and 4) and pyridazine (nitrogens 1 and 2).

| | |
|---|---|
| Glutathione | Glutathione is a tripeptide with a gamma peptide linkage between the amine group of cysteine (which is attached by normal peptide linkage to a glycine) and the carboxyl group of the glutamate side-chain. It is an antioxidant, preventing damage to important cellular components caused by reactive oxygen species such as free radicals and peroxides.<br><br>Thiol groups are reducing agents, existing at a concentration of approximately 5 mM in animal cells. |
| Indole | Indole is an aromatic heterocyclic organic compound. It has a bicyclic structure, consisting of a six-membered benzene ring fused to a five-membered nitrogen-containing pyrrole ring. Indole is a common component of fragrances and the precursor to many pharmaceuticals. |
| Quinine | Quinine is a natural white crystalline alkaloid having antipyretic (fever-reducing), antimalarial, analgesic (painkilling), and anti-inflammatory properties and a bitter taste. It is a stereoisomer of quinidine which, unlike quinine, is an antiarrhythmic. Quinine contains two major fused-ring systems: the aromatic quinoline and the bicyclic quinuclidine. |
| Adenosine monophosphate | Adenosine monophosphate, also known as 5'-adenylic acid, is a nucleotide that is used as a monomer in DNA and RNA. It is an ester of phosphoric acid and the nucleoside adenosine. AMP consists of a phosphate group, the sugar ribose, and the nucleobase adenine. As a substituent it takes the form of the prefix adenylyl-. |
| Ribonuclease | Ribonuclease is a type of nuclease that catalyzes the degradation of RNA into smaller components. Ribonucleases can be divided into endoribonucleases and exoribonucleases, and comprise several sub-classes within the EC 2.7 (for the phosphorolytic enzymes) and 3.1 (for the hydrolytic enzymes) classes of enzymes. |

## 24. The Chemistry of Life: Organic and Biological Chemistry

1. _____ is the chemical compound with the formula CH3CN. This colourless liquid is the simplest organic nitrile (hydrogen cyanide is a simpler nitrile, but the cyanide anion is not classed as organic). It is produced mainly as a byproduct of acrylonitrile manufacture.

   a. Acetonitrile
   b. SEAgel
   c. Ceration
   d. Congelation

2. _____ is an a-amino acid with the formula $C_6H_5CH_2CH(NH_2)COOH$. This essential amino acid is classified as nonpolar because of the hydrophobic nature of the benzyl side chain. -_____ is an electrically neutral amino acid, one of the twenty common amino acids used to biochemically form proteins, coded for by DNA. The codons for -_____ are UUU and UUC. _____ is a precursor for tyrosine, the monoamine signaling molecules dopamine, norepinephrine (noradrenaline), and epinephrine (adrenaline), and the skin pigment melanin.

   _____ is found naturally in the breast milk of mammals.

   a. Bile bear
   b. Phenylalanine
   c. Buffalo coat
   d. Catgut

3. _____ is a naturally occurring organic compound with antioxidant properties. It is a white solid, but impure samples can appear yellowish. It dissolves well in water to give mildly acidic solutions.

   a. Ascorbic acid
   b. Buffering agent
   c. Carbonate alkalinity
   d. Charlot equation

4. _____ is a simple polyol (sugar alcohol) compound. It is a colorless, odorless, viscous liquid that is widely used in pharmaceutical formulations. _____ has three hydroxyl groups that are responsible for its solubility in water and its hygroscopic nature.

   a. Bleach
   b. Camphine
   c. Glycerol
   d. DEET

5. . _____ is a weak organic acid with the formula $C_6H_8O_7$. It is a natural preservative/conservative and is also used to add an acidic or sour taste to foods and drinks. In biochemistry, the conjugate base of _____, citrate, is important as an intermediate in the _____ cycle, which occurs in the metabolism of all aerobic organisms.

a. Citric acid

b. Benzotriazole

c. Bipyridine

d. Catechol

**1.** a
**2.** b
**3.** a
**4.** c
**5.** a

---

## You can take the complete Chapter Practice Test

**for 24. The Chemistry of Life: Organic and Biological Chemistry**
on all key terms, persons, places, and concepts.

### Online 99 Cents

### http://www.JustTheFacts101.com

Use www.JustTheFacts101.com for all your study needs

including Facts101's online interactive problem solving labs in

chemistry, statistics, mathematics, and more.

# Other Facts101 e-Books and Tests

## Want More?
## JustTheFacts101.com...

**Jtf101.com provides the outlines and highlights of your textbooks, just like this e-StudyGuide, but also gives you the PRACTICE TESTS, and other exclusive study tools for all of your textbooks.**

**Learn More.** *Just click*
*http://www.JustTheFacts101.com/*